Confucianism in China

ALSO AVAILABLE FROM BLOOMSBURY

Chinese Religion: A Contextual Approach, Xinzhong Yao
Confucius: A Guide for the Perplexed, Yong Huang
Religion and Orientalism in Asian Studies, Kiri Paramore

Confucianism in China

An Introduction

TONY SWAIN

Bloomsbury Academic
An imprint of Bloomsbury Publishing Plc

B L O O M S B U R Y
LONDON • OXFORD • NEW YORK • NEW DELHI • SYDNEY

Bloomsbury Academic

An imprint of Bloomsbury Publishing Plc

50 Bedford Square   1385 Broadway
London   New York
WC1B 3DP   NY 10018
UK   USA

www.bloomsbury.com

BLOOMSBURY and the Diana logo are trademarks of Bloomsbury Publishing Plc

First published 2017

© Tony Swain, 2017

British Library Cataloguing-in-Publication Data
A catalogue record for this book is available from the British Library.

ISBN: HB: 978-1-4742-4244-8
PB: 978-1-4742-4243-1
ePDF: 978-1-4742-4246-2
ePub: 978-1-4742-4245-5

Library of Congress Cataloging-in-Publication Data
Names: Swain, Tony, author.
Title: Confucianism in China : an introduction /
Tony Swain. Description: New York : Bloomsbury Academic, 2017. |
Includes bibliographical references and index.
Identifiers: LCCN 2016058161| ISBN 9781474242448 (hardback) |
ISBN 9781474242462 (epdf)
Subjects: LCSH: Confucianism–China. | BISAC: RELIGION / Confucianism. |
RELIGION / Eastern. | HISTORY / Asia / China.
Classification: LCC BL1840 .S93 2017 | DDC 181/.112–dc23
LC record available at https://lccn.loc.gov/2016058161

Cover design: danileighdesign.com
Cover image: China, Shandong Province, Qufu City. International Confucius Cultural Festival. Birthplace of Confucius, the great philosopher politician and educator of the 6th–5th centuries BC, and Unesco World Heritage Site. © Christian Kober / Getty Images

Typeset by Newgen Knowledge Works Pvt Ltd., Chennai, India.
Printed and bound in India

For Elizabeth Rieger

Contents

Illustrations

Notes on pronunciation, translation, and Chinese dynasties

The first English introduction to Confucianism appeared in 1691. It was not a great start. *The Morals of Confucius a Chinese Philosopher* was just a translation of a French book. And that French book was merely a popular abridgment of a Latin book. Those days, China and Confucianism seemed very remote indeed.

Things had changed by the nineteenth century, when British armed forces, merchants, and missionaries were camped in China. But just as Confucianism was becoming relevant, the tradition itself appeared to die. Interest waned. A well-known trilogy by Joseph Levenson, entitled *Confucian China and Its Modern Fate* (1958–65), summed up the prevailing view: It was all over.

Only in the past forty years has the study of Confucianism really taken off. Currently, it is running hot. New translations are constantly appearing, reinterpretations are refining our understanding, and, most importantly, we now have solid documentation of a major revival of Confucianism unfolding in China.

Three hundred and twenty-five years after our first faltering effort, this book introduces today's English-speaking reader to Confucianism in China.

I have not tried to make Confucianism accessible by dumbing it down. Rather, I have attempted to introduce the complexities of a sometimes challenging tradition in a clear and coherent way. I have assumed little knowledge of Chinese history and none of the Chinese language. But if you are totally new to things Chinese, there are a few very basic matters to explain before we begin.

The Chinese language and Pinyin. A person of average literacy in Chinese can recognize about 3,500 characters. For the convenience of English-speaking readers, we transcribe the way characters are pronounced in Mandarin using the letters of the Roman alphabet.

The problem is, there are several different ways of doing this. Pinyin is adopted in the People's Republic of China and is now almost universally used in English-language books. But most older publications used the Wade-Giles system, and James Legge, whose translations I sometimes quote, had another system of his own.

I always use Pinyin. When I quote sources using alternative conventions, I simply convert them to Pinyin.

How to pronounce Pinyin. Pinyin is reasonably intuitive for English-language readers satisfied with ballpark pronunciation. If you want to pronounce words correctly, there are websites that will let you hear them. Online dictionaries (e.g., MDGB at www.mdbg.net) work well, or you can try an internet search for "Pinyin charts with audio." Meanwhile, here is a rough-and-ready guide to some of the trickier sounds.

q = <u>ch</u>eese

x = <u>sh</u>eep

z = be<u>ds</u>

c = ca<u>ts</u>

zh = <u>j</u>am

ai = <u>eye</u>

ao = c<u>ow</u>

ei = s<u>ay</u>

en = f<u>un</u>

ia = <u>ya</u>rd

ie = th<u>e air</u>

ou = d<u>ough</u>

ui = w<u>ai</u>ter

ue = <u>you</u> <u>airhead</u>

uo = w<u>ar</u>

Translating Chinese concepts. On the whole, scholarly English translations of Confucian texts are good. I use what I consider to be the best available translations, but sometimes my quotations differ slightly from the original. In most cases, this is to ensure consistency when rendering important philosophical terms. Throughout this book, therefore, I am "following" the cited translation rather than adhering strictly to it. In the few cases where I felt substantial changes were required, I have stipulated that a passage has been "modified."

Dynasties. Were you beginning school in late dynastic China, you would almost certainly be studying the *Three-Character Classic*. It would teach you basic literacy while introducing you to key Confucian concepts. But about a third of that little Classic is devoted to acquainting students with China's dynasties. As this book progresses, you will come to appreciate that thinking in dynasties was integral to the Confucian view of history. I will introduce the dynasties as we go, but you will probably need to flick back to this list from time to time.

Xia Dynasty	c. 2100 – c. 1600 BCE
Shang Dynasty	c. 1600 – c. 1045 BCE
Zhou Dynasty	c. 1045–256 BCE
Qin Dynasty	221–206 BCE
Han Dynasty	206 BCE–220 CE
Period of Disunion	220–581
Sui Dynasty	581–618
Tang Dynasty	618–907
Five Dynasty Period	907–960
Song Dynasty	960–1279
Yuan Dynasty	1271–1368
Ming Dynasty	1368–1644
Qing Dynasty	1644–1912

PART ONE

Introductory chapters

Each of the four parts of this book begins with a précis and a summary of its individual chapters. You can, of course, read these consecutively for a running summary of the whole. This part contains two introductory chapters.

Chapter 1 examines the thorny problem of "Confucianism" as a "religion." It explains why "Confucianism" was an unfortunate Western invention (we will soon be abandoning the word) and it goes on to consider how a tradition with deeply religious concerns might yet not be "a religion." Conceptual clarity is very important for appreciating the unique features of Confucian religiosity. In the final part (Chapters 8–10) you will learn that Western notions of "Confucianism" and "religion" have, nonetheless, been shaping the tradition for more than a century.

Chapter 2 offers an overview of Confucian belief and practice. It applies definitions established in Chapter 1 while accentuating the distinctive contours of Confucian religiosity. I explain that Confucian beliefs are not centered in supernaturalism (gods, spirits, the afterlife, etc.), but instead focus on the possibility of nurturing human nature so as to achieve moral perfection. I then turn to learning and ritual, the primary methods of self-cultivation. Although this chapter is based on the pre-imperial and imperial eras, it will become very apparent in the final part of this book that modern revivalists are endeavoring to adapt these beliefs and practices so as to make them compatible with today's sociopolitical realities.

1

On Confucianism and religion

Obituaries were the only thing being written for Confucianism in China in the late 1970s. Less than forty years later, everyone is wondering just how big the comeback will be. Some are filled with trepidation, others with enthusiasm, but no one is contesting that Confucianism is once again on the ascent.

This is a domestic revival that the world cannot ignore. In three decades, China has risen from having a GDP that was just over 6 percent of that of the United States to having the second-largest economy in the world. It has passed 50 percent of the USA's GDP and is projected to overtake it in about a decade. This economic acceleration has at its disposal the largest population of any country, almost one-fifth of all the people on the planet. China's space program, which is currently the most active in the world, is as much a symbol of the country's growing national pride as it is a scientific enterprise. The Gobi desert city of Jiuquan was the launch site for the first Chinese astronaut into space in 2003. The city gate proudly proclaims, in Chinese and English: "Without Haste, Without Fear, We Conquer the World."

This slogan was actually coined in the 1950s when nuclear capabilities were being developed in Jiuquan, and it then belonged to a very different and decidedly militant era. Today, China's power is dependent on trade and requires cordial relationships with commercial partners just as it requires a stable and harmonious workforce. If China is currently poised to conquer the world, it will do so softly.

It is in this world of "soft power" that Confucianism is once again flourishing. It is no coincidence that the primary instruments for promoting China to the world, found in more than ninety countries, are known as Confucius Institutes. There is absolutely no doubt that the Chinese government will continue to employ things Confucian in order to advance the country. Quintessentially Confucian concepts such as humaneness (ren) and harmony (he) have become fixtures in official pronouncements, party members formally attend ceremonies celebrating Confucius' birthday, and Confucian literature has found its way back into the education system at all levels. Indeed, rumor has it the current leader of the Chinese Communist Party (CCP) is having a "love affair with Confucius" (*Time*, October 30, 2014).

The real question is: Just how far might this go? The extreme case is currently being championed by Jiang Qing who will settle for nothing less than a Confucian government to replace the CCP. His comprehensive plan, were it implemented, would not merely return Confucianism to the position it held in imperial times but would give it vastly more authority and unprecedented institutional power. You would have to be a reckless punter to back Jiang Qing's horse, but no matter the odds against him, the fact remains he has been allowed to approach the starting post. He is tolerated by the government and being permitted to promote his ideas.

There are other signs of renaissance. In schools and parks, with small groups or even private tutors, people in China are coming together to recite Confucian Classics. How many people? The figures swing wildly from one to one hundred million, but 10–20 million people would probably be a fair estimate. Again, there are phenomena like Yu Dan's television series and book on the sayings of Confucius. Twelve million copies of her book sold in China (it is available in twenty-eight other languages), which makes it the most popular book interpreting the ideas of a religious thinker or philosopher ever written. And then there is this: millions of entrepreneurs in China are convinced that Confucianism is good for business. Capitalism may seem an unlikely bedmate for Confucianism, but the seminars and training courses on this very topic continue to be booked out.

China will never reach its potential, the revivalists say, unless it fully embraces Confucianism. They insist there is no alternative because Confucianism is what shaped the nation and defines what it was, and is, to be Chinese. Variations on the mantra "Confucianism is the essence of Chinese culture" are recited over and over by the activists.

Whether or not their claims are justified, it certainly is impossible to comprehend China today without having a sound grasp of Confucianism. And to understand contemporary Confucianism requires an awareness of the history that shaped the tradition. I will be devoting my last three chapters to the modern era, but to get there we must first go back two and a half thousand years and establish the historical foundations on which current developments rest.

***

The history of Chinese Confucianism is long and complex, and it is useful to have at hand a map of the terrain that lies ahead. In the next chapter I will provide a concise overview of the Confucian tradition to help orientate readers as they pass through the chapters that follow. But first, I need to clear up a few things.

Many modern Chinese revivalists claim that Confucianism is a religion. The first book devoted to proving this was entitled *On Confucian Religion* (*Kongjiao lun*) and it appeared in 1912. The author, Chen Huanzhang, presented some insightful arguments, but this one was a howler: "All books by Westerners list Confucius first when mentioning the founders of Chinese religions; they also first list Confucianism when mentioning the religions of China. When comparing world religions and their founders, they always list Confucianism and Confucius. It has long since been a fact that Confucius was a founder of a religion" (Gan 2013: 28).

And there you have it, Confucianism is a religion because it is in Western textbooks on world religions. But how did it get there and was its inclusion just a colossal blunder? That is what I want to discuss in this chapter.

So, *is* Confucianism a religion? The problem is not finding the right answer. The real issue is whether the question is worthy of an answer at all. Joseph Adler describes the position of those presenting a worst-case scenario: "To ask whether Confucianism is a religion is ... wrongly put on both counts, in their view: there's no such thing as Confucianism and there's no such thing as religion" (Adler 2014b: 5).

I, for one, have no problem finding signs of "Confucianism as a religion" in China. My only concern is that I cannot locate them before the late nineteenth century. There were no Chinese equivalents to "religion" or "Confucianism" until they were introduced to the country by the West, along with missionaries, secular philosophies, invading armies, and unequal trade agreements. *Zongjiao* was coined in the 1880s as a translation for the English word "religion" and at much the same time we gain our first real glimpses of *Kongjiao* or "Confucianism."

The fact that these terms were both shaped by Western intellectual concerns is unsettling to many scholars. Here are two of the more memorable protests. In 1963, Wilfred Cantwell Smith wrote in *The Meaning and End of Religion* that "we may simply observe ... that the question 'Is Confucianism a religion?' is one that the West has never been able to answer, and China never able to ask" (Smith 1963: 86). More recently in *Manufacturing Confucianism,* Lionel Jensen said: "To employ the term 'Confucianism,' which we know lacks accuracy, in situations where accuracy is desired, is to create confusion. There is as much that is genuinely Chinese in Confucianism as there was in chinoiserie" (Jensen 1997: 144).

In the following sections, I examine in turn the concept of "Confucianism" and the issue of the religious nature of Confucianism. Having clarified some of the conceptual problems, I will then, in the next chapter, offer a concise overview of what we will by that stage be referring to as the Way of the Ru.

"Confucianism"

Let me begin with an anecdote. Some years ago when I was in Qufu, the hometown of Confucius, I came upon a bilingual tourist brochure that made perfect sense in Chinese but that sounded absurd when translated into English using standard entries from a Chinese-English dictionary. It read: "Confucius trained as a Confucian."

A literal translation of the Chinese would read: "Confucius trained as a *Ru*". Whether this is historically correct is uncertain, but at least it is not a logical impossibility. Every sinologist knows that "Confucian" is a thoroughly inaccurate rendering of Ru, and more and more are choosing to leave the word untranslated. Throughout this book I too will be adopting the Chinese term. In this section, I explain why I think this is a necessary shift and also show how Western scholarship became conceptually disoriented.

"Confucianism" is obviously derived from the name Confucius and suggests the -ism of the man and his followers. Before tackling that misconception, we have to note briefly that even the name Confucius is unfortunate. As Jensen shows in *Manufacturing Confucianism,* it was coined by Jesuits in the seventeenth century as the Latinized form of Kongfuzi. This was rather peculiar, as "Confucian" texts almost never refer to him thus, although it was used in spoken Chinese and popular literature (Meynard 2015: 78). In scholarly Chinese, Kongzi (Master Kong) and Fuzi (That Master) are both common, but the amalgam Kongfuzi is extremely rare. From now on, therefore, I will be using Kongzi rather than Confucius, although I admit this a minor issue. With "Confucianism," the stakes are higher.

Jensen seemed simply to assume that insofar as the Jesuits created Confucius, they also invented Confucianism, but in this he was mistaken (Standaert 1999; Sun 2013: chapters 1 and 2). "Confucianism" had to wait more than another two centuries. In the 1860s, it occasionally pops up in books by Protestant missionaries serving in south China, but it was only in 1877 that a fellow missionary, the great translator and scholar James Legge, began to give the word currency. A few years later in 1880, he offered this very revealing definition:

> I use the term Confucianism as covering, first of all the ancient religion of China, and then the views of the great philosopher himself, in illustration or modification of it, his views as committed to writing by himself, or transmitted in the narratives of his disciples. The case is pretty much as when we comprehend under Christianity the records and teachings of the Old Testament as well as those of the New. (Legge 1880: 4)

What is very evident is that Legge is shaping his "Confucianism" in the mold of Christianity; Kongzi is the fulfillment of the ancient religion of China that preceded him; his is a Chinese gospel that completed the Old Testament of the East. Legge, in short, has conflated a tradition with one man. This is perhaps appropriate when that person's very being is definitive of a faith, such as a Christ or a Buddha, but it will become apparent why manufacturing "Confucianism" was a most unfortunate and misleading way of renaming the way of the Ru. Later in the same book, Legge (1880: 123) admitted, "China does not owe its national religion to Confucius. He received it, as did others, from prehistoric times," and Norman Girardot quite rightly concludes that Legge's only justification for "Confucianism" was "his own scholarly license" (Girardot 2005: 314).

The clearest way to explain why "Confucianism" was and is inappropriate is a brief historical synopsis of the Ru and their shifting relationship with Kongzi. First, however, let me define "Ru." Although its origin is obscure, the word "Ru" eventually came to mean "scholar." "Scholar" would be the most direct English translation, but it could be misleading, as there were many scholars in imperial China who were not Ru, *shi* being a frequently encountered term for "scholar" in this more general sense. The Ru were scholars devoted to a particular corps of texts that were believed to have been written by sages and to thus have scriptural authority. As these books (discussed in detail in

Chapter 5) are referred to as the Classics (*jing*), I will occasionally follow those who translate Ru as "Classicist." This can still cause confusion, as there were other *jing* outside the Ru canon that had great authority, and so for the most part I will simply leave "Ru" untranslated. Sinologists who are hesitant to take this step usually balk because the term "is unfamiliar and potentially confusing or simply not informative to English-language readers" (Major et al. 2010: 8n. 9), but an introductory book such as this is an ideal place to make the transition.

I use "Ru" in place of "Confucian," and while I thus avoid "Ruist," I cannot sidestep "Ruism." I am not concerned that this word might seem strange and ungainly (the same could have once been said of "Daoism"), but it does conflate several different things. The closest Chinese equivalents to "Ruism" are *Rujia,* the school (*jia*) of the Ru, *Rujiao,* the teaching (*jiao*) of the Ru, and *Ruxue,* the learning (*xue*) of the Ru. Each of these have separate nuanced meanings lost when they are conflated, but to avoid overburdening the reader, I simplify this to "Ruism," except on those occasion when the distinctions are important. I am aware that the use of a single term runs the risk of reifying the tradition and ask readers to recall Hoyt Tillman's (1992: 10) words of caution: The "*ru* were simply scholars engaged in classical learning of the ancients, and the term was more vague and elastic" than any "modern 'ism' with doctrinal uniformity, documented membership, or party program."

So, then, who were the Ru, and did their historic relationship with Kongzi justify the Western invention of "Confucianism"?

I. Before Kongzi (pre-551 BCE). The defining feature of Ru in imperial times was, as I have just mentioned, their devotion to the Classics, but as Ru predate the formation of the canon, this could not have originally demarcated them. Early references certainly do note their love of learning, but equally they observe their association with ritual and music so that a second-century BCE text caricatures them as "singing to stringed instruments and dancing to drums so as to make music; turning, bestowing, diminishing, yielding so as to practice rites" (Major et al. 2010: 500).

We cannot be certain if the Ru preceded Kongzi. The oldest use of the character for "Ru" is a lone passage in the *Analects* (the compilation of Kongzi's sayings, discussed in Chapter 3), in which Kongzi says: "Be a gentleman *ru*, not a petty *ru*" (6:13). As this is the only occasion in which he uses the word, it remains unclear precisely what it meant to him. Those who maintain that the Ru predated Confucius are thus obliged to speculate. The etymology of the character for *ru,* for instance, suggests it is composed of compounds signifying "person" and "weak" or "soft," hence possibly originally meaning "weaklings" or "softies." It has been variously conjectured that the word first referred to the old Shang dynasty (1766–1122 BCE) ritualists who mildly submitted to and served their new Zhou dynasty (1122–256 BCE) overlords, that it was a derogative term for Zhou ceremonial experts who were weak in comparison to martially trained warriors, or that it alluded to the softness and flexibility of ancient quasi-shamanic dancers (Eno 1990: appendix B).

These hypotheses need not be mutually exclusive, and feasibly there was a lineage of transformations in court ritualism from early dancing shamans and magicians through to professional ceremonial experts and finally to scholars who studied and taught ritual techniques and philosophy. All this remains conjecture, however. Whether Kongzi stood out as a preeminent figure in a long-standing association or rather began a new order is thus uncertain. What is clear is that music, ceremony, and education were indicative of the early Ru, and these were features that remained characteristic.

II. From Kongzi to the Early Han Dynasty (551 BCE to second century CE). We are on more solid terrain in the era immediately following Kongzi. It seems clear that, even if the Ru predate him, in the centuries following Kongzi's life he was widely recognized as the rejuvenator and leader of the Ru in their contemporary form. It is significant, however, that most references we have to Kongzi as the leader of the "Ru" come from authors who themselves did *not* identify as Ru, and the word "Ru" in fact appears very infrequently in early Ru writings. This perhaps reflects a derogatory origin to the word (weaklings, softies). How, then, did Kongzi and his immediate followers refer to themselves? As far as we know, they did not.

Later sources from the Han dynasty do sometimes refer to "Kongzi's school" (*Zhongni zhi men*) and "Kongzi's disciples" (*Kongzi zhi tu*) to designate Kongzi and his band of followers, and I dare say such expressions could very easily have been used in their own day. I would not at all object to these being rendered "Confucians," but significantly the Chinese phrases were used to specify a category quite distinct from what we today classify as "Confucians." Kongzi's immediate circle was *not* synonymous with the "Ru" more generally. As Nicolas Zufferey has noted, "In the view of ancient Chinese authors, to be a follower of Confucius and to be a *ru* were two different things, even if, of course, the two were not mutually exclusive" (Zufferey 2003: 368).

III. Han Dynasty (207 BCE – 220 CE). While Kongzi was widely recognized as the leader who had revitalized the Ru, he did not present himself as a founder of a new school and he was not perceived as such. In the *Analects* he said, "I transmit but do not innovate" (7:1), and it was agreed that what he espoused was a Way that had reached its zenith in the Early Zhou dynasty (1045–771 BCE) but which had gone into decline. Whether or not this was the case, it was understood that Ru predated Kongzi, and that his role had been to resuscitate a withering tradition. As the *Hanshu* (1st century CE) said, while the Ru took Kongzi to be a great teacher, they "regarded [kings] Yao and Shun as the ancestors of their school, and King Wen and King Wu as brilliant exemplars" (Fung 1948: 32–3). Xunzi likewise said: "The Ru model themselves on the former kings" (Hutton 2014: 53).

By the time of the Han dynasty, some 250 years after his death, Kongzi was no longer invariably center stage among the Ru. In the early Han, observes Michael Loewe, "there are very few cases in which Kongzi's sayings were cited as authority to support a point of view or a proposal" (2011: 335). He is forced to insist that "a straight translation of *ru* ... as 'Confucian' has begged too many questions" (2011: 2). Zufferey too notes the conspicuous lack of references to Kongzi in official edicts and memorials and adds that this is "very hard to account for if Confucianism represented the core of the *ru shu,* if, as tradition has it, the *ru* were originally followers of Confucius—Confucians" (Zufferey 2003: 367–8).

Yet this precise period when Kongzi was waning was the moment when Ruism was in ascent. As we will see in Chapter 5, it was at this juncture that the Ru gained imperial patronage that secured their position in China for the next two thousand years. It was at this time too that "Ru" took on the primary meaning of "Classicist" as the core of their curriculum was now set as the study of the Five Classics. Significantly, the *Analects* of Kongzi was not among them and may not yet have existed in its current form.

For the Han in particular, we can see that the word "Confucian" emphasizes a man who, no matter how significant, was seen as secondary to the preeminence of the texts. Many Ru in the early Han were little interested in Kongzi and were anything but "Confucian." As the dynasty unfolded, Kongzi's status again began to rise, but in a most telling manner. He was not primarily revered as the leader of the Ru or as a great philosopher, but rather as someone who had his hand in the creation of the all-important Classics. He was said to have edited the books and to have authored one himself. This is certainly a great prestige, but priority was always to the texts. The Classics were not revered because they revealed the wisdom of Kongzi; rather, Kongzi was revered because of his service in giving birth to the Classics. In the Han it is very clear: the Ru were Classicists, not Confucians. Indeed, in the period prior to the Tang, the Duke of Zhou was usually considered to be the preeminent sage of Ru history.

IV. Song to Ming Dynasties (960–1644). Kongzi's status again declined with the collapse of the Han, and his authorship was no longer seen as a defining feature of a Classic. A third-century text thus maintained that "if a book has lasting relevance, it becomes a classic … The fact that a book was not written by Confucius surely does not preclude its becoming a classic" (Nylan 2001: 18). There were, of course, many significant shifts in the fortunes of the Ru in the 750 years following the Han dynasty (Chapter 6), but these pale in comparison with the radical changes of the Song dynasty. This was the era that saw the emergence of what is known in English as "Neo-Confucianism." What is most distinctive of this revival was that it sought to put aside much of over a millennium of Ru tradition to reconnect with Kongzi and his early followers. This led the great sinologist Jacques Gernet to the opinion that "what is commonly called Neo-Confucianism from the Song onwards should actually be considered as the earliest form of Confucianism" (cited in Cheng 2001: 101).

There is no question that Kongzi's thought as recorded in the *Analects* became focal at this time. It, along with three works attributed to a disciple, Kongzi's grandson, and a disciple of that grandson known in the West as Mencius (Latinized from Mengzi), were promoted as the Four Books that would thereafter join the Five Classics on the curriculum of the Ru. Could we not at least call this final third of the history of the Ru "Confucianism"?

Although I do not deny a reasonable case could be made for this, its only real merit would be in allowing us to salvage the West's invention of "Confucianism" rather than learning to adopt Chinese ways of designating the tradition. We must keep in mind that the Song dynasty revivalists did not think of themselves as "Confucians." It will come as no surprise to learn that "Neo-Confucianism" is not a literal translation of any

Chinese category. Given how ubiquitous the term has become, it may be more surprising to learn that, despite a few isolated earlier instances, it only became commonplace in academic parlance in the 1950s (Nylan 2001: 365; Elman 2002: 526).

The Chinese words translated as "Neo-Confucianism" are primarily *Daoxue* (Learning of the Way), *Lixue* (Learning of Principle), and *Xinxue* (Learning of the Heart-Mind). They were actually separate, albeit overlapping, movements that "Neo-Confucianism" lumps together. The Chinese terms noticeably prioritize philosophical concepts, not the personhood of Kongzi. The phrase that came closest to "Confucianism" at this time was perhaps *shengxian zhi dao* or "the Way of the Sages and Worthies," but this was used in a more general sense rather than as a designation for a movement, and it should be noted it does not single out Kongzi but includes others both before him (such as the Duke of Zhou) and after (Mengzi).

Although there were names for the new philosophical currents from the Song onward (none of which meant "Confucian"), these were subcategories, and their exponents continued to regard themselves, first and foremost, as Ru.

V. The Fall of the Empire (late nineteenth century). The Ru became ever more firmly entrenched from the Song dynasty onward, as training Classicists was the focus of formal education, and excelling in examinations became the primary means to securing government appointments. In the nineteenth century, however, when the empire was in tatters due to Western incursions, the institution of Ruism for the first time faced wholesale criticism and it was blamed for China's failure to adapt to modern challenges.

It was at the very juncture when the Ru were losing their millennia-old role in governing the country that we get out first real glimpse of what might legitimately be called "Confucianism" (*Kongjiao*). It is no coincidence that this was occurring precisely as James Legge was inventing "Confucianism." Nor is it accidental that no one seemed to refer to *Kongjiao* without mentioning Christianity in the same breath. I will discuss this in detail in Chapter 8 and can only offer a few salient pointers here.

In the middle of the nineteenth century, a revolution broke out, which was very nearly successful in transforming China into a quasi-Christian state. The so-called Taiping Uprising was led by a man claiming to be Jesus' younger brother, and while the rebels had some sympathy for Kongzi, who they claimed actually believed in the Chinese version of the Biblical god, they were entirely dismissive of the Ru who they said had distorted this truth and so contributed to the country's woes. Significantly, the Taiping's second-in-command had been Legge's most esteemed assistant and confidante (Legge 1904: chapter 8). Even after the rebellion was contained, there was a tendency among reformers to argue for a return to Kongzi as an alternative to institutional Ruism, which was quickly becoming an anachronism. The journalist and Taiping sympathizer Wang Tao was a pioneer in the call for going back to Kongzi to replace Ruism in order to help China adapt to the modern world. And Wang Tao was James Legge's professional colleague, long-time collaborator, and personal friend (Girardot 2005: 60). China and the West were co-inventing "Confucianism."

It was, however, the exceptionally influential Kang Youwei who took up this idea and gave it currency. Kang believed China required a religion that would play a role equivalent to Christianity in the West. This was *Kongjiao* that we can, for the first time, reasonably translate as Confucianism (although Confucius-ism would be more accurate). Kang had his moment when he persuaded the Qing emperor to implement his ideas, but this came to a rapid end when the emperor was effectively deposed. His campaign to establish *Kongjiao* proceeded without imperial support, however; it persisted long after the empire itself had collapsed, and even today some prominent revivalists continue striving to fulfill Kang Youwei's mission.

China invented Confucianism (*kongjiao*) in the late nineteenth century at the same time the West was manufacturing Confucianism; it is a modern term and is appropriately applied only to the modern era. "Confucianism," however, remains an unsatisfactory term even for the overall developments in China since the end of the empire. Kongzi continues to loom large and has become a symbol of Chinese nationalism, but for the most part the revivals that have occurred since the twentieth century continue to be referred to as contemporary manifestations of *ruxue*, *rujia*, or *rujiao*—that is, of what I term Ruism. The main philosophical developments, discussed in Chapters 9 and 10, are termed New Ru Learning (*Xin Ruxue*) and, quite frankly, they owe more to Song and Ming dynasty thought than they do to Kongzi's own teachings. The Classics and the Four Books remain pivotal, and while Kongzi is vitally important, the tradition that continues to unfold should nonetheless be understood as the way of scholars or Classicist, that is, as the Way of the Ru.

"Religion"

While the legitimacy of "Confucianism" is primarily a Western concern, the question of whether "Confucianism," or *Rujiao*, is a "religion" has been debated both in the West and in China for over a century. Answering it is a devilishly tricky business. Indeed, I doubt there is a correct answer, only answers that at any particular historic moment are more or less useful.

The world has no clearly demarcated boundaries but that words have created them. With some categories and classifications there seems to be widespread cross-cultural agreement, but others are idiosyncratic and do not at all refer to self-evident aspects of "reality." "Religion" belongs to the latter group. Brent Nongbri has reminded us that "the isolation of something called 'religion' as a sphere of life separated from politics, economics, and science ... in the broad view of human cultures, ... is a strikingly odd way of conceiving the world" (2013: 1–2). None of the languages of the world's "religions" originally had a word that approximated "religion," and the idea of "religion" in fact only emerged with the Western Enlightenment. Jonathan Z. Smith would go so far as saying that "religion is solely the creation of the scholar"s study," and "has no independent existence apart from the academy" (1982: xi).

In pre-nineteenth-century China, the closest approximates to "religion" were per-haps *dao* or "way," which I will discuss a little later, and *fa* or "law," a Chinese Buddhist rendering of the Sanskrit *dharma*. But it was two other words, *zong* ("lineage" or "sect") and *jiao* ("teaching") that were brought together in the late nineteenth century to create a new word to translate "religion."

Zongjiao has caused a lot of conceptual mischief. It certainly does not resonate with the vast majority of Chinese people. The World Values Survey question asking respond-ents if they belong to a religion has the Chinese easily winning the prize for being the most irreligious people on earth (only 6 percent said yes), with the runners-up trailing a long way behind (Estonia at 25 percent) (Inglehart et al. 2004: question F024). A more nuanced survey came up with a similar figure for Chinese people claiming to be reli-gious (8.7 percent), yet a hefty 56.7 percent reported having had what can only be called religious experiences (Yao and Badham 2007). People, it seems, were stumbling over a word, and dictionary definitions of *zhongjiao* tend to have negative connota-tions. Many fieldworkers have learned that asking locals in China about their "religion" will only elicit disclaimers, but asking them about, for instance, their "customs" will readily open up enthusiastic conversation about what researchers consider to be their religious life (Tam 2011: 31).

Zongjiao was a word made for scholars and politicians. It was invented at much the same time as *Kongjiao* or "Confucianism," and initially the two words were inseparable. It was Kang Youwei, once again, who co-joined them. Kang's motiv-ation for creating *Kongjiao* to replace Ruism was what he saw as the need for a "religion" to serve China in a way comparable to Christianity in the West. With the looming collapse of the empire and the loss of the institutional function of the Ru, Kang saw "religion" as a new vehicle for an old tradition. "Confucianism" as a "reli-gion" was created to unify and uplift a country under siege. At this stage, religion was implicitly defined as anything that looked like Christianity. As Vincent Goossaert (2011: 184) has observed, the Chinese "paradigm of ['religion'] was imposed from the West and modeled on Protestant Christianity: an organization of individual con-verts/believers, separate from other social institutions, based on scriptures, theology, and ethics, and geared towards action in the world (charity, education, publications, proselytizing)."

Although *Kongjiao* did not stick and people for the most part continued to refer to Ruism (i.e., *Rujiao, Rujia, Ruxue*, etc), "religion" and the question of whether Ruism is a religion remain an enduring legacy of Kang's innovations. Political agendas were and are invariably conspicuous. Kang had said it was a religion because he wanted to see *Kongjiao* instituted as state religion. His critics equally adopted the Christian template of "religion," but they argued that the historical facts of Ruism failed to meet the cri-teria, and therefore it could not be rejuvenated as state religion. The critics won and later, in the 1950s, when the CCP announced their official list of recognized *zongjiao* in China, Ruism was not included (the "Five Major Religions" are Buddhism, Daoism, Islam, Christianity, and Catholicism. Ruism is, however, recognized as a sixth religion in Hong Kong).

The question of the religious nature of Ruism returned to intellectual stage in the changing political climate after Mao's death. In 1978, Ren Jiyu, the founder and director of the Institute of World Religions, reexamined the historical evidence and concluded that Ruism in fact had served as a religion in imperial China. As his proclamation was made when Marxist denouncement of religion was still commonplace, the verdict was intended to further emphasize the irrelevance of Ruism to modern China. At the time, his views provoked some fierce criticism, but among his younger followers were those who upheld his basic thesis that Ruism was religious, but who cast it in a more sympathetic light.

At much the same time, the ideas of a group of scholars promoting what came to be known as *Xin Ruxue* (New Ru Learning) were becoming popular in China (see Chapter 9). The most important "second generation" of these thinkers had departed for Hong Kong and Taiwan when the Communists came to power in 1949, but in the politically relaxed atmosphere of the 1980s their ideas were being imported back to the mainland. These scholars had developed a more nuanced understanding of "religion," but it was their followers, the so-called "third generation," most of whom completed their education at Harvard, who made real advances in refining the discussion about the religious dimensions of Ruism. Of them, Tu Weiming has been the most influential on both Western and Chinese scholarship, and I will return to his thought a little later.

First, however, we need to go back to consider the vicissitudes of "religion" in the Western world. Scholars like Tu Weiming have been informed by both Chinese debates and Western academic developments, and we too require some understanding of how the idea of "religion" has evolved in the West.

* * *

Talal Asad (2002: 146) has astutely observed that "'religion' is a modern concept ... because it has been linked with its Siamese twin 'secularism'." Prior to the Enlightenment, the word religion was used to denote piety and a respectful attitude toward the sacred—that is, the quality of being religious. It was not, however, used to refer to a thing that could be isolated and defined as a phenomenon clearly demarcated from, say, science, philosophy, politics, or economics. There surely was fierce conflict generated by contrasting true religion with false or idolatrous religion, but there was no effort to isolate religion from non-religion. As Nongbri (2013: 4) recently wrote, "The very idea of "being religious" requires a companion notion of what it would mean to be "not religious", and this dichotomy was not part of the ancient world."

It was two seventeenth-century developments that precipitated our modern notion of a definable thing called religion. One was the fragmentation of Christendom by multiple reform movements and the subsequent struggle between Catholics and Protestants known as the Wars of Religion. Their settlement, in 1648, saw the word "secularization" adopted for the first time to refer to the separation of church and state power (previously *secularis* had been used for priests who served the community at large rather than a religious order). In the context of the folly of war, there also emerged philosophers who began to be skeptical of all those who claimed to be the rightful upholders of true religion and who thus began isolating religion as a thing to be eradicated. The second development was colonial expansion, a quest for wealth that was itself partially motivated by the financial drain of the wars and the competition between nation-states. The known varieties of idolatry were about to expand exponentially.

Although this has not been adequately researched, a tantalizing possibility is that the Ru at this time played a pivotal role in the emerging Western concern to identify and define the separate and discrete domain of "religion." The very Jesuits who bequeathed us "Confucius" also pioneered the distinction between religion and non-religion in one of the longest controversies in the history of the Catholic Church. The Jesuits had no hesitation in declaring Buddha an "imposter," Buddhists "idolaters," and Daoists "magicians." There was "false religion" (*falsae Religionis*) enough in China, but they looked very differently upon Kongzi and the "sect of the literati" and were willing to don the garb of the Ru and partake in rituals venerating the sage and other ancestors. Had these Jesuit missionaries themselves become idolaters? Their critics feared this was so, but they themselves responded that the ceremonies were civil rather than religious; they were no more than acts of respect to a great man who acknowledged the true God and taught moral values compatible with those of Jesus (Figure 1). The "Rites Controversy" lingered for over a century, and rather than distinguishing true and false religion, it hung upon differentiating religion from non-religion. Word of these allegedly non-religious Chinese philosophers administering the state greatly impressed European thinkers like Leibniz, Rousseau, and Voltaire who were reshaping the Western mind; here was living proof that a secular philosopher's republic could be realized. Nicolas Standaert has suggested that the Jesuit distinction between religious and civil ceremonies "was taken over and reformulated by eighteenth century European thinkers who, among others, took China as a place where 'religion' was not needed. This birth of non-religion led to the birth of the modern category of religion" (Standaert 1999: 129).

Once religion had been identified as a discrete phenomenon, once it had been seen as a thing that could be isolated and distinguished from other cultural domains, it was only natural that the familiar form of Christianity would initially be definitive. Despite all subsequent attempts to develop a cross-culturally inclusive alternative, an increasing number of scholars believe that the initial Christocentric prejudice will forever remain ingrained in "religion." Two very recent and germane quotations illustrate this. Nongbri singles out our own particular case when he writes: "Most of the debates about whether this or that '-ism' (Confucianism, Marxism, etc) is 'really a religion,' boil down to the question of whether or not they are sufficiently similar to modern protestant Christianity" (Nongbri 2013: 18). The same point is made by Jason Josephson in *The Invention of Religion in Japan*, which is particularly relevant insofar as the Chinese word *zongjiao* was in fact coined indirectly from the English "religion" via the Japanese *shūkyō*. Josephson is convinced. "The word 'religion' is a fundamentally Eurocentric term that always functions, no matter how well disguised, to describe a perceived similarity to European Christianity" (Josephson 2012: 9).

FIGURE 1 *"Festival or Sacrifice in Honor of Confucius."*

This engraving from 1765 is perhaps the oldest surviving Western depiction of a sacrifice to Kongzi. The figure at right looks at the viewer as if soliciting our response: Is this "religion" or merely "civil" ceremony?

The composition seems to be a mixture of observation and fancy. The heart-shaped sunshade (*shan*) and halberds (*yue* and *fu*) are correct, but the lone musician behind the altar playing a horn (*suona*) is out of place. Horns were common in other rituals, but drums, bells, stone chimes, zithers, flutes, and small wind instruments made of clay and gourd were used during Kongzi sacrifices. Court hats like these were not usually worn. The dishes could be grains and vegetables presented as minor offerings, but a whole ox, pig, and goat were the primary sacrifices to Kongzi.

From its inception through to the late nineteenth century, religion was understood to be a belief in and worship of a supreme being, perhaps with a few attendant doctrines such as an afterlife and moral retribution, along with the organizational equivalents of a priesthood and a church. During this period, there were really only four religions: Christianity, Judaism, Islam, and the undifferentiated rest known variously as Idolatry, Heathenism, or Paganism. This state of affairs began to shift in the final quarter of the nineteenth century with the emergence of disciples such as anthropology, sociology, and the comparative study of religion.

For our purposes, 1877, the very year in which James Legge began to write freely of "Confucianism," was vital. In that same year Max Müller, the founder of the "science of religion," secured a publisher for what was to become a fifty-volume work known as the *Sacred Books of the East*. Legge was willing to accept Confucianism as a religion because he mistakenly believed the Ru Classics upheld a kind of monotheism. Müller had been greatly impressed by the recent translations of some of the Classics by his fellow Oxonian and persuaded him to make further translations for his series. Legge's "Texts of Confucianism" filled four volumes of the *Sacred Books of the East*, and so Confucianism now joined the growing ranks of recognized World Religions. This status was reinforced when the World Parliament of Religions held their inaugural meeting in Chicago in 1893. Several scholar-officials from the Qing court were invited to represent Confucianism, and so the tradition was once again prominently paraded as an official world religion (Sun 2013: chapter 2). At this stage it was not at all clear precisely why it was a religion, and the main Chinese delegate in fact said it was not (Pung 1893: 378–9), but people nonetheless became accustomed to its presence. As religious studies developed, a chapter on Confucianism would become a default inclusion in books on the religions of the word, even if authors felt obliged to note they felt uneasy in doing so (Sun 2013: chapter 4).

At the same time as the "great world religions" were expanding, so too were the ethnographies of the beliefs and rituals of tribal peoples. Although the logic was clearly circular, the need to establish a more embracive definition of "religion" that would do justice to all these "religions" was becoming urgent. Two such definitions were immensely influential. In 1871, the anthropologist Edward Tylor argued that a definition requiring "the belief in a supreme deity" and other "partially-diffused doctrines or rites ... has the fault of identifying religion rather with particular developments than with the deeper motive which underlies them." To remedy this, he therefore suggested "as a minimal definition of Religion, the belief in Spiritual Beings" (Tylor 1958: 8). Tylor's primary intent was to ensure the "lower races" of the world were covered by his definition, and in this regard he was quite successful. But the Ru had no more interest in spirits than in God. Something more subtle would be required.

Although the great sociologist Émile Durkheim was thinking of early Buddhism rather than "Confucianism," he was quick to remind those who had adopted Tylor's position that "there are great religions from which the idea of gods and spirits is absent, or at least, where it plays a secondary and minor role." To remedy this, in 1912 he famously opted instead for "beliefs and practices relative to sacred things" as the core of an inclusive definition of religion (Durkheim 1961: 45, 62). The net of Durkheim's definition managed to capture Buddhism while retaining the religions of "lower races," but from it Ru could still escape.

Durkheim maintained that "sacred things differ in nature from profane things [and] have a wholly different essence"; the sacred and profane are, by his definition, mutually exclusive domains (Durkheim 1961: 57). It might be said that it was precisely this separation that Ru found so problematic in Buddhism. It was the otherness of Nirvana and the Buddhist renunciation of this world that was so frequently at the heart of Ru criticism. Although he does not explicitly mention Durkheim's definition, another giant of sociology, Max Weber, observed in 1915: "The Confucian wished neither salvation from life, which was affirmed, nor salvation from the social world, which was accepted as given." Was Confucianism, then, a religion? As if to accentuate the growing conceptual chaos, Weber, who refused to define religion, nonetheless felt confident that "Confucianism was indifferent to religion" and said so in a book that readers of the English translation know as *The Religion of China: Confucianism and Taoism* (Weber 1951: 156, 146).

Confucianism was caught in a strange religious limbo from the early twentieth century until the 1980s. It was dutifully rolled out with the other world religions in general texts, although it always seemed necessary to make some apology for its presence. Meanwhile, China specialists showed little interest at all in the religious aspects of Confucianism. The shift that began in the 1970s was due to increased dialogue between Western and Chinese scholars. The turning tide was marked by a manifesto written in 1958 by four exponents of New Ru Learning, which targeted the failure of the West to appreciate the religious nature of Chinese philosophy. The authors do no speak of gods or spirits, nor of a sacred realm separate from the profane, yet nonetheless they argue that core Ru concepts are "pervaded by [religious] sentiments, and hence [are] quite different from occidental atheism" (Chang 1962: 461). One of the authors of this manifesto was Mou Zongsan, the most important Ru philosopher of the twentieth century. He was a passionate advocate of the religiosity of Ru thought and he was also the chief inspiration of the "third generation" of New Ru Learning (*Xin Ruxue*) scholars who trained and taught in the United States (see Chapter 9). Their influence has changed the game.

The definition of religion that currently dominates the study of Ruism, and indeed religious studies more generally, is one derived from the existentialist theologian Paul Tillich (see Smith 2010). In 1954, Tillich wrote: "Religion, in the largest and most basic sense of the word, is ultimate concern ... Ultimate concern is manifest in the realm of knowledge as the passionate longing for ultimate reality" (1959: 7–8). While ultimate reality is in many traditions synonymous with the sacred, this need not be so. Ru did not distinguish sacred and profane realms, but they most certainly did envision an ultimate reality in which everyday life was perfected and where mundane activities themselves became holy acts. I will explain this more fully in the next chapter, but for now it is enough to observe that a definition akin to Tillich's has become widespread in scholarship considering the religious aspects of Ru tradition.

Often Tillich's influence is explicit. Liu Shuxian, who is recognized as one of the third-generation exponents of New Ru Learning and whose works are very influential both in China and the West, wrote his doctoral dissertation on Tillich. He recalls that while he "rejected Tillich's view that we should have faith in an ultimate transcendent god," he nonetheless "felt excited about uncovering the implicit ultimate concern of the Confucians transmitted through generation after generation" (Liu Shuxian 2003: 133). Cheng Zhongying, also identified as a New Ru Learning scholar, likewise nods to Tillich when defining "religion to be an activity involved with the problems of relating to the *ultimate*" (Cheng Zhongying 1991: 451).

An influential modified version of Tillich's definition was developed by Fredrick Streng (1982) (who, incidentally, also made a comparison between Tillich and the New Ru Learning philosopher Tang Junyi). Noting that an absolute reality might merely be a metaphysical postulate, he added that a religious orientation actually seeks to engage that reality and work toward its realization. For Streng, religion was thus a "means of ultimate transformation" (1985: 1–8). This definition was in turn taken up by Rodney Taylor in *The Religious Dimensions of Confucianism*, which many feel encapsulates a growing consensus of opinion; it permeates, for example, the two-volume collection of essays on *Confucian Spirituality* that appeared in 2003–4. The idea of religion as a means to ultimate transformation resonates with other modern Ru philosophers who, as far as I am aware, do not specifically mention Tillich's definition. For example, Mou Zongsan said: "Whatever ... leads a person to purify his life to the highest state by practice can be called a religion" (Tang 2002: 340), while Tu Weiming (1985: 133) says that to be religious, in the Confucian sense, is to be engaged in "ultimate self-transformation as a communal act." Tu has been very instrumental in reviving the study of Ru tradition in China, and a liberal understanding of the religious aspects of Ruism is now becoming evident among a younger generation of mainland scholars.

I find definitions such as these useful, and they inform my references to religion throughout this book. I hasten to add, however, that I do not believe we have at last found what truly defines religion. Chasing a correct definition of religion is a fool's errand. As there was no concept of religion in premodern societies, we cannot simply gather together all those things clearly labeled "religion" and then discern their commonalities. Rather, we impose *our* preconceived scholarly concept of religion on the data. Different definitions create varying research possibilities, ask unique questions, and suggest divergent interpretations; they may seem more or less promising, relevant, incisive, or useful to a generation of researchers, but this does not make them more or less correct or true. This is reminiscent of Thomas Kuhn's famous analysis of scientific paradigms and he is well worth misquoting here: "We may ... have to relinquish the notion, explicit or implicit, that changes of [definition] carry [scholars] and those who learn from them closer and closer to the truth" (T. Kuhn 1962: 170).

A definition of religion that embraces Ru tradition certainly has it merits, both within the Chinese context and at a broader comparative level. In China from medieval times on, for example, it was common to say that the "three teachings" (*sanjiao*) of the Ru, the Buddhists, and the Daoist were a "unity" (*heyi*). If we are willing to treat Daoism

and Buddhism as religion, then it seems sensitive to Chinese views to adopt a definition that keeps the triad together by also embracing the Ru. This is not to say that they
were seen as the "three religions" in China (a common mistranslation), but they were
seen as three teachings that were essentially in accord. If we continue to employ
the Western idea of religion to investigate Chinese traditions, then a definition broad
enough to include Ruism seems a tool less inclined to fracture the subject to which it
is being applied.

At a comparative level, defining religion so that it is inclusive of the Ru creates excit-
ing new ways of thinking of religion more generally. Tu Weiming articulates this nicely
and indicates how accommodating Ru tradition might actually revitalize the study of
religion:

> It should be obvious that some of the conceptual apparatuses widely employed in
> religious studies are inadequate in dealing with the Confucian tradition. Virtually all
> familiar exclusive dichotomies have lost their explanatory power: spirit/matter, body/
> mind, sacred/profane, creator/creature, and transcendence/immanence. We need
> to develop a new method, formulate a new procedure, and cultivate new symbolic
> resources to meet the challenge. (2010: 273–4)

Religion, religious tradition, or Way?

My discussion of definitions of religion has thus far tended to conflate two things
that we now need to clearly separate. Are we defining "a religion" or are we defining
what it is to be religious? For example, the great psychologist and philosopher William
James once famously defined religion as the relation people have "in their solitude"
to whatever they consider to be the divine (James 1902: 30). Whatever its merits as a
definition, this could never be used to define "a religion." To be "a religion" requires an
institutional presence and a community that is drawn together by that institution. This
is the alternative notion of religion Émile Durkheim had in mind when he said, "In all
history, we do not find a single religion without a Church" (Durkheim 1961: 59).

It is the latter idea of "a religion," the defined entities that are collectively said to
form the religions of the world, that is particularly problematic. It is especially this side
of "religion" that is alien to the pre-Enlightenment world. There are scholars who still
feel it is a concept with some merit, but in the case of Ru tradition there is a growing
consensus that it is useless. I believe we can confidently answer the old question—
"Was Confucianism *a* religion?"—with an emphatic no, although given the developments currently unfolding in China, it might yet become one.

Ruism is unique among the designated "world religions" in its lack of institutional
structure. It had no church, no priesthood, no conversion rites, no formal gatherings
of the faithful. Above the level of the family, and with the possible exception of private
academies in later dynasties, the only real institutional form that might qualify Ruism
as "a religion" would be the imperial apparatus of state. In older Western literature and

in the views of several Chinese scholars we will meet in Chapters 8 and 10, Ruism was thus said to constitute the state religion of China.

The number of scholars who have identified Ru tradition as China's state religion suggests that this is an easily made mistake. After all, as we will see in later chapters, the state formally recognized Ru teaching, patronized education in the Classics, selected bureaucrats based on their ability to master these scriptures, used their texts to determine ceremonial protocol, and employed Ru in executing state rituals. Furthermore, Kongzi and other sages and worthies were enshrined in state-owned temples, and the emperor himself sometimes attended the sacrifices to them performed at the capital.

Ru tradition was clearly very closely aligned with the state, and this is an absolutely vital facet of any history of the Ru. But there was no form of Ruism that was explicitly manifest as state religion. Yes, Ru officiated in state rituals, but so too did Daoists and Buddhists. True, Kongzi, other sages, and past Ru worthies received state sacrifices, but there were an impressive number of gods and venerated people of the past who were thus recognized. Ru education and examination in the Classics was profoundly important to the running of the state, but the state was not merely an expression of Ru values, a fact that many a Ru felt acutely and lamented. I will discuss this further in the next chapter.

C. K. Yang (1911–1999), himself schooled in Ru Learning (*Ruxue*) as a child and trained in sociology in both China and the United States, made the helpful distinction between religions that have their own autonomous institutional structures and a tradition like that of the Ru, which is a "diffused religion, with its theology, rituals, and organization intimately merged with the concepts and structures of secular institutions and other aspects of the social order" (Yang 1961: 20). As a "diffused religion,"—or better, as a diffused tradition with religious concerns—Ruism had a symbiotic relationship with the state. The state was a host body in which Ruism thrived, and the Ru in turn contributed mightily to the well-being of the state. There was mutuality between Ruism and the state, but not identity; Ru tradition has never provided the state religion of China.

Ruism, therefore, did not develop the autonomous institutional organization that would allow it to be recognized as "a religion." The only contemporary scholars I am aware of who insist otherwise are those in China who wish to see *Rujiao* recognized as state religion (*guojiao*) and who are seeking an ancient precedent, but as Wing-tsit Chan said in response to those with similar agendas and who had made similar claims at the beginning of the twentieth century: "All these arguments . . . can only lead to the conclusion that Confucianism is religious, but they do not prove that Confucianism is a religion" (Wing-tsit Chan 1969: 16).

Ru tradition might be profoundly religious, it may contain many religious dimensions and facets—without it, however, being "a religion." This is now a common conceit. Here, I offer quotations from two influential New Ru Learning scholars making this distinction. Mou Zongsan groped for a contrast of this kind when he said that Ruism is not religion in practice because it lacks certain structural features, but "in principle it has a highly religious character. Indeed, it has a most perfect religious spirit" (Mou Zongsan

1981: 39). Tu Weiming is more precise in a passage that culminates in his definition of being religious previously quoted.

> The problem of whether Confucianism is a religion should not be confused with the more significant question: what does it mean to be religious in the Confucian community? The solution to the former often depends on the particular interpretive position we choose to take on what constitutes the paradigmatic example of a religion … The question of being religious is crucial for our appreciation of the "inner dimension" of the Confucian project … Being religious in the Confucian sense can be understood as being engaged in *ultimate self-transformation as a communal act*. (Tu Weiming 1985: 132–3, adapted from the original which specified "Neo-Confucianism")

It may seem a trivial distinction, but in fact there is every reason to insist that Ruism historically was not a religion (*zongjiao*), but that this does not preclude it from being a tradition with deeply religious concerns, that is, with being a religious tradition (*zongjiao xing de chuantong*) (Adler 2014b: 10–12).

In this book I focus on Ruism as a religious tradition, by which I mean it was and is a tradition that manifested an intent to transform individuals and, ideally, humanity by engagement with an ultimate concern. And unlike the very unfamiliar idea of "a religion," this more general notion of a tradition with religious purpose is not entirely foreign to Chinese thought. In particular, the term *dao* was traditionally used in a manner compatible with (although not identical to) a broad understanding of a religious tradition.

Dao, which literally means a way, path, or road, is also used in several other senses. It can be used to refer to a particular manner or method, just as we would say in English, "That is the way it is done." This, however, can be extended to designate a group who share a particular way of doing things, which comes close to what we might call a tradition. There were, for instance, various sectarian movements considered to be "Ways" (such as the *Taiping dao* or the "Way of Great Peace"), and in its early reception Buddhism was sometimes referred to as "the Way of the Buddha" (*Fodao*) (Campany 2003: 300–5). Although the Way of the Ru (*Rudao*) is mainly a modern appellation, in early times the Ru were associated with various "Ways." Kongzi's disciples said their master had learned from the "Way" of the sage kings Wen and Wu (*Analects* 19:22), and Mengzi said Kongzi's great achievement was to revive the "Way of the sages." As Mengzi says this to contrast Kongzi's teachings with those of subsequent rivals (*Mengzi* 3B9, 7B26), he possibly was using the "Way of the Sages" to actually designate the tradition of the Ru.

Way was thus used in China to identify traditions, but it was further used to refer to the supreme principle of existence and to an "ultimate concern"; indeed, it was to become virtually synonymous with the "Supreme Ultimate" (*taiji*) in later Ru philosophy. *Dao* is a concept so fundamental to Ru thought that the great Song dynasty revival of the tradition was designated Learning of the Way (*Daoxue*) (Chapter 6). They had much precedent in prioritizing *dao*. Kongzi had said: "He has not lived in vain who dies the day he is told about the Way" (4:8), and Mengzi used *dao* to signify a cardinal facet of existence and the means for living a righteous life (e.g., 2A2; 7A42). Calling the Way an "ultimate reality" might be misleading, however, if this was interpreted to mean it was some separate reality to strive toward. Dao here still retains the primary meaning of a "way," and it is thus an ultimate process or path; the Ru did not venerate the Dao as an isolated object of worship, but rather sought to follow it and proceed according to dictates. I will pursue this matter further in the next chapter.

"The Way of the Ru" is meant to simultaneously suggest both the tradition of the Ru and the ultimate concern of the Ru, and together I see these as approximating the Western idea of a religious tradition. For reasons I trust I have now made clear, this is not at all to suggest Ruism was "a religion" with its own discrete institutional structures that set it apart from secular domains.

Having dealt with the terminological problems created by "Confucianism" and "religion," we can now to turn to The Way of the Ru itself.

2

The Way of the Ru

Contemporary revivalists appreciate that Ruism is an unusual religious tradition. In an age when most religions have been found wanting, however, they sense the world is hungry for something exceptional. The Way of the Ru, many advocates maintain, is a religious tradition uniquely suited to modern humanity.

This claim has been rehearsed for more than a century. Standing on the threshold of modern China, Kang Youwei declared that Kongzi had established the religion that "suits the present world best." Religions relying on gods belong to the past, he said, but as human "intelligence gradually develops, divine authority gradually loses its hold" (Hsiao 1975: 114).

Half a century later, a manifesto proclaiming that the world urgently required a revival of Ru values somewhat more diplomatically said much the same thing. The authors claimed that the West needed to learn that divinity is not some "external transcendental being" and that "God" should instead be "identified with the human heart-mind, made manifest through our bodies as the direct communication between the life-spirits of all authentic being" (Chang 1962: 479–80, modified).

These challenges to theism demanded, and from their authors received, definitions of religious life inclusive of Ruism. But new definitions were just a preliminary. Their real business was reintroducing this unexpected "religious tradition" to China and announcing it to the world. They hoped it would cause quite a stir.

Likewise, we too must now move on from definitions to introduce the Way of the Ru. And yes, it does unsettle the standard model of religion: a Heaven deficient in gods but filled with humanity, an ultimate reality residing in everyday things, a ritual life that was an extension of good manners, and self-cultivation techniques that included reading books, sitting quietly, and going to school. My job in this chapter is to convince you these can be holy things.

This overview of Ru beliefs and practices is intended to help orient readers and focus their expectations for the detailed history that follows. Needless to say, a concentrated reduction of two and a half thousand years cannot do justice to every variety of Ru tradition. There most certainly were voices not in accord with my generalizations; the details and dissent will become apparent in the ensuing chapters.

I begin by presenting a nucleus of cardinal beliefs. This is followed by two sections on Ru methods of self- and communal cultivation. To avoid overwhelming readers with too many unfamiliar names at this early stage, I will only draw examples from the most authoritative of texts and the views of acknowledged titans in the tradition.

Doctrine

In the previous chapter we saw that the Way was, for Ru, an ultimate path to be followed. It is now time to ask: from where did that path emanate and to where might it lead? For the sake of clarity, I will itemize a core of Ru doctrine under headings taken from six of the most important terms in their lexicon.

Tiandao, The Way of Heaven. Although the *Analects* says Kongzi was unwilling to discuss his views on "the Way of Heaven" (*tiandao*) (5:13), when Ru refer to the Way they certainly understand this to be synonymous with the Way of Heaven. Although rich and nuanced, this was not a particularly problematic concept for Ru, but it was one that bedeviled Western scholarship, and so initially we must clear up some misconceptions.

We need always recall that the first Western scholars of Ruism were missionaries and for them "Heaven" was heavy with connotation. To make matters worse, *tian* was a concept that was related to, and largely came to supplant, an earlier one of *shangdi*, "high god" or "lord on high." From the Jesuits on, *shangdi* was frequently interpreted as being cognate with the Biblical deity and *tian* too was understood to refer to god. And indeed, it is *possible* to read some passages in the *Analects* as having traces of a fading notion of a god-like Heaven (or was Kongzi speaking figuratively? Heaven only knows!) but if we dwell on them we will miss the point.

Critics can provide clarity. Mozi was born around the time Kongzi died and he *did* think of *tian* as a god. He complained that Ru "take Heaven not to be all-seeing" (Johnston 2013: 323). Evidently, they had a reputation for saying that *tian* was not a personal, watchful god. Even if individual Ru sometimes contemplated the possibility of a god, gods or spirits (see below), this was not essential doctrine, and Mozi has one Ru categorically saying: "there are no ghosts and spirits" (Johnston 2013: 321–2). Kongzi himself usually refused to discuss such things (6:22, 7:21, 11:12). On such matters most Ru were not so much agnostic as *anti*-gnostic as they felt this line of inquiry was unhelpful and inappropriate. Ru showed no overt interest in unknowable realms, which led Xunzi to remark that "only the sage does not seek to understand Heaven" (Hutton 2014: 176). Heaven was not a god who intervened, responded to prayer or spoke through prophets. Rather, as Kongzi rhetorically asked, "What does Heaven ever say? Yet there are the four seasons going round and there are the hundred things coming into being. What does Heaven ever say?" (17:19).

For Ru, *tian* was absolutely focal yet one searches in vain for passages suggesting it had any independent ontological substance. It was to borrow Robert Eno's apt phrasing, "a vanishing point, representing the apex rather than the object of reverence" (Eno

1990: 189). *Tian* is in no way other to the natural world. David Hall and Roger Ames have observed that "*tian* is ... a general designation for the phenomenal world as it emerged of its own accord. *Tian* is wholly immanent, having no independent calculus of phenomena that constitute it" (1987: 207).

Although *tian* is entirely natural, it cannot be adequately translated as "nature." Rather, *tian* is an inherent pattern, a coherence or reason that impels existence as it takes form. From the Song dynasty on, this was conveyed by the concept of *tianli* or Heavenly Principle. While the difference is subtle, the idea that Heaven is the form-ing principle of existence rather than the manifest world per se allows *tian* to be acknowledged as an ultimate reality to be engaged through religious transformation. Tu Weiming has thus said Heaven is the source of "ultimate self-transformation," which makes all major Ru thought "profoundly religious" (Tu Weiming 2010: 214). But thus far, Heaven seems no more tangible than the Way. Indeed, as the great Song dynasty thinkers were to say that "Heaven is the Way," we seem to have gone nowhere at all (Cheng Yi in Chan 1963a: 570).

Xing, Human Nature. Although Heaven in theory informs the order of all things, Ru were in practice primarily concerned with how it worked through humanity and provided the basis for authentic human morality. The essence of the Way of the Ru is perhaps best captured by the enormously influential opening words of the *Doctrine of the Mean* (*Zhongyong*): "What Heaven (*tian*) decrees is *xing*, to follow *xing* is the Way (*dao*)." Here we can see that following the Way of Heaven is realized by introducing a third concept, *xing*, which mediates between *tian* and *dao*. *Xing* refers to "the nature" of a thing, but in this context it signifies "human nature" (*renxing*). Heaven's imma-nence as the inherent coherence of existence is manifest as our innate human nature; to follow the Way of Heaven is to be true to our intrinsic selves.

In the *Analects*, *tiandao* and *xing* were brought together only by Kongzi's reticence to discuss them—"one cannot get to hear [the Master's] views on human nature and the Way of Heaven" (5:13). Much of the subsequent history of Ru thought was devoted to filling that silence. And while Heaven itself was not to be scrutinized, our Heaven-derived human nature was discussed, hotly debated, and exposed to various cosmological theories. Was *xing* good, bad, or mixed? If good, as was the dominant orthodoxy, why do we stray from our true selves? How does human nature evolve from Heavenly Principle (*tianli*) and how does this relate to *qi*, the essential stuff of which the world is composed? How do we discern human nature—by examining people in the world or by turning inward to reflect on our inner heart and mind? The various answers to these questions occupy a good deal of the chapters that follow.

For Ru, understanding and following the Way of Heaven is to understand and fol-low our authentic human nature. Mengzi quite clearly affirms that "a man who knows his own nature will know Heaven" (7A1). Indeed, for him it is as though Heaven's entire cosmic process is manifest in human nature. He said: All the ten thousand things (i.e., all things) are there in me. There is no greater joy for me than to find, on self-examination, that I am true to myself." (7A4). For a good many Ru, although not all, it would quite correct to say that Heaven essentially *was* the authentic nature of humanity. Zhu Xi, the most influential philosopher of the imperial era of China, thus said "Heaven and people are the same thing" (Wittenborn 1991: 59). From Song times on, this was acknowledged by the expression *tianren heyi* or the harmonious unity of Heaven and humanity.

The Ru disinclination to investigate Heaven in its more ancient sense of a separate, perhaps anthropomorphic, realm is offset by their great enthusiasm for investigating Heaven as human nature. It was even possible to know the will of Heaven this way, and so perhaps Mozi was a little too hasty in declaring that Ru believed Heaven was unseeing, for, as Mengzi said, "Heaven sees with the eyes of its people. Heaven hears with the ears of its people" (5A5).

Because Ru tradition was concerned with human nature and its ethical manifest-ation, there was a tendency in older Western scholarship to see "Confucianism" merely as a rational system of morality that was lacking in religious sensibility. It was this misapprehension that was at the heart of the critique of the scholars who wrote the manifesto mentioned at the beginning of this chapter (see Chapter 9 for details). They insisted on the deeply religious nature of Ru thought and reminded their readers that

> human nature reflects the nature of Heaven; the morality of humanity is also that of Heaven. What humanity does to perfect its own nature is also what gives praise to the manifold manifestations of the universe. Because of this, the Song-Ming Ru equate [the principle of human nature] with heavenly principle, the human heart-mind with the cosmic heart-mind. All these express once more the idea of the one-ness of heaven and humanity [*tianren heyi*]. (Chang 1962: 464, modified)

The religious dimension of the Way of the Ru resides precisely in the fact that moral cultivation is the transformation of the self by engaging with the ultimate and Heavenly authority of our own human nature.

***Ren*, Humaneness.** Mou Zongsan, the foremost exponent of contemporary New Ru Learning, once said the essence of the Way of the Ru could be reduced to just three words: *Tiandao, xing*, and *ren* (Mou 1981: 28). We have discussed how the Way of Heaven is manifest as human nature, and now we must turn to see how *ren* com-pletes the triad.

If the Ru ultimate concern is to cultivate and make manifest our authentic human nature, the obvious next step is to ascertain just what defines and constitutes our true selves. Buddhists would say our nature was an inner Buddha nature best nurtured by "leaving the family" (the Chinese expression for joining the *sangha*) and remaining distant from ordinary social relationships. Daoists also recommended withdrawal from society, and some were renowned recluses. In contrast, a fundamental premise of Ru thought is that human nature is essentially relational and that cutting ourselves off from cardinal relationships is tantamount to diminishing who we truly are. For Ru, to be human is to engage with others and the path to self-perfection is that of perfecting the way we treat our fellows. This is encapsulated by the paramount Ru virtue known as *ren*. Kongzi said a man of *ren* "helps others to take their stand in so far as he himself wishes to take his stand, and gets others there in so far as he himself wishes to get there" (6:30).

Ren has the connotation of benevolence or altruism or even, in a unique sense, love. But none of these terms quite captures *ren*. The Chinese character for *ren* (仁) is composed of the radical meaning "person" or "human being" (人), identically pro- nounced *ren*, together with "two" (二), suggesting the sentiment that arises from people relating to one another. Both Mengzi and the *Doctrine of the Mean* made the pun: "*ren* means *ren*," which we can capture in English by rendering it as "being human means to be humane." To retain the connotation that the moral virtue of *ren* is intrinsic to our natures as human beings *(ren)*, it is thus usual (in recent scholarship) to find it translated as humaneness or humanity. Mengzi is clear that realizing humane- ness as our nature is to manifest the Way of Heaven: "*Ren* means *ren*. When these two are conjoined, the result is the Way" (7b16).

Altruism is hardly unique to Ru thought. Both Jesus and Mozi taught universal love (*jian'ai*) and the Buddha loving-kindness (*mettā*, Chinese *ci*) and compassion (*karuṇā*, Chinese *cibei*) to all. *Ren* is quite different from these universal kinds of altruism, however. It does indeed extend to reach all people and can go yet further—Mengzi expanded it to embrace the welfare of animals, Wang Yangming widened it further to the care of plants, stones, and tiles, while Kang Youwei even admitted to a frustrated urge to reach out to extraterrestrials with *ren*. But Ru were very critical of any notion of love or compassion or care that *started* from a universal premise. For them, to love everybody universally is to truly love nobody at all. Cheng Yi, one of the great revival- ists of the Song dynasty put it thus: "A man of humaneness (*ren*), of course, loves universally. But one may not therefore regard universal love as humaneness" (Chan 1963a: 559).

For Ru, *ren* begins with our most proximate and concrete relationships and in par- ticular those with members of the family into which we are born, so that Kongzi said that "filial piety and brotherly respect are the root of humaneness *(ren)*" (1:2). Family relationships are followed by those with people we befriend, marry, or serve through employment. In the patriarchal and hierarchical world of dynastic China, these became formalized as the Five Relationships (*wulun*) between father and son, ruler and sub- ject, husband and wife, older and younger (based on older and younger brother), and between friends. Mengzi, who provides our first reference to these relationships as a group, says they were instated by ancient sage kings. They were to remain fundamen- tal to Ru thought and practice until the end of the empire.

For Ru, we nourish our selves by devoting ourselves fully to the most fundamen- tal relationships in our life. Rather than beginning from an abstract notion of universal love, *ren* starts from immediate and primary embodied ties. From there, like expanding ripples in a pond, it is said to extend to everyone. The classic statement of this is found in the opening section of the *Great Learning* (*Daxue*): "The ancients who wished to manifest their clear character to the world would first bring order to their states. Those who wished to bring order to their states would first regulate their families. Those who wished to regulate their families would first cultivate their personal lives" (Chan

1963a: 86–7). And, inversely, self-cultivation is achieved by learning to manifest *ren* in all our engagements, starting with our family, people in our proximate world, communities, and from there state, nation, the world, and even, perhaps, beyond. We will return to this all-important continuum later in this chapter.

Li, Ritual. *Ren* begins with our closest relationships and expands from there to the furthest reaches, but this is not just a matter of extending circles of positive affection or loving feelings. Because *ren* is based on specific relationships, each manifestation of *ren* also requires a specific form—that is, it must be ritualized. All cultures to some degree have some ritualized ways of displaying differentiated kinds of positive regard – today we might nod hello, shake hands, give a hug or a kiss on the cheek to greet someone, each appropriate to a specific relationship or context. But Ru upheld the importance of ritualizing every interaction. One of their ritual texts calculated that "the important rules are 300, and the smaller rules 3000," which means there were almost as many forms of *li* as there were words in an average person's day-to-day vocabulary (Legge 1885: vol. 27, 404). Theirs was a comprehensive ritual language.

Ru maintained that humaneness (*ren*) was inseparable from ritual (*li*). I quoted Kongzi saying a person of *ren* "helps others take their stand in so far as he wishes to take his stand," but he also said to "take your stand on the rites" (8:8) and "unless you study rites you will be ill-equipped to take your stand" (16:13). For him and for Ru thereafter, ritual was the fundamental embodiment of *ren.* Kongzi said: "To return to the observance of the rites through overcoming the self constitutes *ren* ...; Do not look unless it is in accordance with the rites, do not listen unless it is in accordance with the rites; do not speak unless it is in accordance with the rites; do not move unless it is in accordance with the rites" (12:1). Rites were empty, however, if they were not genuine expressions of humaneness: "What can a man do with the rites who is not *ren*" (3:3).

Li is ritual in the broadest and most inclusive sense. It ranges from behavior covered by terms such as propriety, etiquette, decorum, manners, and protocol (dress, posture, proper speech, greetings) through to rituals regulating transitions in life (coming of age, marriage, death), sacrifices to ancestors and gods, and major state ceremonies, all of which are discussed later in this chapter. In every case, the focus is on the correct form of relationship. The sacrifices to ancestors and gods did not demand that they actually exist, as I will later explain. Ru maintained the importance of relating properly with family elders, even if they were long dead, and showing reverence to the divine powers of the world, even if there were no gods. The sacrifices sought no magic response from the recipients. Rather, the transformative power of the rituals worked by cultivating the humaneness of those performing the ceremonies.

If *ren* is love, then it is love with distinctions. The *Doctrine of the Mean* states this clearly: "*Ren* (humaneness) is [the defining characteristic of] human beings *(ren)*, and the greatest application of it is being affectionate towards relatives ... The [commensurate] degree of affection we ought to feel for our [various] relatives ... gives rise to *li* (Chan 1963a: 104). In short, *Li* maintains appropriate gradations of *ren*.

There was a tension in early Ru thought as to whether *li* was natural or artifice (see Chapter 4). Mengzi did not devote a great deal of attention to *li*. He saw it as being grounded in the relationship between parents and children and older and younger brothers (4A27) and says that, like *ren*, *li* is a part of our nature (*xing*); "they are in me originally." (6A6). Xunzi, who discussed *li* at length and had a far more comprehensive view of its function, saw it as separate to our nature; "Ritual cuts off what is too long and extends what is too short. It subtracts from what is excessive and adds to what is insufficient. It achieves proper form for love and respect" (Hutton 2014: 209). The orthodoxy for most of the imperial era was something of a compromise, accepting Mengzi's organic theory of the innate origin of *li* with *ren* in human nature but applying this in Xunzi's comprehensive manner. How this fusion was achieved is an important part of our story.

The ritualism of the Ru was one of their defining features. It can be looked at sympathetically as a way that seeks to transform everyday interactions into religious acts, as Herbert Fingarette argued in *Confucius: The Secular as Sacred*. But modern Chinese critics have argued that what Ruism in fact did was a sleight of hand that took traditional Chinese social values that were elitist, hierarchical, and patriarchal and imposed them on a nation by insisting they were intrinsic to human nature and authentic manifestations of humaneness. To their mind, Ru ritualism was a conservative force sustaining the status quo and hindering progress toward an egalitarian and more truly humane world. I will be considering those critiques, along with modern Ru responses to them, in the final chapters.

Shengren, the Sage. Were *ren* just love, a good heart might suffice. But, as Cheng Yi said, "love is a feeling whereas humaneness [*ren*] is the nature [*xing*]" (Chan 1963a: 559). As we have just seen, Ru maintained that ritual is intrinsic to humaneness, but ritual is a comprehensive and complex art. A good heart is still required, but it is not enough. Learning to live ritually requires great devotion to self-cultivation. Further, while ritual might belong to human nature and be "in me originally," as Mengzi said, it is at best latent. Who had taken this potential and refined it into the perfected forms of the comprehensive ritual codes? This, surely, required uncommon insight into the depths of human nature.

Ru maintained that only a perfected person has the penetrative wisdom to perceive the true workings of the Way of Heaven manifest in humanity as the workings of *ren* and *li*. The word *shengren* is usually translated as "sage," but this does not really capture the Ru idea of ultimate human potential. *Shengren* are indeed wise, but it is a wisdom that is born of consummate moral cultivation and the exemplary qualities of *shengren* are manifest in an almost more-than-human power to influence others to embrace goodness. Buddhist Boddhisatvas and Daoist immortals were also called *shengren*. It literally means a holy (*sheng*, holy, sacred) person (*ren*) and "saint" (from the Latin *sanctus*, sacred) possibly better conveys the meaning to English readers.

Past exemplary sages and the ultimate human aspiration of becoming a sage were so fundamental to Ru tradition that it was sometimes alternatively referred to as the Way of the Sages (*shengren zi dao*) or the Sagely Way (*shengdao*). It has frequently been observed that Ru Classics are aberrant in the world of religious scripture for lacking creation myths, but in their place are chronicles of China's early dynasties and the appearance of *shengren* at critical junctures in history. When they ruled, the world was at peace, their absence opened the way for wickedness, and studying the rise and fall of dynasties was a means of discerning the decree of Heaven (*tianming*) as it was made manifest through the human past. History itself was thus holy writ. Kings Yao, Shun and Yu (Yu founded China's first Xia dynasty, c. 2100 – c. 1600 BCE), Kings Tang (founder of the Shang dynasty c. 1600–1045 BCE), Wen and Wu (founders of the Zhou dynasty, c. 1045–256 BCE), and in particular the Duke of Zhou (who ruled in place of his brother Wu's son) were venerated as the great sage-rulers of the past (Chapter 3). Kongzi is said to have based his teachings on the Way of the ancients (19:22), and he believed sages belonged to the golden age of the past (7:26). Although some of his followers considered he too was a sage (9:6), Kongzi explicitly denied this was so (7:34).

By the time of Mengzi, Kongzi had joined the rank of the sages – "ever since man came into this world, there has never been another Confucius" (2A2). Much later, Mengzi's own name would be added to the register of *shengren*. With Mengzi, sagehood also became an ideal to which all people could strive. He said that "all men are capable of becoming a Yao or a Shun" (6B2) and this was reiterated by Xunzi who argued that "anyone on the streets can become a Yu" (Hutton 2014: 254). This was a widely acknowledged theoretical possibility, and many a devout Ru spent their lives striving toward sagehood.

The sage ideal is pivotal to the religious dimension of Ru thought and practice. Older scholarship that searched for a god-like Heaven failed to observe that the Way of Heaven is embodied in the sage. This is very clear in the writings of Xunzi (see Chapter 4). On first reading, Xunzi seems to have a thoroughly naturalistic idea of *tian* that appears to be like our idea of "nature." He was thus often presented as having stripped Ruism of any religious sentiment. But when he discusses past sages he rhapsodically praises their "godlike" (*shenming*) clarity of vision and their uncanny powers of comprehension and influence. The sages left a path that, if followed, would transform this world of conflict and dissatisfaction into one of pure beauty, joy, and accord. Indeed, the sage is for him and many Ru a co-creator with Heaven. His disinclination to look back or beyond to investigate *tian* itself was due to his insistence that we should instead look forward and within to the completion of the cosmogonic process. As Tu Weiming put it, "the god-like sage is the co-creator of the universe" and brings the potentialities of the Way of Heaven to fulfillment. In this sense, the Ru ideal is "the full realization of humanity as heaven"s own ultimate transformation" (Tu 1989: 97–8). In Xunzi's words: "The sage is the pitch pipe of the Way [and] ... the Way for all people under Heaven rests in him" (Hutton 2014: 60).

Xue, Learning. The sages opened a path leading back to our authentic natures (*xing*). True learning (*xue*) was to follow their Way. Zhu Xi put this clearly: "*Xue* means 'to emulate.' Human nature [*xing*] in all cases is good, but in becoming aware of this goodness, there are those who lead and those who follow. Those who follow in becoming aware of it must emulate what those who lead in becoming aware of it do" (Gardner 2003: 31). Learning, in other words, is following the Way of the Sages.

Sages, however, were not a living presence for Ru. Kongzi said he had never met a sage, Mengzi said Kongzi was a sage and lamented he had died two hundred years earlier, and Mengzi in turn was identified as a sage long after his passing. Sages dwelt in the past. There was no way to summon them, no spiritual entities that lived on to beseech. But there were books. Zhu Xi once remarked that reading was "like speaking with [the sages] face to face" (Gardner 1990: 129).

Being a Ru, being a "scholar" of the Classics, was thus seen as a primary method for refining the self. Studying the Five Classics, and later the Four Books, was regarded as the ultimate means of self-cultivation insofar as the texts were understood to contain the gnosis of the sages. *Xue* certainly has a broader meaning than the study of books, but reading was the most significant of all the religious methods of the Ru.

"Sage Classics" does not really do justice to *shengjing*. It comes closer to "Holy Scriptures," which is precisely why these days the term is used to refer to both the Classics and the Christian Bible. What gives the Classics their scriptural authority is that they were said to have been written or selectively edited by sages. I will discuss the authorship and contents of the Five Classics (*wujing*) in Chapter 5 and provide a detailed analysis of the contents of the Four Books (*sishu*) in Chapters 3 and 4.

There was no church or priesthood to stand between Ru and their scriptures; it was a direct and unmediated engagement between a person and texts written or selected by sages. There were, however, teachers to help students become immersed in scripture. Training men to become Ru through an imperial education system may not seem like a religious undertaking, and we will soon see that in practice it was often primarily a means to employment, prestige, and wealth, but the underlying assumption was that learning (*xue*) was a Way for transforming the self. Learning was not directed toward acquiring particular task-related skills and Ru were rather proud of their lack of specific expertise. As Hall and Ames have observed, for Ru *xue* "refers to an unmediated process of becoming aware rather than a conceptually mediated knowledge of a world of objective fact' " (1987: 44). Kongzi captured this with deceptive simplicity: "Men of antiquity studied to improve themselves" (14:24).

***

We have traced some fundamental teachings in the Way of the Ru to arrive at the supreme importance of learning. This is the juncture where we turn from theory to practice. Religious traditions don't just propose an ultimate reality; they strive to connect. Ru efforts to engage absolute values defined them more than did any one doctrine. It was *Rushu*, the methods or "arts of the Ru," that set them apart. For convenience, I will divide these into two broad categories that should come as no surprise. We have already established their theoretical significance: they are, of course, learning (*xue*) and ritual (*li*).

Learning

Reading. The man who is traditionally said to have masterminded the Classics being adopted by the state was Dong Zhongshu (Chapter 5). Dong was the most celebrated Ru of the first half of imperial China. He often secluded himself in his study, occasionally teaching an inner circle of disciples from behind his curtain. He was so absorbed in the Classics that for years students never saw his face and he never saw his garden (Watson 1961: vol. 2, 400–1). Zhu Xi, whose philosophy prevailed during the final six hundred years of imperial China (Chapter 6), once said: "The only good thing in life is to read" (Ching 2000: 128). Ru were "scholars" and for them reading was a sacred art.

Ru were not reading ordinary books, of course. They were engaging with scripture (*jing*) containing the words of sages. Yet even this does not suffice. Insofar as the genius of sages was their ability to perceive the essence of worldly things, especially human nature (*xing*), studying the Classics was really reading the self.

Ru scriptures envision no other world—they eschew the realms of Daoist immortals; they promise no Buddhist Nirvana or Western Paradise. In theory at least, they tell you nothing you could not work out for yourself by observing the world and, in particular, by contemplating your own nature. The *Great Learning* thus says that self-cultivation begins with "investigating things," and the *Analects* counseled people to "learn widely . . . and reflect on what is at hand" (19:6). Zhu Xi agreed that "book learning was of secondary importance" to grasping the essence of the world we inhabit, but he was quick to add: "The reason [a person] must engage in book learning is that he hasn't experienced much" (Gardner 1990: 128). Most of us lack the insight of sages and we require their assistance to penetrate "what is at hand."

The prominence of reading as a religious practice admittedly fluctuated throughout Chinese history. In later chapters we will see that Tang and Qing dynasty scholars sometimes had a more secular attitude toward the Classics, while in the Ming there were those who believed books were only supplementary to the immediate expression of our innate natures. For most, however, scripture remained *the* primary agent of transformation.

Zhu Xi devoted considerable attention to the art of reading. We have already noted that he saw reading as being akin to a "face-to-face" encounter with sages and he was eager to ensure such an opportunity was not wasted. Students certainly should not rush, skim, dart, or skip. Rather, they were to take a small section and read and recite it over and over until it had fully penetrated their being. Only then should they progress to the next passage. They were instructed to reflect on what they had read as Kongzi himself had insisted that learning without thinking was futile (2:14), but this was deep contemplation not critical assessment. You do not wrangle with sages. Zhu said: "In reading, we must first become intimately familiar with the text so that its words seem to come from our own mouths. We should then continue to reflect on it so that its ideas seem to come from our own minds." In this way, the text "will become a part of us" (Gardner 1990: 135, 133). In a mysterious way he could never fully explain, Zhu said recitation greatly facilitated this internalization process. The student was slowly remade by scripture. As they systematically worked their way through a carefully graded sequence of Classical texts, their understanding progressively became aligned with that of the sages.

There was just one snag.

Concentration. Xunzi was first to suggest a set corpus of Classics be employed in training Ru. He encouraged people to study, embrace, apply, ponder, and always obey these texts. Learning, he said, "begins with reciting the classics … and ends with becoming a sage" (Hutton 2014: 30, 5). But Xunzi was concerned. Sages were exceptional and their perfect teachings could be easily misconstrued by a student's very imperfect mind. His solution was to find good teachers and diligently employ ritual, but the hazards remained.

As we will see in Chapter 4, Xunzi believed the sages' uncanny perception was due to the fact that their minds were perfectly tranquil and centered, undisturbed by personal desire or petty distraction. These very qualities were also required to penetrate the words of the sages. The *Great Learning* thus opens by declaring that people must achieve calmness, tranquility, and peaceful repose (Chan 1963a: 86). During the revival of the Song dynasty, these qualities were constantly exalted. True learning required people "concentrate on one thing," set aside desire, and become "vacuous and tranquil" (Zhou Dunyi in Chan 1967: 123). "Sages and worthies have uttered thousands and thousands of words from their desire that people should recover their lost minds" (Cheng Hao in Chan 1967: 126), but a lost mind would itself struggle to make sense of their teachings. Zhu Xi thus said: "Modern scholars are unable to empty their minds and take a step back to slowly look over the teachings of the sages … Instead, they directly take their own ideas and force them into" the mouths of the sages (Wittenborn 1991: 81).

How might a reader's mind be prepared so as to receive the wisdom of sages? Zhu Xi believed good posture and recitation both helped restrain the mind: "If our mouths recite it, our minds will feel calm" (Gardner 1990: 147). More significantly, there was a form of Ru meditation known as quiet-sitting (*jingzuo*) that Zhu's predecessors had begun to employ and which he himself endorsed for clarifying and calming the mind. On one occasion he recommended "half a day of quiet-sitting and half a day of reading" (Taylor 1997: 45), and although this was just a formula he had suggested to a particular disciple, it was thereafter often quoted as a general prescription (Chan 1987: 28).

Quiet-sitting was certainly common among Ru from the eleventh century on, but it was always auxiliary to reading. One concern was that "from Confucius and Mencius upward, there was no such doctrine" as "sitting in meditation" (Zhu Xi in Chan 1963a: 608). Furthermore, try as many assuredly did, there really was no denying a significant Buddhist and Daoist influence. Zhu Xi was careful to differentiate *jingzuo* from the practices of the other faiths. He claimed Buddhists feared the world and retreated into meditation while Daoists feared death and used it to escape mortality. Ru, in contrast, used quiet-sitting as a preliminary practice to ready the mind for study and moral engagement with the world. This subordinate role is reflected in the almost total absence of descriptions of how to actually perform quiet-sitting. In the context of this silence, Zhu Xi's perfunctory advice to sit "with your eyes focused upon the tip of the nose and the mind focused upon the abdomen" was almost garrulous (Taylor 1997: 59).

If the tranquil minds of sages had produced the Classics, would not any tranquil mind perceive with the same clarity, thus rendering scripture redundant? This was a view alternate to Zhu Xi's associated, in particular, with the Ming scholar Wang Yangming who had reached his own enlightenment after prolonged meditation. We might anticipate Wang's followers would be very keen on quiet-sitting, as indeed many were (Chen 2015). But again, there was a proviso. Wang insisted that our inherent nature, even though it be encountered in solitary meditation, was a nature that was *inherently* familial and communal. He thus became concerned when his followers seemed to prefer meditating to fulfilling their social commitments; they had, he said, "degenerated into lifelessness like dry wood" (Chan 1963b: 217). Wang thus eventually discouraged the practice.

A late Ming offshoot of Wang's teachings went so far as to suggest that if we all have sage potential within us, then perhaps we just need to spontaneously let it out. Meditation was anathema to these radicals. Traditionalists saw them as crazed heretics and so increasingly promoted quiet-sitting as an antidote to their wild eccentricities (Taylor 1979). The practice of *jingzuo* was thus consolidated by the orthodox, although once again in a manner subservient to study and learning from the Classics.

No specific method of quietude was ever definitive of Ru tradition, although it was persistently agreed that the mind must be restrained and centered. On the whole, this was more a general attitude than any one set practice. From the Song dynasty onward, this orientation was captured by the word *jing*, which more generally means "reverence" but in this context signified a single-minded "concentration" on the perfection of the self. As one of the greats of that era said, "If one wants to avoid confusion and disturbance, [one's] mind must have a master. What can be its master? Concentration and concentration only" (Cheng Yi in Chan 1967: 144).

Zhu Xi once said: "Concentration is the essence of preserving the mind. Extending knowledge is the merit of advancing one's learning. Both mutually interact and issue forth" (Wittenborn 1991: 97). Recalling that for Zhu "extending knowledge" was first and foremost learning from the words of sages, we can see how reading and concentration entwined to become the preeminent methods of self-cultivation.

Examinations. The desire to become a sage was the ultimate reason to study. The most common reason was to get a job. The tension was there from the outset. Kongzi said: "It is not easy to find a man who can study for three years without thinking of earning a salary" (8:12). For two thousand years, devout Ru continually complained about students who pursued learning to obtain wealth, prestige, appointments, and power. There is no denying material reward was a major incentive to study the Classics.

The Classics became a recognized path to official appointment in the Han dynasty. This was without doubt a significant historical moment, but it has been greatly exaggerated (Chapter 5). A Classical education was not yet a major conduit into government and examinations were used inconsistently. With the fall of the Han, formal education became even less important as powerful families came to monopolize the court. It was only with the demise of these families that the famous Chinese civil service examinations truly emerged. There were signs of vigorous growth during the Tang dynasty, but they finally blossomed in the Song.

Education and examinations became increasingly structured. A boy hoping to be admitted into a district school would usually begin his studies at the age of seven. He would start with the Four Books before progressing to the Five Classics. His goal was to commit them to memory, and it would take around six years for an average student to rote-learn the nearly half a million characters (Figure 2). After passing several preliminary examinations, a young man was accepted as a "student member" (*shengyuan*) of the civil service, but his studies had just begun and he was not yet qualified to hold office. The tests were grueling and the attrition high. The success rate varied greatly depending on employment demand, but perhaps 1 percent of *shengyuan* would pass the provincial examinations and of them one in thirty would get through the municipal and palace examinations to become a *jinshi* or "advanced scholar" (see Chaffee 1995; Elman 2000, 2013; Lee 2000; Miyazaki 1981).

Devout Ru were of course in favor of the Classics being used for training and selecting men to administer the country. On the surface, the state education system seemed perfectly to implement the *Great Learning*'s ideal of utilizing learning to bring order to the world. The reality was something else. Even in the context of Han dynasty examinations, Yang Xiong had felt the need to say: "For the great man, the Way is the goal of learning, whereas the object for the petty person is profit" (Yang 2013: 17). Noted Ru of the Song and subsequent dynasties were invariably critical. They did not approve of the prominence of examinations in the education system and they were concerned that the undeniable rewards for success meant students had become preoccupied with obtaining degrees. Knowing students would have to live with examinations, Zhu Xi recommended indifference: "If Confucius were to come back to life now, he would not avoid the examinations; but surely they would not disturb him." Likewise, in 1518, Wang Yangming wrote this advice to two young examination candidates: "If you can fix your aim, in all your pursuits fully express the Dao, and be influenced in thought neither by desire for success nor by fear of failure, then, though you study for the degree, this will be no real hindrance to you learning to become virtuous men" (Nivison 1975: 230, 240).

Could a state education system ever be "religious"? In theory, certainly, although by the end of imperial times Kang Youwei was blaming the examinations for having destroyed "our sagely religion" (Gan 2013: 21). Nonetheless, the curriculum was scripture devoted to the perfection of the self and society, the training was an all-consuming discipline of internalizing these texts and their values, and the education process was itself ritualized, complete with ceremonies venerating sages (discussed below). But rulers didn't require sages, they needed bureaucrats who were highly literate, articulate, intelligent, and, above all, loyal. This, primarily, was what examiners were looking for. And rulers knew how to entice. Emperor Zhenzong (r. 977–1022) once wrote

FIGURE 2   *A late nineteenth-century classroom.*

Courtyards of private homes were sometimes used by wealthier families, but classes were often held in cramped and dingy rooms. Over about six years, students faced the herculean challenge of rote-learning the Four Books and the Five Classics, after which they faced the even greater challenge of passing the various tiers of examination.

Teachers were typically men who had failed to pass examinations and so secure an official appointment. Teaching was neither prestigious nor imaginative. The teacher at right is checking the written text as a boy "backs the book" and recites passages from memory. If he succeeded, he returned to his seat to continue memorizing. If he made mistakes, the teacher was expected to be harsh. As a very popular school primer called the *Three Character Classic* said: 'To teach without severity is the teacher's laziness."

a poem called "Encouraging Learning" (*Quanxue pian*), which became a favorite for coaxing young men into their books. The Classics, it says, are the sure path to wealth and women.

There was no need to change the curriculum, but there was increasing dissatisfaction with the pedagogy. Academies were one Ru response to this concern.

Academies. No sooner had the Han dynasty began to formally patronize Ru than there were those among them who wished to opt out. Disengaged scholars (*yishi*) were withdrawn but by no means reclusive and they frequently established small study communities devoted to lecturing and discussion. These retreats were known as "houses of essence" (*jingshe*). The term continued to be used, but from the Song dynasty onward *shuyuan* or "book schools" became the more common name for their latter-day descendants. These were the famous Ru academies.

At their height in the Song, academies were establishments with a deeply religious commitment. Like Buddhist and Daoist refuges, they were often built in peaceful remote locations. Some academies in fact were disused temples or monasteries and one haven rehabilitated by Zhu Xi contained an inscription reading: Zhu Xi "built a retreat here, using a Daoist hut … [But] Zhu Xi was a [*Ru*]. He used his learning to conduct himself in his locality and improve his disciples. He was not like the improper [Daoists] who sequester themselves in the mountains and valleys." The inscription is telling. While Ru might have had very different ultimate values, the self-transformation they sought was every bit as comprehensive as that of their predecessors who, "clothing themselves in air and eating fungus," were seeking to metamorphose their bodies so as to become immortal (Walton 1993: 351).

Academies had some non-negotiable rules of conduct that became increasingly prominent in later dynasties. Zhu Xi preferred keeping these to a minimum, however. He respected the integrity of students, and rather than employing rules he sought to motivate them with "proclaimed exhortations" (*jieshi*). The *jieshi* posted in Zhu Xi's White Deer Grotto Academy (*Bailudong shuyuan* – Figure 3), were profoundly influential and were adopted or adapted by most academies (Lee 2000: 594–607). They were a selection of quotations distilling the essence of Ru tradition; according to Wing-tsit Chan, "there is no better summary of Confucian morality" (1989a: 398). They are worth quoting in full.

> Between father and son, there should be affection.
> Between ruler and minister, there should be righteousness.
> Between husband and wife, there should be attention to their separate functions.
> Between old and young, there should be proper order.
> And between friends, there should be faithfulness. (*Mengzi* 3A4).
> The above are the items of the Five Teachings.

> Study [the way to be authentic] extensively, inquire into it accurately, think it over
>   carefully, sift it clearly, and practice it earnestly. (*The Doctrine of the Mean* 20)
> The above is the order of study.

> Let one's words be sincere and truthful, and one's deeds be earnest and reverential
>   (*Analects* 15:6).
> Restrain one's wrath and repress one's desires. Move toward the good and correct
>   one's mistakes *(Yijing,* hexagrams 41 & 42).
> The above are the essentials for self-cultivation.

> Rectify moral principle and do not seek profit. Illuminate the Way and do not calcu-
>   late on results (Dong Zhongshu in *Hanshu* 56).
> The above are the essentials for handling affairs.

Do not do to others what you do not want them to do to you (*Analects* 15:23).

If you do not succeed in your conduct, turn inward and seek for its cause there (*Mengzi* 4A4).

The above are the essentials for dealing with others (Chan 1989a: 397)

Zhu then added his own words reminding students that the true purpose of Learning was self-cultivation; memorizing texts, passing exams, and seeking appointment were incidental things.

Shuyuan were "book schools" and their library of texts was pivotal. They were centers for study and reflection, and a hall was dedicated to lecturing and discussing student's questions. Academies were also devoted to ritual. There were, of course, sacrifices to the sages and worthies as well as the patriarchs of the academy's particular lineage, but there were also shrines to patrons and noteworthy officials. As the latter tended to be men who had been rejected, dismissed, or punished, there was actually something softly subversive about some academies.

FIGURE 3 *White Deer Grotto Academy.*

This photo, taken in 1905, captures the tranquility and isolation of the academy that is lost today. It was initially a retreat built by a Tang dynasty poet who had a white deer as a companion. Zhu Xi turned it into the most famous of all Ru Learning academies. It was destroyed several times, and these building date from the Qing dynasty.

The academy was a place of pilgrimage for devout Ru. A Western visitor in the mid-nineteenth century wrote: "The retreat is at the base of a mountain two thousand feet high, and many of the neighboring hills are covered with fir trees. A mountain torrent, flowing through the ravine, adds to the romantic beauty of the scene" (Gray 1878: 168n. 1).

The autonomy of academies could worry rulers. The early Ming emperors made an effort to curb their secluded independence so that academies became progressively urbanized and were increasingly used to groom students for examinations. Later in the Ming, Wang Yangming and his disciples revitalized academies as sanctuaries devoted to pure learning and once more they proliferated in isolated areas. Their popularity paired with their remoteness again caused alarm, and from 1537 onward edicts were issued to contain them. This concern continued into the final Qing dynasty when the establishment of academies was temporarily prohibited. But once their autonomy had been curtailed, they were officially promoted to offset a decaying and decrepit school system. Although moral self-cultivation was still emphasized, in the end academies were fettered to the examinations, at which point their numbers soared. There were some 7,000 academies at the end of the empire.

Ritual

A lifetime of learning might seem very inward looking, as indeed it was. But for Ru there was no real divide separating the inner self and the outer world. In the section on *ren*, I quoted the *Great Learning*'s famous continuum extending from the self to family, state, and ultimately to the world. This was a cardinal tenet frequently rehearsed. Mengzi had said "the Empire has its basis in the state, the state in the family, and the family in one's own self" (4A5), and the same sentiment is at least implicit in the *Analects* (e.g., 2:21, 14:42). It was reiterated down the centuries, still echoing in the eleventh century when, for example, Zhou Dunyi said: "In order to see how a ruler governs his empire, we observe the government of his family. In order to see how he governs his family, we observe how he governs himself" (Chan 1967: 202).

According to Ru, all social interaction should be morally governed. *Ren* or humaneness was the paramount virtue but, as we have seen, ritual was *ren*'s embodied form. I will, therefore, now introduce Ru ritual life both within the family and the state before concluding with ceremonies celebrating the Way of the Sages itself.

Family. Genuine affection was, of course, the ideal foundation on which to build a family, and Kongzi had had been critical of seemingly filial acts that lacked true reverence (2:7). Authentic feelings were indispensible but they were insufficient. "Family reverence" or "filial piety" (*xiao*) also required appropriate forms of ritual (*li*) so that Kongzi also said: "When your parents are alive, comply with the rites in serving them; when they die, comply with the rites in burying them; comply with the rites in sacrificing to them" (2:5).

When the Classics discuss family, they dwell on *li*. Sometimes this comes closer to good manners—how to dress for, greet, inquire after, and care for parents (e.g., *Liji*, Legge 1885: vol. 27, book 10)—but a significant proportion of the Classics, and some extremely influential later Ru manuals, were devoted to major ceremonial occasions (Ebrey 1991b). There was no absolute divide between formal ritual and daily etiquette, however. The *Classic of Filial Piety* (*Xiaojing*), an immensely popular little text that eventually was added to the canon, depicts Kongzi explaining that "serving parents in their daily lives" naturally flows into "sacrificing to them" when they are dead (Rosemont and Ames 2009: 111).

Most family rituals (*jiali*) were "rites of passage" marking important transitions in life—becoming and adult, getting married, and dying. "Ritual," Xunzi once said, "is that which takes care to order living and dying" (Hutton 2014: 206). These rites symbolically refashioned individuals so they could assume their proper place at each successive stage of life. Every culture has rites of passage and they mostly consolidate core religious values. God, for example, is central to Christian baptisms, marriages, and funerals, but what Ru family rituals valorized was the sacred significance of family itself, in particular an ongoing succession of fathers and sons.

Zhu Xi was the author of the most popular of all books on family rituals, a late dynastic best seller, and he well understood that "the intimacy between father and son is the acme of [human] nature and human feelings" (Wittenborn 1991: 114). Even educated children would know the words from the *Classic of Filial Piety*: "In human conduct there is nothing more important than filial piety; in filial piety there is nothing more important than venerating one's father; in venerating one's father there is nothing more important than placing him on a par with Heaven" (Rosemont and Ames 2009: 110). All family rituals were in fact directed toward one things—the deification of parents, particularly fathers, who continued in perpetuity as family ancestors.

Although they were a final rite of passage, funerals were by far the most important and extended over three years (generally twenty-five months). From the outset, these protracted ceremonies were seen to define the Ru. Kongzi (*Analects* 17:21) and Mengzi (3A2) both recommended three years of mourning while Mozi ridiculed Ru for their "elaborate funerals and prolonger mourning" (Johnston 2013: 323) and an early Han text said that "lavish burials and lengthy mourning" distinguished the Ru (Major et al. 2010: 500). Ru saw funerals as a time when families could obtain catharsis for their profound loss through ritually regulated grieving, but more enduringly it allowed filial devotion to be redirected from the parent's dead body to a wooden tablet bearing their name. Over three years and through a series of sacrifices, parents metamorphosed to become ancestors. The Classics say their tablet was thereafter installed in an ancestral temple, but in later times this was replaced by an offering hall included within each home. This hall became the heart of family ritual; erecting one, said Zhu Xi, was the first priority when any virtuous person built a home (Ebrey 1991a: 5). The offering hall embodied filial loyalties which endured beyond death and the spirit tablets of successive generations of eldest sons were essentially venerated as gods. There were no hard-and-fast distinctions between gods and spirits (both are "*shen*") in Ru liturgical instructions. Ancestors were greeted daily, received incense and food, and were informed about and consulted on all major family matters.

All other rites of passage were actually defined by this cult of family ancestors. Coming of age was celebrated by "capping" boys aged between fifteen and twenty and "pinning" girls at the time of their engagement. In the former case, three different caps were successively placed on the youth's head as he was admonished: "abandon your childish thoughts, and comply with the virtues of manhood" (*Yili*, Steele 1917: vol. 1, 14). Capping originally took place within the ancestral temple, but the offering hall of later times was too small for such purposes, and the initiated youth was therefore brought before his ancestors and living elders at the conclusion of the rites. Attending to them would be foremost among his "virtues of manhood." Ru perhaps had no priesthood, but every eldest son presided over the cult of his family's ancestors.

Marriage was the next major life-cycle ritual. Men did not take wives; families took daughters-in-law. In marriage, women underwent a far more significant transition than did men. The ceremony culminated in her being ritually presented in turn to her new husband's parents, senior relatives, and ancestors. She now had filial responsibilities to them and was admonished: "Be careful and reverent. Day and night, never disobey the commands of your parents-in-law" (*Yili*, Steele 1917: vol. 1, 39). She assisted her husband in serving his ancestors as well as bearing him sons to perpetuate his lineage—not producing a male heir, Mengzi had warned, was the most unfilial of all failings (4A26). The *Rites Records* clearly proclaims that filial piety and ancestors were the raison d'être of marriage: "The ceremony of marriage is for the good of two surnames [i.e., families] so as to serve in the ancestral temple and continue the line of descendants" (Legge 1885: vol. 28, 428).

Ancestors and Spirits. Given the absolute importance of ancestors to all family rituals, we must pause to consider in more detail the place of gods and spirits in the Way of the Ru. Did they believe their ancestors actually lived on after death? Were spirits real? It is almost impossible to pin Ru down on this. In the *Analects*, Kongzi said to sacrifice to gods and spirits "as if" they were present (3:12) and that people should keep their "distance from gods and spirits while showing them reverence" (6:22), neither of which much help us. Ambiguity would remain the norm. According to the *Rites Records*, Kongzi also said: "In dealing with the dead, if we treat them as if they were entirely dead, that would show a want of affection, and should not be done; or if we treat them as if they were entirely alive, that would show a want of wisdom, and should not be done" (Legge 1885: vol. 27, 148). Xunzi said the symbolism of grave goods communicated much the same thing. Hats with no string to tie them, belts without buckles, vessels that were empty, musical instruments left untuned all conveyed both a filial compulsion to continue serving yet an awareness that "these things will not be used" (Hutton 2014: 212). Over a millennium later, Zhu Xi reiterated that grave goods expressed the "idea of not being able to bear the thought the parent is dead, [although] in fact these are useless things" (Ebrey 1991a: 110). He also said spirits were something "even sages found ... hard to explain" and added: "One should not say there is really something; yet one should not say there isn't really something" (Ching 2000: 62–3).

Until recently, most scholars were inclined to present Ru as treating spirits as impersonal natural forces (Chan 1963a: 789–80) or symbolic "manifestations of ethical concerns" (Tu 1989: 46). In many cases this is an accurate assessment, but several recent studies have shown there is solid evidence some Ru did affirm the reality of gods and spirits (Adler 2004, 2008; Gardner 1995; Sommer 2003; Tillman 2004; Wilson 2014). I want to suggest this was not a major difference of opinion, which I will illustrate by looking at Zhu Xi's views. Zhu is an obvious choice because his interpretations defined later orthodoxy and because, most unusually, he *was* willing to discuss spirits (see Gardner 1996).

Zhu Xi theories about spirits are quite messy and sometimes self-contradictory. He was speculating and he knew it. But yes, he thought spirits were probably real, although he tried to show they were not supernatural but were constituted of the very same substance as worldly phenomena. The "vital stuff" or *qi* of every living thing dissipates upon death, but if death is traumatic it can leave a residual ghost, and even with natural death *qi* lingers for a while like smoke in still air, slowly diffusing. Zhu conjectured that as "fathers and grandfathers, son and grandson, all share the same *qi*" (Ebrey 1991a: 105), rituals performed by members of a patriline might somehow reaggregate their ancestor's *qi* so that the spirit would, after a fashion, actually be present at the sacrifice. And, it should be emphasized, present *only* at the sacrifice, for "as soon as the praying and sacrificing have ended," the ancestor's *qi* "too suddenly disperses" (Gardner 1996: 117).

Zhu Xi's spirits seem so insubstantial, we wonder why he bothered. Perhaps he was trying to present a viable alternative to the spiritual enticements of Daoism and Buddhism (Gardner 1995: 611). Perhaps too he felt that the possibility of reintegrating an ancestor's *qi* would ensure participants were completely immersed in the ritual. When Zhu Xi said that "by fully exercising authenticity (*cheng*) and reverent concentration (*jing*) we're able to summon their *qi* so that it coalesces right here" (Gardner 1995: 608), we sense that the promise of spirits was intended to heighten the moral resolve of those gathered to venerate departed family.

Zhu Xi's conjectures actually do little more than accentuate the orientation of the *Rites Records*. The "Meaning of Sacrifices" (*Jiyi*) chapter reasserts the axiom that sacrifices were merely an extension of service to living parents and it explains how these rituals concentrated a son's thoughts so he could once again almost hear and see his parents: "As he gave full play to his love, they seemed to live again; and to his reverence, they seemed to stand before him. So seeming to live and stand out, so unforgotten by him, how could his sacrifices be without the accompaniment of reverence" (Legge 1885: vol. 28, 211).

The manifestation of filial piety and authentic reverence were the perennial core of sacrifices – in Zhu Xi's words: "In sacrifices, the emphasis is on fulfilling sincere feelings of love and respect" (Ebrey 1991a: 166). The manifestation of spirits was incidental. Zhu Xi thus said: "The matter of spiritual beings is naturally a secondary one … [which is] difficult to grasp, but there's no need to. Better to expend your efforts on the urgent matters of daily life" (Gardner 1995: 599). Centuries later, when Wang Yangming was asked if spirits existed, he replied that the matter had always intrigued him, but really, he "did not know what to say" (Ching 1972: 4). Clearly, this was not crucial doctrine.

For all the uncertainty, one thing most certainly did survive death: the profound filial attachment children retained for their parents. This was the crux of the matter; the metaphysics of it all did not much matter. The *Doctrine of the Mean* placed its emphasis precisely: "To serve the dead as they were served while alive, and to serve the departed as they were served while still with us: *this is the height of filial piety*" (Chan 1963a: 104).

State. Capping initiated a young man into his ceremonial duties to family, but it also marked the beginning of his formal responsibilities in the wider world. He had another father to serve. A crucial Ru premise that has been dubbed the "parallel conception of society" (Kutcher 1999: 3) maintained that the family redoubled so that the emperor, son of Heaven, was father to the people. Self-cultivation led to filial piety, which itself transposed to become loyalty to the ruler. The *Rites Records* states: "There is a fundamental agreement between a loyal subject and his service for his ruler and a filial son and his service for his parents" (Legge 1885: vol. 28, 236–7). For Ru, to be fully human was to be politically engaged. Zhu Xi therefore insisted that "originally self-cultivation and serving one's lord were not two different things. We cannot treat them as two things" (Wittenborn 1991: 141).

As we pass from "regulating the family" to "bringing order to states," we naturally anticipate Ru deploying ceremonies for sustaining the empire just as they used rituals to consolidate families. This was indeed the theory, but in practice things did not go smoothly.

For the first 700 years, Ru were very vocal about state ritual. Kongzi had maintained that restoring the rites of the sage-kings was the key to reforming society, and this was reiterated by great Ru from Xunzi to Dong Zhongshu. In particular, the king had two primary ritual responsibilities. As the living heir, he was of course responsible for sacrificing to his dynasty's family ancestors, but as "Son of Heaven" he and he alone was responsible for sacrifices to Heaven and Earth (Legge 1885: vol. 23, 225). The *Doctrine of the Mean* put this succinctly: "If one understands the ceremonies of the sacrifices to Heaven and Earth and … to [the royal] ancestors, it would be as easy to govern a kingdom as to look at one's palm" (Chan 1963a: 104).

The last 700 years of imperial China were another matter. By this time, Ru were actively employed in scripting state rituals yet their verve had cooled. *Reflections on Things at Hand* (*Jinsilu*) was an immensely influential compilation of quotations that Zhu Xi selected in 1175. It was the preeminent statement of orthodoxy during latter imperial China. It employs the *Great Learning*'s paradigm and discusses self-cultivation and "the way to regulate the family" before moving on to "governing the state and bringing peace to the world" (Chan 1967: chapters 6, 8). *Reflections* stresses family ritual (Chan 1967: 229–30) and has a great deal to say about the moral virtues of Ru in office, but it is noticeably quiet about ceremonies of state.

The only significant exception is a passage that sheds light on the overall omission. It acknowledges that "in ancient times, sage-rulers instituted ceremonies," "sage-kings created music," and through these "government reached its perfection" so that "the world was transformed and brought to completion." But it goes on to lament that ceremony and music had since become degenerate and so were unrecognizable and had a detrimental affect (Zhou Dunyi in Chan 1967: 218–19). It almost reads like a statement of resignation. In conversation, Zhu bemoaned the demise of government

ritual: "In ancient times, rituals were a specialist field and were always kept up as such
… From the ancestral temples and the palace halls above to the scholars and villagers
below, ritual regulations were very clearly articulated. It was still so during the Han and
Tang times. But now, there is not a single expert" (Ching 2000: 88).

Over the centuries, Ru had been continually impeded from realizing their state ritual ideals. The simple fact was, the form these rituals took was ultimately decided by
emperors. Ru were duly consulted, they planned proceedings, they were obliged to
participate, but they were not in control. They were employed as the state's ritual archi-
tects, but it was not their house. It was a challenge from the outset.

Emperor Wu (r. 141–87 BCE) is often seen as the man who established "Confucianism
as a national religion" in China (Hu 1929: 27), but his state rituals owed as much to
specialists in esoteric arts known as "Method Masters" (fangshi) as they did to the
Classics. Like China's First Emperor before him, Wu performed spectacular rituals to
Heaven and Earth on Mount Tai known as feng and shan sacrifices (Lewis 1999b). The
First Emperor had actually appointed seventy Ru to oversee these ceremonies, but
they ummed and ahhed so much he was forced to sack the lot (Watson 1961: vol. 2,
23). Although some Ru had managed to convince themselves otherwise, the truth
was the Classics made no mention of these rituals, which they eventually were forced
to concede. Nonetheless, emperors continued to periodically perform feng and shan
sacrifices for the next thousand years.

Some Ru had been uncomfortable with these innovations from the outset. They certainly endorsed ceremonies to Heaven and Earth, but they were uneasy with the feng
and shan sacrifices, which seemed to send the emperor scrambling up Mount Tai to
reach Heaven so he might become an immortal (Puett 2001: chapter 5). By mid-Han,
Ru were dispatching memorials to the emperor beseeching him to return to the rituals
stipulated by the Classics. They asserted that "in supporting the order of Heaven, nothing is more important than sacrifices and offerings," and so it was imperative these be
in accord with the models bequeathed by sages (Puett 2003: 327).

Mid-Han, Wang Mang in fact did proclaim his desire to adhere to the Classics
(Bujard 2011: 798), but that ended disastrously when he was deposed as an illegiti-
mate "usurper" (Chapter 5). Soon thereafter, Buddhism and Daoism were on the rise
and were destined to have a monumental impact on China's state cults. At first glance,
it seems like the Ru began regaining control from the Tang dynasty onward. They were
given official responsibility for writing ritual codes that expanded upon the sometimes
very sketchy descriptions of state ritual in the Classics (the oldest surviving is from
732 and it still includes feng and shan sacrifices). It is quite correct to say these ritual
codes generally expressed a "traditional Confucian outlook on cosmology and society"
(McMullen 1987: 186). This is only to be expected of works scripted by Ru. There were,
however, very real "gaps between ritual texts and ritual performances" (McDermott
1999: 4), and Tang rulers were also very keen to ritually align their state with Daoism
and, less consistently, Buddhism.

Emperors and Ru shared a cosmology in which sagacious kings were pivotal.
The contention developed with interpretation. The paragons of ritual for Ru were the

FIGURE 4 *Altar of Heaven.*

Every tourist to Beijing pays a visit to the "Temple of Heaven," but most of their photographs miss it. *Tiantan* actually means Altar of Heaven, and the Classics stipulated certain altars remain uncovered, "open to receive the hoarfrost, dew, wind, and rain, and allow the influence of Heaven and earth to have full development upon it" (Legge 1885: vol. 27, 425). The iconic tourist shot, which looks very similar to this altar but crowned with a magnificent triple-gabled circular building, is the adjacent Hall of Prayers for Good Harvest (*qiniandian*). This complex became a public park in 1918, but during the Ming and Qing dynasties it had been reserved for the emperor and his attendants. The sacrifice to Heaven was the most important of all state rituals and was performed at the time of the winter solstice. This photograph shows the altar in the late Qing dynasty.

sage-kings of antiquity who had bequeathed the Classics. Emperors, on the other hand, were more concerned with their own embodiment of Heaven's mandate to rule. For emperors, sacrifices to their ancestors (hereditary legitimization) and Heaven and Earth (cosmic legitimization) were first and foremost ways to validate their rule and consolidate power (Figure 4). Ru, in contrast, saw Classical ritual forms as restraints that checked autocracy and impelled rulers to govern virtuously.

State rituals, especially those to dynastic ancestors, Heaven, and Earth, were subject to ongoing dispute (Zito 1997: 127–30). To give just one example, the first Ming emperor was very critical of Ru ritualists who, he said, followed "ancient models stubbornly and resist change" (Lam 1998: 49). In response, he appointed Daoists to perform the music and dance accompanying his rituals. (Taylor 1998: 877). Ru could be persistent, but if a ruler dug in his heels, there was little to be done. Banishment and execution were among emperors' methods of persuasion.

The Classics were obviously a major source of precedent for official ritual, but this does not mean state ceremonies were therefore "Confucian." The realities of ritual politics were far more complex. John Lagerwey has gone so far as to suggest that "with regard to the legitimization of dynasties, Confucianism never held a candle to Daoism" (Lagerwey 2010: 19) but Buddhism, "shamanism," and "popular religion" were each also incorporated in significant ways.

While early Ru had been optimistic about the power of state ceremonies to transform the world, in latter eras stark political reality dampened their enthusiasm. State rituals were thus pushed to the periphery of Ru religious vision. Ru employed by the Ministry of Rites (*libu*) certainly did their duty by scripting ceremonies while trying to persuade rulers to remain faithful to the Classics, but the great reformers, philosophers, and revivalists we will be meeting in the later part of out history (Chapters 6 and 7) were, for the most part, attending to other ways of transforming the world.

The Sage. The sacrifices to Heaven, Earth, and dynastic ancestors were the most important imperial rituals, but there were many others. One of the Classics, the *Rites of Zhou*, had distinguished between great, middle, and minor sacrifices (*dasi, zhongsi*, and *xiaosi*), and from the Tang dynasty onward this division was employed in official ritual codes.

Only the emperor could perform great sacrifices, but others officiated at the lower levels, and individual Ru certainly executed many state sacrifices to various gods. These were designated duties, however, and "there is little evidence to suggest that these cosmic divinities were meaningful in the unofficial intellectual or religious lives of the scholars" (McMullen 1988: 116). There was one exception. Among the secondary sacrifices, performed twice a year, was a ritual intended for every Ru. Although the emperor might attend, it was otherwise reserved for officials who had graduated, current students and promising potential candidates. Here was a ritual most definitely *not* mentioned in the Classics—sacrifices to Kongzi himself.

According to the Classics, Kongzi's family should have performed his sacrificial rites, but it was traditionally believed his disciples, devoted to him like a father, lingered at the gravesite and continued making offerings to their deceased master (*Mengzi* 3A4). A small cult began to grow at Qufu, sustained by both family and the faithful (Yang and Yang 1979: 26–7). Centuries later, Han emperors would often financially support the cult and occasionally even drop by to participate while touring their domain.

Initially, ceremonies to Kongzi were only performed at Qufu, but from the third century sacrifices were sometimes made to him in the capital, as they were to the Duke of Zhou. The Duke of Zhou was at the time the foremost sage in the Way of the Ru, and when Kongzi was first installed in a state temple, in 619, he was actually introduced as the Duke's assistant. Almost immediately thereafter, however, Kongzi was given his own temple in the capital and became the primary paragon of education. By 630, every prefectural and county school had been ordered to erect a temple to Kongzi, justified by a passage in the Classics stating that when establishing a school "offerings must be set forth to the earlier sages and the earlier teachers" (Legge 1885: vol. 27, 347–8). Kongzi's elevation was almost certainly political. It occurred at a time Tang rulers were trying to use examinations to break the power of aristocratic families, and Kongzi, whose status derived from his capacity for learning and teaching, was preferable to the Duke whose authority derived from his royal pedigree (McMullen 1988: 33).

Introducing Kongzi into temples throughout the land raised some uniquely Chinese questions. There was no obstacle to inaugurating a ritual recipient, as the Classics allowed for new sacrifices to people who had greatly benefited the public good (*Liji*. Legge 1885: vol. 28, 207–8). Nor was there much need for liturgical innovation, as ceremonies all followed a very predictable pattern. The devil was in the detail.

As we will see in later chapters, Ru maintained that the prime function of ritual was to demarcate social standing, among the living as well as the dead. In sacrifices, this was conveyed by the oblation as well as by the numbers of ritual vessels, bronze bells, jade chimes, and dancers. The first priority was therefore to determine Kongzi's rank. This would vary down the centuries, but a basic Goldilocks principle prevailed: too low would be disrespectful, but too high and Kongzi would require a great sacrifice, which would place him beyond the jurisdiction of Ru. Exalted King of Culture (*Wenxuan wang*), Ultimate Sage (*Zhisheng*), and First Teacher (*Xianshi*) were frequent components of his various titles.

Had Kongzi become a god? For some, the answer was yes. Kongzi temples (*Kongmiao*) looked very similar to Buddhist and Daoist temples and they inevitably attracted unofficial worshippers. Some thought Kongzi a bodhisattva. Apparently, he would even grant fertility to women who snuck in to expose themselves before him (McMullen 1988: 34). Many Ru themselves entertained occult beliefs, and in Chapter 8 we will observe these overflowing into popular religious movements. But prominent Ru eschewed this supernaturalism, and Kongzi was not officially recognized as a deity.

This explains the fact that when aspiring Ru sought divine aid in passing exams, they did not turn to Kongzi but to Daoist and Buddhist gods. From the Song dynasty on, scholars often solicited the help of the Daoist deity Wenchang, patron of the literary arts (Kleeman 1994), while Guandi (a deified general from the Han dynasty) was very popular among those seeking examination miracles during the Ming and Qing (Elman 2000: 299–303). Individuals who were Ru frequently believed in Gods and spirits, but they did not avow them *as* Ru, nor did they find justification for their beliefs in the texts which defined Ru Learning.

The resistance to deifying Kongzi can also be observed in another detail of his sacrifices: the manner in which he was represented. From at least the sixth century, the Qufu temple contained a sculpture of Kongzi, very probably inspired by Buddhist icons. State temples adopted this practice, and his image would reflect his current rank so that, for example, were he "King of Culture" he would be in royal regalia. Ru like Zhu Xi were opposed to these icons, which were not endorsed by the Classics and were obviously historically inaccurate (Murray 2009: 382). Most of all, Zhu Xi and many likeminded Ru did not like the fact that images gave the impression the recipient was about to "creep and crawl" down to grab their sacrificial offering (Sommer 2002: 107). The protests continued into the Ming dynasty when it was clearly articulated that the real purpose of the rituals was moral self-transformation: "The Way of sacrificial offerings ... is called humaneness, filiality, authenticity, and reverence; that is all" (Qiu Jun

1421–95, cited in Sommer 2002: 121). In 1530, the emperor finally gave the order that in every temple save the one in Qufu images be removed and replaced with inscribed tablets. Kongzi's royal titles were also removed; he was now simply the Ultimate Sage and First Teacher (*Zhisheng xianshi*).

There is no denying many Ru were "idolaters," and some were so desperate to retain their icons of Kongzi that they concealed them behind false walls. The orthodox understanding, however, was that the intended focus of temples was not the embodied sage but the body of texts associated with his name. Kongzi temple (*Kongmiao*) was thus largely interchangeable with "culture temple" (*wenmiao*), calling to mind Kongzi's words: "is not culture (*wen*) invested here in me" (*Analects* 9:5). As one Ming dynasty Ru put it, "The sacrifice … is not directed to Confucius personally, but rather to his teachings and to the Way" (Chu 1998: 171).

Unlike other temples, Kongzi temples were everywhere inscribed with lengthy inscriptions from the Classics—inside and out, on walls, pillars, archways, and ceilings (Wilson 2002a: 266–8). Again, the pre-eminence of Classical doctrine was evident in an ongoing debate over the identity of Kongzi's associates who would receive lesser sacrifices, beginning with 22 in the Tang and growing to 162 by the late Qing. They were not lesser gods, but rather representatives of an orthodox line of textual interpretation. Today, the centrality of the Classics, learning, and study can easily be observed by visiting the Kongzi temple in Beijing. Inscribed on 198 stone tablets before the main gate is a reminder of the aspirations and achievements of those who entered the temple before you: the names of some 50,000 men whose devotion to learning allowed them to pass China's highest examinations.

* * *

This overview of Ru beliefs and practices has been confined to China prior to the fall of the empire in 1912. When we reach the final three chapters discussing the eschewing eras, we will quickly realize that most modern manifestations are revivals of practices discussed in this chapter. Contemporary advocates are trying to reintegrate the Way of the Ru with state education and government structures; they promote learning through reciting and memorizing the Classics; they seek to revive ritual in interpersonal interaction and even, to some extent, restore family rituals; they are trying to reintroduce academies and other comparable institutions. Most conspicuously, the rituals to Kongzi have survived to become a major national spectacle.

Everything seems familiar, yet nothing is left unchanged. To truly understand the vicissitudes of time, however, we must observe these developments in historical context. It is now time to go back and tell our story from the beginning.

PART TWO

The First Epoch: Zhou to Han dynasties

The notion that Ru tradition falls into three major epochs was first proposed by some of the scholars we will be meeting in Chapter 9. There are other ways of divvying up China's past and none of them can claim to be "true." Time is not delivered bundled in chapters. I adopt the three-epoch model simply as one helpful way of conceptualizing our data.

This first epoch was the era in which Ru tradition emerged and consolidated. It was a time when Ru were contending with other philosophical schools, culminating in the Han dynasty rulers' decision to officially patronize Ru learning. By the end of the first epoch, Ru were recognized "scholars" devoted to a canon of Classics and their beliefs and practices were sanctioned by the state.

Chapter 3 introduces a lineage of ancient sages who were paradigms of virtue for the Ru. Kongzi said he was transmitting their legacy, and Kongzi's life and teachings form the core of this chapter. The final sections consider the generations that immediately followed Kongzi. I look at traditional Ru accounts of the "transmission of the Way" and compare these with the evidence provided by recent textual discoveries.

Chapter 4 introduces two titans among early Ru: Mengzi (Mencius) and Xunzi. I show how their ideas had been refined by debate with adherents of other doctrines, and I highlight the cardinal differences between their philosophies. I suggest their respective views demarcate a philosophical schism running through the Way of the Ru that endures to this day.

Chapter 5 is devoted to the "victory of the Ru" that occurred in the Han dynasty, although I argue that this assessment has been greatly exaggerated. In the Han, Ru transformed from being ritual masters to becoming "scholars," men devoted to studying a canon of scripture. These all-important texts are introduced in this chapter. I also look at vital changes to cosmology that occurred at this time. This is exemplified by the thought of Dong Zhongshu, the most esteemed Ru of the Han. I close with the political vicissitudes of Ru Learning in the mid to late Han.

3

A history of sages

In a recent book surveying the most influential people in history, Kongzi did not even make the top one hundred. He was beaten by Joseph Smith and Elvis. The book has reputable authors and a prestigious academic publisher, but it also has one fatal flaw. Its data, analyzed by a sophisticated algorithm, is confined to internet sources in the English language (Skiena and Ward 2013). The Western world seems to easily forget there are almost three native Mandarin speakers to every native speaker of English. Were it possible to quantify influence at a genuinely global level, there is every chance Roger Ames and Henry Rosemont would be proven correct: "Confucius . . . is probably the most influential thinker in human history" (Ames and Rosemont 1998: 1).

Kongzi was and is a master of transformation, however. We will meet and re-meet him throughout this book. He was a teacher among teachers, the greatest of sages, China's uncrowned king, and just occasionally a god. He was a humanist philosopher, a moral metaphysician, a mystic, and a monotheist. He defended absolute monarchy, anticipated liberal democracy, and was a socialist revolutionary. He warned people to keep distant from spirits and descended as a spirit to possess mediums; he was a sexist and promoted gender equality; he wrote nothing and virtually everything that mattered. Today, he is a relic of China's feudal past and the person best suited to lead the country into the twenty-first century.

There is in fact little reliable evidence about the "real" Kongzi's life. Sima Qian's biography of him was considered authoritative in China, but it was written more than three centuries after Kongzi's death and must be used with caution. The few biographical glimpses found in the recorded sayings of Kongzi (*Lunyu* or *Analects*—see discussion below) are our best bet. The more probable incidences are these: Kong Qiu, as he was named, was born in 551 BCE in the state of Lu. His family had a noble pedigree but had fallen on hard times, and he said he "was of humble station when young" (9:6. *Analects* quotations follow Lau 1979). He was orphaned at an early age but must have been raised by people of reasonable means, for he was not hindered in his resolve at the age of fifteen to dedicate himself to learning (2:4). He appears to have been a *shi* or scholar-official who filled low-ranking civil posts—Ru may have been a subset of the *shi* at this stage, although this is uncertain. He initially held minor offices keeping records of stores in the granary and of animals at pasture. Being a great advocate of loyalty to rulers, he was unsettled by the overthrow of the Duke of Lu and so, at age thirty-five, he briefly left his home state, returning to be appointed police commissioner some-time later. When he was in his mid-fifties, he traveled to various states offering his advice to rulers and finding none willing to accept his services. So, at the age of sixty-eight, he resignedly returned home to devote himself to learning and teaching. Twenty-seven of his disciples are named in the *Analects*, but there is probable evidence he had around seventy followers. He died in 479 BCE, but there are no reliable records of his last days or his funeral.

Given this unremarkable biography, Kongzi's impact is unexpected. Although wise, he denied he was a sage (7:34). He was willing to admit he had an indefatigable love of learning but compared to those born with uncanny intuition (16:9) he could only boast a "lower level of knowledge" (7:28). He was not irresistibly charismatic, but was rather a proper and measured man, "cordial yet stern, awe-inspiring yet not fierce, and respectful yet at ease" (7:38). Unlike "Confucius say" jokes, he seems to have made no attempt at pithy wit, and the one book he was traditionally believed to have authored has been described as "the driest chronicle that has ever been written" (Hu 1968: 48). And if you are picturing heart-throb Chow Yun-fat from the film *Confucius* (Chapter 10), I had better add that an early source said his "appearance was such that his face looked like an ugly mask" (Hutton 2014: 33).

For all this, Kongzi yet felt he was perhaps destined to reform the world. This had nothing to do with his sense of his own importance; rather, he believed he acted with Heaven's (*tian*) authority. Others claimed that Heaven was about to use the Master as "a wooden tongue for a bell" to rouse the empire (3:24), and Kongzi himself professed to have come to understand the decree of Heaven by the age of fifty (2:4). *Tian* was without doubt the ultimate source of authority for Kongzi. Any capacity for excellence that people had came from *tian* (8:19, 9:6), and it imparted human virtue just as it con-trolled life (7:23).

As we saw in the Introduction, however, Kongzi's *tian* was no personal God. He said Heaven forever remained silent (17:19), and his followers said he himself remained silent about Heaven (5:13). How then could he claim Heaven's authority, how could he profess to know what Heaven decreed? An answer to this is implicit in a passage we might mistakenly think merely shows Kongzi being humble and modest. It is rather an assured declaration of authorization. It says: "I transmit but do not innovate; I am … devoted to antiquity" (7:1).

To appreciate the potency of transmission, we must examine the Ru view of the past and come to appreciate their esteem for history. History, I suggest, was the mythology of the Ru, and the dictates of Heaven were found inscribed in human history.

A mythology of sage-kings

Every person in Imperial China who had any education, and many of those who did not, knew how history began. Ru scriptures, the Classics, are profoundly historical. If, as tradition held, Kongzi wrote one of them called the *Spring and Autumn Annals* (*Chunqiu*), it is surely significant that he bypassed the opportunity to set down his philosophy to instead become China's first named historian. For the Ru, more perhaps than any religious tradition, history matters. Their remaining Classics achieve their scriptural status, in part, because they contained the earliest documents of China's past. As Wang Yangming (Chapter 7) would say, Kongzi's "*Spring and Autumn Annals* also is a Classic, while the other five Classics are also histories" (Chan 1963b: 23. The Classics will be discussed in detail in Chapter 5).

The most ancient times described in the Classics are those mentioned in the "Great Commentary" to the *Classic of Changes* (*Yijing*). The alleged author, once again, is Kongzi. The curtain raises in early antiquity when Fuxi ruled the world and instigated the methods of hunting and fishing (Figure 9). Some time later, Shennong or "Divine Farmer" came to power and developed agriculture. "After Lord Shennong perished," it continues, "the Yellow Emperor, Lord Yao and Lord Shun applied themselves to things" (Lynn 1994: 78).

The *Shujing* or *Classic of Historical Documents,* in turn, picks up with Yao and Shun. Shun subsequently left the kingship to Yu the Great who had brought order to the world by channeling away floodwaters that inundated the land. From Fuxi to Yu, men had become kings by virtue of their wisdom, righteousness, and worthiness. But the *Documents* next describes a momentous shift that would change the subsequent history of China. When Yu passed on the throne to his son, China's first dynasty, the Xia (c. 2200 – c. 1600 BCE), was born. The *Documents* does not explain why this shift occurred, but the event highlights a tension in Ru ideals of kinship; should succession be determined by virtue alone, or does family and the quintessential bond between father and son take precedence?

With the founding of the Xia, history began to take on a familiar form of dynastic cycles that begin harmoniously and then gradually dissipate into corruption, depravity, and chaos. When the Xia reached its lowest point, Tang, a man of virtue, usurped the throne to usher in the Shang dynasty (c. 1600–1046 BCE). The pattern repeats. Half a millennium later, King Wen of Zhou saw that the Shang house had lost its moral authority to rule, although it was his son, King Wu, who actually overthrew it and so began the Zhou dynasty (1045–256 BCE). When Wu died, his son was too young to rule, and so Wu's brother, the Duke of Zhou, acted as regent. The Duke of Zhou, loyally serving the king but not seeking to usurp the throne, was to become a paradigm of service for Ru.

Fuxi, Shennong, and Huangdi in remote antiquity (other names were added in later sources), but more importantly kings Yao, Shun, Yu, Tang, Wen, Wu, and the Duke of Zhou, were the lauded sage-rulers of the Ru. They were not only the subject of the Classics but were also claimed among their authors. Fuxi, Wen, and the Duke of Zhou (and later Kongzi himself) consecutively added layers to the *Changes*. The Duke of Zhou was also said to have composed the oldest section of the *Odes Classic* (*Shijing*), hymns praising Wen and Wu, as well as producing the *Zhouli*, which describes Zhou court rituals.

To this lineage of sages Kongzi's own name would eventually be added; indeed, he would be recognized as the supreme sage (*zhisheng*). By his day in the decline of the Zhou dynasty, a new variant of the sage paradigm was emerging; neither a sage-king who sought a sagacious successor nor one who trusted in family and dynastic descent, but rather, closer to the example of the Duke of Zhou, a sage who did not rule in his own right but was of service to those in power. This was to be the charter of the Ru and their history of sages was the myth on which it was founded.

***

The stories from the Classics were accepted as an authentic picture of China's past for over two thousand years. Only around the turn of the twentieth century did a new breed of scholar begin suggesting there was something not quite right about them, either as history or as myth.

As the comparative study of religion and mythology emerged in the West, the picture of the past presented by the Classics began to look aberrant. Max Müller, a pioneer, felt obliged to observe that "the religion of the Chinese seems to have left the mythological stage … It seemed to be a prosaic and thoroughly unpoetical religion" (Girardot 1976: 294). The earliest texts from every other ancient civilization were populated by gods who created the world and ordered the cosmos. China's oldest texts, foremost among them those destined to become Ru Classics, begin far from the beginning with a history of sage-kings. There was no real creation myth, gods and ancestors remain offstage, and miraculous events are little more than the occasional wondrous pregnancy.

What had happened to China's myths? In the 1920s, scholars in China and the West converged in their suspicion: the Ru had disguised early myth by dressing it as history. In China, this new scholarship emerged in the context of the New Culture Movement (see Chapter 8), which saw Ru tradition as an obstacle to China's progress. To contest the validity of Ru views of history was to undermine Ru social and political authority.

Although Ru themselves had occasionally questioned the authenticity of some of their texts, this was the first instance in which the historical legitimacy of the entire canon was disputed. The movement was known as the Doubting Antiquity School (*yigupai*), and they were well aware they had undertaken "a great act of destruction" (Gu Jiegong, cited in Schneider 1971: 61). Their verdict was that the era of the dynastic sage-kings (Xia, Shang and Early Zhou) was devoid of all historic substance, and the stories of men like Fuxi, Shennong, and Huangdi were pure mythology. At much the same time, Western scholars were following the lead of Henri Maspero in asserting that sage-rulers had been created by stripping gods of their supernatural features until they appeared completely human, a process rather unhelpfully known as "reverse euhemerization." Ru "history," he said, was "nothing but the name of history; actually there are only legends, sometimes mythological in origin" (Bodde 1961: 373).

All this revision was based on revisiting existing texts, but in the late nineteenth century the Chinese were eating their words—quite literally. In 1899, it was realized that old bones being prescribed as medicine were sometimes inscribed with a very ancient script. It took decades to trace their origin and undertake excavations, but it was soon realized people had been consuming one of China's greatest archeological resources. The so-called "oracle bones" (although about half are turtle belly-shells) had been used for divination and the subject of inquiry, answers, and even occasionally the actual outcome of events were inscribed on the bones. The almost shocking realization was the kings for whom the divinations were being performed were precisely those the historical records had recorded as the final rulers of the Shang dynasty. Although there was no direct corroboration of the earlier Shang kings, the widespread assumption now is that the historical records probably do name authentic rulers. There is no such consensus on the Xia, some continuing to think it purely mythological while others believe its remains have already been unearthed.

Since the oracle bones were discovered, Chinese archaeology has steadily progressed. Among the great discoveries are several astounding textual caches, some of which are discussed later in this chapter. As these have tended to authenticate texts once thought forgeries, support traditional dating, and even perhaps vindicate lines of transmission assumed to be fabrications, there is now a general swing among Chinese scholars toward "believing antiquity" (xingu). On the whole, Western scholars remain more cautious.

***

Kongzi maintained that he was transmitting the way of the sage-kings and was not responsible for any radical innovation. This was echoed by the early Ru who were renown for declaring "the noble man follows but does not create" (Johnston 2013: 191). Archaeological evidence promises a means for adjudicating upon the truth of this claim. Unfortunately, current scholarship has not at all reached any consensus. Indeed, opinion still runs the gamut from extreme forms of "doubting antiquity" to largely accepting the Ru theory of continuity.

Rather than here detailing this scholarly disunity, I will briefly look at the question of whether the Classics contain myth or history from an alternate perspective. Often, the implicit assumption is that "truth" is the decisive criterion: if it is true, it is history; fabricated, and it is myth. I suggest that truth can be a distraction, and these stories are *both* history and myth.

History, as I am using the word, is a way of trying to understand things by observing how they unfold and develop in time; history is, as Cicero famously said, "a witness that testifies to the passing of time." The Classics contain history simply by virtue of the fact that they look like history. Myths are here understood to be narratives that serve as sacred exemplars and are deferred to in the process of engaging ultimate reality. The fact that the stories of the sage-kings were evoked over and over whenever Ru sought to justify their beliefs and practices suffices to make them myth.

Most people's myths do not look like history. Indeed, Mircea Eliade, the twentieth century's most influential historian of religion, argued that myths were archetypal stories used to overcome the human "terror of history." They provided a timeless template that was ritually used to periodically wipe clean the unpredictable contingencies of time—what happened "in the beginning" rendered history ephemeral (Eliade 1954).

Eliade's model is useful for us precisely to the extent to which it fails our data. It alerts us to the possibility that the absence of a creation myth, the lack of an "in the beginning," may actually be purposeful and powerful. If there is no sacred reality that transcends time, then the absolute must be located within the world of past events and within human history. This is precisely what Ru mythology seeks to establish.

History in the Classics, in particular the chronicles of sage-kings, is temporalized mythology. Rather than a timeless *revelation* of divine order, the absolute is reached by the *observation* of history. As the Great Commentary to the *Changes* simply says, "The sages had the means to perceive the activities taking place in the world" (Lynn 1994: 68).

Heaven (*tian*) is the supreme authority of the Classics, but this is no God who existed before creation, brought things into being, and thereafter communicated its will through prophets. Heaven remained forever aloof, which in hard times felt like cruel indifference. (Many a passage in the *Odes*, as well as the genuinely old sections of the *Documents*, describes Heaven as inconstant, contrary, callous, and distant). The will of Heaven was rather known through history itself. The doctrine of *tianming* or the "decree of Heaven" maintained that Heaven's mandate could be observed in the rise and fall of kings and dynasties. Heaven sustained the virtuous sage-kings who began new dynasties and withdrew its support from corrupt kings at the time of a dynasty's fall.

There was no personal covenant that Heaven made with Chinese Kings. The *Documents* records the Duke of Zhou saying that "Heaven is not to be trusted," and he could but try to remain virtuous and hope "Heaven will not have occasion to remove the mandate received by King Wen" (Chan 1963a: 7). Mengzi would later make the impersonal nature of Heaven's mandate perfectly clear. He said only Heaven could confer the Empire upon a king, and when asked if this meant Heaven gave "detailed and minute instructions," he replied: "No. Heaven does not speak but reveals itself through its acts and deeds." He then proceeded to explain how the patterns of history were a vestige of Heaven (5A5).

It was no oversight that saw Kongzi presented as China's first named historian rather than as its first philosophical author, and it was no false modesty when he said his wisdom was transmitted and not his original creation. Kongzi's ultimate authority might be Heaven, but his Heaven was known only through history and honored best by transmitting the Way of history's sages.

FIGURE 5 *Portrait of Kongzi.*

This image of Kongzi is a rubbing from a stele kept in the Kongzi temple in Qufu. It is believed to be based on a portrait by the Tang dynasty artist Wu Daozi (c. 680 – c. 760). In 1974, Kongzi's seventy-seventh lineal descendent acknowledged this image as the one he personally associated with the sage. It thus became the archetype for the statues of Kongzi that began proliferating soon thereafter.

Across the top it says: "Portrait of First Teacher Kongzi, engaged in teaching." The vertical inscription reads: "His virtue equals Heaven and earth; his Way crowns past and present; he edited and explained the Six Classics; he left a standard for ten thousand generations."

Kongzi and the return to ritual

Anyone might appeal to history, and in Kongzi's day just about everyone did. He had no monopoly on the past and his rivals used it too. Mozi, born around the time Kongzi died, was the first systematic critic of the Ru and he makes his case using a formulaic, almost obsessive repetition of the sages-kings' stringed names, "Yao, Shun, Yu, Tang, Wen and Wu." In early China, the challenge was not to appeal to history but to possess it. The Ru would eventually triumph in this regard, but in Kongzi's time "their" Classics remained unowned, uncanonized, and to some extent unwritten.

Kongzi's philosophy was based on his understanding of China's mythic history. He does not develop sustained rational arguments (as the early Greeks did), nor does he appeal to divine decree (as the monotheistic faiths had done). For the most part he is recorded as simply stating his views in short aphorisms, but when he does reach for support, he turns to history. History, for Kongzi, was "evidence" (3:9) of the "Way of antiquity" (3:16).

Before proceeding to examine how Kongzi read China's past so as to transform its future, we need to briefly pause to consider *our* historic evidence. How do we actually know what Kongzi taught? Of the books later canonized as Classics, he was said to have written the *Spring and Autumn Annals* and the appendices to the *Changes*, while many sections in the *Rites Records* are presented as his words. These are very doubtful attributions. The sole source most scholars use to reconstruct his teachings is the *Lunyu* or "Selected Sayings," known in the West as the *Analects*. It is common practice to use the *Analects* as though it reliably relays Kongzi's thinking, but this is a bold leap of faith of indeed. The book is a pastiche of short sayings attributed to the Master, or sometimes his disciples, and as it now exists it lacks coherent structure. It was traditionally assumed to be based on notes recorded by various first- or second-generation disciples, and the *Analects* appears to be a compilation of their multiple little "books." It certainly is not the work of a single author. Modern scholars agree it contains multiple layers from different hands and eras, but they often disagree on the number of strata and their possible dates (chapters 3–9 are generally accepted as the most authentic, chapters 16–20 as the least so). It may well have taken shape some two hundred years after Kongzi's death, although we in fact have no positive evidence for its existence until the first century before the common era. When I discuss the "views of Kongzi," it must be understood that this is more accurately the views of the *Analects*. Given its multiple authors, it may well be that the *Analects* itself lacks a single viewpoint and we are imposing concord upon disparate voices. But the *Analects* is the best we have.

Kongzi saw that the Zhou dynasty was in decline, and his solution was to return it to its former glory when Heaven's mandate had been freshly bestowed. Punning on the name of King Wen or "Culture King," he said: "With King Wen dead, is not culture (*wen*) invested here in me?" (9:5). Kongzi's Way was derived from "the Way of King Wen and King Wu" (19:22) and his ultimate ambition was to see a restored Zhou dynasty (17:5).

Although Kongzi took the early Zhou as his ideal, he also greatly admired the examples set by Yao, Shun, and Yu. These ancient kings who modeled themselves on Heaven (8:19) were for him history's great examples of virtue and the capacity for sagacious rule (6:30, 14:42). Their way of governing had a mysterious power (*de*) to it, for while they remained aloof (8:18), they could achieve things without taking action. Shun had to do nothing (*wuwei*) "but hold himself in a respectful posture and face due south" to keep his realm in order (15:5). Kongzi, furthermore, seems to imply the initial transmission by sage-to-sage abdication was preferable to the subsequent father-to-son succession of dynastic rule (3:25, 20:1). For all this, he took the early Zhou as his Golden Age.

There were several reasons for this. First, the Zhou was the current Heaven-bestowed dynasty, and Kongzi's intention was simply to honor Heaven's mandate. Second, he believed the early Zhou had incorporated the best of the Xia and Shang dynasties. He said: "The Zhou is resplendent in culture (*wen*), having before it the example of two previous dynasties. I am for the Zhou" (3:14, cf 2:23). Third, pragmatically, he said that although he could discuss Xia and Shang rituals in broad terms, there were "not enough records" to "support what I say with evidence" (3:9).

Kongzi believed the sage-kings of the past had created exemplary civilizations, but he did not look to a new sage ushering in a new age as a solution to current woes. He was no rebel. Rather, he wished to revive the culture of the early Zhou. As we have seen, the early Zhou was "resplendent in culture," and Kongzi said that culture was now "invested here in me." And for him the stabilizing core of culture (*wen*) was ritual (*li*). He recommended that people should be "widely versed in culture but brought back to the essentials by rites" (6:27). Ritual ensured cultural continuity. Kongzi was willing to adapt rituals to the times so long as the substance was retained (9:3), and that nucleus was what preserved culture. When asked what the culture of the future would be like, Kongzi replied: "The [Shang] built on the rites of the Xia. What was added and what was omitted can be known. The Zhou built on the rites of the [Shang]. What was added and what was omitted can be known. Should there be a successor to the Zhou, even a hundred generations hence can be known" (2:23).

When Kongzi looked back for a way forward, it was thus not beliefs or doctrines, but ritual practice that he primarily sought to restore. The harmony brought about by ritual, says a disciple, was the most beautiful and valuable thing in the Way of the former kings (1:12). These rites, Kongzi believed, had the capacity to totally transform the realm. Law and punishment were only required in the absence of an authentic ritual life (12:13, 12:19), but "if a man is able to govern a state by observing the rites ... what difficulties will he have?" (4:13, cf. 14:41). The rites sought no supernatural intervention, but they did have a deeply mysterious capacity to totally transform the living. Kongzi thus said: "Guide them by edicts, keep them in line with punishments, and the common people will stay out of trouble but have no sense of shame. Guide them with virtue, keep them in line with the rites, and they will, besides having a sense of shame, reform themselves" (2:3).

In the *Analects*, Kongzi does not offer a theory of how ritual works, but we can surmise some of his understanding. First, it should be noted that he regularly paired ritual (*li*) with music (*yue*) and he was as determined to return to the best in ancient music, that of the virtuous sage kings (9:15, 15:11), as he was to reform the rites. Sublime music had an overwhelming emotional impact on him (7:14, 8:15), and the aesthetic aspect of both music and ritual should never be underestimated. *Li* and *yue* were typically found working together as the music to which he referred was primarily ceremonial performance.

Later Ru theories of ritual and music seem to be anticipated in the *Analects*. *Li* and *yue* conjoin to produce a harmony of differentiated elements. Music primarily evokes harmonious unity: "It begins in unison. When it gets into full swing, it is harmonious, clear and unbroken. In this way it reaches its conclusion" (3:23). Harmony is the ultimate goal, but "to aim always at harmony without regulating it by the rites" simply will not work, Kongzi said (1:12). While not stipulated as such, it is clear from Kongzi's usage that *li* reinforces social *distinctions*; rulers and subjects relate according to the rites (3:19), children serve their parents, alive or dead, according to the rites (2:5). Kongzi himself applied different ritual behaviors to people depending on their rank at court (Book 10, *passim*), and he was once appalled by a family using eight rows of ceremonial dancers, as this number was reserved to distinguish the status of the ruler (3:1). Later Ru texts would make this the complementary nature of *yue* and *li* more explicit: "Similarity and union are the aim of music; difference and distinction, that of ceremony" (Legge 1885: vol. 28, 98).

Ritual, paired with music, was thus an instrument of cultivation designed to create a society in which all members harmoniously fulfilled their prescribed roles. It would be no exaggeration to say that for Kongzi, life should be lived ritually: "Do not look unless it is in accordance with the rites; do not listen unless it is in accordance with the rites; do not speak unless it is in accordance with the rites; do not move unless it is in accordance with the rites" (12:1). Kongzi saw the ideal community as a ritual performance. To his mind, this was not merely efficient; it was morally just, aesthetically rich, and deeply sacred; it was the "human community as holy rite," as Herbert Fingarette once aptly described it (1972: chapter 1).

The single thread

Thus far, it might seem that Kongzi was aspiring to little more than formality, aesthetically pleasing at best, at worst superficial displays devoid of authentic substance. There were soon critics enough in China who said just this. This was not Kongzi's own understanding, of course. He said: "Surely when one says 'The rites, the rites,' it is not enough merely to mean presents of jade and silk. Surely when one says 'Music, music,' it is not enough merely to mean bells and drums" (17:11). He believed ritual and music embodied virtue and, in particular, the quintessential virtue of *ren* or humaneness, defined in the Introduction. Ritual was useless without *ren*: "What can a man do with the rites who is not *ren*? What can a man do with music who is not *ren*?" (3:3). Ritual may be empty without humaneness, yet it is also the means to its realization, so that Kongzi also said that "to return to the observance of the rites through overcoming the self constitutes *ren*" (12:1).

Ritual is empty without *ren*; to realize *ren*, return to ritual. Which is primary, *ren* or *li*? Our minds naturally seek priority, but the *Analects* suggests the dichotomy is a false one. When an official questioned Kongzi's ideals by arguing that "the important thing about the noble person is the stuff he is made of" rather than the trappings of refinement, a disciple replied: "The stuff is no different from the refinement; refinement is no different from the stuff. The pelt of a tiger or a leopard, shorn of hair, is no different from that of a dog or a sheep" (12:8). Like pattern and pelt, *ren* and *li* can be spoken of separately but in reality they are inseparable.

Kongzi once said his teaching had "a single thread binding it all together" (15:3). That thread was *ren*. It does require a little untangling, however. In another passage that refers to this "single thread," a disciple explains that the Master's doctrine was based on *zhong* and *shu* (4:15). *Zhong* and *shu* are not separate virtues; rather, they are phases or aspects of *ren*. The concept of *shu* is clarified in another section, which says: A person of *ren* "helps others to take their stand in so far as he himself wishes to take his stand, and gets others there in so far as he himself wishes to get there. The ability to take as analogy what is near at hand can be called the method of *ren*" (6:30). While often translated as "consideration," *shu* is a method of taking "what is near at hand,"—that is, ourselves—as a measure for understanding what others would or would not desire; it is a kind of empathy, although based more on analogical thinking than on intuition or feeling. Having projected from our own experience so as to identify what others would wish for, we then act with *zhong*, a term often used to mean "loyalty" to a ruler but more generally meaning to serve with devoted care (Goldin 2008).

Ren or humaneness, Kongzi's supreme virtue, is a deep and active concern for the well-being of others based on our shared human experience and a deep consideration of others' needs. This perhaps sounds like love, and Kongzi indeed does once define *ren* as loving people (*airen*) (12:22). But although essential, "love" is insufficient.

The thing that distinguishes *ren* from love is precisely that which unites *ren* with ritual. Ritual, as we have seen, sustains social distinctions, and *ren* is love, which is grounded in these very distinctions. Kongzi was a great believer in social differentiation—"Let the ruler be a ruler, the subject a subject, the father a father, the son a son" (12:11)—and the primary importance of asymmetrical relationships was one of the most stable and enduring axioms in the entire history of Ru thought.

We saw that *ren* was defined as "do not impose on others what you do not desire," often admired as Kongzi's negative version of Jesus' Golden Rule. There are deeper differences than a change in sign, however. Although the following example is not from the *Analects*, it perfectly reveals why *ren* is more than generalized love. In the *Doctrine of the Mean*, Kongzi is presented reiterating that *zhong* and *shu* converge in not doing to others what we do not wish upon ourselves, but he then proceeds to give specific examples. He says: "There are four things in the Way of the noble person, none of which I have been able to do. To serve my father as I would expect my son to serve me: that I have not been able to do. To serve my ruler as 1 would expect my ministers to serve me: that I have not been able to do. To serve my elder brothers as I would expect my younger brothers to serve me: that I have not been able to do. To be the first to treat friends as I would expect them to treat me: that I have not been able to do" (Chan 1963a: 101).

For Kongzi, doing or not doing unto others was always dependant on precisely who the other was. Acting with devoted care (*zhong*) toward others by empathizing with their needs (*shu*) *given their specific social standing*, was precisely what ritual was seen to embody. Kongzi did not begin with abstract moral values but built on tangible human relationships, which is perhaps what he meant when he said, "I start from below and get through to what is up above" (14:35). And for Kongzi, the root of both *ren* and *li* was the family.

The relationship between children and parents, particularly fathers and sons, was fundamental. *Xiao* or "filiality" was easily defined: "Never fail to comply" with your parents (2:5). This primary relationship was then extended to others so that "it is rare for a man whose character is such that he is good as a son and obedient as a young man to transgress against his superiors" (1:2). In full, these two passages also show that *xiao* is the root of *li* and *ren*, for to comply with our parents is to "comply with the rites in serving them" (2:5) and "being good as a son and obedient as a young man is ... the root of *ren*" (1:2).

Kongzi did not begin with abstract moral principles, but rather with the genuine sentiments that emerged out of concrete relationships. The family and filiality provided the archetype, but the parent-child dynamic was extended throughout society wherever subordinates served those above. Humaneness (*ren*) was thus seen as authentic expression of cardinal asymmetrical human associations, and the legacy of sage-kings was the ritual forms in which harmonious distinctions were perfectly embodied.

* * *

Was there anything new in Kongzi's vision? Was he correct when he said "I transmit but do not innovate"? Nothing I have discussed thus far would have surprised his audiences, yet Kongzi's very words betray him. His undeniable innovation was the very fact that *he* was transmitting. He might equally have said: "I transmit, therefore I innovate." In China, Kongzi was considered to be not only the first named historian and first philosopher, but also the first teacher (*xianshi*). As Benjamin Schwartz (1985: 76) observed, "what may well be new ... is the notion that commoners such as Confucius may *teach* other commoners *how* to achieve *ren*—how to become 'noble men'." Following Kongzi, there was nothing particularly new in the ceremonies being performed, the valuation of virtue or the recognition of the importance of basic family ties, but the presence of a new class of men who had *learned* to cultivate these things would eventually transform a country.

In the *Analects*, the quality that most distinguishes Kongzi is his capacity for *xue* or learning, and it was the one thing he was willing to admit he excelled at (5:28, 7:2). He denied he was a sage, he denied he had mastered *ren*, but he affirmed he was indefatigable in learning and teaching (7:34). It is very fitting that "learning" is the first word the Master says in the *Analects*.

Learning was a radical concept but one that perfectly addressed changes that began unfolding in the middle of the Zhou dynasty. The development of iron technology, which had revolutionized farming and warfare, was a major factor. Improved productivity provided a surplus and instigated a new market economy. In the old feudal order, the king and the extended royal family in theory owned and ran the country, but new sources of wealth and power saw that system crumbling. Increasingly, individuals without pedigree were being employed by the state and the *shi*, the class to which Kongzi belonged, based their claims not on hereditary but on their capacity to serve.

For Kongzi, learning was a means for transforming the character of a person. In earlier usage, as seen in the *Odes* and *Documents,* a *junzi* (literally "son of a lord") belonged to the nobility, but Kongzi mainly used the word to refer to someone who had a highly refined and noble character. The *junzi*, the noble person, was Kongzi's attainable ideal. Sagehood (*sheng*) was an unrealistic aspiration, and Kongzi never expected to meet a sage (7:26); it was perhaps something he thought reserved for kings. Becoming a *junzi,* however, was possible, even though Kongzi admitted that even this had eluded him (7:33). There are many passages lauding the qualities of the *junzi*, but these can perhaps be reduced to just one: "The *junzi* never deserts *ren*" (4:5).

The *junzi*, a person of consummate humaneness, was the ultimate goal of learning, even if this goal was rarely achieved. And learning was, of course, based on the Way of antiquity. Kongzi said that the *junzi* stood in awe of the decree of Heaven (*tianming*) and the words of the sages (16:8), and this is precisely what Kongzi taught. His curriculum seems to have been based on ritual and music, and his foremost "texts" were the *Odes* and *Documents*, although it is uncertain to what extent these correspond to the books we now know. He thus said: "Be stimulated by the *Odes,* take your stand on the rites and be perfected by music" (8:8). Genuine learning, of course, involved thinking (2:15), but thinking was secondary to leaning from the ancients (15:31). There was only one purpose to learning. It was not to "impress others" (14:24), gain wealth and power (8:12), or even become knowledgeable about practical things (9:2). "Men of antiquity," Kongzi said approvingly, solely "studied to improve themselves" (14:24).

Kongzi thought education was an end in itself, but he also saw it as essential training for those who served rulers, and the *Analects* says: "When a man in office finds that he can more than cope with his duties, then he studies; when a student finds he can more than cope with his studies, then he takes office" (19:13). It is hardly incidental that Kongzi spent much of his life trying to persuade rulers to implement his ideas.

Were he successful then, as we have seen, he believed he might revive the glory of the early Zhou dynasty.

Kongzi thought he had failed. But the idea that people could cultivate their selves by *learning* the Way of the sages was carried on by his immediate disciples, transmitted by later Ru and destined to forever transform the history of China.

Transmitting the Way

This chapter began with a myth of history. According to Ru from a later age, the myth resumed. After the Master's death, various followers continued to relay his teachings. Among them was Zeng Shen, better known as Zengzi (505–435 BCE). Zengzi is one of only two disciples regularly referred to as *zi* or Master in the *Analects*. He is described as a paragon of filial piety (1:9) and devoted care (1:4) and is quoted frequently; his words, for instance, help explain the "single thread" to Kongzi's thought (4:15). Zengzi, in turn, was said to have trained Kongzi's own grandson known as Zisi (Kong Ji, 481–402 BCE), and a pupil of Zisi then went on to teach Mengzi (372–289 BCE), who is discussed in detail in the next chapter.

When medieval Ru began consolidating their lineage, Zengzi, Zisi, and Mengzi were counted as sages in the "transmission of the Way" (*daotong*). After 1267, these three, along with Yan Hui—depicted in the *Analects* as Kongzi's favorite who had died young (2:9, 11:9–11)—were recognised and represented as the Master's Four Associates (*sipei*). Their sculpted images (or spirit tablets) can still be seen flanking the Master in temples today (Figure 6).

Zengzi was traditionally said to have authored the *Great Learning* (*Daxue*), and Zisi a work called the *Zhongyong,* known in English as the *Doctrine of the Mean* (hereafter, *Mean*). They, together with the *Analects* just discussed, and the *Mengzi*, which follows in the next chapter, would form the Four Books that were to become the core of the later Ru curriculum. The *Great Learning* and *Mean* are both short, stylistically similar works that were incorporated into the forty-nine books (imagine "chapters") of the *Rites Records*, one of the Ru Classics. They discuss themes absolutely essential to the Ru, yet undeveloped in the *Analects*, namely the manner in which *xue* or learning accomplishes its transformative purpose, and how the Way of Heaven is made manifest to humanity.

To keep the quartet together, I will now discuss the *Great Learning* and the *Mean* here, but I must warn you that this is very possibly anachronistic. I will explain this a little later, but first let me introduce these texts.

The *Daxue* or *Great Learning* is an essay on cultivating the self to become a person of greatness. It begins by establishing "three main guidelines" (*san gangling*), which seem to resonate philosophically with the character or Zengzi as he is described in the *Analects*. The essence of learning to be great, the essay says, "consists in manifesting the clear character, loving the people, and abiding in the highest good." This is followed by what is the central and most influential part of the text, a sequence of "eight

FIGURE 6   *The Four Associates.*

Since the thirteenth century, Kongzi temples have flanked the Master with his Four Associates (*sipei*). Typically, they were represented by "spirit tablets"—wooden placards bearing honorific inscriptions. In Kongzi's hometown temple in Qufu (Figure 19), however, they were portrayed by large sculptures.

Kongzi himself faces south, the seating position of kings. Mengzi (top left) and Zengzi (top right) are to the west, Yan Hui (bottom left) and Zisi (bottom right) to the east. Yan Hui was Kongzi's favorite disciple, but the other three were selected to legitimize a particular *daotong* or "transmission of the Way." With those of Kongzi, their teachings were contained in the Four Books that formed the core of the curriculum for the final six centuries of imperial China.

specific points" (*ba tiaomu*), which show how a person who begins with the "investigation of things" can ultimately transform self, society, and the world. I alluded to this continuum several times in the previous chapter. The key passage states:

> When things are investigated, knowledge is extended; when knowledge is extended, the will becomes sincere; when the will is sincere, the mind is rectified; when the mind is rectified, personal life is cultivated; when personal life is cultivated, the family will be regulated; when the family is regulated, the state will be in order; and when the state is in order, there will be peace throughout the world. (Chan 1963a: 86–7)

This passage, allegedly the words of Kongzi, forms a framework for the subsequent sections of commentary. There is very little on the first two steps (some text is perhaps lost), but the sections on making the will sincere, rectifying the mind, and cultivating personal life make it clear they are each concerned with rising above self-interested subjectivity and insular feelings. Just as it is inappropriate to adjudicate upon color or smell because we personally like or dislike them, the *Great Learning* says, so too we must transcend fear, anxiety, anger, partiality, and affection in making decisions.

The sixth step is the hub. All the self-cultivation that preceded is now applied to the primary and most immediate form of social relationship—the regulation of the family, which is the archetype of all human association. If the previous steps have refined individuals, paring them down so they are not distracted or driven by concerns for the self, this has only been so that they might reengage in true affiliation with others, initially in the context of the family but the regulated family in turn becomes the model of the state and ultimately of the world at peace.

All learning leads people to recognize the supreme importance of filial piety (*xiao*): "the noble person without going beyond the family, can bring education into completion in the whole state" (Chan 1963a: 91). The world can be rectified by fully understanding and extending the importance of family. This is the message of the *Great Learning*, and it is thus consistent, even if unlikely, that Zengzi was also said to be the author of another very influential little Ru book called the *Classic of Filial Piety* (*Xiaojing*), which eventually found its way into the canon.

***

Whereas the *Great Learning* begins with the investigation of things and builds up to link the self to family, community, and the world, the *Mean* starts by boldly proclaiming the identity of the self and Heaven. Kongzi had been reticent to discuss "human nature and the Way of Heaven" (5:13), but the *Mean* has no such qualms. The ideas expressed in the opening words would come to define Ru tradition: "What Heaven (*tian*) imparts to people is called human nature (*xing*). To follow our nature is called the Way (*dao*). Cultivating the Way is called education" (Chan 1963a: 98).

This passage declares that to pursue the *dao* is to cultivate our inherent natures. "The cultivation of the person is to be done through the Way, and the cultivation of the

Way is to be done through humaneness," the text says, and then immediately presses these words to their etymological conclusion by stating that "*ren* is *ren*," or the virtue of humaneness (*ren*) is intrinsic to human beings (*ren*) (Chan 1963a: 104).

Although the *Mean* asserts the identity of human nature and the supreme virtue of *ren*, it is obviously not suggesting that people are faultless. Rather, it observes that one of the most difficult challenges we face is to authentically be ourselves. Human nature is an inner core that can easily be obscured. "Mean" is probably misleading to the extent that it suggests merely avoiding extremes. *Zhong* is rather a moral "centre" that must be retained as an "unwobbling pivot" (Ezra Pound's inspired translation) for balancing our lives.

The secret to realizing our Heavenly natures, our true humaneness, is embedded in a word that does not appear in the *Analects* but which is fundamental to the *Mean*. *Cheng* is quite often rendered "sincerity" but this does not fully capture it. For the moment, while observing its immense importance, I will leave *cheng* untranslated:

> *Cheng* is the Way, of Heaven. To think how to be *cheng* is the way of man. He who is *cheng* is one who hits upon what is right without effort and apprehends without thinking. He is naturally and easily in harmony with the Way. Such a man is a sage.
>
> It is due to our nature that enlightenment results from *cheng*. It is due to education that *cheng* results from enlightenment. Given *cheng*, there will be enlightenment, and given enlightenment there will be *cheng*. (Chan 1963a: 107)

From these passages it is evident that *cheng* derives from Heaven and is intrinsic to our nature, its inherent existence allowing us to achieve enlightenment and sagehood and thus to effortlessly intuit what is right so that we live in accordance with the Way. While in some contexts it has the connotation of being "sincere," it also bespeaks of profound reality and truth. The English words "integrity" and "authenticity" come closer to grasping the wider dimensions of *cheng*, with the implication of being complete and whole in the former case and true to our nature, genuine and real in the latter.

Whereas the *Great Learning* rather pragmatically spoke of the investigation of things to cultivate ourselves and thence the family, state, and world, the *Mean* proclaims the path of authenticity so that we realize the intrinsic, almost mystical unity of ourselves and Heaven. In this vision, the authentic person even takes precedence over the phenomenal world of "things" that might be investigated:

> Only those who are absolutely authentic (*cheng*) can fully develop their nature. If they can fully develop their nature they can then fully develop the nature of others. If they can fully develop the nature of others, they can fully develop the nature of things. If they can fully develop the nature of things, they can assist in the transforming and nourishing process of Heaven and Earth. If they can assist in the transforming and nourishing process of Heaven and Earth, they can thus form a trinity with Heaven and Earth. (Chan 1963a: 107–8)

The person of authenticity who has formed "a trinity with Heaven and earth" is a sage, an ideal that appears here as an achievable goal. To form a trinity with Heaven and earth is to partake in a way that is "extensive," "deep," "high," "brilliant," "infinite," and "lasting" (Chan 1963a: 109). The sage is someone in harmony with the natural principles regulating the world and with an uncanny power and virtue (*de*) that can mysteriously transform humanity. In short, the sage "is a counterpart of Heaven" (Chan 1963a: 112).

This portrait of the sage, which seems almost Daoist in tone, is brought back to Ru reality by one assumption. Human nature, while Heaven derived, is intrinsically communal. Indeed, at a fundamental level, there is no separation between Heaven and humanity. The essay stresses that sagehood and the way of Heaven must be discovered in the common mundane world of human relationships. Just as the *Great Learning* had done, the *Mean* singles out filial piety so that someone "wishing to cultivate his personal life ... must not fail to serve his parents" (Chan 1963a: 105). The path to self-realization is thus one where the centered self is embodied in common, everyday relationships. Reflecting this understanding, *Zhongyong*, which puzzled even scholars in imperial China, should perhaps be rendered as something like: *Maintaining the Centre* (zhong) *in Everyday* (yong) *Affairs* (compare Tu 1989; Ames and Hall 2001).

Guodian

The *Great Learning* and the *Mean* were destined for greatness. That occurred after 1313, however, more than one and a half millennia beyond the time of their alleged authors. They were certainly important earlier insofar as they were incorporated into the *Rites Records*, but we know that Classic was still taking shape at least until 78 BCE. What we need to ask is whether they actually tell us anything about the era between Kongzi and Mengzi.

Until recently, the scholarly consensus suspected they were actually written much later, but grave robbers have changed quite a few minds. Three astounding caches of texts have been unearthed in Hubei Provence from tombs sealed in about 300 BCE. Two of these were recovered in poor condition from the black market and acquired by the Shanghai Museum in 1994 and Tsinghua University in 2008. Although they promise further evidence for our discussion, I will be focusing on the other, better-preserved cache the robbers left behind in a tomb in a village named Guodian. Professional archaeologists recovered it in 1993. These recent discoveries contain China's oldest copies of philosophical texts, and in the resultant "fever" of analysis Zisi's name is regularly being mentioned. These are the discoveries, mentioned earlier, that have inclined more than a few scholars toward once again "believing antiquity."

We can probably dismiss the association between the *Great Learning* and Zengzi as this was first made as late as the twelfth century CE. The *Mean*, however, was initially attributed to Zisi by Sima Qian in the second century BCE. To appreciate why the Guodian texts are being linked with Zisi, you will need to keep two things in mind. First, Xunzi, who we will meet in the next chapter, was a fervent critic of the teachings of Zisi and Mengzi who he called "stupid scholars of this vulgar age [who] yammer all about" an "extremely deviant" doctrine of *wuxing* or "Five Conducts" (Hutton 2014: 41–2). Second, there was a belief that not just the *Mean* but also three other books in the *Rites Records* (together, books 30–33), including one called "Black Robes" (*Ziyi*) were all by Zisi and were taken from his book called the *Zisizi*. As these chapters are all stylistically similar, and as the claim was made at a time when the now lost *Zisizi* was still in circulation, this could be true (Cook 2012: 113), although it might just as easily mean the *Zisizi* was a forgery that had poached four chapters from the *Rites Records* (Hu 2008: 540).

With these points in mind, you can imagine the excitement when it was realized that the Guodian corpus contained a version of "Black Robes" and a work named *Wuxing* or *Five Conducts* (also uncovered in a tomb at Mawangdui in 1973). Furthermore, another text that has been named *Nature Comes via Mandate* (*Xing zi ming chu*) contains passages that are strikingly similar to opening lines of the *Mean*. There is even a short text describing Zisi himself bluntly advising one Lord Mu, who later texts claim he had tutored. As the tomb was closed around the time that Mengzi himself died, and providing the deceased had not chosen to be laid to rest with a stash of new releases, we can assume the texts are significantly older than 300 BCE and so belong to the period between Kongzi and Mengzi.

Many continue to hope that the Guodian texts represent the Zisi school and perhaps even contain sections of the *Zisizi*. The possibility of having discovered largely unknown texts revealing the thought of one of the most influential early Ru who also happened to be Kongzi's grandson—merit by both worthiness and filiation—is incredibly alluring. But the uncertainties are many; there is even serious doubt as to whether Zisi actually was Kongzi's grandson (Csikszentmihalyi 2004: 94–100).

Assignation aside, what we do now undoubtedly possess is evidence for Ru thought during an era that was previously unrepresented. I will consider three of the more illuminating Guodian texts, and my focus is on light they shed on changes to Ru tradition between the time of Kongzi and Mengzi.

The text that perhaps shows the greatest affinity with Mengzi is called *Wuxing* or *Five Conducts*, the very term for the doctrine that Xunzi had denigrated in the teachings of Zisi and Mengzi. As we will see in the next chapter, Mengzi was to argue that the virtues of *ren* (humaneness), *li* (ritual), *zhi* (wisdom), and *yi* (righteousness) were all intrinsic to human nature (*xing*). The *wuxing* turn out to be precisely these four with the addition of a fifth and privileged virtue of *sheng* or "sagacity." The first four working in concert, we are told, pertain only to goodness (*shan*), but with the fifth included a person achieves true virtue (*de*): "Goodness is the Way of mankind; virtuosity is the Way of Heaven" (Cook 2012: 488). The text emphasizes that these five must work from "within" and not be mere artifice, and to this end it stresses cultivating the inner self. This focus on the interior nature of virtue is very much in keeping with Mengzi's views, as we will see. I will spare the reader from further analysis of this text, however – the remainder readily calls to mind Xunzi's description of the *wuxing* doctrine: "murky" with "no proper arguments" (Hutton 2014: 41).

Xing zi ming chu or *Nature Comes via Mandate* has attracted a lot of attention. As another version was found among the Shanghai Museum Corpus, this may have once been a well-known work. The title was selected by modern scholars from an early passage in the text, which says that "[human] nature comes via mandate, and this mandate is sent down from Heaven" and goes on to argue that the Way is realized by cultivating out Heaven-given natures (Cook 2012: 700). This, of course, sounds remarkably similar to the opening lines of the *Mean*, which explains why this text initially generated so much excitement.

Upon closer inspection, however, *Nature Comes via Mandate* turns out to be more completely in accord with the views of Xunzi, the great critic of Zisi and Mengzi. What it actually says is that human nature is derived from Heaven, and the emotions (*qing*) such as joy and sorrow, anger and grief, are definitive of our nature. Xunzi too says just this: "Human nature is the accomplishment of Heaven. The [emotions (*qing*)] are the substance of the nature" (Hutton 2014: 244). Neither the *Xunzi* nor *Nature comes via Mandate* are renunciatory texts and the latter positively celebrates emotion and seeks to elevate it to new heights. Everyone shares in having emotions, it says; where people differ, and sometimes differ wildly, is in what makes them happy or sad. While "oxen are born to spread out, and geese are born to line in formation," human inclinations are not innate, but are rather learned (Cook 2012: 703). It is the *xin* or heart-mind (*xin* is literally "heart" but controls both thoughts and feelings) that guides human nature so that raw emotion is cultivated to respond to the dictates of righteousness (*yi*). This is what distinguishes those whose likes and dislikes are base from those whose tastes are noble.

The idea that emotions, and from them desires, define our natures and that our natures require the restraints of heart-mind were fundamental to Xunzi's thought, as we will see in the next chapter. So too *Nature Comes via Mandate* anticipates Xunzi's proposals for cultivation. Xunzi is remembered for having advocated ritual and music as the best instruments for shaping people, and *Nature Comes via Mandate* likewise champions music as the quickest and most immediate tool for refining the heart-mind. It says that ritual and music are natural expressions of human emotion, but the sages had gathered and distilled them to a "refined pattern" so that they in turn guide the emotions toward righteousness (*yi*). Without for a moment renouncing emotions, music—which incorporated rhythm, melody, the words of odes and even historic themes enacted through dance—can harness our emotions so as to lead us toward moral fulfilment.

The two examples I have considered suggest the Guodian corpus does not tie tidily to any one lineage or school, which is surely to be expected in a time of transition. Lineages only appear clearly with hindsight. Rather, we do better to look to these texts for broader tendencies in evolving Ru thought. The discussion of the relation between Heaven, human nature, and the heart-mind is very apparent in the works discussed thus far, although conspicuously absent from the *Analects*. Clearly, these were things subsequent Ru felt needed amplification. As we will soon see, they were further consolidated by the philosophies of Mengzi and Xunzi and they were to remain fundamental to Ru thought thereafter.

Some other Guodian texts anticipate developments of an even later date. One of the distinctive features of Ruism in the Han dynasty, to which Chapter 5 is devoted, was the manner in which a fivefold classification of phenomena in virtually every domain was used to explain how differing cosmic elements corresponded to and resonated with one another. It is just possible that the *wuxing* (five conducts) laid the foundation for this as the primary form of this classification—usually translated as the Five "Phases" or "Processes" (earth, fire, wood, water, and metal)—is in fact identically called *wuxing*. It is written with the same characters (五行) and only context makes the meaning distinct (Holloway 2009: 45–8). In the *Wuxing* text of Guodian, however, actual correspondences were not pursued.

In another text called the *Six Virtues* (*Liu de*), however, this correlative way of thinking is very evident. The text begins with six paired positions that people occupy in the world: husband-wife, father-son, ruler-minister. These, we are told, correspond to six paired duties: to lead and to follow, to instruct and to learn, to direct and to serve. With these also correspond six paired virtues: *zhi* (wisdom) – *xin* (fidelity), *sheng* (sagacity) – *ren* (humaneness), *yi* (righteousness) – *zhong* (loyalty, devoted care). The text explores multiple ways of reconfiguring these social positions, duties, and virtues to create the impression of an all-embracing web of connection and correspondence.

And amid the categories appears yet another sixfold group that was most unexpected, our earliest reference to the body of books that were to be canonized as the Ru Classics in the Han dynasty—the *Odes, Documents, Ritual, Music, Changes*, and *Spring and Autumn*—although these could not have been identical to the versions we know, which were evolving for centuries yet. As I suggest in Chapter 5 when discussing the canon, it is very likely that when one of these Classics was "lost," it was a deliberate move to ensure the Five Classics were consonant with the Five Processes (*wuxing*). Here, the correspondence between the Six Virtues and a prototype of the Six Classics seems to indicate the germ of the idea that scripture must correlate with every facet of the cosmos.

***

How can we determine what really happened between the time of Kongzi and Mengzi? Should we doubt or believe antiquity? The reason there is no simple answer to this question is because of something I have stressed throughout this chapter: for Ru, history had mythic authority. As such, we can expect they had a vast repertoire of data based on their observations of history, an assumption verified by old bibliographies listing books now lost and new discoveries of books already lost to the bibliographers. We should not underestimate the "evidence" available to early Chinese historians. But we must expect their data to have been constantly reworked in order to reveal desired patterns in the past. They were not striving for objectivity; they were searching for traces of Heaven.

While later myths of the "transmission of the Way" (*daotong*) from Zengzi to Zisi to Mengzi suggest a tidy lineage of disciples relaying and developing Kongzi's teachings, the recent discoveries present a more complicated picture. Indeed, while the former view might be considered "Confucian," the Guodian corpus seem to reflect the views of less sectarian Ru. It is surely significant that while the texts are replete with references to sage-kings, virtue based on distinction, and the importance of ritual and music—all quintessentially Ru attributes—Kongzi himself is conspicuously absent. The only exception to this might be in *Black Robes if* "the Master said" in fact means "Kongzi said," but Ru themselves had questioned this interpretation (of the canonical version) since the Song dynasty (Cook 2012: 355–6n. 2).

While a lack of evidence to the contrary is hardly positive proof, I suspect that at this time Kongzi had yet to be widely recognized as a great sage, and for many he was an ever receding memory of a revered master who had revived Ru tradition. As far as we know, it was Mengzi who began reinventing Kongzi as a sage. It is time to meet this man who would himself come to be known as the "Second Sage" (*yasheng*).

4

Two paths: mysticism and ritual

The Ru certainly had enemies. Here is a description of Kongzi from a follower of Yang Zhu: "You devise maxims, concoct aphorisms, tendentiously cite King Wen and King Wu, and with that branching tree of a cap on your head and a hide of a dead cow's ribs around your waist, by your verbose phrasings and lying explanations you get your dinner without having to plough" (Graham 1981: 235). And now, Mozi on the early Ru: "They are like beggars. They hoard food like field mice. They stare like billy-goats. They rise up like castrated pigs" (Johnston 2013: 191).

Perhaps we should expect dirty play from their opponents, but the Ru could be equally scathing of one another. Xunzi, who we saw in the previous chapter describing Zisi and Mengzi as "stupid Ru of this vulgar age," was not finished. Targeting three prominent disciples of Kongzi whose own disciples were "perverse, hollow and smug," he said those following Zizhang were pretentious in dress, speech, and deportment, those emulating Zixia just mutely gawked "as though holding something in their mouths," while adherents of Ziyou did nothing but stuff themselves with food and drink (Hutton 2014: 45–6).

This factionalism was already becoming evident in the *Analects*. Book 19 is made of quotations from the three disciples just mentioned, along with Zengzi and Zigong, and occasionally the bickering seems to be barely beneath the surface. Little wonder that Han Feizi (280–233 BCE), a sometime student of Xunzi, would say that the Ru were so divided it seemed farcical they claimed to uphold the way of ancient sage-kings; how could these men possibly know what Yao and Shun had said thousands of years ago when they couldn't even agree on what their own Master had recently taught? (Watson 1964: 118–19).

The influence of rival philosophies

This divisiveness and argumentation perfectly matched the political realities of the time. A few years before Kongzi's death, the Zhou dynasty had entered its final bloody

centuries known as the age of the Warring States (481–221 BCE). The once relatively harmonious league of cities governed by the ruling dynasty's nobles was fragmented into independent states with their own monarchs, each vying for supremacy.
Campaigns and devastating wars were rife, but battles were also being waged for
minds, and some rulers positively encouraged intellectual dispute.

Nowhere was this more apparent than at the famous Jixia academy (*Jixia xue-
gong*) founded in the mid-fourth century BCE in the state of Qi. The Qi kings sought
to attract vagrant scholars by offering them luxurious accommodation, generous sti-
pends, and a place to preach. They came, sometimes in their hundreds, to debate
their views in a privileged atmosphere, free from the burden of political responsibility. Among its prestigious guests were the two Ru to whom this chapter is devoted,
Mengzi and Xunzi.

We can readily see that Mengzi's and Xunzis thinking had been honed by opposition. Although they, like Kongzi, constantly draw on examples from the mythic history
of sage-kings as "proof," they also develop sustained rational arguments to defend
their views against assailants. At the same time, they show that Ru thought was
consolidated and enriched by appropriating and reworking their critic's philosophical vocabulary. This was the beginning of an ongoing process; first it was Mozi and
Yang Zhu, in imperial times Buddhism and Daoism, today it is a new pair dubbed Mr.
Science and Mr. Democracy. Ru thought has been repeatedly refined in the crucible
of enmity.

Mozi's (ca. 470 – ca. 391) followers were very real competition at court, and their
attacks on the Ru were well aimed. Their primary critique was of the gradations of
love in the Ru understanding of *ren*, and of the excessive music and ritual required
to reinforce gradations and distinctions. Mozi instead taught universal love (*jianai*).
He believed that Heaven was the source of that love and Heaven, to him, was a
knowing and intervening god. His Heaven said: "Those I love, these men love without partiality" (Johnston 2013: 128). It is tempting to see Mozi as China's precursor to Jesus—he was even perhaps a carpenter—but Mozi was ever the pragmatist.
He promoted universal love purely because it was an expedient solution to division
and strife. Mengzi and Xunzi were resolute in rebutting Mozi, as his followers were
genuine rivals for patronage, but a positive Mohist influence is also very apparent,
particularly in Mengzi's philosophy. While Mengzi continues to insist the family is
the fundamental source of *ren*, he takes care to emphasize that it radiates out to all
people. Mengzi shows more explicit concern for the well-being of the masses than
we can find in the *Analects*; he was probably as democratic as a Ru of his day could
be. While emphasizing the need for ensuring the distribution of life's necessities, he
remains surprisingly silent about music and ritual, which again appears a concession
to Mohist critiques.

Yang Zhu (440–360 BCE) did not start a "school," and those who agreed with
him were certainly not competing for jobs. Yangists distrusted anyone with political
ambition, saying that "only the man who cares nothing for the empire deserves to

be entrusted with the empire" (Graham 1981: 224). This is a very clear snapshot of Kongzi, Mozi, and Yang Zhu taken in the early Han dynasty:

> Singing to stringed instruments and dancing to drums so as to make music;
> Turning, bestowing, diminishing, yielding so as to practice the rites;
> Having lavish burials and lengthy mourning so as to send off the dead:
> These were established by Confucius, but Mozi opposed them.
> Universal love, honoring the worthy,
> Esteeming ghosts, opposing fatalism:
> These were established by Mozi, but Yangzi opposed them.
> Keeping your nature in tact, protecting your authenticity,
> Not allowing things to entangle your form:
> These were established by Yangzi, but Mengzi opposed them. (Major et al., 2010: 500–1)

Yangists maintained that the ways of the Ru and Mohists were doomed because they were inauthentic and went against human nature (*xing*). Yangists were attacked for being selfish hedonists, but it is fairer to say they denounced ambition and celebrated being true to themselves. Mengzi's important response to this was to show that Ru values and ideals in fact were authentic expressions of human nature. We saw this stance beginning to take shape in some of the Guodian texts, but it was Mengzi who was remembered for championing this view.

Before proceeding to our two philosophers, I need to say something about an anti-Ru school of philosophy that did not exist: Daoism. Early Daoism is often presented as an amalgam of the doctrines of the *Daodejing* and the *Zhuangzi*. Mengzi mentions neither of these works. Xunzi criticizes them both but he does not pair them, nor does he associate them with any particular school of thought. Despite traditional Chinese and lingering modern claims to the contrary, there is in fact no evidence that "Daoism" had yet been conceived. Rather, we have several independent texts that were later brought together and retrospectively identified as constituting a Daoist school of philosophy.

A traditional view of Daoism was that it emerged in opposition to Ruism. Were this true, we would be hard-pressed to explain several things. Although the Guodian corpus seems predominantly Ru, among its texts were three fragmentary forms of the *Daodejing*. Why were they buried together? As we will see, Mengzi and a "Daoist" text called *Neiyi* or *Inward Training* seem to be in almost total accord. Why would Mengzi blatantly endorse a rival school of thought? Xunzi has obviously adopted ideas akin to those found in the *Daodejing* and the *Zhuangzi*. Would he have done this if their ideas were seen as being intrinsically anti-Ru?

These questions are only problematic if Daoism existed. At this stage, the *Daodejing* (or an early form of it), the *Zhuangzi* (or at least the older "Inner Chapters") and the "*Neiyi*" had no clear affiliation with any school of thought. Nor are they as self-evidently anti-Ru as they are often assumed to be. As this chapter unfolds, I will have occasion to show how their ideas were freely adopted to enrich the teachings of Mengzi and Xunzi.

Mengzi on our innate goodness

Little is known of Mengzi's life. He was named Meng Ke and he was born very close to the hometown of Kongzi some two hundred years after the Master (possible dates are 372–289 BCE). He admired Kongzi immensely, claiming that he was a sage and that, "ever since man came into this world, there has never been one greater than Confucius" (2A2. *Mengzi* quotations follow Lau 1970). Of all the pre-imperial Ru, Mengzi was the most "Confucian." The stories of his childhood from later sources are unreliable, although their recurrent reference to the formative influence of his virtuous mother may reflect some reality. As I have mentioned, tradition has it that he was a pupil in the school of Zisi and his thinking certainly shares the *Doctrine of the Mean*'s deep yet subtle religiosity. He traveled to various states seeking political patronage, but in a world where leaders were clamoring for military supremacy, this staunch critic of oppressive warfare found little favor. He thus devoted himself to study and teaching, including a stint at the Jixia academy, and his doctrines were collected by his followers into the seven books of the *Mengzi*.

As was the case with the *Mean*, so too Mengzi was keen to explore two things that Kongzi was reluctant to discuss: Heaven and human nature. He repeats the Master's dictum that "Heaven does not speak" but adds that it "reveals itself through its acts and deeds" (5A5). As we have seen, this accounts for the sacredness of history in Ru tradition, and the *Mengzi* is replete with exemplary tales of sage-kings responding to Heaven's mandate, evinced by the people harmoniously embracing their rule. He thus approvingly quotes the *Documents*: "Heaven sees with the eyes of its people. Heaven hears with the ears of its people" (5A5).

Mengzi said history revealed the mandate of Heaven, but *tian* could be equally understood by knowing ourselves. The following concise passages are cardinal to Mengzi's philosophy and take us to the crux of his teachings.

> For a man to give full realization to his heart-mind (*xin*) is for him to understand his own nature (*xing*), and a man who knows his own nature will know Heaven (*tian*). By retaining his heart-mind and nurturing his nature he is serving Heaven (7A1).
>
> All the ten thousand things are there in me. There is no greater joy for me than to find, on self-examination, that I am true to myself. (7A4)

Mengzi resolved Kongzi's silence about Heaven and human nature by proclaiming their identity. *Xing* refers to an object's or person's tendencies or characteristics, and while it certainly includes people's basic needs and cravings, it can be broadened to also include any ethical predispositions or moral propensities they might have. Mengzi did not at all deny that "appetite for food and sex is nature" (6A4) and he readily admitted that humans and animals have much in common in their natures. Humans and animals do differ, however.

What separates us from other beings is *xin*, a word literally referring to the organ of the "heart" but which incorporates the connotations of both "heart" and "mind" in English. All animals share the basic senses and urges, but *xin* is unique to humans and so defines us. The heart-mind is not just our aptitude for intellectual investigation. Rather, it includes our capacity for moral reflection and serves to fathom both "reason and righteousness" (6A7). Mengzi's first step in countering those who rejected Ru values because they were contrary to human nature was to insist that morality in fact was natural: "Reason and righteousness please my heart-mind in the same way that meat pleases my palate" (6A7). Thus, to return to the cardinal passage quoted above, "for a man to give full realization to his heart-mind is for him to understand his own nature."

Because the heart-mind with its propensity for "reason and righteousness" was innate to humanity, Mengzi had no hesitation in proclaiming that human nature was good. By "good" he meant that traditional Ru virtues such as *ren* (humaneness), *li* (ritual), *zhi* (wisdom), and *yi* (righteousness) were not exterior to our nature but emerge from its inherent disposition. His famous illustration of this was the case of a person who sees a child fall into a well and is moved by a sense of compassion to save it, with no ulterior motive. Cases like this proved to him that the "heart-mind of compassion" is integral to human nature and without it we would not be human. *Ren* (humaneness) is *ren* (human), says Mengzi, matching the pun of the *Mean*. Likewise, the "heart-mind of shame," the "heart-mind of charity," and the "heart-mind of right and wrong" are definitive of human *xing*. He then aligns these natural dispositions with the virtues, so that "the feeling of compassion is the sprout of humaneness (*ren*); the feeling of shame is the sprout of righteousness (*yi*); the feeling of courtesy and modesty is the sprout of observance of rites (*li*); the feeling of right and wrong is the sprout of wisdom (*zhi*)" (2A6).

Although Mengzi is asserting that goodness is in our very nature, he is, needless to say, not claiming that all people are good in practice. He calls our innately good heart-minds our "original" or "true" *xin* (6A8, 10). The "sprouts" of the previous quotation, while inherently destined to grow to goodness, may be distorted, stunted, or die. When discussing lazy and violent individuals, he explains that their bad behavior is "due to what ensnares their hearts" (6A7), and he uses the analogy of barley seeds that grow unevenly because of differences in soil and rainfall. To say "the sage and I are of the same kind" (6A7) is not, therefore, to say we are identical in maturation, for the sage is a person whose seed of humaneness has grown to full potential. There are many things Mengzi cites that can retard our growth—false teachings, worldly pursuits, lack of application, conflict with other base parts of our nature, even overzealousness—and so to bring our capacity for perfect goodness to fruition, to become sages, requires diligent self-cultivation.

The essential task of self-development was, for Mengzi, to give the heart-mind the place of priority in the person, to locate it at the pinnacle of our natures, and to allow it to rule over the self (6A14). His unqualified support for the moral heart-mind's right to supremacy is evident when he claims he would choose duty over life itself (6A10) or ritual and protocol (*li*) over sex, and while we might be tempted to smile at the latter example, we must be prepared for Mengzi's rejoinder to men who would say their desire for a woman is more important that *li*: therefore, "would you drag her away by force?" (6B1) Quite simply, the heart-mind must be given primacy and wholeheartedly employed. "Seek it and you will get it: let it go and you will lose it," he said (7A3, 6A6).

Nourishing the heart and mind

Mengzi does not persistently speak of actual methods of self-cultivation, and when he advises rulers on how to be humane, he does so in a very pragmatic way, much as though he was suggesting to them ways to improve agriculture (1A3, 1A7, 3A3). There is, however, one important exception to this rule when he delves deeply into the mysteries of consolidating the paramount position of the heart-mind. Before turning to that long passage, it is worth observing some cultivation practices that are conspicuously absent in the *Mengzi*. To appreciate the omissions, you should recall that education and ritual-music were fundamental to Kongzi's program, as they were in Xunzi's philosophy (below) and, indeed, to the subsequent history of the Ru. It is therefore quite remarkable that while Mengzi might advise rulers to "exercise due care over the education provided by the village schools" (1A3), he does not at all highlight learning (*xue*) as a path to moral development. Again, although he speaks of *li* frequently as an attribute of the heart-mind, if we compare the *Mengzi* with the *Analects*, then, as Robert Eno observed, "we cannot help but be struck by the absence of any claim that the practice of *li* is the path to sagehood" (Eno 1990: 108). When Mengzi advises a king that it doesn't matter if he prefers popular or ancient music so long as he shares his enjoyment with the people (1B1), we sense he is skirting close to heresy. Overall, Mengzi's silence regarding traditional Ru devotion to ritual and music as well as his advocacy of diligent care for basic needs of the masses is strongly suggestive of Mozi's influence, although this, of course, is never explicitly acknowledged.

Not only is Mengzi rather disinterested in discussing learning, ritual, and music as means of cultivation, but when he does turn to consider the way to develop the heart-mind, his teachings are quite exceptional. Section 2A2 begins with Mengzi claiming that since the age of forty his heart-mind had not been stirred by worldly ambition or desire. As he expands on this, he introduces *qi* as a major concept in Ru philosophy. His ideas, rudimentary and unintegrated, would be revived and developed during the Ru renaissance of the Song dynasty (Chapter 6).

Qi originally referred to vapor or steam but soon came to include the air we breathe. By Mengzi's time, as well as designating vital breath, it also signified the essential and primary substance constituting all things. In its refined form it was understood to have

generated the heavens, in its coarse form earth, and between them all things, including humanity. Mengzi defined it haltingly. He said: "It is difficult to explain. This is a *qi*
which is, in the highest degree, vast and unyielding. Nourish it with integrity and place
no obstacle in its path and it will fill the space between Heaven and Earth." This *qi* that
fills Heaven and earth is the same *qi* "that fills the body" (2A2), and Mengzi seems to
have had a very concrete and corporeal understanding of how cosmic *qi*, particularly
that of the morning air, could naturally regenerate our physical and moral being (6A8).

It is quite evident that Mengzi's understanding of the way to cultivate *qi* is very similar to ideas expressed in a short treatise called *Inward Training (Neiye)*, which somehow became embedded as a chapter in the *Guanzi*, an eclectic work (perhaps a Jixia
Academy miscellany) mainly about statecraft. There it remained buried and overlooked
until it was textually "excavated" by modern scholarship. Dating from around 350–300
BCE, *Inward Training* is China's oldest text advocating the use of meditative breathing in order to achieve mystical union (Roth 1999: chapter 4). Although it might look
very "Daoist," it belongs, as A.C. Graham observed, "to an early phase before the
breach between Confucianism and Daoism opened" (Graham 1989: 100). It certainly
expresses no anti-Ru sentiments and it even approvingly refers to *ren* and *yi*, and
advocates the *Odes*, music, and ritual (Roth 1999: 88, 222n. 59). Although it very much
looks like these explicitly Ru statements were inserted at a later date, this in itself
indicates a Ru desire to appropriate this text as their own.

Inward Training says that "all the forms of the heart-mind" are naturally infused with
and nurtured by *qi*, but this process is blocked by desires generated by the emotions.
"If you are able to cast off sorrow, happiness, joy, anger, desire, and profit-seeking /
Your heart-mind will revert to equanimity" (Roth 1999: 50). Mengzi likewise maintained
that *qi* must be freed to work its inherent purpose. This is not something to be done
but an undoing, a stilling of hindering activity so that *qi* can spontaneously revitalize our
nature. "There is nothing better for the nurturing of the heart-mind than to reduce the
number of one's desires," he said (7B35). By stilling desire, *qi* will be allowed to revitalize our heart-mind so that our latent nature, containing the virtues of humaneness,
ritual, wisdom, and righteousness (*ren, li, zhi*, and *yi*) will become manifest.

Both *Inward Training* and the *Mengzi* emphasize the importance of not interfering
with *qi*'s natural flow. Mengzi uses the analogy of plant growth when discussing the
effects of *qi* on the heart-mind. In one passage he compares the felling of trees on
a mountain to the way people deplete their true heart-minds (6A8). He also dwells
on an inverse organic image by warning against the dangers of impetuous cultivation, which he likens to someone impatiently pulling rice sprouts up to hasten their
growth: "While you must never let it [*qi*] out of your heart-mind, you must not for-
cibly help it grow either" (2A2). This is entirely in keeping with the thought of *Inward
Training*: "Do not push it! Do not pull it! … And that Way will naturally come to you"
(Roth 1999: 94).

As we have seen, Kongzi stressed the importance of education and correspondingly
said that others were "unlikely to be as eager to learn as I am" (5:28). In contrast, when
Mengzi was asked what it was he excelled in, he replied "I am good at cultivating my

flood-like *qi*" (2A2), which reflects his own alternative focus on nourishing the inner self. He quite evidently has other sources of inspiration besides the Master's teachings, and tellingly, the idiosyncratic expression "flood-like" (*haoran*) *qi*, is also found verbatim in *Inward Training* (Roth 1999: 74).

***

It remains, finally, to consider Mengzi's attitude toward cultivating the moral community. Through self-cultivation a person strived for sagehood, and the ideal ruler was, of course, a sage, but Mengzi's political philosophy addresses the inevitable need to govern in the absence of sage-kings.

Mengzi insisted that Heaven bequeathed the empire upon a ruler and he did not contest the supreme importance of kings. His attitudes were, nonetheless, more democratic than those of other premodern Ru. Without neglecting devotion to family and king, he was as concerned for the commonweal as was Mozi; indeed, whereas for Mozi universal love springs from utilitarian necessity and pragmatic simplicity, Mengzi comes across as someone touched by genuine compassion. "The people are of supreme importance," he said (7B14). Mengzi was quite clear that "only the benevolent man is fit to be in high position" (4A1) and he had no qualms with kings being overthrown if they lacked the virtue appropriate to their position (1B8). The mandate of Heaven could certainly be withdrawn but the agent of Heaven was the people themselves. We have already quoted Mengzi saying: "Heaven sees with the eyes of its people; Heaven hears with the ears of its people." Again, when asked how Shun received the empire, he replied, "Heaven gave it to him and the people gave it to him" (5A5).

For Mengzi, *ren* is the most important virtue that a ruler could possess. Before proceeding, we must pause to examine his understanding of *ren*. Mengzi defined *ren* using the "golden rule" in its positive form: "Try your best to treat others as you would wish to be treated yourself, and you will find that this is the shortest way to *ren*" (7A4). This was something that he said should be extended to the care for widows and widowers, the old and orphaned (1B5), and even animals, as the humane person "cannot bear to see them die, and once having heard their cry, he cannot bear to eat their flesh" (1A7).

We have seen that Mengzi maintained that *ren* emerges from our innate "heart-mind of compassion," but it, along with other virtues, not only has its place of origin but also its primary manifestations. Thus, he said, "the content of *ren* is the serving of one's parents" (4A27). There can be no doubt that he saw the love of a child for its parents as the most basic form of humaneness, and while we might extend *ren* to all people, we do not feel the same immediate attachment to them (7A45). This was the essence of his criticism of Mozi's "love without discrimination," which undermined the concrete foundations of affiliation and love. For Mengzi, real humaneness must emerge from real relationships with real people and must not be derived from some moral maxim that transcends the world of embodied humanity.

There is, however, an unintended twist to the way Mengzi employs the idea of filial piety in the political domain. First, Mengzi explicitly recognized the king as an extension of the father or, in some cases, the "father and mother" (1A4). Thus, pursuing his critique of Mozi, he says, "Mo advocates love without discrimination, which amounts to a denial of one's father. To ignore one's father on the one hand, and one's prince on the other, is to be no different from the beasts" (3B9). Again, the origin of kingship in the family and kinship is implied when he says:

> There are no young children who do not know loving their parents, and none of them when they grow up will not know respecting their elder brothers. Loving one's parents is humaneness; Loving one's elders is righteousness. What is left to be done is simply the extension of these to the whole empire. (7A15)

Passages like these might prime us to expect Mengzi is about to proclaim that ministers and the masses must be taught *ren* so they will revere the ruler as a filial child reveres its parents. This, after all, was not an uncommon stance in the history of Ru thought.

Book 1 of the *Mengzi*, which records dialogues during his early travels, alerts us that Mengzi was temperamentally disinclined toward such a conclusion. What is evident in that first book is how rarely he gives rulers advice on how to educate, cultivate, or refine those below them, but instead how bluntly he points out the ruler's own failings and suggests ways they might better serve the people. This is reminiscent of the brief description of Mengzi's predecessor Zisi in the Guodian corpus (Chapter 3). While Mengzi certainly does not say so explicitly, it nonetheless seems that by stressing the importance of the ruler's capacity for *ren* he was placing the onus of responsibility on the king himself in caring for his "family." For Mengzi, the ruler's sole purpose is to care for those in his charge.

> You can never succeed in winning the allegiance of men by trying to dominate them through goodness. You can only succeed by using this goodness for their welfare. You can never gain the Empire without the heart-felt admiration of the people in it. (4B 16)

If "loving one's parents is humaneness" and if humaneness is also treating others as we ourselves would be treated, then it would seem the following passage advises that the way to win the empire is for the ruler to serve the people with the *ren* that a child feels for its parents.

> There is a way to win the Empire; win the people and you will win the Empire. There is a way to win the people; win their hearts and you will win the people. There is a way to win their hearts; amass what they want for them; do not impose what they dislike on them. That is all. (4A9)

FIGURE 7 *Mengzi's Temple.*

Although it is not as grand as Kongzi's temple in Qufu (Figure 19), Mengzi's home-town temple in Zoucheng, less than 30 kilometers away, is these days far more tran-quil. There are sixty-four buildings in the complex, which center around the Hall to the Second Sage (*Yasheng dian*), pictured here.

This was originally just the site of Mengzi's tomb, and a temple was only added in the Song dynasty when his status began to soar. The present Hall was built in the Qing dynasty after its predecessor was destroyed by earthquake. It required further restoration following the Cultural Revolution.

In the final analysis, Mengzi's image of ideal government is, like Mozi's, simply a matter of the ruler looking after the needs of the people in very practical ways such as equitable distribution of resources, good agricultural practice, sound education, sensi-ble taxation, and avoiding the disastrous folly of offensive warfare. These are the prag-matic applications of the adage that we must care for others as we would ourselves wish to be tended.

***

Needless to say, Mengzi's idealism was his undoing. His critique of warfare, his rel-egation of rulers to the place of lowest priority—"last comes the ruler" (7B14)—his support for rebellion against unjust government, his relentless demands on king's moral fiber, as well as his rather vague notions of personal cultivation, which lacked all the interventionist muscle of education and ritual, ensured his teachings would be ignored by those struggling to gain supremacy over the Warring States of China.

We are now approaching a fork in the Way of the Ru. The four main texts we have thus far examined—the *Analects*, *Great Learning*, *Doctrine of the Mean*, and *Mengzi*—would one day be known as the Four Books that formed the core of the Ru curriculum. This occurred over a millennium later, however (Chapter 6). For the moment, China required a hard-headed kind of Ruism that placed minimal demands on leaders but promised to discipline, educate, cultivate, and so transform an unruly populace. Rather than the Four Books, the initial texts sustaining the ideology of the empire were the Five Classics, and, as we will see in the next chapter, these were established alongside a rigorous regime of education and ritual cultivation. More than any other person, this system was inspired by Xunzi, whose teachings are the subject of the remainder of this chapter.

The divergence between Mengzi and Xunzi opens a rift running through the entire history of the Ru. In the Han dynasty (Chapter 5) and the final Qing dynasty (Chapter 7), Xunzi's influence was predominant even if this was not always formally acknowledged. From the Song to Ming dynasties (Chapters 6 and 7), Mengzi was hailed as the "Second Sage" and his thinking prevailed. And today, as will become evident in Chapters 9 and 10, their respective positions are being aligned with the ways of "inner sageliness" (*neisheng*) and "outer kingliness" (*waiwang*), a major division in the modern Ru revival.

For now, our story leaves Mengzi behind. His day will come (Figure 7).

Xunzi contra Mengzi

The man whose teachings were to have the most immediate impact on preparing Ruism to become China's state ideology was Xun Kuang, who is usually referred to as Xunzi or "Master Xun." His philosophy is recorded in the *Xunzi*, a compilation of thirty-two "chapters" that very probably began as separate little treatises. While Xunzi is often said to have developed a rationalist form of "Confucianism," this does not do justice to the originality and independence of his thought. Although he does once in passing refer to Kongzi and his disciple Zigong as "sages" (42 – references are to pages in Hutton's 2014 translation), he does not eulogize Kongzi to the extent that Mengzi had, nor does he mention or quote him with particular frequency. The exception to this is chapters that seem to have been appended by Xunzi's disciples (chapters 27–31), yet significantly these claim that Xunzi himself was a sage and even Kongzi "did not surpass him" (343).

The exact dates for Xunzi's long life are difficult to ascertain, but he was probably born around 310 BCE in the state of Zhao in the center of northern China and died in or some time close to 215 BCE. Like Mengzi, he journeyed to the Jixia Academy where he was exposed to a spectrum of philosophical views. Again, like his predecessor, Xunzi traveled to various states to discuss his thought on government. He was appointed magistrate of the Chu city of Lanling, although this was probably an honorary position that made few demands on him. Instead, he spent most of his later years teaching and writing.

Xunzi is best known for his opposition to Mengzi's theory of human nature: "Mencius says: people's nature is good. I say: this is not so" (252). This blunt refutation might predispose us to anticipate the two philosophers diverged at every junction, but in fact they agree on many fundamental points. Both, for instance, believed that people are composite creatures consisting of basic drives and their heart-mind (*xin*). Both too maintained that the heart-mind should govern us, that, in Xunzi's words, "the heart-mind is the lord of the body and the master of one's spirit and intelligence" (229). Both readily acknowledged they lived in a world devastated by unbridled base desire, greed, and violence, and both agreed that it was possible, in theory at least, for all people to rise from this state to become sages: "Anyone on the streets can become a [sage like] Yu," said Xunzi (254).

Mengzi and Xunzi did not arrive at their contrasting positions because they disagreed about the evidence before them revealing human tendencies toward good or bad behavior, but rather because they strategically adopted different definitions of *xing*. While *xing* is typically translated as human "nature," we must be careful not to confine this to fixed innate qualities. *Xing* can also be used to signify a general tendency or predisposition as when we say in English that "it is the nature of people" to do certain things. Because this was a rather flexible concept, it was easy for Mengzi and Xunzi to employ it very differently by exploiting the vagueness of definition. For the sake of brief comparison, I will compress their views into a pair of syllogisms that draw out their implicit assumptions:

Mengzi: People's *xing* is defined by what is *unique* to humans and separates them from other forms of life. This is the heart-mind, which, he argues, is the origin of moral reason.

> Human nature is heart-mind
> Heart-mind is good.
> Therefore human nature is good.

Xunzi: People's *xing* is defined by the *total overall manifestation* of human predispositions. This is, evidently, a host of tendencies, desires, and needs that are invariably at odds with each other and with the tendencies, desires, and needs of other people.

> Human nature is conflicted.
> Conflict is bad.
> Therefore human nature is bad.

While Xunzi's conclusion is frequently translated as "human nature is evil," this overstates and distorts his position. His basic view is that it is a natural tendency for people to be "deviant, dangerous, unruly, and chaotic" (252), which he deems to be *e*, a word signifying things that are disagreeable. It is conflict, the lack of harmony and accord, that Xunzi primarily laments.

Xunzi needed people to be bad in order to justify his program for human cultivation that was fundamentally different from that of Mengzi. Mengzi, as we have seen, repeatedly employed organic images of shoots sprouting or trees struggling to grow, and the path to human completion was portrayed as one in which indwelling tendencies were nurtured to fruition. Xunzi employs very different imagery; he wants his trees felled and shaped. It is not our natures that turn our woody selves into useful beings, but something exterior, imposed on us for our betterment. And the main tools he recommends are precisely the ones Mengzi neglected: education and, in particular, music and ritual.

Mengzi believed that *li* or ritual was a natural expression of the heart-mind of "courtesy and honesty," although he actually had very little to say about ritual practice as such. For Xunzi, *li* was not natural but "artifice" (*wei*), something invented by humans yet nonetheless exterior to their nature. "The craftsman carves wood and makes utensils. Yet how could the wood of the utensils be the craftsman's nature?" he asked (253).

Rituals, in Xunzi's view, are not designed to simply block or oppose some innately "evil" essence in people; rather, they are constructed to bring our conflicted desires and drives into harmonious accord so that they might be satisfied.

> Ritual cuts off what is too long and extends what is too short. It subtracts from what is excessive and adds to what is insufficient. It achieves proper form for love and respect, and it brings to perfection the beauty of carrying out righteousness. Thus, fine ornaments and coarse materials, music and weeping, happiness and sorrow— these things are opposites, but ritual makes use of them all. (209)

It is important to observe that Xunzi is decidedly not saying desire per se is bad, nor, contra Mengzi, even that we should limit desires. He acknowledges that "human nature is the accomplishment of Heaven" (244) and that emotions and desires are a part of our Heaven-bestowed nature. He has no intention of rejecting any gift from *tian*, and the challenge was not to renounce desires but to fulfill them in the most harmonious manner: "When the Way advances, then one approaches complete fulfillment" of all desires, he said (244). As I noted in the previous chapter, Xunzi's understanding of emotion and desire is in fact very similar to views expressed by the Guodian text *Nature Comes via Mandate* (see Goldin 2005: chapter 2).

According to Xunzi, *li* was introduced into the world by ancient sage-kings in order to harmoniously satisfy human desires.

> From what did ritual arise? I say: Humans are born having desires. When they have desires but do not get the objects of their desire, then they cannot but seek some means of satisfaction. If there is no measure or limit to their seeking then they cannot help but struggle with each other. If they struggle with each other then there will be chaos, and if there is chaos then there will be impoverishment. The former kings hated

such chaos, and so they established rituals and righteousness in order to divide things among the people, to nurture their desires, and to satisfy their seeking. They caused desires never to exhaust material goods, and material goods never to be depleted by desires, so that the two support each other and prosper. This is how ritual arose. (201)

Far from having a pessimistic image for humanity, Xunzi's delights in human potential. Nor was he preaching the drudgery of duty, but instead promising that those who live in accord with *li* would enjoy life in ways previously unimaginable. There is a strong aesthetic tone to his imagery, and living ritually is portrayed as an avenue to beauty, joy, and fulfillment. In one instance, he likens uncultivated human nature to a diet of coarse greens—dregs and husks that barely sustain life. Having never tasted better, a person could not imagine other foods and would persist in their eating habits, but were they introduced to the finest dishes, they would immediately appreciate their superiority and freely choose them in preference to their old fare (28). Ritual begins with emotions and desires, he says, but "reaches full development in giving it proper form, and finishes in providing its satisfaction" (204). *Li* is life's banquet.

Heaven and the sage

Rituals were the legacy of past sages. Before pursuing Xunzi's analysis of *li*, we need to appreciate his notion of the sage. He did not believe a sage's nature was different to that of other people. "The noble person and the petty man" have the same nature (26), and likewise "anyone on the streets can become a [sage like] Yu" (254). This might at first appear to contradict his thesis that human nature was bad, but the key word to the second quotation is "can." He says all people with two feet "can" walk to every corner of the earth, although, of course, very few indeed actually do this (255). Likewise, all people can become sages, but this is no desideratum; it is not intrinsic or essential to human nature, and so it is an infrequent occurrence. It remains a universal capacity, however, open to all people who are cultivated by *li*.

The sage is a person with the same nature as other humans, who has chosen to use his heart-mind as tirelessly as a person who has committed their feet to transverse the globe. For Xunzi, heart-mind is morally neutral and is the organ that controls the body by ordering, selecting, and organizing (229). We might, therefore, expect Xunzi to depict the sage as someone who has used their heart-mind to accumulate vast amounts of reasoned knowledge, but his explanation is in fact the very inverse of this. As we will see, this unexpected twist seems very likely to indicate the influence of two "Daoist" philosophers he had occasion to criticize: Laozi and Zhuangzi.

Xunzi's sage is someone who, having begun life with the same conflicted nature that all people share, learns to develop their heart-mind so that it becomes free of all prejudicial error and can impartially weigh all matters (227). To reach this evaluative centre, people must apprehend the Way (*dao*), and to fathom the Way the heart-mind must achieve a state of "emptiness, single-mindedness, and stillness" (228). Xunzi is, of course, aware this is the very antithesis of the usual notions of the mind that is full of information, divides and distinguishes things, and is actively engaged in thinking. But these very pursuits can cloud thought as memory, reason, and active thinking muddy the waters of the heart-mind. The metaphor was Zhuangzi's, who said, "None of us finds his mirror in flowing water, we find it in still water" (Graham 1981: 77). Xunzi says when the intellectual sediment has settled, the heart-mind, no matter how many things it knows, receives each new impression as though empty and clear (231); no matter how different things might be, the heart-mind is single-minded and unified because it "does not let one idea harm another idea" (228); no matter how active, the heart-mind does not get carried away with its own movement, but is always still.

While there are parallels between Xunzi and Zhuangzi—who spoke of the developed person having a "heart-mind like a mirror" reflecting everything as if new, seeing all things as one and maintaining enduring stillness (Graham 1981: 98)—the most striking similarity is between Xunzi and the *Daodejing*'s description of the sage. Given the resemblance of Xunzi's central tenants to ideas expressed in *Nature Comes via Mandate*, we can perhaps appreciate why the short variants of the *Daodejing* were interred with it at Guodian. The *Daodejing* says:

I do my utmost to attain emptiness;
I hold firm to stillness.
The myriad creatures all rise together
And I watch their return. (Lau 1963: chapter 16)

Again, it says a person "without stirring abroad ... can know the world" (47). Xunzi says this of the person who embodies the Way by making their heart-mind empty, single-minded, and still:

He sits in his chamber yet sees all within the four seas. He dwells in today yet judges what is long ago and far away in time. He comprehensively observes the myriad things and knows their true dispositions. He inspects and examines order and disorder and discerns their measures. He sets straight Heaven and Earth, and arranges and makes useful the myriad things. He institutes great order, and the whole world is encompassed therein.

So vast and broad is he! Who grasps his true limits?
So lofty and broad is he! Who grasps his true virtue?
So active and varied is he! Who grasps his true form?

His brilliance matches the sun and moon. His greatness fills all the eight directions. Such a one is called the Great Man. (229)

The sages were, for Xunzi, people whose calm clarity of heart-mind perceived the proper order of things and in particular the patterns that could harmonize human relationships. These they recorded as the canons of *li*. Their superior heart-minds allowed them to complete and fulfill the creative process that was instigated by Heaven. The sagacious ruler "observes Heaven above, and applies this knowledge on Earth below. He arranges completely everything between Heaven and Earth and spreads beneficence over the myriad things ... He has spirit-like (*shenming*) powers of intelligence" (77). No Ru philosopher prior to Xunzi had employed the term *shenming*, spirit- or god-like, although it is found in the *Zhuangzi*. It was generally reserved for the gods, but Xunzi uses it to suggest the sage's marvelous and mysterious gnosis, a wisdom that takes the hypernatural to a level that matches any supernatural or divine knowledge.

The joyous dance of the Ru

Having considered the cosmic role of the sage as Heaven's co-creator who "completes all things," it is time to return to the legacy of past sages who recorded their flawless insight in books, music, and rituals. Xunzi all but lists the books that were to be canonized as Ru Classics in the Han dynasty, omitting only the *Changes*. Yet in Xunzi's plan for human cultivation, these books were not as important as ritual and music, not because they were less perfect, but because they were more susceptible to misuse.

"The sage is the pitch pipe of the Way," and the books record their wisdom, Xunzi said. "The *Odes* tells of his intentions. The *Documents* tells of his works. The *Rituals* tells of his conduct. The *Music* tells of his harmoniousness. The *Spring and Autumn Annals* tells of his subtlety" (60). Xunzi believed "all things between Heaven and Earth are complete" in these books (5) and that they contained the "greatest considerations under Heaven" (29). He encouraged people to read, repeat, investigate, and reflect on these texts (30). Their purpose, he said, "begins with becoming a well-bred man, and ends with becoming a sage" (5).

Xunzi was, nonetheless, cautious about the way these books might be used. The "vulgar Ru," he said, tended to treat them as disembodied texts and so conflate their words with the teachings of the Mohists and other wayward doctrines. To take precautions against this, he advised people "to exalt ritual and righteousness and to put the *Odes* and *Documents* second" (63). Because the books can be exceedingly difficult to fathom, they are readily misinterpreted, and Xunzi believed it vital that students have a good teacher. Thus, he said, when seeking an education, "nothing is more expedient than to draw near to the right person." Failing this, the next best route is "exalting ritual." Without one or both of these, book learning can easily become superficial or distorted and as useless as "trying to measure the depth of the river with your finger" (6). The analogy does not for a moment question the immense depths of the books but merely points out that they will be as shallow waters to someone incapable of fathoming their reaches.

Rather than the path of textual learning, which could descend all too easily into false intellectualism, Xunzi placed his faith primarily in ritual and music. Here too you will notice his thought is very close to the ideas expressed in *Nature Comes via Mandate*. My exposition will begin with his views on major ceremonies, move toward more personal and intimate aspects of *li*, and then conjoin ritual with music to culminate in a key image in Xunzi's religious thought, the cosmic dance.

Xunzi was primarily concerned with ritual's capacity for perfecting human relationships. While *li* had the ability to complete all creation by guiding people as they ordered their physical environment, its main function was to bring sound structure and measured proportion to the social world. Ritual achieves this end by introducing differentiation and division on the one hand and constraint on the other.

Many of Xunzi's examples of ceremonial differentiation served to define hierarchical relationships from the Son of Heaven down to common laborers. "What is meant by 'differentiation'?" he asks, and replies: "It is for noble and lowly to have their proper ranking, for elder and youth to have their proper distance, and for poor and rich, humble and eminent each to have their proper weights" (201).

These distinctions were maintained by quantitative differences marking levels of ritual prestige. Kings, for instance, sacrifice to seven generations of ancestors, lesser rulers to five or three generations depending on the size of their territories, while laborers should not possess a family ancestral temple at all (203). Again, a king's coffin has seven layers, a lord's five, a minister's three and an official's two (207).

Ceremonial gradations thus serve to reinforce and consolidate the basic hierarchical division of labor, which Xunzi believed was essential for overcoming the chaos of equality. Equality, for Xunzi was the bane of harmony for it only led to the masses squabbling over finite resources; in Xunzi's words, "Desires are many, the things to satisfy them are few" (83). The resources of Heaven, while finite, can be extended to satisfy all people by refining the "hundred skills" and raising capable men to high rank. *Li* paves the way for this process, and Xunzi said, "To have social divisions is the root benefit for the whole world" (85). Ritual was thus the foundation for sound economics.

Division, differentiation, and structure are the primary features of the social dimension of ritual, but when Xunzi turns to the individual and rites of passage—"ritual is that which takes care to order living and dying" (206)—his emphasis is mainly on regulation, constraint, and proportion. Ritual not only erects the framework of society but also shapes and trims each person to be attached to the scaffolding. At the personal level, Xunzi's concern was with passion, desire, and emotion, the wildcards of individuality. He particularly dwelt on the problem of death, which is such a raw moment that it is certain to intensify all affectivity. Funerals, then, become an urgent context in which it is essential to "make clear what is righteous with regard to the living and the dead" (212). Xunzi argues that it is obvious that human emotions need space to be expressed, and rituals serve to ensure moderation and constraint so that unbridled feeling does not usher in a state of destruction and chaos. Joy and sorrow are natural but potentially dangerous and should be harnessed just as the ruler regulates the resources of the environment. Ritual "makes use of music and happiness in such a way as not to lead to perversity or laziness. The way it makes use of weeping and sorrow is such as not to lead to dejection or self-harm. This is the midway course of ritual" (209).

In the case of funerals, mourning into the third year is stipulated, as grief is a proper expression of filial love, yet it must then cease lest a truly devoted child grieve endlessly. The rites thus require a time to express sadness and then "ritual breaks off the mourning" (213). As we saw in Chapter 2, the symbols of the grave also seek to reach the "middle state" by treating the dead *as if* alive. To not wish that deceased parents were still living would be unfilial but to treat them as though they in fact were still alive would deny the transition they have made to death. Thus, while the mound is a symbolic house, it is a paradoxical dwelling. The corpse is dressed, but imperfectly, with no sash buckle, hat pin, or strings; food utensils are presented but they are empty; carvings are left unfinished, musical instruments untuned, and carriages have no horse or tackle to draw them (211–12). Later sacrifices also serve to mediate between natural feelings of "remembrance and longing" (215) and the need to keep emotions contained by fixed limits and orderly restraints.

Xunzi's ritual program could sound regimented and unspontaneous even to ancient Chinese audiences, but this was certainly not his own understanding. Rather, he believed the careful and disciplined cultivation he advocated would culminate in the satisfaction of human desire and a state of sustained joy. This becomes particularly apparent when we observe his discussion of the relationship between ritual and music, which he always saw as a complementary couple. *Li* and the distinction it introduced to the world were not an end in themselves but a means to create perfect accord, a joyous coming together of humanity and a harmony, which was best captured by the spirit of music. "Music ... is unchanging harmony, and ritual is unalterable order. Music unites that which is the same, and ritual distinguishes that which is different. Together the combination of ritual and music governs the human heart-mind" (221).

Edward Machle has insightfully argued that *yue*, which included not only instrumental musical and singing but also the integral contribution of dance, was the fundamental metaphor for Xunzi's entire philosophical venture. If music embodies Xunzi's vision of a world that has been transformed by *li*, then that world is one of delight and happiness. "Music is joy," says Xunzi (218). There is a graphic pun here, for while music (*yue*) and joy (*le*) had from an early age been pronounced differently, they were originally the same word and continued to be written with the same character (樂). Xunzi is hardly the dour disciplinarian he is often accused of being and is quite adamant that "people cannot be without joy, and their joy cannot be without shape." His only qualification was that "if it takes shape and does not accord with the Way, there will inevitably be chaos" (218), and chaos, we know, was for Xunzi the root of all misery. To sustain joy it must be regulated by *li* and if there is a goal to which Xunzi's teachings all lead it is to ushering the world toward a state of ordered joy.

Xunzi frequently refers to music in ways that make it clear he saw it as a microcosmic form of a world of orderly joy. The purity of a noble person's music, he said, "resembles Heaven, his broadness resembles the Earth, and the way he postures and revolves has resemblance to the four seasons," (221). In another passage he makes an even more concrete correlation between the instruments, dancers, and the cosmic process.

> The drum is the lord of music, is it not? Thus, the drum resembles Heaven. The bells resemble Earth. The stone chimes resemble water. The [wind instruments called] *yu, sheng, xiao, he, guan,* and *yue* resemble the sun, moon, and stars. The [percussion instruments called] *tao, zhu, fu, ge, qiang,* and *qia* resemble the myriad creatures.

The passage pronounces that the "meaning of the dance" is that "the way of Heaven is all-encompassing," and while he does not say so explicitly, in Xunzi's musical cosmos the dancers surely are humanity (222).

Xunzi's cosmic dance is a carefully choreographed, disciplined, and skillful performance. The dancers move to the music, and the music, in particular the drum sounding the cosmic beat, represents Heaven. The dancers' responsibility is neither to scrutinize the intentions of the drummer ("only the sage does not seek to understand Heaven" [176]) nor to try persuade him to change the beat (Xunzi's ongoing critique of "magical" efforts to control Heaven), but rather to learn to move in complete harmony and accord with the given rhythm.

Only when Heaven and humanity work harmoniously together, only when dance is in accord with music, will the process of creation be complete. The sage might be likened to the dance leader whose heart-mind is so attuned to the Heaven-like pulse he can uncannily intuit how the movements should be choreographed. While this is something Xunzi does not explicitly say, there is little doubt that when he makes his enraptured observations of the sublime beauty and joy of the dance he senses this resonating with his vision of humanity trained in the art of ritual and through it completing the cosmic process that begins with the harmonies of Heaven.

> How does one know the meaning of the dance? I say: The eyes do not themselves see it, and the ears do not themselves hear it. Nevertheless, it controls their postures, gestures, directions, and speed. When all the dancers are restrained and orderly, exerting to the utmost the strength of their bones and sinews to match the rhythm of drum and bell sounding together, and no one is out of step, then how easy it is to tell the meaning of this group gathering. (222)

***

Xunzi believed he understood the way to usher this utopian society into political and social reality. Ideally, the country would be ruled by a sage-king, but more realistically and immediately the Ru themselves would inject the sagacious element into politics by altruistically serving the monarch. Xunzi takes the Duke of Zhou's selfless service as an archetype for the Ru. He says Ru never seek power for themselves but serve as needed and when requested. They model themselves on the ancient sage-kings, exalt morality and ritual, and tirelessly devote themselves to their lords. If they are appointed, they faithfully serve; reject them, and they obediently withdraw. They are not swayed by enticements of wealth or prestige, and even if they are landless, desti-tute, and starving they will continue to uphold their standards (Hutton 2014: chapter 8).

Xunzi's portrait of the Ru was flattering and executed to ensure they appeared attractive to rulers. Unlike the Mohists, who Mengzi and Xunzi constantly attack, they were not threatening the existing social structure with a dangerous doctrine of univer-sal love, but instead offering a means to deepen the people's appreciation of hierarchy and loyalty to superiors. Contrary to the Yangists, who Mengzi discredited and Xunzi simply ignored, they were dedicated to the ruler and his realm and had no thought for themselves. And opposing Laozi and Zhuangzi, who Xunzi critically mentions while borrowing their ideas, their gaze was not far away, but focused on immediate social and political concerns.

Xunzi possibly lived to witness the unification of China in 221 BCE but he died before Ruism became state ideology in the Han dynasty (206 BCE–220 CE). Because Xunzi's name was tainted by association with his pupil Han Feizi, his contributions were not always freely acknowledged, but his impact is undeniable. His extensive dis-course on music and ritual and his insistence that learning from the Classics required guidance from teachers were soon to become standard practice. Indeed, as Xunzi's writings have apparently been incorporated into one of Classics (the *Rites Records*) and as the words attributed to Kongzi in the Classics seem spurious, most of the Ru in the Han may well have memorized more of Xunzi's actual words than those of the Master himself. More than any other person in pre-imperial times, Xunzi was the archi-tect for the state deployment of the Ru (Goldin 2007).

In the next chapter we will pursue the Ru into the imperial era. Before proceeding, I want to close this chapter with a comparative observation about the religious nature of the thought of the three main thinkers we have thus far discussed, Kongzi, Mengzi, and Xunzi. While opinion is now shifting, it was once common to portray Xunzi as the pre-imperial scholar who finally stripped Ruism of the last vestiges of religion to produce an entirely secular worldview. By contrast, I would suggest Xunzi succeeded in drawing to completion religious possibilities that were only embryonic in Kongzi's teaching. For the first time, Xunzi fully conceived of the Way of the Ru as a truly reli-gious tradition.

If, as I suggested in the Introduction, religion is defined openly as an ultimate real-ity that people seek to engage in order to transform themselves and their world, then Xunzi's religious vision was comprehensive. Kongzi, in contrast, would appear to be the least religious of the pre-Han Ru philosophers, for while his notion of *tian* per-haps retained more anthropomorphic overtones, his theory of transformation through education and ritual was but weakly tied to this ultimate reality, and the quest for human perfectibility or sagehood remains undeveloped in the *Analects*. Mengzi (with the *Mean*) opened up the possibility of a genuinely religious worldview by explicitly equating human nature with *tian* so that Heaven, as our inner self, becomes a supreme reality we can aspire to fully engage. Sagehood, the ultimate realization of our true selves, was certainly for Mengzi a religious pursuit. His path to self-transformation, vaguely defined in terms of cultivating *qi*, was, however, not firmly assimilated into his doctrines—indeed, his mystical moments seem somewhat ad hoc and strangely anomalous to his overall teaching. It was left for later Ru to take his germinal ideas and thoroughly integrate them.

While it was certainly not the only solution, Xunzi consolidated his ideas by segregating human nature from *tian* and maintaining that self-cultivation required the external transformative disciplines of education, ritual, and music. These were the unsurpassed legacy of past sage-kings. In his vision, the sage actually brings Heaven to completion and is intrinsic to the cosmic process. Heaven itself remains inscrutable, and we will miss his faith if we seek to fathom it. Xunzi's religiosity resides with the sage, and when he speaks of the transformative power of sagehood, he is lucid, systematic, and entirely uncompromising.

5

From ritual masters to Classicists

There is a lot riding on the history of early imperial China. The Han (206 BCE–220 CE) is often seen as the dynasty that defined a nation. The word "Han" conjures as much; after all, the Chinese are the Han people (*Hanzu*) who speak the Han language (*Hanyu*). Those wishing to revive Ru tradition insist that Ru beliefs and values determine what it is to be Chinese, and to sustain their arguments they need to show that the Ru prevailed from the outset of the imperial era.

Prior to the Han, the Ru had been a small elite competing with adherents of other political persuasions. This was about to change, say traditional accounts. The momentous shift came to known as "banishing the hundred [philosophical] schools and the victory of the Ru arts" (*bachu baijia duzun rushu*). This was implemented by Emperor Wu, we are told, but he in turn acted on the advice of Dong Zhongshu, the most famous Ru of the Han dynasty. Because of this, some see Dong as second only to Kongzi in determining the entire history of the Ru.

It has been reasserted in some recent Chinese scholarship that the adoption of Dong Zhongshu's proposals marks the moment when "*rujia* thought became the shared intellectual framework for the whole nation" (Ma Zhenduo et al., cited in Makeham 2008: 114). This is an assumption amplified by revivalists we will meet in Chapter 10. Jiang Qing insists China must once again adopt Ru religion because from ancient times to the "Han empire and until 1911, a great religion has existed in China, namely, Confucian religion (*Rujiao*)" (Jiang 2013: 48). Kang Xiaoguang is even less restrained: "Confucianism was the most successful religion in history. The emperor was its pope, the whole of government was its church, and all the officials were its believers ... The gentry that ruled society were also believers ... and the masses were also to receive an education in Confucianism" (Kang 2006: 116).

In this chapter, I provide an overview of recent scholarly evaluations of this comprehensive "victory of the Ru," which suggest it is little more than a fabrication created by "cherry-picking" data and "splicing together facts and factoids" (Nylan 2007: 770). The growing critical consensus is "that there was no such thing as Han Confucianism (in the sense of a coherent body of doctrine), that the notion of a 'Han Confucian Synthesis' is at best an oversimplification, and that the idea that Dong Zhongshu presided over the 'triumph of Confucianism' during the reign of Emperor Wu is simply illusory" (Queen and Major 2016: 12).

If this is so, then subsequent dynasties must also be reconsidered. Traditional histories suggest that having reigned supreme in the Han, the Ru sunk into a Dark Age from which they only began to reemerge in the tenth century. But as Michael Nylan (1999: 42–3n. 34) observes, "imperial support for Confucianism in the Han was often at a level comparable with the supposed 'Confucian Dark Ages.'" In other words, we might still be well over a millennium short of the time when the Ru fully entered the light. This interpretation obviously weakens the historical foundation for the claimed unity of Ru ideology and Chinese values.

Reassessing the events of the Qin and Han dynasties is a tricky business, however. While we have quite a few texts from the era (see Loewe 1993), there are only two main sources providing detailed narratives of historical events. They are magnificent, rich resources that draw heavily on state archives and other histories now long lost, but they are not neutral accounts. Modern scholars, of necessity, are almost fully dependant on these two sources and so rely on critical readings that attend to their internal contradictions as well as the divergences between the two texts.

Let me introduce our historians, whose works would come to be almost as important as the Classics themselves to the Ru. Sima Qian (145–86) is China's most famous and esteemed historian. His *Records of the Historian* (*Shiji*) traces China's history from the eve of the Xia dynasty to about 90 BCE. This monumental work in 130 chapters provided a paradigm for later historians. About two hundred years later, Ban Gu (32–92 CE) wrote the *History of the Former Han* (*Hanshu*). His intent was to extend, expand, and revise Sima's history. As he was employed by the state and confined himself to one dynasty, his work became a model for all subsequent official dynastic histories.

We need to keep a few things in mind when reading Sima Qian and Ban Gu. First, as we have seen, history was the premier political and religious genre in China; it was understood to be a record of Heaven's mandate (*tianming*) unfolding through time. Writing history was the business of sages, and both our historians subtly suggest they thought themselves a latter-day Kongzi, the alleged author of the *Spring and Autumn Annals*. Sima said his work aimed at nothing less than discerning "the principles behind ... success and failure" in "all that concerns heaven and man" (Watson 1958: 66). Second, not surprisingly, Sima Qian and Ban Gu are both very sympathetic to the Ru cause. Ru were upholders of antiquity and their sages were devoted to history, so it is natural that our historians identified with them. Third, although they saw their vocation as immensely important, they also knew it was extremely dangerous. Rulers were their patrons, and history legitimized their rule. One bad review could cost you your life, and both men experienced the perils of politics (Ban Gu died in prison, Sima Qian was castrated). Their accounts are biased toward the "legitimate" Han rulers while their rivals cannot win a trick.

The cumulative effect of these factors raises the suspicion that our historians are subtly passing judgment on events by aligning the rise and fall of rulers with their support for or neglect of the Ru. The current revisionist histories tend to indicate that neither the oppression nor the endorsement were ever so extreme. Overall, they suggest that in the Qin and for much of Han Ru were, in fact, not particularly prominent at all.

Unification and the canon

We begin in 221 BCE when, after a series of campaigns that lasted less than a decade, the king of Qin subjugated his rivals and heralded himself Shi Huangdi, First Sovereign Emperor. Barely a decade after his coup, China's First Emperor was dead; a few years more and his dynasty was in tatters. In Ru history, there could be no more lucid testimony to his tyranny than Heaven's mandate being so ruthlessly and summarily withdrawn.

The Qin was followed by the long and prosperous Han dynasty. During the Han, Ru began telling a story that is still being told today, for instance in school texts in Hong Kong, Taiwan, and Singapore. It says the First Emperor, in his ruthless quest for military supremacy, detested the cultured and moral ways of the Ru. To ensure their teachings did not hinder him, he ordered their Classics be burnt and to set an example, he had 460 Ru buried alive. *Fenshu kengru*, "burning the books and burying the Ru," is an expression that has echoed down the centuries (Figure 8).

This story is based on Sima Qian's account, but not his actual words. Sima indicates that at this time the Ru were in fact in disarray and hardly worth singling out. The First Emperor did not target "their" Classics, which Ru were yet to appropriate as their own, but rather the *Odes* and *Documents* and any philosophy that "uses antiquity to criticize the present" (Watson 1993: 55), which was all but universal practice. Other eventual Classics, such as the *Changes*, were exempt, and copies of all the proscribed books were carefully retained for court use. The First Emperor's inscriptions, furthermore, indicate he was not lacking in sympathy for Ru values (Kern 2000). The scholars who incurred his wrath were not exclusively Ru, and the sentence was precipitated by men charged with securing the elixir of immortality, hardly a Ru specialty. As for their gruesome fate, this was perhaps no more than a misreading of Sima's word *keng* ("pit"), which can mean either to bury or put to death. Merely being executed by the First Emperor was hardly claim to fame.

Whatever his excesses, the First Emperor had increased unity. He greatly improved transportation throughout the realm and standardized currency, weights and measures, and, most importantly, the written language. He also believed a single system of law was essential and so endorsed views retrospectively identified as a philosophical school of Legalism (*fajia*). Two of the Emperor's infamous advisers, Han Feizi (c. 280–233 BCE) and Li Si (c. 280–208 BCE), insisted on the importance of law. They had both been pupils of Xunzi but had derived a very different conclusion from his premise that human nature could not be trusted. They turned against Ru ideals of cultivation in favor of the impartial application of law and punishment. Li Si, who had recommended the

FIGURE 8 *Burning the books and burying the Ru.*

This scene from an eighteenth-century album depicts the orthodox view that the First Emperor ordered the burning of the Classics and Ru to be buried alive. This is loosely based on Sima Qian's account, but Sima did not specify that Ru were buried and he said the emperor followed advice to burn private copies of "the writings of the hundred schools of philosophy" (Watson 1993: 55), that is, of every philosophical persuasion.

Ironically, while the First Emperor became the villain in Ru myths of early imperial China, the hero, Dong Zhongshu, adopted very similar tactics. Dong too advised an emperor to prohibit all teachings *except*, of course, those of the "Six Disciplines and the Arts of Confucius" (Queen and Major 2016: 644).

book burning, wrote to the Emperor saying that "when laws are applied," there is no possibility of "the empire being in disorder" (Watson 1993: 197). Meanwhile, the Qin dynasty was collapsing all around them.

The initial Han emperors were equally militant, but as the dust of war settled, it was recognized that an enduring empire required more than martial and criminal law, if for no other reason than that these were impossibly expensive as long-term measures.

The years of war had created massive inflation and swept away half the population. Rulers clearly needed more efficient strategies, perhaps a "how-to" book for running an empire. This niche market was about to be filled (see Lewis 1999a: chapter 7).

Earlier rulers had encouraged philosophical debate by creating institutions like the eclectic Jixia academy, where intellectual battles echoed the wars of state. With unity, the focus shifted to bringing advisers together to create a grand synthesis, an encyclopedic text to guide a unified land. The first of these slightly predates the First Emperor's triumph. It was sponsored by Lü Buwei (291–235 BCE), a powerful Qin minister who, according to Sima Qian, hosted up to 3,000 debaters of various persuasions and from their contributions compiled and edited a work known as *Mr Lü's Spring and Autumn Annals* (*Lüshi chunqiu*). He felt it so perfectly comprehensive that he offered a huge reward to anyone who "could add or subtract a single character from it" (Watson 1993: 163). Sima did not bother critiquing the book. Rather, he slandered its compiler by suggesting the First Emperor was secretly Lü Buwei's bastard son.

A century later, just prior to the Han's official patronage of the Ru, another encyclopedic work based on the collective wisdom of myriad advisers was produced at the request of Liu An (179–122 BCE), the reigning emperor's cousin. The resultant *Huainanzi* also professed to be comprehensive: "extend it to the world and it will leave no empty spaces" (Major et al. 2010: 867). It can reasonably be called a Daoist book insofar as Daoism as a philosophical school that conjoined the *Daodejing* and *Zhuangzi* was invented at Liu An's court. But the *Huainanzi* is as a syncretic work that blends Daoist ideals of "not doing" (*wuwei*) with a softer, more organic form of Legalism. This kind of Daoist-Legalist amalgam, known as Huang-Lao, was quite popular with some early Han rulers.

How could Ru compete in this textual marketplace? It is important to note that at this juncture, "Ru" did not yet connote "Classicist." Rather, what then distinguished Ru was primarily their devotion to the ritual and music of antiquity. True, they were known for studying the *Odes* and *Documents* as testimonies to the past. Furthermore, as we have seen, some Guodian texts and the *Xunzi* had expanded this textual corpus to incorporate all of the eventual Ru Classics, and this body of five or six books was well established by the time of unification. But as Michael Nylan reminds us, "The Five Classics were hardly the preserve of the ethical followers of Kongzi. They functioned as the common cultural coin for all educated people" (Nylan and Wilson 2010: 70). These books were not exclusively theirs to profess.

That was about to change. Although careful recent studies of the Ru in the early Han have shown that Kongzi was no longer particularly prominent, he was still respectfully acknowledged as the Master of the Ru. At the very time the encyclopedic texts began to appear, it was for the first time announced that Kongzi himself had in fact written or compiled, added commentaries to, and revised all the books, thus essentially appropriating them for the Ru. Our earliest attestation to this comes from Sima Qian. As Liang Cia notes, this "made the Five Classics—which were formally taken as the common cultural heritage of all educated men—the private intellectual property" of Kongzi and the Ru who followed him (Cai 2014: 54). One of the Classics, the *Rites Records*, even contains a late insertion entitled "Explaining the Classics" (*Jingjie*) in which Kongzi himself describes how the scriptures perfectly complimented one another and collectively generated the exemplary community (Legge 1885: vol. 28, book 23).

With his new status as author-compiler of the Classics, Kongzi required a befitting promotion. He had previously been acknowledged as a sage, but now tales of his near omniscience spread and he was increasingly recognized as an "uncrowned [sage-] king" *(suwang)* whose conception and birth had been marked by miraculous portents announcing his destiny. This too we find in Sima Qian's *Shiji,* which contains our oldest biography of Kongzi,

The Imperial Academy

The first Han emperor was said to have had little use for Ru save for occasionally urinating in their caps. An exception was made for Lu Jia (d. 178 BCE), mainly because he was an engaging conversationalist. Lu Jia is traditionally seen as a precursor to Dong Zhongshu and second only to him among the early Han Ru. An often retold tale is that when the emperor taunted him by saying he had won the empire on horseback with no recourse to the *Odes* and *Documents*, Lu Jia replied: "But can you rule it on horseback?" The emperor, no doubt losing interest, suggested Lu "try writing something" on the subject, and the resultant book, *New Discussions* (*Xinyu*), at least received his "Bravo!" (Watson 1961: vol. 1, 277–8). A work claiming to be this book survives, although its authenticity is questionable. Its basic argument is "that if a ruler governs with virtue, the multitude will turn to him, if he relies on laws, the people will fear him" and revolt. It even suggests schools and academies be established to "teach and guide the people" (Ku 1988: 108–9). While he anticipated reforms that would occur later in the dynasty, Lu Jia had no effect on the policies of the first Han emperor.

Sima Qian tells us the rulers that followed, "little by little," allowed Ru into their court, although they preferred the Daoist-Legalist synthesis of Huang-Lao. Then, early in his immensely long reign, Emperor Wu (r. 141–87 BCE) had a sudden change of heart. He appointed professors (*boshi*) for the Classics, established an Imperial Academy, and recognized Ru performance in mastering one or more Classic as a selection criteria when making official appointments. This was traditionally seen as a comprehensive and ideologically exclusive reform. Were this so, there might be some cause to agree with Hu Shi when he declared that this was the moment of the "establishment of Confucianism as a national religion" (Hu 1929: 27).

As I mentioned earlier, the man who was traditionally said to have suggested this plan to Emperor Wu was Dong Zhongshu. Dong was a very influential philosopher (I discuss his ideas later), and it was perhaps due to his reputation as a teacher that he was respectfully credited with having swayed the emperor. Ban Gu reproduced three memorials that Dong submitted to Emperor Wu in 134 BCE recommending the aforementioned innovations, but something seems amiss. Some have questioned whether Ban Gu is literally quoting archival documents (Loewe 2011: 121); others accept them but assume they were simply ignored by the emperor. Dong was not a high-ranking official who had the emperor's ear and he appears to be a minor player throughout the rest of the *Hanshu*. Although Sima Qian was a great admirer of Dong, his senior contemporary, he makes no mention of these memorials.

Sima Qian does, on the other hand, quote a memorial of 124 BCE by Gongsun Hong recommending examination in the Classics be increasingly used to select officials. Given that Sima agreed with Dong's estimation that Gongsun Hong was nothing but a "servile flatterer" (Watson 1961: vol. 2, 411), he would have been more than willing to give credit to Dong Zhongshu instead. Clearly, Sima had no knowledge Dong played any significant part in these reforms. Although Gongsun Hong *was* of high rank, his memorial was written too late to have instigated the changes. For want of evidence, we can only say that there was a gradual shift and that multiple unknown Ru contributed to the process (Zufferey 2003: 295–335).

But how radical was the change? Had Emperor Wu really converted to "Confucianism as a national religion"? This all-too-common claim is based on verbal muddling. There is every difference between a state religion on the one hand and adherents of a religious tradition being supported and employed by the state on the other. Han emperors were not so much promoting Ru religious values as they were engaging the services of Ru. Ru, of course, had strong Classics-based opinions about how state rituals should be performed, but their views were not always heeded and the ceremonies were not "theirs"—they were the rituals of the dynastic rulers, alive and dead, performed to the powers sustaining their domain (Bujard 2011).

Furthermore, recent research consistently indicates that the Imperial Academy was anything but a thoroughly implemented system of education for training and selecting officials. Emperor Wu was certainly not a total convert, and although he quickly appointed the five professors of the Five Classics (*wujing boshi*), he did not actually establish the Academy (*taixue*) for over a decade. Moreover, for some time yet the Ru filled but a tiny fraction of the top posts. Sima Qian does his best to portray the Ru of his day as a coherent and influential group, but his extensive lists of important officials betray him. A simple headcount indicates that Ru very rarely achieved high rank. Throughout Emperor Wu's reign, family connection, military achievement, and wealth continued to be the prime criteria for appointment (Cai 2014: chapter 1).

But while Sima might not accurately depict what actually occurred, he presents an image of the Ru that reveals important shifts in their self-identity. After relating the events that led to state-sponsored Ru learning, he goes on to present lineages of scholarly transmission for each of the Five Classics. Examined carefully, it becomes evident he is cobbling together bits and pieces and weaving pedigrees "out of thin air" (Cai 2014: 111). Invention aside, what is significant is the fact that these genealogies were now considered necessary. The previous association of masters and disciples was being supplemented by lineages of disciples bound by their devotion to a chosen text.

This reflects a new dimension to what it meant to be a Ru. Ru continued to avow ritual, of course, but their primary focus increasingly shifted to studying a canon of texts and writing commentaries on them. In brief, this was the moment that the Ru transformed from being ritual masters to becoming Classicists. The Academy might not have been a major path to political influence, but the Ru had nonetheless reinvented themselves to conform to its dictates.

The Five Classics

This juncture when studying the Classics had come to define the Ru is an apposite occasion to introduce these texts. The actual content of the canon continued to evolve throughout the Han and beyond. Here I will offer an inclusive list of the Five Classics, including works added well after Emperor Wu's reign (see Nylan 2001).

Classics by numbers can cause some initial confusion. As there were actually three canonical books of rites, and the *Spring and Autumn Annals* appears in three commentarial forms, they were also counted as the Nine Classics (*jiujing*) from the Tang dynasty onward. Add the *Analects*, *Mengzi*, *Classic of Filial Piety*, and China's oldest dictionary (*Erya*), and you get the Thirteen Classics (*shisanjing*) of the Song dynasty.

Throughout Chinese history, there was also ongoing reference to the "Six Classics" even though there were ever only Five. This was a kind of homage paid to a text that had gone missing in action, destroyed by the fires of Qin. The Six were never a part of any curriculum, as the *Music* was "lost" before any canon was settled.

The remembrance of fallen textual comrades can powerfully consolidate the solidarity of those that have survived. That the *Music* was lost worked well as myth, but it is unlikely to be true. I will offer an alternative explanation a little later, but first we will meet the remaining Five.

Odes. The *Shijing* (English translations Karlgren 1974, Legge 1871, and Waley 1996) is a collection of 305 odes. They date from around 1000 BCE down to the decades just before Kongzi. Sima Qian claims that Kongzi selected them from some 3,000 pieces, but there is no solid evidence he in fact played any editorial role. He was, however, aware of the work which he mentions more than any other, and as he speaks of "three hundred *Odes*" (2:2), it seems that he was referring to a collection roughly comparable to the received edition. A fixed, written version of the text may not have emerged before the time of unification, however.

Many of the *Odes* are refined versions of folk songs dealing with daily life, agriculture, and the perennial themes of falling in love, broken hearts, and the hardships of war. There are also courtly pieces that treat dynastic legend, the life of royalty, and the performance of sacrifices. There was a long-standing tradition, dating back to Kongzi, which saw the *Odes* as allegorical lessons in virtuous living. *Analects* 2:2 thus alludes to an *Ode* describing sure-footed stallions and concludes: "The *Odes* are three hundred in number. They can be summed up in one phrase, swerving not from the right path."

The "Great Preface" to the *Odes*, added in the late Han, offered an alternate explanation for how the *Odes* transformed people. It says odes serve "to regulate the relation between husbands and wives, to perfect filiality and respect, to enrich human relations" and ultimately to uphold order even to the point of "moving Heaven and earth," but this is primarily achieved by the aesthetic power of music.

> Emotion moves within and takes shape in words. Words are not enough, and so one sighs it. Sighing is not enough, and so one draws it out in song. Drawing it out in song is not enough, and so all unawares one's hands dance it and one's feet tap it out. Emotion is manifest in voice. When voice is patterned, we call it tone. The tones of a well-governed age are peaceful and happy; its government is harmonious. The tones of a chaotic age are resentful and angry; its government is perverse. (Mair 1994: 122)

For the author of the "Great Preface" it is the resonating power of pattern (*wen*) in words and music which transforms people, not didactic instruction. In this regard, James Liu once nicely observed that Ru Classics were to some extent scriptural "not so much because they taught people how to behave as because they embodied the Dao in beautiful language" (Liu 1975: 25).

Documents. Not only does the *Analects* describe Kongzi and his followers studying odes; it also refers to them examining official documents or *shu*. These would have been important recorded cases, a kind of political precedent, that any aspiring diplomat would need to be familiar with. While Sima Qian claims that Kongzi edited these cases into the *Shujing* or *Documents Classic,* also known as the *Shangshu* (*Venerated Documents*) (English translations Karlgren 1950 and Legge 1865) no such work existed in his day, and the *shu* he referred to were probably a loose and informal body of historical records.

As the importance of precedent increased, rival collections appeared and both Mengzi and Xunzi expressed misgivings about some of the *shu* circulating at their time, as well as approvingly quoting documents not found in our *Shujing*. The first standard edition of the *Shujing,* containing twenty-nine documents, only appeared in the mid-second century BCE, just prior to Emperor Wu's decision to endorse the Ru. Because it contained documents transcribed in the style of writing that only came into use during the Qin dynasty, it is known as the Modern Script (*jin-wen*) *Documents.* This was said to be a truncated version of the one hundred documents that Kongzi had allegedly collated, and the fires of Qin were blamed for the loss. Later in the Han, various Ancient Script (*guwen*) fragments emerged, the most famous being ones "found" hidden within a wall of Kongzi's old home. By the fourth century CE the work had expanded to forty-five documents, but the Ancient Script additions appear to be forgeries, albeit ones that quite possibly contain some genuine historical data.

The *Documents* has a torturously tangled editorial history, and it must suffice to simply note some general features. The chapters are conventionally classified into six genres. The first two chapters are elevated to the status of exalted canons (*dian*). The remainder are divided into recorded consultations (*mo*) between the ruler and ministers, instructions (*xun*) or advice from ministers to the king, the king's proclamations (*gao*) to the people, declarations or oaths (*shi*) made by the ruler on the battlefield, and decrees (*ming*) conferring special rights and responsibilities on individuals.

The various documents span the period from the eve of the first Xia dynasty down to the Zhou about a century before Kongzi's birth. I summarized the *Shujing*'s view of the past in Chapter 3, where I explained its importance as mythic history manifesting the qualities of sagacious rulers and the workings of Heaven's Mandate (*tianming*).

Rites. Ritual was a defining feature of the Ru. It is hardly surprising, therefore, that ritual is the focus of one part of the canon, although three books eventually came to be contained therein: the *Ceremonies and Rites* (*Yili*), *Zhou Rites* (*Zhouli*), and *Rites Records* (*Liji*). Although the original core of each book was traditionally attributed to the Duke of Zhou and their editing to Kongzi, they are obviously composed by several authors with distinct styles. Again, while older material has been incorporated, the final editing and much of the content is clearly from the Han dynasty.

To modern readers, the *Yili* and *Zhouli* come across as the most systematic and the least engaging. The *Zhouli* (no English translation, but Gingell 1852 is a Qing dynasty abridgement; French translation Biot 1851), another Ancient Script text, is allegedly a very detailed contemporary account of the administrative bureaucracy that operated in the golden age of the early Zhou, although it probably was produced somewhere between the Late Zhou and early Han. It was destined to obscurity until it was promoted by Wang Mang (see discussion that follows). In contrast to the *Zhouli*'s state focus, the *Yili* (English translation Steele 1917) deals with domestic ceremonies in the life of the lower aristocracy. Without offering commentary or explanation, it outlines rites of passage such as capping, marriage, and funerals as well as providing detailed descriptions of the protocol to be observed when visiting fellow officers, giving a banquet, or engaging in a bout of archery. It is the oldest of the three rites canons.

The forty-nine books of the received edition of the *Liji* (English translation Legge 1885) also contain many descriptive accounts, ranging from lofty state sacrifices through to domestic ceremonies. What sets it apart from the other two books on *li*, however, is it engages in exegesis and addresses the philosophy and function of ritual and education. Frequently, it is Kongzi himself who is presented explaining these things, and his life and teachings are considerably embroidered in this Classic. The *Great Learning* and the *Doctrine of the Mean* are included in this diverse collection, as is *Black Robes* (Chapter 3). Extracts from the *Xunzi, Mr Lü's Spring and Autumn Annals*, and other works also seem to have been surreptitiously incorporated. The *Liji* continued evolving until the second century CE. Seen as a single text, it appears entirely disjointed and sometimes self-contradictory. It is best viewed as a Han dynasty miscellany wherein each book must be considered independently.

Changes. Few people in the West have heard of the Ru Classics except, of course, for the *Yijing*, more familiarly written *I Ching* (English translations Lynn 1994 and Wilhelm 1967 among countless others, many best avoided). Richard Smith makes this comparison: "For the past two thousand years or so, among all the works in world literature only the Bible has been more extensively commented upon than the *Changes*" (2008: xiii).

The *Yijing* is also part of the Daoist canon and is the only book to achieve this dual scriptural status. There are also Buddhist versions. Popular from the outset, during medieval times its appeal further increased, shaping the Ru renaissance, new forms of Daoism, and the entire gamut of Chinese culture. It not only continues to inspire people in the East but can be found in virtually every Western bookstore catering to readers of "esoteric" literature.

Given this story of staggering success, it is somewhat sobering to realize Ru of the Zhou dynasty showed little interest in the *Changes*. Mengzi never mentions it, and although Kongzi came to be regarded as its editor and commentary author, there is only one passage in the *Analects* that *might* refer to it (7:17), but that virtually every modern translator agrees does not. Xunzi at least referred to it on two occasions, but significantly when he came to make his pioneering suggestion that a curriculum of named books be promoted, the only thing conspicuous about the *Changes* is its absence.

In origin, the *Yijing* was a divination prompt book. "Reading" the cracks in bone and shell are the best-known methods of divination in ancient China, but other techniques were also used, including the manipulation of yarrow stalks. In ways that are unclear, this evolved into a method where the stalks merely directed the diviner to one of sixty-four set "answers." These take the form of hexagrams, stacks of six horizontal lines that are either solid or broken (later, interpreted as *yang* and *yin* lines). Varying the order and number of solid and broken lines yields a total of sixty-four possible hexagrams. Each hexagram is named and has a short and enigmatic statement that is followed by brief commentaries on each of the six lines.

This basic core of the *Yijing* may have been established as early as the tenth century BCE. Some eight hundred years later, roughly at the time of unification, a series of commentaries known as the "Ten Wings" were added by various authors providing metaphysical and moralistic interpretations of the hexagrams. In Ru thought, the *Changes* was valued not so much as a divination tool as it was for revealing moral responses to the ebb and flow of the cosmic pulse. A Han text found buried with the *Yijing* thus has Kongzi saying that although he sometimes used the *Yi* for divination, he was primarily concerned with "observing its virtue and propriety" (Shaughnessy 1996: 241).

The *Changes* was so highly regarded, it was given the most ancient pedigree of all the Classics and was said to contain the cumulative wisdom of four sages. It began in pre-dynastic times when the cultural hero Fu Xi observed the patterns of heaven and earth and distilled them into eight trigrams (Figure 9). King Wen, founder of the Zhou dynasty, paired the trigrams to form the sixty-four (i.e., eight by eight) hexagrams to which he added statements, while his son, the Duke of Zhou, is credited with the line commentaries. Finally, none other than Kongzi himself was said to have composed the Ten Wings. These traditions have been recognized as legendary by critical Chinese readers for more than a millennium.

FIGURE 9   *Fuxi inventing the trigrams.*

This is a Ming dynasty picture of Fu Xi drawing trigrams by Guo Xu (1456 – c. 1529). The Great Commentary to the *Yijing*, allegedly written by Kongzi, explains how Fu Xi discovered the trigrams with his sagacious insight into patterns inherent in the world.

"When in ancient times [Fu Xi] ruled the world as sovereign, he looked upward and observed the images in heaven and looked downward and observed the models that the earth provided. He observed the patterns on birds and beasts and what things were suitable for the land. Nearby, adopting them from his own person, and afar, adopting them from other things, he thereupon made the eight trigrams in order to become thoroughly conversant with the virtues inherent in the numinous and bright and to classify the myriad things in terms of their true innate natures." (Lynn 1994: 77)

Spring and Autumn Annals. It is difficult to exaggerate the aridity of the *Chunqiu* or *Spring and Autumn Annals* for the unsuspecting reader. Essentially, it sets down the bare details, in point form and without connecting narrative or interpretative commentary, year by year, the significant events that occurred in the state of Lu from 722 to 481 BCE. Most of it is concerned with local affairs, conflicts with neighbors, and unusual natural occurrences. Very probably, it is an official chronicle written at the court of a local ruler to be added to the state archives. In the eleventh century, Wang Anshi (Chapter 6) frankly and controversially declared that it was just a "fragmented and messy court report" (*duanlan chaobao*).

Because Lu was Kongzi's home state and because the *Spring and Autumn* ends just three years before his death, it is not totally surprising the book eventually came to be ascribed to him. Until recently, it was assumed that Mengzi first made this claim

(*Mengzi* 3B9). Strangely, nobody voiced their agreement until the time of Sima Qian. As "spring and autumn" was commonly used in titles to signify "annals" or "history," it may well be that Mengzi was not actually referring to the Classic that we know. Furthermore, when other pre-Han sources clearly *are* referring to our Classic, they never mention Kongzi as its author. It may have been Sima Qian himself who first interpreted Mengzi as saying Kongzi had written the actual *Chunqiu* of the canon, an assumption that thereafter was universally accepted by Ru (Cai 2010). For this attribution there is, however, "not one shred of literary or archaeological evidence" (Nylan 2001: 257).

The explanation that developed in the Han was that, as a low-ranking official, Kongzi could not freely express his views, and so he chose to conceal them using "subtle phrasing" (*weiyan*), his true judgments hidden behind the seemingly neutral language of his text. Deciphering these secret messages required very imaginative commentary skills indeed.

Three canonical commentaries accompany the *Spring and Autumn*: the *Gongyang*, *Guliang*, and *Zuo*. They are traditionally, but unconvincingly, said to have been written or orally transmitted by Kongzi's followers. The *Gongyang* and *Zuo* nonetheless seem to genuinely date from the Zhou dynasty, although the *Guliang* is from the Han.

The *Gongyang* (English translation Miller 2015) and *Guliang* (not available in any European Language; some passages are translated in Malmqvist 1971–7) are similar in style (they are both Modern Script texts) and take the form of questions and answers designed to disclose the "praise and blame" that Kongzi was passing through carefully selected words. The fine nuances of terms or the decision to include or omit an event were clues to his hidden judgments. These two texts were largely overlooked after the Han dynasty, but the *Gongyang* has made a remarkable comeback in the modern era, as we will see in later chapters.

In contrast, the *Zuo* (English translations Durrant, Li, and Schaberg 2016, and Legge 1872; selections in Watson 1989), an Ancient Script text, does not consistently analyze the *Spring and Autumn* and was perhaps in its original form not even a commentary. Rather, it was a detailed and comparatively lively history that just happened to span roughly the same period of time. It is considered a literary masterpiece and it is China's most ancient work of narrative history.

***

Ru claimed they maintained the Way of the Sages. They insisted this was transmitted through music and ritual on the one hand and in texts on the other. But it was ritual and music that were primary to Kongzi, and even though Xunzi esteemed sagacious texts, he too gave priority to ritual. With the state recognition of a defined canon and patronage of Classics-based education, however, the Ru predominantly became Classicists trained to specialize in scriptural interpretation. From this point on, most of their writing would take the form of commentary, annotations on the Classics, and footnotes to the words of sages.

Thankfully, the ensuing two millennia of scholarship is not pure pedantry, although frankly, much of it is. It is, nonetheless, quite impressive just how many new ideas could be read out of, or into, the Classics. This becomes apparent when we turn to the thought of Dong Zhongshu and his followers.

Correlative cosmology

We must assume Dong Zhongshu (c. 179 – c. 104) was promoted as the man who had masterminded Emperor Wu's reforms out of respect for his reputation as a teacher. His name came to be virtually synonymous with Han Ru philosophy. In the twelfth century, Zhu Xi (Chapter 6) reflected: "Of the Han Confucians the purest was Dong Zhongshu ... No one could compare to him" (Wittenborn 1991: 172). Sima Qian tells us Dong was so devoted to the *Spring and Autumn Annals* and its *Gongyang* commentary that he rarely ventured beyond the curtains of his study, and for years students never saw his face. "All the other scholars looked up to him as their teacher" (Watson 1961: vol. 2, 410).

In order to highlight what was novel in Dong Zhongshu's thought, let me for a moment return to Xunzi. As we saw, Xunzi showed how a sage-king could create a perfectly harmonious society by employing education, ritual, and music. He also believed such a ruler would ensure the natural world would provide everything that people required. There was nothing magical to this, it was just a matter of good management of Heaven's natural resources. Why, then, do rain sacrifices produce rain? Because it was about to rain anyway, he said. What do comets and other natural anomalies mean? Nothing, they are just uncommon but insignificant moments in the interplay of *yin* and *yang*. "Hunchbacked shamans and lame-footed seers" might profess "to assess the *yin* and *yang*, to divine the omens and portents, to drill the tortoise-shells and lay out the hexagrams" of the *Yijing*, but this nonsense was no business of Ru (Hutton 2014: 178–9, 78).

And now, Sima Qian on Dong Zhongshu:

> Dong Zhongshu studied the various natural disasters and portentous happenings recorded in the *Spring and Autumn Annals* and on the basis of his study attempted to discover the principles behind the operations and interactions of the *yin* and *yang*. Thus he concluded if one wished rain to fall, one should shut off the *yang* forces and free those of the *yin*, while if one wished the rain to cease, one should do the reverse. (Watson 1961: vol. 2, 410)

Dong Zhongshu was indeed renown for assessing the *yin* and *yang*, making prognostications from natural anomalies, and performing sacrifices to produce rain. This sort of thing was common Ru practice in the Han. In the twentieth century, Hu Shi chided them for having incorporated ideas that were "primitive and crudely superstitious" (Hu 1929: 40); we can almost imagine Xunzi once again muttering: "stupid Ru of this vulgar age."

Such uncharitable assessments do not do Han Ru justice. To better appreciate their innovations, we need to discuss a monumental shift in the Chinese worldview that roughly coincided with unification. Befitting the time, China believed it had discovered the equivalent to that holy grail of modern physics, a grand unified theory of everything. This was the theory that everything that existed could be understood as the interplay of *yin* and *yang* and the operation of the Five Phases or Processes (*wuxing*) associated with wood, fire, earth, metal, and water, which move (*xing* means "to move") in predictable cycles.

Sima Qian said the theory was the brainchild of Zou Yan (c. 305 – c. 240), but there simply is not enough evidence to adjudicate on this. What we can say is that *yin-yang* appears earlier in the textual record, while *wuxing* bursts on to the scene just prior to unification. The two encyclopedic works discussed earlier, *Mr Lü's Spring and Autumn Annals* and the *Huainanzi*, are both saturated with *yinyang wuxing*. We might expect the Classics to predate these innovations, but they are represented by some late inclusions. *Yinyang*, for example, is central to the cosmology of the "Great Commentary" to the *Yijing*, while *wuxing* is employed in a book in the *Documents* called the "Great Plan" and, more systematically, in the "Conveyance of Rites" and "Monthly Ordinances" of the *Rites Records*. It is also found in the final quarter of the *Zuo* commentary to the *Spring and Autumn Annals*. There was, therefore, precedent in the Classics for applying this theory. And Dong Zhongshu was traditionally considered to be one of its greatest exponents.

The perceived value of the theory was that it could be applied to predict future events and to act in ways that could alter outcomes. There are three basic premises:

1. Every class of thing is grouped into fives (and/or twos—here I focus on the *wuxing* dimension). There are the primary categories (wood, fire, earth, metal, and water), five colors, five notes (the pentatonic scale), five directions (counting the center), odors, tastes, senses, shapes, planets (visible to the naked eye), organs, mountain peaks, and so on to include all things. The *Rites Records* mentions sixty-two quinary sets—there were even five ways to turn the royal boat. The classification extends to social and moral realms—there are five cardinal [relationships] (*wulun*) and five constant [virtues] (*wuchang*). It was, by the way, Dong Zhongshu who was credited with adding the fifth virtue of *xin* or trustworthiness to Mengzi's other four (*ren* humaneness, *yi* righteousness, *li* ritual, *zhi* wisdom; see Chapter 4).

2. Things belonging to the same phase group correspond to and influence one another. This is due to a resonance between entities that share an essential commonality. A work attributed to Dong Zhongshu says: "All things avoid what is different from them and follow what is similar to them ... This is clear from the evidence. Now suppose you tune and play a [zither]. Pluck the note *gong*, and other *gong* notes will respond to it ... Among the five notes, each one that matches will sound spontaneously. This has nothing to do with spirits" (Queen

and Major 2016: 438). This premise makes it possible to influence something by manipulating other things belonging to the same category, which is still a fundamental principle of traditional Chinese medicine.

3. The phases move in predictable cycles of "generation" (e.g., wood generates fire) and "overcoming" (water overcomes fire). This third premise added a temporal dimension to the theory, which was particularly important to rulers. Dynasties too were categorized according to *wuxing*. Sima Qian tells us the First Emperor was a great believer and made corresponding adjustments to his reign to ensure that his dynasty (water) successfully overcame the Zhou (fire) (Watson 1993: 43). Signs of increased reverberating activity indicated a new dynasty was in ascent. *Mr Lü's Annals* thus records how a fiery-red crow landing on a Zhou altar was understood by King Wen to signify the Zhou was in ascent over the Shang (metal-white) (Knoblock and Riegel 2000: 283).

Before I return to Dong Zhongshu, let me make good my promise to explain why the *Classic of Music* was "lost." Given their supreme responsibility for transforming and completing the world, the Classics too had to partake in this fivefold classification. A Report written in the latter part of the Han asks the question: Why are there Five Classics? Answer: Because there are five constant virtues. Again: Why are there five constant virtues? Because of there are Five Phases (*wuxing*) (Tjan 1949–52: vol. 1, 608, 566). Remember, Ru were famous for learning texts verbatim and many of them had been orally transmitted. Recall too this was a time when fraudulent versions of Classics were regularly being "discovered." Make no mistake, if the Ru had wanted the *Yuejing*, they would have "found" it—indeed, a *Music* Classic was briefly "discovered" and canonized during Wang Mang's reign (discussed later) (Dubs 1955: 192). If it ever existed as an actual book, the *Music* was probably a short piece now tucked away as the "Record of Music" (*Yueji*) chapter of the *Rites Records*.

Dong Zhongshu

The most important book presenting the Ru application of *yinyang wuxing* is *Luxuriant Gems on the Spring and Autumn Annals* (*Chunqiu fanlu*), traditionally attributed to Dong Zhongshu. This attribution is problematic, however. Han sources list three works by Dong, all lost, and obviously the *Chunqiu fanlu*, which survives, was not among them. As there are no references to *Luxuriant Gems* prior to the sixth century, it has long been suspected to be a forgery, although it probably incorporates genuine material from Dong's lost books.

The main touchstone used to locate the "real" Dong Zhongshu is chapter 56 of Ban Gu's *History of the Former Han*, which contains Dong's memorials to Emperor Wu (translated in Queen and Major 2016: appendix B). There, he employs *yinyang* correlations, but he does not apply *wuxing*. The later, we now assume, was introduced by his followers.

For Dong, Heaven (*tian*) was the ultimate source of all that is. The Way (*dao*) derives from Heaven and operates via the polarities of *yin* and *yang*. This accords with the cosmology of the "Great Commentary" to the *Changes*, which says: "The reciprocal process of the *yin* and *yang* is called the Dao" (Lynn 1994: 53). In Dong's words, "The most important aspect of Heaven's Way is *yin* and *yang*" (Queen and Major 2016: 625).

As with those applying *wuxing* theory, Dong's *yinyang* taxonomy categorizes all things from the most coarsely material to the most refined intellectual and moral realities. Humans are likewise formed by the workings of *yin* and *yang*. Dong deploys this in a clever way to resolve the tension between Mengzi and Xunzi regarding human nature. In Chapter 4, I showed that their divergence was based on their using *xing* (nature) in ways so dissimilar they might almost be two different things. Dong said they were, in fact, different things. Xunzi was describing human disposition due to the influences of emotion (*qing*), whereas Mengzi was discussing our tendencies due to nature (*xing*). The former is generated by the operation of *yin*, the later *yang*, and humans are therefore both good and bad: "Heaven has its dual manifestation of *yin* and *yang*; the self also has a dual nature of greed and humaneness (*ren*)" (Queen and Major 2016: 348).

Another related tension that Dong resolves with his cosmic dualism is that between cultivating people through education (*yang*) and controlling them by law (*yin*). Both, he said, are required. Dong avoids being seen as equal part Legalist and Ru by arguing that in the workings of *yin* and *yang*, there is always far more *yang*. Heaven (*yang*) sends forth heat and earth (*yin*) sends forth coolness, but life requires a hundred times more of the former. Likewise, a ruler should privilege moral instruction as "coercive punishment cannot be relied on to order the age, just as *yin* cannot be relied on to complete the year" (Queen and Major 2016: 625). While secondary, law was nonetheless essential, and so Ru, like Dong, also employed the *Spring and Autumn Annals* as a repository of legal precedent when judging cases brought before them.

Dong's ideas on education and law applied to ordinary people, but kings were extraordinary. Dong in fact saw the king as the central pillar supporting and conjoining the entire cosmic order. He argued this was evident in the very character for king (王, *wang*) which shows the sovereign, represented by the vertical stroke, linking three lines symbolizing Heaven (*yang*), Earth (*yin*), and humanity dwelling between. Only a true king, he said, "could take the central position between Heaven, Earth and humankind and act as the thread that joins and penetrates them" (Queen and Major 2016: 399).

Dong, of course, acknowledged that Heaven could bestow and withdraw its mandate to rule, but in his system Heaven can also communicate more specifically. In his memorials to Emperor Wu, it is clear that Dong believed a king's virtue quite literally affected the natural environment. A good ruler creates harmony among people, which in turn influences that balance of *yin* and *yang* in the natural world. Then, he says, "*yin* and *yang* will be harmonious; the wind and rain will arrive in their appropriate seasons ...; the five [kinds of] grain will reach fruition; the subsidiary crops will flourish" (Queen and Major 2016: 626). Inversely, environmental strife indicated the failings of the ruler. There is insufficient evidence to determine Dong's precise methods for interpreting natural calamities, but it is apparent that in scale, time, and location they correspond to the moral lapses that trigger them (Arbuckle 1991: 189–217). It is also difficult to be certain precisely how Dong believed these events emanated from Heaven. He regularly speaks of Heaven sending forth calamities to reveal its "mind," "desires," "concerns," and so on. Possibly Dong had reconfigured *tian* as an intervening deity, which might suggest the influence of Mozi, but equally possibly he used anthropomorphic expressions to describe an essentially impersonal process. This remains unclear.

What is clear is that Dong places the burden of ordering and sustaining the world squarely on the king's shoulders. If the king's virtue is sufficient, this will reverberate throughout the human and nonhuman world. For Dong, like Mengzi before him, kingship demanded stewardship. It was a task befitting a sage, and, even more than the ancient sage-kings, Kongzi was his archetype. Dong, perhaps for the first time, declared that Kongzi was a sage who had remained an "uncrowned king" (*suwang*).

This raised a problem. If Heaven decrees who will rule and if Kongzi was meant to be king, why had his regency not occurred? The evidence is not entirely clear, but it seems Dong circumvented this problem with a theory of predictable patterns of history in which sages only become kings at the beginning of dynastic cycles. Mid-cycle, an exemplary ruler employed a sagacious "uncrowned king" as the power behind the throne. Dong Zhongshu perhaps imagined himself filling precisely this role for Emperor Wu. Needless to say, the emperor had other plans.

Omens, abdications, and usurpers

While the chapters in *Luxuriant Gems* employing *wuxing* theory are not by Dong Zhongshu, they probably incorporate the writings of several generations of his followers over the next century or so. His own ideas represent a germinal stage in the development of doctrines that were to expand, permeate all of Han Ru thought, and generate vast literature, the majority of which has not survived.

By the mid-Han, around the beginning of the common era, there had developed a body of writing supplementing the Classics (*jing*). *Jing* literally means "warp," and these new treatises were called *wei* or "woof," as they wove themselves into the "warp" of the Classics. They later became linked with oracle texts called *chen,* and together *chenwei* are generally known as Ru "apocryphal" texts (Fung 1953: chapter 3). Many professed to be written by Kongzi himself. Later considered to be seditious, they were systematically destroyed from the fifth century on (Chapter 6), but from remaining fragments and occasional quotations in other works we can see they were a thoroughgoing and systematic development of Dong Zhongshu's germinal ideas. Indeed, as only the first half of *Luxuriant Gems* actually takes the form of a commentary on the *Spring and Autumn Annals*, some of the remaining sections could well be based on those apocryphal texts. What distinguishes them from Dong's own thought is the addition of *wuxing* theory which, of course, immensely increased the permutations of signs that could be used when determining cosmic patterns and reading Heaven's intent.

As this apocryphal tradition grew in strength, Ru increasingly became associated with reading omens and prognosticating. Some believed it was incumbent on rulers to elicit ongoing signs that Heaven continued to support their reign. They acknowledged that Heaven had initially bestowed the empire upon the Han, but they did not necessarily see this enduring in perpetuity. One of Dong Zhongshu's second-generation disciples interpreted an omen to signify the emperor should abdicate, for which he was, not surprisingly, executed. In making his proclamation, he evoked Dong's name, and it is possible Dong too had envisioned a Han abdication (Arbuckle 1995). This notion perhaps lingered harmlessly enough during the first part of the Han, but the frequency of such suggestions was on the rise, and events would unfold that made it most threatening (Ch'en 1986: 773).

The troubles seemed to follow a sudden increase in Ru power. It has recently been suggested that a witchcraft scare during emperor Wu's last years was responsible for their rapid and momentary ascent. Dominant families were eradicated en masse to contain the sorcery, and Ru simply stepped in to fill the vacuum (Cai 2014: chapter 4).

Far from being loyal upholders of the status quo, Ru thereafter were frequently seen supporting potential and real usurpers. Huo Guang (d. 68 BCE) had served emperor Wu and acted as regent after his death. He styled himself after the Duke of Zhou and depended heavily on portents supplied by Ru to depose the emperor (a Chinese first) and find a suitable replacement. Later, the new emperor would himself use Ru to remove the now all-too powerful Huo Guang. It was in the context of this constant search for Heavenly endorsements for major political upheavals that Ru apocryphal literature truly came to the fore (Cai 2014: chapter 5)

Then, in the middle of the Han, we finally meet a ruler who wholeheartedly wished to make Ru teaching central to his domain. To my mind, Wang Mang was the only ruler in all of Chinese history who came close to implementing Ruism as a "state religion." Having previously served as regent, Wang Mang ruled in his own right from 9 to 23 CE. This fervent supporter of Ruism, who claimed descent from the sage-rulers Huangdi and Shun (who had loyally served his predecessor before being handed the throne) and who greatly admired the Duke of Zhou (another faithful servant), intended nothing less than realizing Kongzi's dream of reestablishing the golden age of the Zhou dynasty.

The great irony is, Wang Mang was universally condemned by all subsequent Ru and in recent times has been blamed for corrupting Ru Learning for two thousand years. In his day, however, Wang Mang had immense support. His great mistake was not that he "humbly and reluctantly" obeyed Heaven by forcing the young heir apparent to abdicate the throne so that he could begin his Xin ("New") dynasty, but rather that he lost control so that the Han was restored and continued for a further two centuries. Given state investment in history, it was inevitable Wang Mang would forever be "the usurper" (Thomsen 1988).

Wang Mang's ascent was heralded by a most impressive array of *wuxing*-based omens and portents, which he had collated in a widely distributed book. Many of these had been reported by Ru. Wang Mang himself had a solid Ru education and had previously dressed in their attire; he was a Classicist who genuinely believed in the potential of fully implementing the Ru. He encouraged the accumulation of texts, and many Ancient Script versions of the Classics (notably, the *Zuo* commentary and *Zhouli*) came to light at his time, due particularly to the efforts of the bibliographer Liu Xin (46 BCE–23 CE). Wang Mang also hosted a conference on interpreting the Classics (the prototype of others to follow), had select Classics inscribed in stone (another first – Figure 10), and greatly enlarged the Academy, increasing the number of professors and building ten thousand houses to accommodate Academy students (Dubs 1955: 191–4). Most importantly, he comprehensively promoted the cultural and political protocol of the *Zhouli* (Puett 2010). His wide-ranging reforms, many of which had in fact been previously proposed by Dong Zhongshu, are sometimes considered "socialist" (Hu 1928), but they were then seen to be faithfully restoring Zhou institutions.

Reading between the lines of Ban Gu's thoroughly biased account, it seems "officials supported Wang Mang practically *en masse*" (Bielenstein 1986: 240). Significantly, Ban Gu had so little evidence of overt villainy, he was forced to denounce Wang Mang by depicting a man hiding behind excessive displays of virtue—the First Emperor burned the *Odes* and *Documents* whereas Wang Mang constantly chanted them "to gloss over his wicked words" (Dubs 1955: 473). Yang Xiong (see discussion later here) left us a more sympathetic (but equally biased) comparison in his memorial to Wang Mang entitled "Denigrating Qin and Praising Xin" (*Juqin meixin*). Unlike Ban Gu, he does not need to exaggerate the Han's patronage of the Ru and so offers a fairly even-handed summary: the Han had indeed employed the Ru, but not exclusively and in a fragmentary and half-hearted manner. The Xin, in contrast, is presented as a utopian order based on the Way of the Sages, dedicated to the Classics, rites, and music and implementing the social and political standards of the High Zhou. For this, Yang Xiong suggested Wang Mang's regency be added to the "exalted canons" of the *Documents Classic* (Knechtges 1978).

Wang Mang's downfall may have been simple bad luck, for while he was well supported at court, famine triggered mass revolt among the peasantry. Had his dynasty endured, he might have been remembered as the greatest champion of Ruism in Imperial China. It was not to be. Once defeated, Ru desperately needed to regain Han trust. What we witness at this juncture is a concerted effort among Ru to distance themselves from the doctrine of abdication to instead insist that succession alone was endorsed by Heaven. There was also a scramble to show that the true reading of omens indicated Heaven had never wavered in bestowing its mandate upon the Han (Arbuckle 1994). Ban Gu, writing in the wake of these events, is a case in point. He was at pains to argue that history revealed Heaven's mandate rightfully and eternally belonged to the Han, irrespective of any moral lapses that might occur (Clark 2008: chapter 5).

FIGURE 10   *Stone Classics.*

Inscribing Classics in stone consolidated their authority and provided a standard for correcting the inevitable errors generated by hand-copying manuscripts. It also closed the canon to those trying to promote different versions of Classics.

Wang Mang was the first emperor to order the Classics be inscribed, but not a single fragment has survived.

The next set, known as the Xiping Stone Classics, was carved toward the end of the Han (175–183). They were engraved on forty-six stele over 3 meters high that were erected outside the Imperial Academy. They were destroyed in the battles that ended the Han dynasty, but more than 500 fragments, like the one pictured, have survived.

Other stone Classics were periodically produced thereafter. Best preserved are the Tang dynasty version known as the Kaicheng Stone Classics, now in the Forest of Steles Museum in Xi'an, and the Qing dynasty Qianlong Stone Classics that are housed in the Imperial College in Beijing.

The Later Han

Omenology is a gambler's game that only pays when your predictions transpire. There were players enough willing to risk their hand throughout the rest of imperial history, but Ru began pulling back from the table. To maintain their status whatever the vicissitudes of history might bring, it was imperative that Ru establish themselves as loyal servants to whichever dynasty Heaven chose to instate. Staying neutral demanded keeping clear of prophesy.

This was a stance some Ru began taking after Wang Mang. It did not occur instantly, however, as the rulers of the restored Han still looked to them to provide portents endorsing their return to power. To consolidate this interpretation of the Classics and apocryphal texts, two conferences were held in 51 and 79 CE. The emperor presided over both and pronounced the final decisions, thus asserting control. We have a record of the second conference called the *Comprehensive Discussions of the White Tiger Hall* (*Baihu tong*; Tjan 1949–52), and it draws together much of the thought of the Han and continues to endorse *wuxing* and the importance of portents. Needless to say, it also insists that these reveal Heaven had unambiguously bestowed its mandate upon the Han. The *Baihu tong* did not mark a revival of mantic practice, however. Rather, it was an "apotheosis" of Han Ru doctrine written at the very "time when it had begun to wane" (Kramers 1986: 764).

While there were Ru of the Later Han who continued dabbling in omens and portents, others rejected these arts. This division was once seen as a split between those respectively advocating the Modern and Ancient Script versions of the Classics, but this simplistic correlation has been shown to be an invention of nineteenth-century Chinese scholarship (van Ess 1994, Nylan 1994). Suffice it to say, some Ru began to distance themselves from extraordinary beliefs and practices.

This is well illustrated by Yang Xiong (53 BCE–18 CE), whose thinking anticipates developments to be discussed in the next part of this book. In the build-up to that medieval Ru revival, Han Yu singled out Yang Xiong as the only Han dynasty Ru who had almost got it right (Tiwald and Van Norden 2014: 130). Zhu Xi, the greatest name of that revival, disagreed: "Yang Xiong was most useless. He was truly a stale scholar ... Don't read Yangzi. There is nothing good in what he said." We should not take Zhu Xi too seriously; he was just cranky because Yang Xiong had "lost his integrity by serving Wang Mang" (Chan 1967: 295, 293).

Yang Xiong upheld the supreme authority of the Classics (*Fayan* 7:5, translations from Yang 2013) but he had little time for the "bickering" Ru "ornamenting" scripture to secure jobs (7: 6, 8). Their commentaries, he said, were so full of nonsense that they had virtually turned themselves into shamans (12:10). Yang believed in *yinyang wuxing* and accepted that Heaven's mandate broadly reflected a ruler's virtue (10:11), but he rejected attempts to read Heavenly fine-print and interpret every natural event as a significant portent. He had no time for rain rituals (9:16) or Kongzi supernaturalism (10: 12–13). Yang compared himself to Mengzi who had reopened the Way blocked by Yang Zhu and Mozi (2:20), and like Kongzi, he claimed to transmit but not create (5:18). He believed Ru competition for status and power had estranged them from Kongzi's "easy" Way—easy in that it was straight and clear, though it took a lifetime of total dedication. Its goal was to become a person of nobility (*junzi*), not a diviner in the machinations of the court. In these ways, Yang Xiong was very much a herald of the Ru renaissance that is the subject of the next chapter.

Paired with his rejection of the prognosticating Ru was his endorsement of the Ru recluse: "If a man of worthy speech and conduct fails to meet with the proper time, then he becomes a worthy man in reclusion" (11:21). This is an important shift in the Ru-ruler relationship subsequent to Wang Mang (Berkowitz 2000). Ru had actively interpreted omens as Heaven's warnings and they had supported dynastic overthrow when those warnings went unheeded. This left them with a tarnished reputation with the restoration of the Han. Subsequently, Ru avoided being seen as agents of dynastic change. Rather, they served loyally if they approved of a ruler, and if they felt him unworthy they withdrew and allowed Heaven to sort things out. Thus just after the Han, Huangfu Mi (215–282) wrote his *Accounts of High-Minded Men* (*Gaoshi zhuan*) saying that Sima Qian and Ban Gu had overlooked many of the noblest Ru who had chosen to withdraw from office, although in truth Huangfu Mi was inventing past precedent for a Ru ideal that only became apparent mid-Han (Berkowitz 2014).

The *philosophers* developing Ru thought in the Later Han and beyond tended to be disengaged from politics, and indeed, they were often not even seen as being exclusively or primarily Ru. Many turned to Daoism and Buddhism for inspiration, although they mostly did so while simultaneously acknowledging Kongzi and the Classics. Ru in office, on the other hand, tended to be disinclined to assert any strong ideological stance. Nor were Ru a powerful political force. Pedigree remained far more significant than education in determining status (Ebrey 1986: 633–7), and Later Han emperors became increasingly insular so that in-laws and eunuchs came to control the inner court. Wang Chong (27–97 CE), a friend of Ban Gu, unhappily observed that Ru were generally perceived as being "shallow and incompetent" and that "the authorities do not like to employ them" (Forke 1962: vol. 2, 72).

*** *

The Way of the Ru metamorphosed in the Han. The changes were driven by their new identity as scholars with textual expertise aspiring to be of service to the emperor. With the establishment of the Canon and the Academy, Ru became Classicists and writing commentaries became their primary intellectual medium. Kongzi's brief rise to near-superhuman status should be understood as part of the consolidation of the Ru textual corpus, not as the arrival of "Confucianism."

The Ru certainly transformed themselves in the Han, but China was not transformed by the Ru, and the "victory of the Ru" is an inflated declaration. Ru values were not synonymous with state ideology, and the historical evidence for this period cannot support the equation: Ru Learning (*ruxue*) = China's national identity. Indeed, that formula would only become necessary when confronting values that were *not* Chinese.

The challenges of Christianity, secular humanism, science, and democracy currently motivate claims for the unity of Ruism and Chinese culture, but many of the current arguments were being rehearsed long ago with the arrival of Buddhism.

The coming of Buddhism and, soon after, the emergence of Daoism as a religious movement would once again transform the Way of the Ru. These are events that open the next part of our story.

PART THREE

The Second Epoch: Song to Qing dynasties

The second epoch was precipitated by the emergence of religious Daoism and the arrival of Buddhism. These two faiths had a massive impact and the Ru renaissance of the Song dynasty was a response to their popularity. Reinvented and rejuvenated, Ru Learning would thereafter become *the* major pathway to official life and so flourish as never before.

Chapter 6 begins by examining the challenges of Daoism and Buddhism as well as outlining some important changes to Ru tradition prior to the Song. The main focus of the chapter is the Song dynasty revival known as "Way Learning." The chapter builds to an exposition of the philosophy of Zhu Xi, who was said to have brought Way Learning to a "great completion." Zhu was the most influential thinker in all of imperial China.

Chapter 7 deals with the Ming and Qing dynasties, which were a prelude to truly modern China. In the Ming, there emerged an alternative to Zhu Xi's philosophy, known as Heart-Mind Learning. The most important exponent was Wang Yangming. While Zhu Xi's views continued to define orthodoxy, Wang Yangming was immensely influential and his thinking inspires most modern exponents of Ru Learning. I look at Wang's followers in the late Ming, often considered wild heretics, before turning to the more conservative Ru of the final Qing dynasty. Throughout, I stress that these were dynasties during which Ru Learning increasingly permeated all levels of society.

6

Learning of the Dao

When Enlightenment thinkers first learned of Zhu Xi, he reminded them of the Dutch philosopher Baruch Spinoza (Israel 2007). They both looked like atheists. But while traditional theologians only noticed God's absence, others appreciated their concern to reclaim divine reason within nature. Theirs was the type of religious thought congenial to rationalists and scientists. Einstein famously said, "I believe in Spinoza's God" (Isaacson 2007: 388), and even Richard Dawkins admits he can live with that kind of God delusion (Dawkins 2007: chapter 1). Zhu Xi's religious orientation, if not his actual doctrines, can still seem very relevant today.

But who is Zhu Xi? Few people in the West recognize the name. Yet for the final 600 years of imperial China, he was arguably more important than Kongzi himself. Kongzi might still be the First Sage, but now it was Zhu Xi's Kongzi.

As we will see, Zhu Xi's commentaries became orthodoxy in 1313, and thereafter every aspiring student was obliged to understand the Classics as Zhu had interpreted them. Commentary can change everything. Consider *Analects* 6:30 where a disciple asks Kongzi just what it means to be humane (*ren*). To Kongzi's own answer, Zhu Xi adds that *ren* "speaks of Principle (*li*) which pervades what is above and what is below" (Gardner 2003: 57). Here Kongzi's supreme virtue is explained using a word that does not once appear in the *Analects*. Yet *li*, variously translated as "Pattern," "Coherence," "Form," "Reason," or, most commonly, "Principle" was *the* most important concept in Zhu Xi's own teaching, so important that it is known as *lixue* or Principle Learning.

This kind of Ru Learning is still very much alive in China (Chapter 9). Leading exponents insist that, despite Western claims to the contrary, their beliefs are indeed religious, although in a manner devoid of supernaturalism and congruous with reason and science. Einstein once described himself as a "deeply religious man" who was "striving to comprehend ... the Reason that manifests itself in nature" (Einstein 1956: 11). The words might have been Zhu Xi's. But Zhu went much further, taking Reason or Principle as an ultimate reality to be engaged through religious practices that, he believed, could lead to the perfection of humanity.

This chapter builds to an exposition of Zhu Xi's thought. Zhu, however, lived almost a millennium after the late Han dynasty, where our last chapter left off. The first two sections of this chapter will quickly scroll through the ensuing centuries leading up to the formation of the Song dynasty in 960. I then consider radical changes to the fortunes of the Ru in the Song before turning to focus on one particular tradition known as Way Learning (*daoxue*). Way Learning is another name for Principle Learning and both are known as Neo-Confucianism in the West. Zhu Xi did not invent Way Learning, but he was incontestably its most influential exponent; he was the person traditionally said to have bought it to a "great completion."

Disunion, Daoism, and Buddhism

For three and a half centuries following the collapse of the Han dynasty, China was politically fragmented. For our purposes, it will suffice to refer to this tangled web of kingdoms and mini-dynasties as the Period of Disunion (220–589). From the outset, a small number of aristocratic families became prominent and dominated society. Traditional Ru values were maintained as signs of the cultured status of this elite, but they lacked the deep notion of total self-transformation typical of early Ru thought. Philosophy was now seen as clever repartee, known as "Pure Conversation" (*qingtan*), and Daoist philosophical ideas predominated. Kongzi was still highly regarded, but he was considered a crypto-Daoist whose refusal to discuss metaphysics only proved he understood that "one who knows does not speak" (*Daodejing* 56). The thinking of these privileged savants nonetheless greatly enriched the philosophical vocabulary at the disposal of the later Ru revivalists.

In the following century, China was facing invasion from nomads, and military necessity increasingly dictated policy in the north. As warfare escalated, aristocratic families began taking refuge by withdrawing to the Yangzi delta region in the south, where they continued to prevail. Neither the northern nor southern environment was conducive to Ru tradition, which thrived under stable, centralized government. Buddhism and religious Daoism, on the other hand, flourished.

Precisely how and when Buddhism arrived in China is unknown, but it presumably traveled with traders along the Silk Road and reached China in the middle of the Han dynasty. It spread rapidly through society, and by the Later Han even emperors were sacrificing to the Buddha. Soon after, Daoism began emerging as an organized religious tradition (as distinct from, although related to, earlier Daoist philosophical movements), and Daoist associations actually played a major part in the downfall of the Han. There were two main rebellious sects. The Way of Great Peace (*Taiping dao*) attempted to take over the empire, and the effort to contain the rebels fatally weakened the Han, although they were eradicated in 184. The Heavenly Masters (*Tianshi*) merely sought to secede and form a separate state in the Sichuan region. They surrendered in 215, but only to trade their independence for state patronage from one of the kingdoms of the Period of Disunion. From that moment, Daoism began to spread throughout the court and country, and Daoists to this day trace their institutional history to the founder of the Heavenly Masters.

Daoist and Buddhist scriptures soon inundated a textual world once monopolized by the Classics. *Biographies of Eminent Monks* (*Gaoseng zhuan*), written around 530, shows that the majority of memorable early monks were translators bent on rendering the entire Indian Buddhist canon into Chinese. Daoist scriptures, on the other hand, were dropping from Heaven. The first of these were disclosed to the Heavenly Masters establishing their utopian community, but they soon began appearing among the elite of settled society. Aristocratic families in the south were competing patrons of mediums channeling Daoist scriptures. While these seem esoteric and fantastic when compared to Ru and Buddhists texts, they were of an exceptional literary quality and as such were highly esteemed by the cultured elite. Ru scriptural authority thus now had serious competition. Significantly, the noteworthy religious and philosophical legacies of the Period of Disunion are all overtly Buddhist or Daoist, even when authors do politely acknowledge the Classics and the Sages.

Ruism was struggling. One reason for this was that the established institutions embodying Ru values were the state and the family. There was no Ru "church," and when the state was weak, Ru tradition floundered. Buddhists, on the other hand, had autonomous communities relatively free from both state and family. In China, joining the Buddhist *sangha* is called "leaving the family" (*chujia*), and monks and nuns lived in monasteries that were, at least theoretically, independent of the state. Daoists later began emulating Buddhists monastic practice, but in the Period of Disunion they were already forming cohesive religious communities.

Ru remained a court presence, but a minor one. In the initial years of the Period of Disunion, the primary criteria for making appointments was sheer talent, even though a person be "inhumane and unfilial." When selection criteria later expanded, the primary change was to also recognize individuals who had good pedigree. Being "filially pious and incorrupt" and having a Classical education were, in themselves, rarely reason enough for recommendation (Lewis 2009a: 39, 43).

The remaining haven for Ru values was the family. In this era of competing aristocrats, patriarchs employed Ru ideology in an effort to establish large, powerful, and harmonious families. Collections of stories of exceptionally filial children were a new and very popular genre of this time—variants of these stories were known to everyone in late imperial China, and to a lesser extent they still circulate and continue to edify, and often terrify, children (Figure 14). Caring for parents when alive, and mourning for and sacrificing to them when dead, were now priorities and the tales showed how children should, if necessary, sacrifice government appointment, wealth, and state power for the sake of family. A filial child could quite literally work miracles. This was based on the correlative cosmology of *yin* and *yang* and the Five Processes, but whereas Han thought focused on the emperor's virtue resonating throughout the world, it was now virtuous children who elicited cosmic sympathies producing miracles that saved their families (Knapp 2005).

By the end of the Period of Disunion, the notion that China had Three Teachings (*sanjiao*) was well established. Often, they coexisted harmoniously or melded effortlessly, but Buddhism and Daoism also faced periodic critique and rebuff. This was more apparent in the north where they vied with one another for court patronage and competed to become state ideology. During these doctrinal tussles, Ru Teaching (*rujiao*) was not exposed to the same scrutiny and was itself never rejected; the only complaint Ru could legitimately make was they felt comparatively neglected. Indeed, Buddhists and Daoists, when in competition, often promoted themselves as the rightful partner for the Ru.

Rivalry was intensifying by the time China was poised to reunite. In the sixth century, northern rulers began hosting court debates with the intent of selecting the teaching or teachings most suitable to serve the state. Buddhists critiqued the fanciful extravagances of Daoist beliefs, which they said were excessive, if not plain silly and one report written for a northern emperor was tellingly entitled *Laughing at the Dao* (*Xiaodao lun*) (Kohn 1995). The Daoist retort, echoed by some Ru, was that Buddhism was no more than a religion of barbarians.

The most persistent criticism of Buddhism was that it was neither politically nor culturally Chinese. This concern had been evident from the outset. We can see it in the oldest extant work of Chinese Buddhist apologetics called *Master Mou Settles Doubts* (*Mouzi lihuo lun*), which was written in the late Han. Master Mou was offering responses to common complaints made against Buddhism, and what is very apparent is that the main concerns were not with Buddhist metaphysics but with Buddhist social and cultural practice. Celibacy undermined the importance of family and filial piety (Keenan 1994: articles 10, 15) while shaved heads (9) and robes (11) disregarded Chinese decorum. Buddhism came from a foreign land (8, 14), had texts in a foreign language (5, 8, 23), was not recognized by the Ancients or the Classics (4, 7, 25), and was simply un-Chinese (8, 14).

These xenophobic concerns continued in some circles and they were focal to the later renaissance of the Ru. Ironically, the revivalists would themselves be criticized by subsequent Ru for having merely peddled Buddhism (and, to a lesser extent, Daoism) in Ru disguise. As we will see, this critique has some substance. There can be no doubt that the Way of the Ru was transformed by its encounter with Buddhism and Daoism, and thus transfigured it would come to conquer China.

The Tang prelude to revival

In 581, China was reunified. The short-lived Sui dynasty (581–618) was soon replaced by the Tang (618–907) one of China's most culturally rich and cosmopolitan dynasties. The first Sui emperor had risen to power claiming he was an ideal Buddhist ruler or *zhuanlun* ("wheel turner", Sanskrit *cakravartin*). Reacting against their predecessors, the initial Tang emperors favored Daoism. The Tang rulers had the same family name as Laozi, the legendary author of the *Daodejing* who was now seen as a major god, and they took Laozi as their ancestor and claimed he had miraculously appeared to announce their destined rule (Barrett 1996).

Clearly, there were omens enough to legitimize new dynasties without Ru correlative prognostications. The position of the Ru was consequently less politically vulnerable yet less vital; they continued as an invariably endorsed yet consistently secondary teaching (*jiao*). The initial Tang rulers rated Daoism first among the Three Teachings (*sanjiao*) with Ruism (*rujiao*) a close and complementary second. Buddhism was once again demoted for being foreign and for neglecting family and state, although it too was supported by emperors keen to retain popular approval (Weinstein 1987). Other Tang rulers, in particular Wu Zetian (624–705), China's only ruling empress, were great advocates of Buddhism. And it was in the Tang that Buddhism fully blossomed and became truly sinified. In particular Chan, better known by the Japanese "Zen," was as much Chinese as it was Buddhist (Gregory 2002).

On the whole, Ru in the Tang were quite tolerant of Daoism and Buddhism. Despite a very few, very famous exceptions to this rule, most Ru saw no major conflict and many were in fact themselves Buddhist and/or Daoist practitioners. Overall, being Ru in Tang times tended to be a bureaucratic responsibility that focused on minutiae of ceremony, administration, and routine textual annotation. There was a marked absence of interest in either the utopian transformation of the state or self-transformation to sagehood that in other times distinguished Ruism as a religious tradition. It was as though Ru had conceded ultimate concerns to the Buddhists and Daoists and had accepted their role as their secular partner. In Chinese terms, they were devoted to the "outer" (*wai*) world while the two religious traditions addressed "inner" (*nei*) concerns.

Ru continued to write commentaries, but these focused on the fine points of state ritual and scholarship had to some extent become an "intellectual backwater" (Chen 1992: 18). The most important Tang textual development occurred in the mid-seventh century when the entire canon and commentarial tradition was reviewed, perhaps in response to the consolidation of the Buddhist canon at this time. The Ancient Script (*guwen*) version was formally endorsed and apocryphal texts were condemned. The Han practice or reading omens and claiming Kongzi was an uncrowned king (*suwang*) were officially rejected, both for their seeming supernaturalism and for their potential for fueling political unrest. Overall, there was a mood of mild skepticism toward the Classics at this time.

Ru were not a major presence at the Tang court. In many ways, their sociopolitical situation was a continuation of their circumstances in the Period of Disunion. Powerful aristocratic families remained the dominant force and the vast majority of state appointments were hereditary. Only about 10 percent of officials were selected for their Classical education and even they were appointed to lower clerical posts.

The dominance of great families was an obstacle to Ru and a concern to rulers. It is commonly argued that the use of examinations to select appointees finally broke the families' stranglehold, but while this might have been the intent, it did not actually work. Sui rulers had introduced examinations in an effort to drive a wedge through the aristocracy. Following this, early Tang rulers also promoted Ru Learning and, as we saw in Chapter 2, they began the practice of sacrificing to Kongzi as the patron of education and decreed there should be a temple to him in every school throughout the land. But all that happened was the great families used education and examinations to further consolidate their position. A scholarly degree just added to their prestige without allowing for real competition. The aristocracy had all the resources for education, hand-copied books were prohibitively expensive, and "examinations" were not anonymous so that the relationship between examiner and candidate was actually a kind of strategic patronage geared toward forging favorable alliances (Lewis 2009b: 202–6).

The downfall of the families was complex, but a mid-Tang rebellion certainly facilitated the process. The carnage may not have been quite as bad as some claim, but their claim is that, per capita, this was the greatest atrocity in human history (Pinker 2011: 194). An Lushan (703–57), once a very indulged favorite of the emperor, amassed enough troops to establish his own dynasty in the north of China. The battles to suppress his rebellion, and later wars at the time of the Tang's fall, eradicated many of the traditional family strongholds. By the Song dynasty, their glory was over. This, as we will see, opened the way for the Ru.

The An Lushan rebellion also encouraged Ru to reevaluate their tradition and reconsider their social commitments. There was considerable diversity of opinion, however. Some were liberal and progressive. For example, Du You (735–812) used history to show the need for strong, centralized government. He compiled a massive work entitled *Comprehensive Institutions* (*Tongdian*, 801), and his history of dynastic institutions showed gradual social progress, which, of course, undermined traditional Ru notions of a Golden Age. His younger associate, Liu Zongyuan (773–819), argued early sages had lacked the resources to achieve their goals, which had to await the apparatus of the contemporary state. Appropriate to a time when aristocracy was beginning to wane, Liu was genuinely concerned for the well-being of all people, especially commoners, and in the spirit of Mengzi saw this as a government priority. To this end, he was more than willing to challenge sections of the Classics that stood in the way. He passionately believed Ru tradition could be refashioned so as to ameliorate society, although privately he was drawn to Chan Buddhism (Chen 1992).

But Du You and Liu Zongyuan were not the kind of reformers that later Ru history favored. Rather, the most esteemed name of the Tang was Liu Zongyuan's friend Han Yu (768–824). Han Yu had a then rare quality that made his vision well suited to Ru revival: religious intolerance. He did not welcome Buddhism or Daoism and wished them gone. But to eradicate them, Ru would have to be able to fill the resultant void. This was something the revivalists of the Song sought to achieve, as we will see.

Han Yu's associates thought him the Mengzi of their age. That is, just as Mengzi had denounced Mozi and Yang Zhu to rejuvenate the Ru in the Warring States period, so too Han Yu now championed their cause against Buddhists and Daoists. Han Yu was a government official frequently demoted for his bluntness. He once petitioned the emperor against the "barbarian teaching," saying that even if Buddhism could not yet be fully suppressed, it was most unbecoming an emperor to actually encourage it by having a relic—"this decayed bone, this vile refuse"—brought into the palace. Had not

Kongzi said ghosts and spirits should be "kept at a distance"? Han Yu ended by say-ing that if the Buddha really had supernatural powers, he might prove this by sending down calamites upon Han Yu himself (Tiwald and Van Norden 2014: 123, 125–6). They came. The emperor exiled Han Yu, who was reduced to writing memorials to a trouble-some crocodile in the far south of China (Birch 1965: 253–5).

As Han Yu explained in his very influential little essay "The Original Way" (*Yuandao*), he believed the past thousand years had been a spiritual blunder. The true Way was that of the sages, Yao, Shun, Yu, Tang, Wen, Wu, the Duke of Zhou, Kongzi, and finally Mengzi. After Mengzi, however, the emergence of Daoism and then Buddhism had eclipsed the Way. Xunzi and Yang Xiong "grasped parts of [the Way] but not its essence"; beside them, Han Yu found no other worth praising. His solution was sim-ple: "Burn [Buddhist and Daoist] books. Convert their temples into houses. Illuminate the Way of the Former Kings in order to guide" the people (Tiwald and Van Norden 2014: 130).

Mengzi was being rediscovered by Ru of the late Tang, and it is significant that Han Yu saw him as the last sage to have grasped the Way. The lineage Han Yu named would be central to the revival of the Song dynasty, which claimed to have restored the Way and formed a bridge spanning more than a millennium to reconnect with Mengzi. To those reformers, Han Yu's "The Original Way" was one of the very few things written in the interim of any value.

By the late Tang, many of the ingredients for Ru renaissance were in place. The examination system was established, although it was not a major path to recruit-ment. A few visionaries like Han Yu saw the need for Ru to again embrace ultim-ate values so as to successfully compete with Buddhism and Daoism, but they remained a minority. In the Song dynasty, these subsidiary things would come to revolutionize China.

The empire of the Ru

From the Song dynasty (960–1279) until the empire ended in 1911, the Classics were, as never before, imprinted on the Chinese mind and inscribed in the memory of a nation. Ru Learning (*Ruxue*) was about to arrive.

When the dominance of the great families was finally broken, performance in exam-inations came to replace heredity as the primary path to life as an official. In the Tang, those sitting annual exams had numbered in the hundreds. At the outset of the Song, they soared to about 30,000, and by dynasty's end, the figure was nearing half a mil-lion. Passing at the highest level brought great prestige, employment, and wealth, but failures—the overwhelming majority—had also spent years internalizing the Classics, and many a failure rose to literary and philosophical prominence. Students were glamorous—the hero of romantic literature in mid- to late-imperial China was inevitably a handsome young scholar. The reality was less dazzling. At a rate of 200 characters per day, it would take an average student six years to rote-learn the 431,286 characters

FIGURE 11 *Examination cells in Beijing, 1899.*

Each provincial capital had a complex of thousands of stone prison-like cubicles in which candidates sat examinations. Although they were too small to stretch out, aspirants remained in their cell for three days. The large stoneware pots at the end of the lanes were for fresh water and human waste. Once the main gate (left) was locked, no one could enter or leave. If you died, your body would be thrown over the compound wall.

It was a grueling ordeal that determined a man's future. It was so stressful that collections of stories about life in examination compounds became macabre best sellers. Unlike the texts being examined, these books were filled with tales of ghosts, spirits, and miracles.

of the canon, and that was just the beginning. Many felt it was pure drudgery, and cheating became an art form (Figure 11).

Running such a massive education system based on the Classics demanded new textual technologies. In China, the invention of printing was not a major challenge; all that had been missing was motivation. Initially, the karmic rewards for mass-copying Buddhist sutras was the incentive, but the examinations quickly came to dominate the market. A frustrated book collector in the Ming dynasty observed: "Unless a book is for the examinations, the commercial publishers will not print it" (McDermott 2006: 67). For a few copies it was actually cheaper to employ copyists, but with bulk the price of books could be reduced to one tenth that of manuscripts. Just as we cannot imagine Protestantism without Gutenberg, so too the Ru revival "would certainly never have happened without printing to make books less expensive and more available" (Chaffee 1995: 14).

For the great names among the Song Ru, using examinations to select officials to administer the country was a mixed blessing. Certainly, they approved of the Classics being promoted in government, but inevitably, many aspirants saw learning merely as a means to status and wealth. For passionate believers in the Way of the Sages, passing exams should be secondary to a genuine love of learning. It was, nonetheless, this new cultural capital of examinations that provided a context for those wishing to revive Ru learning as a path to ultimate transformation definitive of religious concerns. Without the examinations, the reformers' ideas would have fallen on barren ground.

* * *

Throughout most of the Song dynasty, there was no orthodox interpretation of Ru thought, yet by dynasty's end Zhu Xi's version of "Way Learning" (*Daoxue*) was poised for victory. Given the association between "Confucianism" and Chinese identity, it is somewhat ironic that this was implemented by the first foreign power to conquer all of China. In Michael Nylan's words, "No coherent system of thought that might be labeled 'Confucianism' existed until a *foreign* dynasty, the Mongol Yuan [1271–1368], enshrined one conservative strain of Song thought called 'True Way Learning' (*Daoxue*) as the single basis of the civil service examinations in 1313" (Nylan and Wilson 2010: 71). This was a momentous shift. From 1313 to the end of the empire in 1911, Zhu Xi's understanding of what it meant to be Ru prevailed. Wing-tsit Chan made the obvious comparison when he observed that "for almost six hundred years" the Ru canon *with Zhu Xi's commentaries* was "virtually the Chinese Bible" (Chan 1986a: 600).

We need to discuss how this unlikely turn of events occurred. Song rulers had initially done little to revise the actual content of education, which they had basically inherited from the Tang. Examinations were used to quickly fill vacant posts, but as the number of candidates rose, the success rate plummeted. As aspirants were increasingly preoccupied with job competition, idealistic Ru became disillusioned and often retreated from office to become private teachers.

The first real reforms were promoted by the privy counselor Wang Anshi (1021–86) who had more than a little in common with Wang Mang (Chapter 3). Both have been considered "socialist," both had radical utopian reform agendas based on the authority of early sage-kings and the ideals of the *Zhouli*, and both were condemned for overstepping their position. Wang Anshi's commentaries on the Classics briefly held a de facto orthodoxy in examinations, but he was opposed by many conservative Ru and his heyday was brief.

As this was the first dynasty in which Ru had been offered a real opportunity to prove themselves, this extremist incident did not look good. It quickly got worse. Following on its heels, the northern half of China was lost to Jurchen invaders, which many believed would have been impossible under good government. Wang Anshi's policies were the scapegoat for this too, and Zhu Xi later claimed the barbarians were victorious because Wang's "reforms were not in accord with the Way" (cited in Kuhn 2009: 61). These two events precipitated a crisis in Ru understanding of their role in society.

Among Wang Anshi's many opponents were two brothers, Cheng Hao and Cheng Yi, who were credited with having revived the Way that had laid dormant since Mengzi. The Two Chengs (as they were known) were the founders of Way Learning or *daoxue*. After the loss of the north, their enthusiastic followers spread their teachings throughout the Southern Song (1127–1279) with its new capital in Hangzhou. Among the converts was a fourth-generation disciple named Zhu Xi.

Advocates of Daoxue were by no means the most numerous Ru, and there was considerable difference of opinion among them (see Tillman 1992). Because Zhu Xi's interpretation eventually became orthodoxy, traditional histories tend to suggest it was simply a case of the cream eventually rising to the top. Modern historians see it differently. Zhu Xi was without doubt brilliant, but sheer stamina and blind luck also played their part. He was possibly the most prolific writer in all of China, and so he out-wrote his opponents; he was an indefatigable wrangler who out-argued them; he was blessed with relative good health and outlived them. Finally, he had the dubious fortune of being the senior representative of Way Learning when it was briefly banned and of dying while the ban was still being enforced. He thus became a martyr and a symbol for the movement's subsequent revival.

This ban had been a minor one, lasting from 1195 to 1202. Way Learning presented no real political threat, and other agendas were at play. The tone of the denouncement was that they were "strange, stupid, snobbish, arrogant" and had the potential to become a "subversive religious sect" (Liu 1973: 497, 500). While wildly exaggerated, these claim did hold just a hint of truth.

Way Learning indeed had some features of a sectarian religious movement. Its exponents were the first Ru to create a significant religious community independent of family and the state. Hoyt Tillman has called this a "fellowship"—"a network of social relations and a sense of community with shared tradition that distinguished them from other Confucians" (Tillman 1992: 3). Their punctilious ritualism and archaic attire easily differentiated them from other Ru, and they maintained very strong bonds between masters and disciples. Masters could fully devote themselves to teaching as they were often freed from financial burden by gifts from students and donations from rich patrons. They held regular meetings, and a master would often have a specially built learning hall (*jingshe*, lit. "house of essence") near to his home. Most importantly, Way Learning Ru pioneered the use of private academies (*shuyuan*) where students not only came to study but also perform rituals, venerate sages, and prostrate themselves before their master (Chapter 2). In short, these Ru had their "church."

It was this autonomy of the Way Learning religious community that was targeted by those crying "false learning." It was this same quality that helped it triumph. The unjustified ban was soon lifted, and Zhu Xi's reputation posthumously soared. At this time Mongol forces were building in the north, but they too patronized Ru. To distinguish themselves from the Mongols, the Southern Song rulers began alternately associating with Way Learning "as a means of bolstering its cultural propaganda" (Tillman 1992: 233). By 1241, Zhu Xi and his predecessors were installed in Ru temples and their teachings were formally recognized by the state. At this time, however, Kublai Khan was on the verge of reuniting China under his Mongol Yuan dynasty (1271– 1368). Way Learning thereafter quickly spread to the north where it was met with all the enthusiasm of "a genuine religious conversion" (de Bary 1981: 23). In 1313, the Mongols declared Zhu's commentaries orthodoxy and made them the basis of Chinese education, examination, and appointment. They would retain this position until the end of imperial China.

Turning inward

As we have just seen, Way Learning Ru had a community or fellowship that allowed them to develop an identity alternative to the traditional Ru employment by the state. Their philosophies reflected this shift. While their thinking was diverse, there was a shared assumption that being Ru was not primarily a concern with statecraft or serving rulers, but first and foremost an act of inner self-transformation. The only authentic reason to study was "learning for one's self" (*weiji zhi xue*) (de Bary 1991a).

Over the centuries since the Han when they were first formally patronized by rulers, Ru had presented themselves as servants of the state. Until the Song, as we have seen, they had only met with minor success, and in the early Song, while fully employed, they had been associated with major disasters. Advocates of Way Learning denounced neither examinations nor politics, but they stepped back and insisted a Classical education was of no avail unless it was primarily directed toward cultivating the self. The ultimate purpose of learning (*xue*) was neither to pass examinations nor to receive employment; it was, in Cheng Yi's words, "to learn the Way of becoming a sage" (Chang 1963: 547).

Exponents of Way Learning found very little to admire in the thinking of the Ru during the 1,300 years since Mengzi. Xunzi had rejected Mengzi and prioritized statecraft, and since then only a few individuals such as Han Yu had longed to reconnect with the early sages. It was, they believed, time to start again.

Way Learning Ru, of course, venerated all of the Classics (which in the Song numbered thirteen and included the *Analects* and *Mengzi*), but they privileged a corpus of Four Books (*shishu*) that made the true intent of the rest of the canon abundantly clear. These books had become prominent before Zhu Xi, but he must be credited with formally uniting them and suggesting they become the foundation of education (Gardner 2007: xxiv). We met these books in Chapters 3 and 4, although they were only recognized as a complimentary quartet in the Song. They are the *Analects*, the

Great Learning, the *Doctrine of the Mean*, and the *Mengzi*, and they were chosen because they focused on the importance of learning in order to become a noble person (*junzi*) and ultimately a sage.

Why had Ru deserted their true calling? Often the answer was the events with which this chapter began, the arrival of Buddhism and the emergence of Daoist religious movements. As both religions focus on self-transformation, it was as though Ru had abandoned this aspect of their tradition and left it to their rivals. Way Learning exponents stressed devotion to self-transformation as the highest priority. In doing so, as we will soon see, they frequently denounced Buddhism and Daoism while simultaneously appropriating their thought; indeed, Way Learning thinkers accused one another of as much when debating their various positions.

***

While they shared this basic orientation, Way Learning Ru were by no means in complete agreement. When presenting their respective views, traditional authority carried weight. Just as evidence of Daoist and Buddhist influence could be grounds for dismissal, so too precedent set by "true Ru" could greatly enhance an argument. But just who were these "true Ru"?

The sages leading to Mengzi were obviously not in dispute. Nor were the Two Chengs, and southern exponents all traced master-disciple lineages back to Cheng Hao and Cheng Yi. Where there was considerable variance was with the individuals who had rightfully preceded the Chengs, if any. Zhu Xi's own position did not voice a consensus, and when he set down his lineage, in 1173, he was partially motivated to do so in order to counter other pedigrees being suggested (Tillman 1992: 114–19). His "five masters of the Northern Song" (*beisong wuzi*) were Zhou Dunyi, Zhang Zai, and Shao Yong, followed by Cheng Hao and Cheng Yi, although Zhu Xi only recognized Zhou Dunyi and the Cheng brothers as actual sages in the transmission of the Way (*daotong*).

A few years later, with assistance from his friend Lü Zuqian (1137–81), Zhu Xi compiled *Reflections on Things at Hand* (*Jinsilu*). The book is a selection of his acknowledged predecessors' sayings with Zhu's unifying commentary. More than half come from Cheng Yi, a quarter from Cheng Hao, a fifth from Zhang Zai, and a very important, curtain-raising 2 percent from Zhou Dunyi. (Shao Yong was excluded, although Zhu Xi later admitted this was an oversight [Chan 1989: 369]). This work would achieve quasi-canonical status. Zhu Xi said: "The Four Books are the ladders to the Six Classics. The *Jinsilu* is the ladder to the four books" (Chan 1967: xl). Over the centuries, it would become *the* handbook for aspiring students and it attracted some fifty commentaries (Chan 1987: 46).

I will now introduce Zhu Xi's chosen predecessors, although, like the *Jinsilu*, I too will omit Shao Yong who was less influential than the other four. I will be focusing on the reasons for their selection, and some of the key concepts I briefly mention will be more fully explained when we later look at Zhu Xi's grand synthesis of their ideas.

The founders of Way Learning

Zhou Dunyi (1017–73). Zhu Xi claimed Zhou Dunyi was the first person since Mengzi to obtain the Way. Zhu also maintained that Zhou was the teacher of the Cheng brothers and that there was therefore an emergent master-disciple lineage in the transmission of the Way. Privately, he admitted the evidence showed only that the Chengs had once "received instruction" from Zhu (Tillman 1992: 115). The Chengs rarely refer to Zhou, and when they do it is without the formal respect due a teacher, even once calling him "poor Zen fellow" (Chan 1963a: 521). As Cheng Yi once declared, it was his brother who had been first to revive the Way (Adler 2014a: 28), Zhu Xi's claim seems fragile.

Zhu Xi was willing to go to considerable lengths to promote Zhou Dunyi, a minor figure who "was not a known philosopher in the eleventh century" (Graham 1958: 156). This was in order to advance one brief text Zhou he had written called *Taijitu shuo* or the *Diagram of the Supreme Ultimate Explained*, which provided Zhu with a cosmology (Figure 12). The choice drew fire. The diagram itself was based on one by the Daoist Chen Tuan, famous for his bouts of drinking and periodic hibernation (Kohn 1990). Worse, Zhou's commentary employs Daoist terminology. Other prominent Way Learning scholars rejected its doctrines and even doubted Zhou Dunyi was the author (Tiwald and Van Norden 2014: chapter 37).

Zhou Dunyi's little text was, nonetheless, selected to open *Reflection on Things at Hand*. Zhu Xi saw it as setting out the cosmological foundation on which Way Learning rested. Most of it is straightforward enough and restates the by now commonplace view that the interplay of *yinyang* and *wuxing* (five processes) produces everything that exists. Nor would anyone have been concerned to learn that the Supreme Ultimate was their source. *Ji*, "ultimate," means the ridge of a roof or a celestial pole and thus an extremity, so that Zhu Xi said, "The Supreme Ultimate is similar to the top of a house or the zenith of the sky, beyond which point there is no more" (Chan 1963a: 641). Kongzi was believed to have first used the term *taiji* in the "Great Commentary" to the *Yijing*: "In change there is the Supreme Ultimate (*taiji*). This is what generates the two modes" of the *yin* and *yang* (Lynn 1994: 65; for a challenging alternative translation of *taiji*, see Adler 2016).

But Zhou Dunyi had not merely referred to this source as *taiji*. His words were *wuji er taiji*. This was controversial. An equivocal translation is "no/not/negative ultimate yet supreme ultimate" where *wuji* could equally mean "not ultimate," "ultimateless," or "ultimate non-being." *Wuji* was first used in the *Daodejing* (28), and later Daoists understood it to be "ultimate non-being" from which all being arises. Maybe Zhou meant as much, which is why some of Zhu Xi's contemporaries rejected it. What is more important is how Zhu Xi read it.

In earlier Ru thought, the dynamics of *yinyang* and *wuxing* were seen as transformations of *qi*, the fundamental stuff that constitutes all physical and psychological phenomena. ("Psycho-physical stuff" is accurate but cumbersome, so I will leave

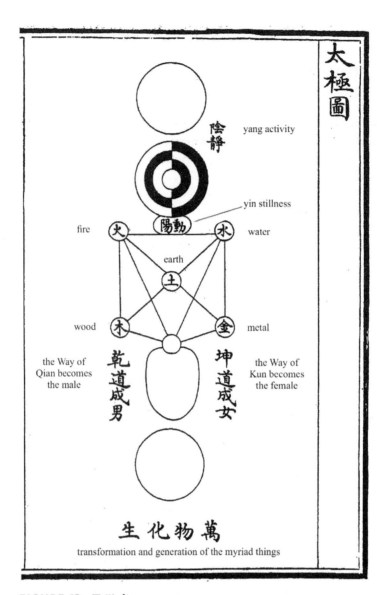

太極圖

yang activity

yin stillness

fire   火   陽動   水   water

earth   土

wood   木   金   metal

the Way of   the Way of
Qian becomes   Kun becomes
the male   the female

乾道成男   坤道成女

生化物萬

transformation and generation of the myriad things

FIGURE 12 Taiji *diagram*.

Zhou Dunyi's commentary reads: "Non-ultimate yet Supreme Ultimate! The Supreme Ultimate in activity generates *yang*; yet at the limit of activity it is still. In stillness it generates *yin* ... The alteration and combination of *yang* and *yin* generate water, fire, wood, metal, and earth ... The reality of Non-ultimate and the essence of the Two [Modes] and Five [Phases] mysteriously combine and coalesce. 'The way of *Qian* becomes the male; the Way of *Kun* becomes the female'; the two *qi* stimulate each other, transforming and generating the myriad things" (Adler 2014a: 168, modified). *Qian* and *Kun* are the names of the first two hexagrams of the *Yijing*.

qi untranslated.) It would seem to follow that *taiji* must be primordial *qi*. This was precisely the conclusion Zhu Xi wished to avoid. The Supreme Ultimate was not a "something," which is why, he said, "*wuji*" had been added. But neither was it Daoist non-being (or Buddhist emptiness) that preceded (or negated) the phenomenal world. Rather, it was an inherent "Principle" or "Pattern" (*li*) immanent in and inseparable from existence. For Zhu Xi, "the Supreme Ultimate is nothing other than Principle" (Chan 1963a: 638). His followers clearly understood this, and a later work defining Way Learning terminology reiterated: "The Supreme Ultimate (*taiji*) simply means Principle (*li*)" (Chan 1986b: 117). This will become clearer when we turn to Zhu's own philosophy.

Zhang Zai (1020–77) would have disagreed with Zhu Xi's reading. For him, the Supreme Ultimate *was qi*. Everything was. Zhang had stripped his philosophy down. All that exists is but a particular manifestation of *qi* that in its original state is formless. He called this original state the Great Void (*taixu*) but by this he just meant it is undifferentiated *qi*. Using his favorite metaphor, he said: "The integration and disintegration of [*qi*] is to the Great Void as the freezing and melting of ice is to water" (Chan 1963a: 503). Even *yin* and *yang* were nothing but words describing the dispersal and coalescence of *qi*.

Zhang Zai's significance to Way Learning rests primarily on two things. First, he pioneered the Song Ru confrontation with Daoism and Buddhism on *philosophical* grounds—"There is only one Way. If this is correct, that is incorrect; if that is correct, I am incorrect" (cited in Kassof 1984: 34). This pragmatic thinker who had formerly been devoted to military affairs, thought Daoists claims that being (*you*) sprang from non-being (*wu*), and Buddhist assertions that phenomenal reality was empty (*kong*) were patent nonsense.

Second, he was revered for a little treatise he wrote on the window of the western wall of his study and which is therefore known as the *Western Inscription* (*Ximing*). If Zhou Dunyi had provided a cosmology for Way Learning, Zhang Zai produced its ethical and metaphysical manifesto. The famous opening words reveal how his all-pervasive *qi* could be the basis of mystical unity and universal care: "Heaven is my father and Earth is my mother, and even such a small creature as I find an intimate place in their midst. Therefore that which fills the universe I regard as my body and that which directs the universe I consider as my nature. All people are my brothers and sisters, and all things are my companions" (Chan 1963a: 497). These sentiments would become a leitmotiv in subsequent Ru thought and provided the foundation for "an ethical mysticism in which ... all men and things [are] intimately related ... through their common substance or *qi*" (Berling 1980: 104).

Cheng Hao (1032–85) and Cheng Yi (1033–1107). Some felt the *Western Inscription*'s claim that the "tired, infirm, crippled, or sick" were all our siblings skirted dangerously close to Mohist universal love or Buddhist compassion for all. Cheng Yi insisted this was not so, and that Zhang Zai, his maternal uncle, was actually saying that the source of *ren* is the family, but this original locus is then *extended* so as to reach everyone. He compressed this into one of the most famous philosophical sayings in all of Chinese history: "Principle is one but its manifestations are many (*liyi fenshu*)" (Chan 1963a: 550).

Cheng Yi took liberty with Zhang Zai's words. While Zhang did sometimes mention a principle or pattern to the movements of *qi*, he had not employed the word as a discrete philosophical concept. Cheng Yi surely knew this, for he once said: "Although I have learned some of my doctrines from others, the concept of the Principle … has been realized by myself" (Chan 1963a: 520).

The doctrine of Li or Principle was *the* central concept of Way Learning philosophy, which, as I have mentioned, is also known as Principle Learning (*Lixue*). Although the word was casually used by their predecessors, it was the Chengs who made it a crowning metaphysical concept. This was something Zhu Xi inherited and consolidated, and thus Principle became the defining feature of what was also known as the Cheng-Zhu School (*Cheng-Zhu xuepai*).

Just as Zhu Xi had read Principle into Zhou Dunyi's Supreme Ultimate, so too the Chengs read it into the *Western Inscription*, which was actually the only thing their uncle wrote that much impressed them. It was Principle that made each thing what it was, and it was Principle that united each individual thing with the cosmos as a whole. Principle was simultaneously the one and the many. Again, this will become clearer when we turn to Zhu Xi.

Before leaving the brothers Cheng I must confess that, like Zhu Xi, I have conflated their thought. It can be difficult untangling them, as they wrote little and their collected sayings unhelpfully refer to them both as "Master Cheng." But they were temperamental opposites—Chang Hao warm and amiable, Cheng Yi grave, humourless, and pugnacious—and their thinking diverged. Cheng Hao made statements like "Principle and the heart-mind are one," which inclined him toward introspection in order to apprehend *li* (Chan 1963a: 536). This tendency was developed by those who believed Principle was in fact inherent in the heart-mind. They are discussed in detail in the next chapter. Cheng Yi, on the other hand, was more inclined to "investigate things in order to understand Principle," and in the twenty-two years he survived his brother he began to grapple with the relationship between Principle and *qi*, the stuff of phenomenal world (Chan 1963a: 556). This approach was developed by Zhu Xi, to whom we can now turn.

Zhu Xi's "great completion"

Zhu Xi (1130–1200) was born in Fujian province and studied with his father, a local official and teacher who died when Zhu was only thirteen. The tragedy of losing his exemplary father, it was said, set him on the path to become a sage. He was subsequently taught by an eclectic range of scholars, Buddhists among them, and Zhu developed a youthful enthusiasm for both Daoism and Buddhism. He was a noted prodigy and passed the highest imperial examinations by the age of nineteen, which allowed him to begin pursuing his own intellectual inclinations some twenty years before the average graduation age. This head-start was extended by his limited engagement with official duties after his mid-twenties. At around this time, he became a student of Li Tong (1093–1163), a third-generation disciple of the Cheng brothers, and underwent a conversion from which he emerged a fervent advocate of Way Learning. For his remaining forty years, he was for the most part free to devote himself to writing and teaching. He had hundreds, perhaps thousands, of students, and some of what he taught is recorded in the *Classified Conversations of Master Zhu* (*Zhuzi yueli*). Zhu's own literary output was phenomenal; he was possibly the most prolific writer in all of Chinese history (Chan 1987: 41).

Zhu Xi felt Zhang Zai's theory that existence was nothing but the congealing and dispersal of *qi* was too amorphous and flirted dangerously with the spontaneously emergent universe of Daoism. Why is it, Zhu would ask, that *qi* variously takes the form of rocks, trees, animals, or humans? With the Cheng brothers, his answer was that there must an underlying "Reason," "Coherence," "Pattern," or "Principle" (*li*) directing the transformations of *qi*. One of Zhu's pupils suggested that perhaps only clearly formed and living things had *li* while things that were indistinct, dead, dried, or decaying had none, but Zhu denied this and staunchly maintained that even these things had Principle: "As there is a thing there is a Principle for it" (Chan 1963a: 649).

While Principle determines the form things assume, it itself has no form. Principle is not something that, in isolation, can be seen, heard, or felt. It is only when *li* acts upon *qi* that embodied, material, sensible objects are produced. Insofar as *li* directs the course of *qi*, Zhu Xi felt obliged to admit *li* preceded *qi*, but he said so reluctantly and he was very careful to avoid misinterpretation. He was not suggesting there was some separate transcendent realm of *li* and he did not want to be seen to endorse Buddhist world negation which, he said, "ignore[s] the universe completely" (Chan 1963a: 647). To this end, whenever he acknowledged that *li* was prior to *qi*, he immediately qualified the statement by saying that this was no more than a logical conclusion, but in practice the two were inseparable. Thus,

> Fundamentally Principle and *qi* cannot be spoken of as prior or posterior. But if we must trace their origin, we are obliged to say that Principle is prior. However, Principle is not a separate entity ... It exists right in *qi*. Without *qi*, Principle would have nothing to adhere to. (Chan 1963a: 634)

There could be, for example, no material bamboos without the Principle of bamboo, but equally, had there never been bamboos existing at all, how could there be a Principle of bamboo? As *li* and *qi* are entirely dependent on one another for their existence, possible dualistic tendencies in Zhu's philosophy are mitigated so as to form an ontological symbiosis; *li* and *qi* are separate entities, but neither exists autonomously.

So far, Zhu Xi had done little more than refine and amplify ideas present in Cheng Yi's teachings. When he incorporated Zhou Dunyi's doctrine of the Supreme Ultimate (*taiji*) into his scheme, however, he was breaking new ground. At one level, Zhu was saying that the Supreme Ultimate is simply the sum of all Principles: "When all Principles of heaven and earth and the myriad things are put together, that is the Supreme Ultimate" (Chan 1963a: 641). An important corollary to this proposition, which may not strike the modern reader as at all obvious, is that all things therefore contain *taiji* within them. Zhu Xi's medieval audience would not have found this surprising, however. This is something I need to pause to explain.

For all his anti-Buddhist diatribe, Zhu Xi was assuming Buddhist ideas. Zhu Xi said, "Buddhists talk of emptiness," whereas Ru talk of "concrete Principle" (Chan 1963a: 648), but it was in fact Buddhists like Fazang (643–712) who had greatly enriched the concept of Principle. Fazang certainly acknowledged "emptiness" (*kong*), which was "based on negation," but he said he preferred to focus on "an affirmative revelation of the Principle (*li*)" (cited in Cook 1979: 368; see also Ziporyn 2013).

To explain this, let me rework Fazang's well-known analogy of a rafter. Imagine being asked to describe to someone the essence of a rafter. To make this interesting, that someone is a nomadic hunter-gatherer who has never seen a house. Suddenly, you realize that to explain a rafter you need to explain a house; after all, without the house a "rafter" is just a piece of wood. And the house as a whole depends on each of its components (tiles, windows, walls, etc.), which are each in turn also defined by the house. If you look at this in a negative way, you might say a "rafter" has no real, permanent essence and is "empty." In its positive form, the same idea could be expressed by saying "rafter" contains within it the Principle of every constituent part of the house and the Principle of the house as a whole. Now, extend the house of the analogy to the entire cosmos. The famous image Fazang used to illustrate this was the Jewel Net of Indra, a magical net strung across space from which at each intersection hung a star-like jewel reflecting in its faultless surface every other jewel. This was Fazang's metaphor for Principle (Cook 1977).

For Fazang, the entire cosmos was the cosmic Buddha, and so everything in the cosmos—person, flower, rock, speck of dust—thus contained Buddha-nature. Zhu Xi's audience was thoroughly familiar with this type of logic. Zhu Xi actually employed another favorite Huayan metaphor to illustrate his argument, but, of course, he replaces Buddha-nature with the Supreme Ultimate:

> Fundamentally there is only one Supreme Ultimate, yet each of the myriad things has been endowed with it and each in itself possesses the Supreme Ultimate in its entirety. This is similar to the fact that there is only one moon in the sky but when its light is scattered upon rivers and lakes, it can be seen everywhere. It cannot be said that the moon has been split. (Chan 1963a: 638)

In this way, each thing contains not only its own distinctive Principle but also the Principle of all that exists; *li* is specific to each thing but is also ultimately one singular indivisible Principle synonymous with the Supreme Ultimate. Cheng Yi's phrase

"Principle is one but its manifestations are many" was redeployed as the credo to encapsulate this doctrine.

Human nature and self-cultivation

Although *li* and *qi* were fundamental to Chinese science (Ho 1985), and Zhu Xi saw no real separation between natural and ethical domains (Kim 2000), in practice he was only concerned with pursuing moral perfectibility. His knowledge of astronomy, harmonics, and medicine were brushed aside when he said:

> The Supreme Ultimate is simply the Principle of the highest good. Each and every person has in him the Supreme Ultimate and each and every thing is in the Supreme Ultimate ... The Supreme Ultimate is a name to express all the virtues and the highest good in Heaven and Earth, man and things. (Chan 1963a: 640)

Like Cheng Yi before him, Zhu Xi maintained that human "nature (*xing*) is the same as Principle (*li*)" (Chan 1963a: 614). Following Mengzi, he also maintained the Principle of human nature was wholly good. The traditional Five Constant Virtues constituting human nature—humanity (*ren*), righteousness (*yi*), ritual (*li*), wisdom (*zhi*), and faithfulness (*xin*)—were likewise said to derive from the Supreme Ultimate residing "within each and every person."

If this were so, Zhu Xi clearly needed to explain the folly, deceit, selfishness, corruption, and cruelty that abounded in the world. It is at this point that he drew inspiration from Zhang Zai. As we have seen, Zhang's universe consisted only of *qi*. In his cosmology, the pure *qi* of the Great Void becomes "turbid" and "obstructed," which results in physical form. Each person is a microcosm of this process. We all have the same undifferentiated "Heavenly nature," but degrees of turbulence and blockage as *qi* congeals results in myriad types of "physical nature." Zhu Xi adopts this theory of obstruction, but, of course, for him our Heavenly nature is not undifferentiated *qi*, but *li*.

Human Heavenly nature is wholly good, but as the Principle of our original nature becomes manifest through the corporeality of *qi*, problems can occur. Our physical natures are thus not always in accord with our original, Heavenly natures. Zhu said, "The nature of all men is good and yet there are those who are good from their birth and those who are [bad] from their birth. This is because of the differences in *qi* with which they are endowed." The *qi* that determines our physical nature can be pure or impure, clear or turbid, and "selfish desire will dominate if the obstruction is great" (Chan 1963a: 624).

Zhu Xi is not entirely opposed to emotions and human desires, but he is at best suspicious of them. He likens our original nature to a body of tranquil water that begins to stir with emotion and swells into troubling waves of passion (Chan 1963a: 631). Some passions might be good (a sage, he says, can be righteously angry), but those that spring from selfish desire are condemned, and we sense that Zhu at heart longs for those still waters of our Heavenly selves.

***

Zhu Xi firmly believed in the possibility of absolute self-transformation that would result in sagehood, and he saw sages as having a comprehensive, almost mystical apprehension of Principle. This could only be achieved through cultivating the heart-mind (*xin*). Zhu was very clear that human nature "consists of Principles embraced in the heart-mind," and the heart-mind was thus the locus of self-cultivation. "Heart-mind means master," Zhu said (Chan 1963a: 631).

While it is unambiguous that heart-mind was paramount for Zhu Xi, his views on what constitutes the heart-mind are inconsistent. This would be the most criticized aspect of his thought. Some suspected he changed his mind over the years, but it is equally possible that he overburdened the concept of *xin* so that, when pushed, he was forced toward conflicting conclusions (Liu 1978: 206). What follows seems to me the dominant position of his mature thought.

Although *xin* alone can embrace Principle, in reality people's heart-minds are rarely all-seeing and are typically confused, distracted, and clouded. Heart-mind is thus not identical to Principle. Just as *li* and *qi* are inseparable yet distinct, so too Principle and heart-mind "are one and yet two" (Chan 1963a: 630). Indeed, as human nature *is* Principle, so too heart-mind belongs to the realm of *qi*, and mental activity was understood to be the product of a very subtle form of *qi*. A heart-mind consisting of perfectly clear *qi* is transparent to Principle, but once again, turbulence can cause obstruction. Zhu could thus say Principle and heart-mind "pervade each other" and Principle "inheres" in heart-mind without assuming their identity (Chan 1963a: 628). This was a position that other Ru would vehemently contest, as we will see in the next chapter.

Zhu Xi's program of self-cultivation was directed toward refining the heart-mind so that it might perfectly discern Principle. His methods sound simple, perhaps even relaxing, so that he once advised a disciple to spend half of each day sitting quietly and the other half reading. These seemingly mundane activities were, however, rigorous religious disciplines.

Jingzuo or quiet-sitting had been advocated by Zhou Dunyi and the Cheng brothers and was regularly adopted by Way Learning practitioners (Chapter 2). For Zhu Xi, the purpose of quiet sitting was to allow the sediment of the heart-mind's mental activity to settle. As he said, the heart-mind "is originally bright. It's just that it gets covered over by things and can't get out from under them" (cited in Gardner 2004: 103–4). Even the seemingly mannered behavior of Way Learning practitioners was a part of this settling process as their ritualized dress, speech, and deportment was understood to be forms of bodily discipline intent on reigning in the heart-mind.

But Zhu Xi was no Zen master. Zen (Chinese Chan) means "meditation," and in Zen, meditation was an end in itself. Zhu took pains to distinguish *jingzuo* from Chan as well as Daoist "sitting and forgetting" (*zuowang*). In their practice, he said, "one seeks the heart-mind with the heart-mind … like the mouth gnawing the mouth or the eye seeing the eye." For him, quiet sitting was preparatory, readying the heart-mind "to investigate things" (Chan 1963a: 604).

Zhu spoke tirelessly of "investigating things" (*gewu*) a priority reflected in the title of his anthology, *Reflections on Things at Hand*, which in turn derives from the *Analects*: "inquire earnestly and reflect on what is at hand" (19:6). While at the broadest level this entailed seeking Principle in all phenomena, in practice Zhu's focus was almost exclusively on the social and moral manifestations of *li*. A person with a serene heart-mind, free from the turbulence of desire, could act in accord with their heightened awareness of Principle.

In theory, an absolutely limpid heart-mind would apprehend Principle in every thing "at hand." For sages this was possible, but it was too much for struggling humanity. There were, however, guides meant to help people recognize Principle in the world. Because sages had lucidly recorded their perspicacity in books, the Classics make *li* transparent even to those just beginning along the Way. "The explanations ... of the sages and worthies," Zhu Xi said, "are very simple" (Gardner 1990: 96).

Reading was so central to Zhu's program of cultivation that later critics would say he was basically obsessed with book learning (Yü 1986: 233). Thus, the chapter on "The Investigation of Things" in *Reflections on Things at Hand* is not an invitation to empirical research, but rather an assertion that in "the extension of knowledge, nothing is more important than reading" (Chan 1967: 88). Quiet Sitting was thus but a method for students to "empty their minds" before beginning "to slowly look over the teachings of sages" (Wittenborn 1991: 81).

Zhu Xi told his followers what to read. He revered the Five Classics and wrote commentaries on all of them save the *Spring and Autumn Annals*, of which he said: "What possible relevance does it have for us?" (Elman 1990: 157). But these texts were challenging and could be easily misunderstood by novices. The Four Books were the core of his curriculum, but even they were graded to avoid possible confusion. He said: "I want people first of all to read the *Great Learning* to set the pattern, next to read the *Analects* to establish a foundation, next to read the book of *Mencius* for stimulation, and next to read the *Doctrine of the Mean* to find out the subtle points of the ancients" (Chan 1967: 102).

Zhu told his followers how to read: slowly and with reverent concentration (*jing*). With an empty mind, sitting upright and chanting with resonant voice, they should approach texts with hallowed attentiveness, going over and over passages until they were thoroughly internalized. This was reading as an act of ritual devotion—"spiritual and bodily exercises that culminate in sage-hood and have strong religious meaning and significance" (Peng 2016: 327). Zhu was adamant that scriptures were the most direct path back to our intrinsic natures, and that reading was therefore an act of self-transformation. The Books' ultimate objective was to bring us back to our true selves:

Book learning is of secondary importance. It would seem that moral Principle is originally complete in man; the reason he must engage in book learning is that he hasn't experienced much. The sages experienced a great deal and wrote it down for others to read. Now in book learning we must simply apprehend the many mani-festations of moral Principle. Once we understand them, we'll find that all of them were complete in us from the very beginning, not added from the outside. (Gardner 1990: 128)

There were meant to be no surprises in Way Learning self-discovery. For all the innovation in cosmology, metaphysics, philosophical vocabulary, and cultivation prac-tice, the eventually disclosed Principle of human nature looks remarkably familiar. Thus, "the teachings of the sages are generally concerned simply with everyday, routine behavior such as filial piety, fraternal respect, loyalty and fidelity. If men are able to practice such behavior, their 'lost heart-minds' will naturally be retrieved" (Gardner 1990: 97). Again,

Man's nature is nothing but Principle ... When [sages and worthies] spoke of the full development of human nature, they meant the complete realization of the moral Principles of the Three Bonds (between ruler and minister, father and son, and hus-band and wife) and the Five Constant Virtues. (Chan 1963a: 613–14)

This endorsement of the Three Bonds and Five Constant Virtues might at first seem to be a conclusion Zhu had reached after a long process of investigation, but other passages make it quite clear they were actually never in question. Thus, for instance, he once said it was unnecessary to study Buddhism and Daoism before dismissing them as "the mere fact that they discard the Three Bonds ... and the Five Constant Virtues ... is already a crime of the greatest magnitude" (Chan 1963a: 646). Some things, it seems, were not open to "investigation."

✱✱✱

Zhu Xi changed the path but not the journey's end, and Way Learning could arguably be seen as just a more sophisticated and comprehensive teaching for reinforcing the sociopolitical status quo. Little wonder that it was readily adopted by rulers. But inev-itably, the new state curriculum employing Zhu Xi's commentaries was subject to the very problems Zhu had sought to solve. For most, studying remained a means to employment, wealth, and status. The cheats did not vanish—they just updated their underwear (Figure 13).

As Zhu's commentaries remained orthodoxy until the fall of imperial China, all sub-sequent Ru were obliged to tussle with his views. Broadly speaking, there were two main critical responses. First, there were those who thought Zhu was not the true representative of Way Learning. Rather, they developed the views of others who had maintained that Principle was not found "in things," but was rather inherent in the heart-mind. That claim was initially proffered gently enough, but the repercussions were momentous. If so, what need for Classics? If true, are we not all latent sages? And if insight comes from within, need we even recognize the preestablished social norms upheld by the Three Bonds and Five Cardinal Relationships? By the late Ming

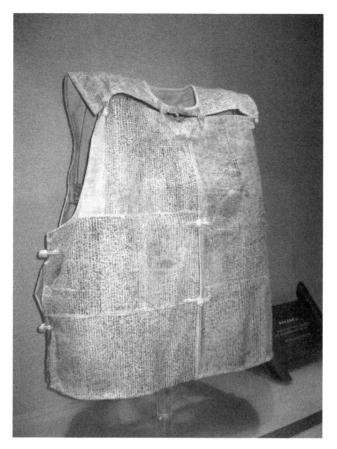

FIGURE 13   *Classics-inscribed underwear.*

With so much riding on passing examinations, candidates were tempted to use every conceivable means to optimize their chances. Many would consult oracles about questions to expect, and omens and the subtle messages of dreams were carefully scrutinized.

Then there was cheating. The logistics of examining around 10,000 men at a time was horrendous. There were no photo IDs, so checks were needed to ensure the candidate was who he claimed to be. There was also the problem of corruptible examiners, so answers (in black) had to be copied (in vermillion) so that handwriting could not be recognized.

And, of course, people tried to smuggle in the works they had failed to memorize. Candidates were checked by guards who were rewarded for finding banned material and punished for missing it, but nothing proved foolproof. Some quipped they could stock a bookshop if only they could retrieve all the illicit texts within a compound.

dynasty, some Ru had become so radical as to be almost unrecognizable. It was this alternative tradition, known as Learning of the Heart-Mind (*xinxue*) (introduced in the next chapter), that continues to inspire most Ru philosophy today.

The final Qing dynasty, in contrast, was very conservative. Some noted Ru of this dynasty were suspicious of all talk of Principle, which they saw as a thinly disguised Buddhism and Daoism. They had far less faith in human nature, although this could be merciful. Principle could be onerous. Dai Zhen (1723–77), who we will meet in the next chapter, said:

> The exalted reprove their inferiors on the basis of "Principle"; the elders reprove their juniors on the basis of Principle; the noble reprove the ordinary folk on the basis of Principle. Although they are wrong, they insist they are following Principle …
>
> When men die because they have violated the law, there are those who have pity for them, but when men die because they have violated Principle, who has compassion for them? (Chin and Friedman 1990: 85)

At the end of the Qing, Tan Sitong (Chapter 8) claimed Principle could "strike into somebody so much terror as to put his soul to death" (cited in Teng 1986: 110).

Whereas Ming *philosophy* is proving most relevant today, the late Qing left a political legacy that continues into the twenty-first century. As we will see in the final chapters, the former pursues the way of the inner sage (*neisheng*) while the latter continues the quest for the outer king (*waiwang*).

7

The Principle of the heart and mind

Many of the distinctive features of contemporary Ru thought began emerging in the Ming and Qing dynasties. There is good reason for this. By the Ming, China was already on its way to modernity.

People today often see China as a debutant superpower. They are unaware that when China first began dealing with the West in the Ming dynasty (1368–1644), China dominated world trade. It was the most populated and urbanized country on Earth and led the way in agriculture, industry, economics, and commerce. China exported in volume (mainly silk and porcelain) but had little interest in Western commodities. It was actually things deriving from Spanish America that made the greatest impact: sweet potatoes, maize, peanuts, and silver. The introduced crops, together with new varieties of rapidly ripening rice from Indo-China and improved agricultural methods, greatly increased China's calorific output. Having hovered at around 60 million since the Han dynasty, the graph of China's population turned to begin its exponential climb during the Ming. But official appointments did not increase proportionately, and there were a growing number of Classically educated men who found themselves out of work.

The silver pouring in from Mexico and Peru was indispensible for Ming coinage. China was developing a moneyed economy to accompany overseas trade, the rise of merchants, wage labor, privatization, and even, perhaps, the "sprouts of capitalism." Trading had previously been considered a very lowly occupation, but it now became respectable, and many Ru found new employment as exemplars of moral principle in business. These *Rushang* or "Ru merchants" were the predecessors of today's Ru entrepreneur (Lufrano 1997).

Ru values progressively penetrated all levels of society. Although *Rushang* lacked the prestige of imperial appointment, they could enhance their status by displaying virtue to those below them—for example, by channeling their wealth into the various *renhui* or "humaneness societies" that mushroomed at this time. Rather than serving the emperor as "father" of the state, they instead tried to attract their own "family" of dependants (Smith 2009). Ru Learning was thus increasingly marketed for local communities and realized through regional associations and popular movements.

These changes inevitably disrupted traditional mores. One eyewitness rather hysterically observed that "even families where the *Book of Odes* and *Book of Documents* are read and households where the [ancient] rites and music are performed are mad for wealth and eminence." He added that husbands and wives were contemptuous of one another, brothers were divided, and parents did not receive proper reverence when they died because a reckless new breed was saying: "These rites were not established for our generation" (Brook 1998: 149–51). Other observers describe these same social transformations positively. Late Ming Ru teachings reflected these changes and deliberately sought to unsettle traditional social norms. They were remarkably liberal, individualistic, accessible, egalitarian, and enamored with freedom—all qualities to be praised.

Or blamed. The final Qing dynasty (1644–1911) roundly condemned the excesses of the late Ming. In many ways, it was its antithesis: pragmatic, empirical, morally conservative, and highly ritualistic. Here was another kind of modernity, rationalist rather than romanticist. China did not begin a homespun scientific revolution, although why it failed to do so remains an unsettled question. In its own way, the Qing dynasty did see Ru beginning to uphold the defining principles of science: reason applied to empirical evidence. This was primarily to *textual* evidence, however, and growing disciples such as astronomy, mathematics, and hydrology only had a supplementary status. The critical approach to the Classics in the Qing was remarkably thorough and impartial, however, and it paved the way for contemporary academic scholarship in China.

Ru of the Qing were not particularly "religious" in their approach to ritual. I will return to this issue at the end of the chapter, but at least to some extent ritual came to be seen less as a means for achieving ultimate social transformation, and more as a cultural embodiment of what it was to be Chinese when living under foreign Manchu rule. This growing association between Ru Learning and "Chineseness" has also carried over into the twentieth and twenty-first centuries.

Despite fundamental differences, the Ming and Qing were both dynasties when Ru teachings, values, and practices increasingly permeated all levels of society. No longer the exclusive domain of the scholar-official elite, many Ru movements focused on the common person. Whether as popular religious movements or local efforts to promote ritual to consolidate Chinese identity, this absorption of Ruism by the masses would prove vital for perpetuating the tradition when, with the collapse of the Qing, the Ru would finally lose state patronage.

Orthodoxy and dissent

The relationship between Ru and the state in the Ming dynasty was by no means straightforward or consistent. The first Ming emperor was himself a commoner, a Buddhist novice who rode to power on the back of a rebellious Buddhist sect. He distrusted "empty phrase makers" and put a halt to examinations for over a decade, as well as executing tens of thousands of officials deemed to be conspiring against him. When the examinations were reinstated, efforts were made to "democratize" the education system. Ming emperors were renowned autocrats who were suspicious of established intellectual cliques and they tried to curb their influence by recruiting officials evenly from across the country. Schooling was broadened to further extend literacy and examination candidate quotas were set in an effort to ensure all provinces were evenly represented. A new lower grade of local examination also greatly expanded the number of students and minor-degree holders. Although more and more people were thus studying the Classics, the overall effect was a steady decline in the quality of scholarship. Ming examinations were simpler and basically just tested a student's rote learning of Zhu Xi's interpretations of the Four Books. Any surviving independence of thought was extinguished by the obligatory examination format known as the "eight-legged essay" (baguwen), which the reluctant scholar hero of China's most famous novel (Honglou meng or Dream of Red Mansions) described as a formula for "blotching together a few classical tags … to hide the fact that [students] haven't got a single original idea" (Cao and Gao 1982: 52).

Although examinations ever-increasingly ensured widespread literacy in the Classics, they were evidently not an avenue to creative philosophical thought or heartfelt moral self-cultivation. It was now almost universally acknowledged that they had become nothing but a means to status, employment, and wealth. Ming rulers, furthermore, remained apprehensive about the value of employing scholar-officials, and Ru frequently felt marginalized from important functions of state.

The most vibrant expressions of Ru values in the Ming thus find expression with independent philosophers who gathered disciples, taught at private academies, and, increasingly, lectured to the bourgeoning masses. The memorable Ru of the Ming had a palpable presence that drew followers to them. Thus, while Ru pursuing office through the examinations were seeking to tap into established pathways of bureaucratic power, independent teachers attracted followers, often in their thousands, through verve, originality, insight, and allure. These are the Ru we will pursue, and I will devote a little more space to their biographies in order to capture something of their charisma.

* * *

Despite the fact that Zhu Xi's commentaries on the Classics were officially sanctioned by the state and as such continued to exert enormous influence, the noted Ru of the Ming were not in full accord with his teachings. Nor has Zhu Xi's thinking been particularly prominent in the post-imperial era. Rather, it was, and is, the views of his critic, Wang Yangming, that captivated Ming thought just as they continue to inspire Ru Learning today. Many consider Wang Yangming to be the greatest philosopher in all of imperial China.

Wang Yangming's thought was not without precedent. His supporters would claim Wang was merely drawing out the true message of Way Learning taught by the Cheng brothers, and in particular Cheng Hao. They also pointed to Zhu Xi's contemporaries who had contested his interpretations. Lu Jiuyuan, better known as Lu Xiangshan (1139–93), stood out. His ideas were so close to those of Wang Yangming that they were said to jointly head the Lu-Wang school (*Lu-Wang xuepai*) alternate to Cheng-Zhu orthodoxy. We have already brushed past Lu Xiangshan. He was the person who wrote to Zhu Xi contesting the value and authenticity of Zhou Dunyi's *Diagram of the Supreme Ultimate Explained*. It is time we became better acquainted.

You may recall that Zhu Xi had said the heart-mind was the site of all self-cultivation and that heart-mind consisted of a fine and subtle form of "psycho-physical stuff" or *qi*. Heart-mind, and heart-mind alone, might apprehend Principle (*li*), but Principle was not at all the same as heart-mind. For Zhu, the job of the heart-mind was to discern Principle as it resided in all of existence, and he was consequently devoted to "investigating things" in order to disclose *li*. In practice, as we have seen, this meant studying the Classics where the sages had rendered *li* lucid and transparent.

Lu Xiangshan was of a very different persuasion, and Zhu Xi knew he had to take his rival's views seriously. Although Lu had passed the highest examinations and held several posts, he was at heart a teacher and so retired to Elephant Mountain (*Xiangshan*) in Jiangxi province, from whence his pen name is taken. Thousands of people came to visit him there, and Zhu Xi once admitted that most of the scholars of eastern China were disciples of Lu. Our two philosophers met at Goose Lake Temple (*E hu si*) in 1175, and Zhu Xi was said to have initially turned pale from what he heard—perhaps it was the barb in a line of a poem opening the proceedings: "Fondness for commentaries brings thorns and thistles / Concern for fine points causes the ground to sink" (Ching 2000: 136). A decade later, they sought to settle their differences through a series of letters, but the intellectual rift remained, although personally their relationship was cordial.

Lu Xiangshan deliberately wrote very little and once said to Zhu Xi: "You ... just talk on and on and end up piling up nonsense" (Ivanhoe 2009: 58). When he was pushed by disciples to set down his philosophy, he shrugged the suggestion off saying "the Six Classics will serve as my annotations" (*liujing zhuwu*). This provocative reply that relegated scripture to footnotes on his life in fact encapsulates Lu's teaching.

For Lu, Classics, wordy philosophy, and investigating things were at best secondary. They were unnecessary because for him the heart-mind was *not* a form of *qi* capable of apprehending and reconciling with Principle, but rather it was Principle itself. He said: "The heart-mind is one and Principle is one. In the final analysis these form a unity; in essence they are one." The heart-mind and this Principle actually do not admit any duality" (Ivanhoe 2009: 48). The heart-mind itself was his ultimate authority; if Classics and doctrines diverged from it, then they were of no avail. There was no need to look further: "The universe is my heart-mind. My heart-mind is the universe" (Ivanhoe 2009: 33).

Lu Xiangshan did not see the need for systematic explanations of what already resided within each person, and as a teacher he was more charismatic counselor than philosopher. Not surprising, what remains of his writing is scant. After Zhu Xi's doctrines became orthodoxy, Lu Xiangshan's ideas were for the most part simply absorbed and tucked away. The trouble only began when his position was revived by Wang Yangming.

Wang Yangming

It is hard to resist reading Wang Yangming's (Wang Shouren, 1472–1529) philosophy as biography. His father looms large. Tu Weiming has described their relationship as "one of the most fascinating examples of father-son competition in traditional Chinese culture" (Tu 1976: 35). Wang Hua was a formidable role model who had topped China's highest examinations, and Wang Yangming struggled to forge his identity in the shadow of his larger-than-life father.

Wang's early years reveal a strong urge to withdraw from society, politics, and family, and his love of learning emerged in tandem with his impulse to retreat. At this stage, he was attracted to the reclusive teachings of Daoism and Chan (Zen) and he never completely abandoned them. Some of his later writings are unintelligible unless the reader is familiar with Daoist terminology, while his love of Chan ran much deeper. He never renounced his respect for the great Zen patriarchs, and so-called "Yangming Chan" is an important part of any comprehensive history of Buddhism in China and Japan.

Many Ru were in fact drawn to Buddhism and Daoism. A common (although superficial) stereotype was that while Ru strived to perfect human relationships, the other two faiths sought salvation through world renunciation and solitary inner self-transformation. The triumph of Cheng-Zhu orthodoxy perhaps looked like a victory for those prioritizing family and community, but while Ru diligently voiced their assent in public, many were furtively drawn to Daoism and Chan. As Mark Halperin's very apt title to a book investigating this issue suggests, these Ru needed to come *Out of the Cloister*. Wang was torn by the tensions between inner and outer realms and he was temperamentally incapable of living a double life.

Wang Yangming eventually passed the highest examination and secured government appointments, but living as a scholar-official drove him to bouts of depression. The Three Bonds were cardinal to his professed ideology, but as a minister, he was quickly bored and often sought to be excused; as a husband, he missed his own wedding day, apparently distracted when a Daoist he met in passing invited him to join him in meditation; while as a son, his father, with a mixture of disapproval and pride, said he was *kuang,* which at best meant he had passionate conviction but at worst signified that he was "wild" or "crazy."

Wang's reclusive urge to dust away "the air of an official" peaked just as his father's career was soaring. In 1502, sick, exhausted, dispirited, he left the capital and spent two years in retreat at Yangming grotto, from whence his pen name derives. When his friends visited him, they believed he "had already acquired the Dao" of the immortals, and his reputation spread as someone who had mastered Daoist secrets of internal alchemy (Tu 1976: 58). Wang, however, knew his ultimate realization was being hindered by a remaining obstacle. For what he had found in the depths of soli-tude, divorced from society and distant from family, was he could not extinguish his feelings for his grandmother and father. A Buddhist might advise him to persist until he freed himself from those final attachments, but Wang began to suspect that solu-tion would be inauthentic. What meditative isolation had taught him was that filial love did not depend on his specific relationship with his father, but rather resided autono-mously within his own inner being. His filiality, in other words, was inherent to his heart-mind (*xin*).

Wang Yangming's insight was essentially a Ru rendition of Chan. Chan maintains that enlightenment is nothing other than the heart-mind awakening to its own original nature. Wang realized that filiality and other bonds were in fact intrinsic to that heart-mind. To let go of his love for his father, therefore, would be untrue to his essential nature:

> Buddhism claims to be free from attachment to phenomenal things but actually the opposite is the case. We, Confucians seem to be attached to phenomenal things but in reality the opposite is true ... The Buddhists are afraid of the burden in the relationship between father and son and therefore escape from it. They are afraid of the burden in the relationship between ruler and minister and therefore escape from it. They are afraid of the burden in the relationship between husband and wife and therefore escape from it ... We Confucians accept [these relationships]. When have we been attached to these relations? (Chan 1963b: 205)

After he returned from seclusion, Wang Yangming resumed office but was soon thereafter flogged and banished to a minor post among the Miao tribespeople in what is now Guizhou province. There, the harsh simplicity of life only served to fuel his inner resourcefulness, and on an eventful night in 1508 he was said to have "rapidly awak-ened ... like a torrent bursting a river bank and rushing to the sea" (Chan 1963b: 265), the Ru equivalent of Chan "sudden enlightenment." While living "among the barbar-ians," he realized "there was nothing in the world to investigate, that the effort to investigate things is only to be carried out in and with reference to one's body and heart-mind" (Chan 1963b: 249).

Wang Yangming had journeyed through Buddhism and Daoism only to return to the Way of the Ru. But his understanding of Ru Learning had been transformed in the pro-cess. This brings us to his relationship with the orthodox teachings of Zhu Xi.

Clearly, when Wang Yangming said, "there was nothing in the world to investigate" he had Zhu Xi in mind; "Zhu Xi's teaching on the investigation of things is forced, arbitrary, and far fetched," he said (Chan 1963b: 12–13). As a conscientious young-ster, Wang had been willing to try to investigate Principle as it indwelled in all things, but he was skeptical. Was this really possible? To test this, he asked his friend to sit day and night before a clump of bamboo until it disclosed its Principle. His friend became sick. Thinking his colleague perhaps lacked stamina, Wang himself tried it, but he too became ill from exhaustion (Chan 1963b: 249). This may not be China's most watertight experimental refutation, but Wang's point is clear enough: there is no Principle "out there" to be found—not just in bamboo but equally in fathers, emperors, and other virtuous beings.

Wang Yangming was not at all denying the existence of Principle and he too is counted among the exponents of Principle Learning (*lixue*), at least in the broader application of that designation. What he was saying was that Principle is not located in the phenomenal world, but rather it resides within the heart-mind. He said: "The heart-mind *is* principle. Is there any affair in the world outside of the heart-mind? Is there any Principle outside of the heart-mind?" And again: "There is no Principle outside the heart-mind; there is no event outside the heart-mind" (Chan 1963b: 7, 33). To distinguish his views from other types of Principle Learning, his thought is most often referred to as Heart-Mind Learning (*xinxue*).

Consider again Wang's experience at Yangming grotto when his filial concerns lingered while dwelling in the depths of solitude. Clearly, this was not dependent on his father's physical presence. Taking this further, Wang Yangming asked: "If the principle of filial piety … is in the person of my parents, is it true that as soon as the parents pass away the heart-mind will lack the Principle of filial piety?" To Wang, it was clear that in "serving one's parents, one cannot seek the Principle of filial piety in the parent … [It] is in the heart-mind, that is all, for the heart-mind and Principle are identical" (Chan 1963b: 99, 7). The same could, of course, be said for all cardinal relationships.

Wang Yangming was primarily concerned with moral Principle, but as his bamboo experiment suggests, he extended his argument to the natural world as well. This has generated considerable interpretative debate. Was he saying that heart-mind was the only thing that existed? (For the philosophically savvy, was he a monistic idealist?) Probably not (see Tien 2010). From the few available passages that shed light on this matter, it seems he was rather saying that it is our consciousness of things that gives the flux of the phenomenal world meaningful structure and Principle. When he was asked what distant trees dropping blossoms on a mountain had to do with the heart-mind, he replied, "Before you look at these flowers, they and your heart-mind are in the state of silent vacancy. As you come to look at them, their colors at once show up clearly. From this you can know that these flowers are not external to your heart-mind" (Chan 1963b: 222). To rephrase a well-known Western conundrum, had Wang been asked, "Do flowers that are seen by no one have color?", his answer in all likelihood would have been no, but that is not to deny there is something "out there" that the heart-mind illuminates as the vibrancy of flowers drifting from trees on a far-away cliff. Readers who fancy some resemblance to Kantian idealism will have their suspicions rewarded in Chapter 9. For now, it is sufficient we appreciate Wang was saying that the Principle of all things resides within the heart-mind: "Without the innate knowledge inherent in man, there cannot be plants and trees, tiles and stones. This is not true of them only. Even Heaven and Earth cannot exist without the innate knowledge that is inherent in man" (Chan 1963b: 221).

Because all things in "Heaven and Earth" exist within the heart-mind, a person who truly apprehends heart-mind achieves a kind of mystical unity with existence (see

Chen 2015). Wang does not reject emotion and desire—"pleasure, anger, sorrow, fear, love, hatred and desire" are "natural to the heart-mind" (Chan 1963b: 229)—but selfish desire, desire based on the illusion of an insular self, cuts us off from our identity with the cosmos. Wang advocated what Mengzi (7A15) had called "innate knowing" (*liangzhi*), which Wang interpreted to mean knowing that is liberated from the fetters of the petty self. Wang said, "The learning of the great man consists entirely of getting rid of the obscuration of selfish desires in order by his own efforts to make manifest his clear character, so as to restore the condition of forming one body with Heaven, Earth and the myriad things" (Chan 1963b: 273).

For Wang Yangming, humaneness (*ren*) is the inevitable response to apprehending the unity of all things and heart-mind. In the following passage, Wang alludes both to Zhang Zai's *Western Inscription* and Mengzi's claim that the humane person cannot tolerate the suffering of others or even animals:

> The great man regards Heaven, Earth and the myriad things as one body. He regards the world as one family and the country as one person. As to those who make a cleavage between the self and other, they are small men. That the great man can regard Heaven, Earth and the myriad things as one body is not because he deliberately wants to do so, but because it is natural to the humane nature of his heart-mind that he do so ... When he observes the pitiful cries and frightened appearance of birds and animals about to be slaughtered, he cannot help feeling an "inability to bear" their suffering. This shows that his humaneness *[ren]* forms one body with birds and animals ... When he sees plants broken and destroyed, he cannot help a feeling of pity. This show that his humaneness forms one body with plants ... When he sees tiles and stones shattered and crushed, he cannot help a feeling of regret. This shows that his humaneness forms one body with tiles and stones. (Chan 1963b: 272)

As the Principle of all things in Heaven and Earth resides within the heart-mind, we might imagine Wang Yangming and his followers spending their days introspectively engaged in meditation or quiet-sitting (*jingzuo*). After all, Wang himself had "day and night sat in silent meditation" until "one night he had a great awakening and jumped around like a crazy man" (cited in Chen 2015: 24). Wang had also encouraged his students to meditate to dissuade them from spending their days debating philosophical minutiae. This was initially effective, he said, but with time "they gradually developed the defect of fondness for tranquility and disgust with activity and degenerated into lifelessness like dry wood" (Chan 1963b: 217). For Wang, inaction was a serious fault. His ambivalence toward meditation must be seen in the context of his conviction that action is integral to the realization of heart-mind.

Wang Yangming is renowned for his insistence that knowledge and action are inseparable (Cua 1982): "knowledge is the beginning of action and action is the completion of knowledge" (Chan 1963b: 30). Wang was acutely aware that Cheng-Zhu orthodoxy had produced generations of scholars who could piously mouth words to pass examinations and yet who remained untouched by what they professed. This was possible because Zhu Xi's doctrine of learning was based on "the investigation of things," and the acquisition of knowledge required a secondary act of moral will to mobilize theory as practice. In contrast, Wang Yangming insisted that the heart-mind was not just a source of knowledge but was itself ultimate reality. Knowing was, therefore, not a process of acquiring information, but was rather an existential encounter. He uses the example of the knowledge gained by seeing the beautiful colors of a flower and the action of loving them and then denies the legitimacy of separating the knowledge from the action: "As soon as one sees that beautiful color, he has already loved it. It is not that he sees it first and then makes up his mind to love it." More importantly, Wang continues, it is insufficient to say someone knows "filial piety and brotherly respect simply because they show them in words." As there is no rift between the knowing self and external objects, any knowledge worthy of the name is a unity "of knowledge and action, which have not been separated by selfish desires" (Chan 1963b: 10–11).

* * *

Despite his radical break with Cheng-Zhu orthodoxy, Wang Yangming continued to uphold traditional Ru social and moral mores. The Three Bond and Five Constant Virtues endure even though he had shifted them from the contingency of the external world to deep within the heart-mind. In doing this, he believed the shallow show of scholarship would be replaced by a unity of knowledge and moral action. This seemed a remedy for superficial learning, but it harbored a real threat to authority.

From the Han dynasty's canonization of the Five Classics to Zhu Xi's elevation of the Four Books, Ru self-cultivation had always begun with the words of sages preserved in scripture. Like Lu Xiangshan, Wang had demoted them to a secondary position. He said: "If words are examined in the heart-mind and found to be wrong, although they come from the mouth of Confucius, I dare not accept them as correct" (Chan 1963b: 159).

Critics could reply that, given the diversity of belief in Wang's day as in all of Chinese history, handing authority over to the heart-mind was surely an invitation to rampant subjectivity. This was certainly the view of Luo Qinshun (1465–1547), Wang's contemporary who (not uncritically) upheld Cheng-Zhu orthodoxy. They exchanged several letters trying to resolve their differences. Luo was concerned that delivering all authority to the heart-mind would lead to relativism and undermine morality. Chan Buddhism, he said, was "confined to the internal," and this created people who "rebel against their sovereign and fathers, renounce wives and children." The Classics were required to safeguard against such things. He said, "Surely the *study* of [the Way] cannot be neglected. I am afraid that one cannot be satisfied with his own views and immediately regard them as ultimate standards" (Bloom 1987: 178, 184). Wang, in turn, insisted that his doctrine of heart-mind would only serve to direct people toward sincerely implementing traditional Ru moral values. But Luo had astutely spied the revolutionary implications of Wang's philosophy, and it was not long before the orthodox tradition of Ming China was under siege.

Heresies of the heart-mind

A seventeenth-century work entitled *Records of Ming Ru* (*Mingru xue'an*) says: "Since Wang Yangming pointed out *liangzhi* [innate knowing] as the principle of all self-realization present in all, accessible to all through contemplation, the road to sagehood was open to everyone." The great Ming popularizers mostly belonged to the Taizhou school, named after the hometown (in Jiangsu province) of its founder Wang Gen (1483–1540). According to *Records,* "The teachings of Master Yangming became popular everywhere under Heaven on account of Wang Gen." Often regarded as radical or leftist, the Taizhou school would transform the Way of the Ru to such an extent that *Records* felt obliged to add: with Wang Gen's disciples "it was no longer within the boundaries of Confucian moral philosophy" (Huang 1987: 100, 165).

Wang Gen was a most unlikely exponent of Ru learning. He came from a family of salt makers and was only educated for a few years at a village school. That did not stop him from discussing the *Analects* and *Great Learning* with anyone willing to oblige, or dampen his determination to become a sage. In 1511, a dream triggered his sudden enlightenment in which he experienced humaneness (*ren*) uniting him with all things in the universe. Despite his lack of education, he felt destined to become a teacher of humanity. He hung a placard above his door declaring he would discuss the Way of the Sages with any passerby and he began wearing clothing styled after the sage-king Yao. Later, he also took up riding in a cart like the one he imagined Kongzi had used.

Wang Gen certainly acknowledged the sages and the Classics, but they were secondary to the inner realization of the heart-mind: "One should use the Classics to prove one's own enlightenment, and use one's own enlightenment to interpret the Classics," he said (de Bary 1991a: 157). This sounds very much like Wang Yangming, but Wang Gen had come to this understanding independently. A friend pointed out the convergence in their thought, and so Wang Gen set off to meet the great scholar, swaggering in dressed in his outlandish robes. Wang Gen came ready to argue, but after several bouts of debate he knew he had met his match and declared himself a disciple. Wang Yangming gave him the name Gen (he was originally named Wang Yin), a hexagram in the *Changes* symbolizing a mountain and which could suggest either enduring strength or unmovable obstinacy.

The essence of Wang Gen's teaching was an idiosyncratic variation on the *Great Learning's* dictum that rectifying the family, state, and world began with self-cultivation. Wang Gen interpreted this to mean people must learn to love themselves: "To make the self secure, one must love and respect the self, and one who does this cannot but love and respect others" (de Bary 1991a: 161). He exuberantly taught this simple, egalitarian, and individualistic philosophy to anyone from state officials to firewood collectors.

Wang Gen's interpretation of Ru doctrine did not require extensive training in Classics and commentaries. He claimed he had "gotten it for himself" and so too could anyone else. Ru had previously been an intellectual elite dwelling in the upper echelons of state power, but Wang Gen was instead working from the "bottom up." His was not just a cult of the "commoner," but rather a movement that cut across traditional social boundaries and reflected the growing social mobility of the late Ming. As one observer at that time noted, this was an era when "the status distinctions amongst scholars, peasants, and merchants have become blurred" (cited in Brook 1998: 143).

* * *

The radical social implications of Wang Gen's doctrines became very apparent with He Xinyin (1517–79). He Xinyin had been following a conventional scholarly path until he heard of Wang Gen's teachings and immediately abandoned his plans for becoming an official. He Xinyin saw people as fully embodied beings for whom desire was essential—after all, even the desire to eliminate desire is a desire, he said. Moral cultivation was, for He, a spontaneous manifestation of our innate nature in which conflicting desires just have to be juggled and balanced. He also insisted that people are inherently social so that humaneness (ren) is a natural manifestation of our innate desire to connect with others. He said: "For the humane [ren] man there is nothing not kindred to him. He enlarges his feelings of kinship for a relative to all, and sees kinship not only in the relation of father and son but in all relations worthy of the feelings of kinship" (Dimberg 1974: 75).

The notion that ren ultimately extended to "all-under-Heaven" was hardly new; it had been prominent throughout the Ru revival since Zhang Zai's Western Inscription. Nonetheless, all previous Ru had agreed that filial piety (xiao) was fundamental and that the Three Bonds (between father and son, ruler and minister, and husband and wife), served as the primary paradigms for other relationships. He Xinyin was the first to challenge this seemingly unassailable Ru dogma. For He, the quintessential relationship on which all bonds should be modeled was friendship. By friendship he meant a communion of people drawn together to discuss life's philosophical challenges, and he regarded the relationship between teacher and student as the ultimate form of friendship. He said: "Only through the relationship of friend and friend can the brave and talented of the land be gathered together to establish a teaching in accord with the principle of humanity, and make all-under-Heaven return to it" (Dimberg 1974: 103). Friendship as a bond between teachers and students thus took precedence over obedience to fathers and loyalty to rulers; pedagogically it was more important than the veneration of Classics.

Members of Taizhou school were indefatigable teachers, and stories of unbreakable teacher-student friendships are a part of the mythology of their movement. They were also great popularizers, and Records of Ming Ru says they "preached to the masses, established schools everywhere … [and] may be called propagators" (Huang 1987: 223). Their ability to draw huge crowds sometimes beggars belief. For instance, a second generation disciple of Wang Gen named Luo Rufang (1515–88) was said to have regularly attracted an audience of four to five hundred, but on one occasion he reportedly had 40,000–50,000 rural listeners and was forced to use shouters to relay what he said to the back rows (Handlin 1983: 42). His delivery was colorful and colloquial, with communal singing and refreshments to ensure his audience remained entertained. This kind of Ru teaching was unprecedented. Wm. Theodore de Bary clearly grasped its momentous significance when he wrote: "With its primary engagement in education, and what might be called proselytizing and propaganda, in the Taizhou school Confucianism for the first time became heavily involved in the sphere traditionally occupied by the popular religions" (de Bary 1991a: 186–7). This was the beginning of widespread Ru movements that became prevalent among nineteenth- and twentieth-century "redemptive societies" (Chapter 8) and a prototype of the grassroot Ru revivals that remain very active today (Chapter 10).

***

How far could those associated with the Taizhou school push tradition and still be recognizably Ru? There were those who indeed did lose interest in being identified as Ru and became "syncretists" combining the Three Teachings, or iconoclasts who identified with none of them. Perhaps the most extreme case of someone challenging virtually every traditional tenet of Ru doctrine yet still hanging by a thread to the Way of the Ru was Li Zhi (1527–1602). Li Zhi was the *enfant terrible* of Ruism. He liked to shock his audience. Here is a description of his character: "He was by nature narrow-minded and he appeared arrogant. His behavior was impulsive, his friends few … His actions deviated from social norms, and the words he spoke conflicted with the feelings in his heart. This was the sort of person he was" (Li 2016: 138–9). We might expect as much from his detractors, but Li Zhi wrote this of himself.

Having only passed the provincial examinations, Li Zhi spent the first half of his adult life serving as an unremarkable low-rank official, but went through a radical life transition after hearing of the teachings of Wang Yangming and the Taizhou school. He quickly began severing the Three Bonds. His parents were already dead, but he left officialdom because he did not like being controlled by his superiors, and he sent his wife and children packing to be free from the ties of marriage. The only association he now valued was friendship, and with He Xinyin he maintained that teachers were supreme friends: "I say that teachers and friends are essentially the same. How could the two be different?" (Li 2016: 25).

Li Zhi decided to shave his head, but not his beard, and to wear Buddhist robes. He also moved into a Buddhist temple with two nuns who some said were his lovers. When asked why he had shaved his head, he gave every answer save that he had become a Buddhist, which he probably had not: it was an attempt to get cooler during summer; he needed to be free from his family; it was a spontaneous act of individualism; it was just a trick to get attention (Petersen 1998: 747). Li Zhi did not just preach relativism; he embodied it.

On a wall in his new Buddhist home hung a picture of Kongzi, and beneath it Li Zhi wrote:

People all consider Confucius to have been a great sage. I too believe he was a great sage. Everybody believes that Laozi and the Buddha were heretics. I too think of them as heretics. The masses do not really understand the difference between a great sage and a heretic. This is because they have become accustomed to certain ideas by listening to the teachings of their fathers and teachers. But then, fathers and teachers do not really understand the difference between a great sage and a heretic, because these fathers and teachers have become accustomed to listening to the teachings of prior Confucians. Moreover, the prior Confucians did not really understand the difference between a great sage and a heretic. They just based their opinions on what Confucius said.

When Confucius said, "As for being a sage, I am not able to become one," this was because of his modesty. When he said, "Rushing into heretical causes is a cause of great misfortune," he was undoubtedly speaking of Laozi and the Buddha. (Li 2016: 289–90)

Li Zhi was obviously undermining every –ism, but there is nonetheless reason for counting him as an extreme Ru radical. His essay "The Three Teachings all Return to Ru Doctrine" (*Sanjiao gui rushuo*) suggest he privileged Ru philosophy, and his thinking was primarily shaped by the ideas of Wang Yangming and key thinkers in the Taizhou school (see de Bary 1991a: 233–57).

Li Zhi was no friend of Ru as scholar-officials, however, and de Bary perceptively observes that Li Zhi actually anticipated the wholesale rejection of Ruism by the New Culture Movement of the twentieth century (Chapter 8) (de Bary 1991a: 212). This is very apparent in a book he published in 1590, called *A Book to Burn* (*Fenshu*), and its sequel a decade later, entitled *A Book to Conceal* (*Cangshu*). In them, he lampoons traditional Ru and their oppressive moralizing. He sought to flaunt virtually every accepted view, not in order to make way for some new orthodoxy, but solely to show all beliefs were mere fashions: "Yesterday it was right, today it is wrong; today it is wrong, and tomorrow it is once again right." His relativism was paired with an uncompromising individualism whereby, in the absence of fixed external authority, each person should be free to do as they please: "Concerning what people view as right and wrong, there is no determined standard. As for people judging others as right or wrong, here too there is no established view" (Li 2016: 317–18).

This is anarchism born of an extreme rendition of Wang Yangming's innate or intuitive knowledge (*liangzhi*). Li Zhi believed human nature was originally untainted, and thus all that was required was that people preserve or recover their "child-like heart-mind" (*tongxin*): "The childlike heart-mind is the genuine heart-mind ... Losing the genuine mind is losing the genuine self" (Li 2016: 107). All talk of Principle espoused by Cheng-Zhu orthodoxy was an inauthentic imposition on the innocence of the child-like heart-mind; it was all "phony." Li Zhi also distrusted the Classics: "Who knows whether more than half these writings are *not* words from the mouths of sages?" he asked, and even if they were accurate records they contained sages' advice for their own times, which may not be relevant to ours. These books had, however, become "a crib sheet for those belonging to the School of Principle, a fountainhead for phonies" (Li 2016: 109–10).

For Li Zhi, as long as it was an authentic expression of the heart-mind, anything went. This entailed embracing emotion (*qing*) and desire (*yu*) as genuine expressions of the self. One of Wang Yangming's more moderate followers described him as say-ing "wine, sex, money, and power" were no obstacle to sagehood, adding: "Who would not want to follow someone who sanctioned such things?" (cited in de Bary 1991a: 262).

A more charitable assessment from a modern perspective might note Li Zhi was a "Confucian feminist" (Lee 2000) who advocated the equal relationship between hus-band and wife as an archetypal human bond, and questioned the necessity of invari-ably bowing to hierarchical authority. Rulers tend not to be charitable, however, and in 1602 he was arrested for licentiousness, maligning Kongzi, and publishing misleading books that, true to their prophetic titles, were banned and destroyed, although this just added to their appeal. Li Zhi, individualist to the end, died by cutting his own throat. As he bled, the horrified jailer asked why he taken such a drastic step. Unable to speak, Li traced his reply across his palm: "What else could a man of seventy do?" (Huang 1981: 220).

* * *

Some later Chinese historians blamed the wild ideas of the Taizhou school for the downfall of the Ming Dynasty, but this was nonsense. It was not just a case of seduc-tive ideologies and vibrant, charismatic teachers that drew the huge followings. The primary appeal was that their new doctrines resonated with lived experience in the late Ming. Agricultural advances had weakened the place of the family as an economic unit, mercantile wealth had added new dimensions to social mobility, and late Ming imperial complacency had made official life un-alluring. Old institutions were found wanting, yet it was a time of prosperity, creativity, and progress when anything seemed possible.

Li Zhi was, for example, less radical than we might imagine in his views on women, as he lived in a world where, for the first time, women were sometimes permitted to study and teach. Most women as wives and concubines still cultivated their intellectual talents from the confines of the "inner chambers" (Ko 1994), but love and intellec-tual companionship were increasingly being promoted as a basis for the relationship between women and men. The sweeping influence of this dangerous idea is seen in the immense popularity of the play *The Peony Pavilion* (*Mudan ting*, 1598), which is a homily on the virtues of emotion (*qing*). The author, Tang Xianzu, was a great admirer of Li Zhi. The heroine of his play, both desirous and the object of desire, is a woman who devotes her days to studying the Classics. To be compatible intellectual partners, men and women required equal education: "Except she lacks ambition for fame and office, instruction of the girl pupil parallels the boys" (Birch 1980: 29). The drama was immensely influential, and when a printed version appeared, it was said that "there was no man of letters or scholar without a copy on his desk" (Lin Yining, cited in Zeitlin 1994:128). Even Kongzi might have approved of it, if we are to believe Li Zhi: "It may have been in hopes of encountering [a person with a woman's body and a man's vision] that the Sage Confucius wandered the world" (Li 2016: 31).

The Three Bonds had apparently become negotiable, and in the late Ming the Classics were seen as being not only compatible with but also a path to women's advancement. Although the Qing dynasty quickly curtailed these liberal views, they were significant in anticipating current attitudes toward gender. Today, even among the most conservative Ru revivalists, I know of no one who advocates returning to promote the authority of husbands over wives.

Returning to the evidence

When the Manchus overthrew China to form the final Qing dynasty (1644–1912), the last thing the new overlords needed were bamboo gazers, mind contemplators, and bald-headed relativists. They faced the daunting task of governing a massive country where Han Chinese outnumbered them fifty to one, and to do so they required a tight and efficient administration. They quickly saw the potential for reviving the gentry, the scholar-official class trained in Ru orthodoxy, to mediate between centralized and regional governments. The Ru they needed were not wild heretics full of "empty talk." This was the time for a tough, practical, no-nonsense Ruism, rationalistic, empirical, staunchly moralistic, and relatively disinterested in metaphysics.

The gentry found themselves in a bind. They obviously believed that China should be ruled by the Chinese, but the late Ming rulers had been disastrous and had alienated Ru as scholar-officials, whereas early Manchu emperors were in fact excellent caretakers who had restored their status. They managed their conflict of interests in several ways. One was to downplay the cosmic significance of kingship. A bold exposition of this position appeared in Huang Zongxi's (1610–95) *Waiting for the Dawn* (*Mingyi daifang lu*), completed in 1662. Huang maintained early sage-kings were men who toiled tirelessly on behalf of the people, but the event of hereditary kingship fueled the misconception that rulers were privileged individuals who owned the land and people: "In ancient times all-under-Heaven were considered the master, and the prince was the tenant … Now the prince is master, and all-under-Heaven are tenants." Huang recommended decentralizing power—"the world is too big for one man to govern"— so that the burden of responsibility fell on Classically trained ministers who acted with the interests of the people at heart (de Bary 1993: 92, 94).

Decentralizing power would allow Ru officials some semblance of autonomy and integrity while they served a foreign regime. It permitted them to claim they were not primarily aiding alien masters, but rather caring for their native charges. This became apparent in the Qing tendency for Ru to increasingly concentrate their attention on local government. This had been occurring in the late Ming, but during the Qing there was a discernible shift in tone. The freewheeling "everyone is a sage" attitude of the late Ming was quickly replaced by a conservative swing promoting traditional moral values and ritual practices (*li*). This too should be seen in the context of Manchu rule. Ritual became a way of defining a distinctly Chinese ethnicity. This was especially pertinent at a time when certain Manchu cultural practices, such as the queue hairstyle (shaved forehead, braided ponytail), was being enforced. Kai-wing Chow nicely observes the tensions involved: "By devoting themselves to the study and practice of proper rituals, Chinese scholars were consciously setting themselves apart from the alien conquerors. They had lost control to the Manchus in the political arena, but they were still able to live as Chinese and to show contempt toward the culturally inferior 'barbarians'." This, perhaps, helped "mitigate the sense of guilt of those who served the Manchus" (Chow 1994: 91, 45).

Once reserved for an elite, since the late Ming Ru ritual practice had increasingly permeated all levels of society (Liu 2013: 4–8). As the *Rites Records* had insisted that "the rules of ceremony do not go down to the common people" (Legge 1885: vol 27, 90), this was a significant reorientation. It could not have occurred without increasing literacy (Rawski 1979) and the growing demand for printed books. The best sellers were works every household could use, foremost of which were almanacs (*tongshu*); as one Qing ritual handbook said, "No household is complete without an almanac" (Smith 1992: 9). Almanacs typically contained accessible collections of sayings of the sages as well as guides to ritual occasions (Li 1993). The importance of filial piety spread through numerous renditions of *Twenty-Four Paragons of Filial Piety* (*Ershisi xiao*), a popular descendant of the stories compiled for elite families during the Period of Division (Chapter 4). There were countless illustrated editions that were intelligible even to illiterate people, and individual paragons were also the subject of popular dramas (e.g., Idema 2009, also Guo 2005). By late imperial times, these tales were known to almost everyone and served as the lay person's *Classic of Filial Piety* (Figure 14). Picture books illustrating the life of Kongzi were another favorite with publishers and these made the Master's own observation of *li* intelligible even to those who could not read and to "many who could never set foot in a Confucian temple" (Murray 1997: 122). Another ubiquitous work that by late imperial times could be "found in almost every home" was Zhu Xi's *Family Rituals* (*Jiali*), or at least a simplified version thereof (Ebrey 1991a: xiii). Zhu Xi wrote the book to redress the influence of Buddhism and Daoism on marriages, funerals, and ancestral rites, and it became the standard reference for these ceremonies in late imperial China.

***

The transition from the spontaneity and eccentricity of the Taizhou school to the formalities of ritual norms obviously demanded major philosophical reassessment. This revision revoked the sovereignty of the individual in favor of formal cultural conventions, and transferred authority away from the inner reaches of the heart-mind in order to reestablish the supremacy of the Classics. As we will see, fidelity to the Classics and the revival of ritual were inseparable in Qing thought.

Although examinations continued to be based on Zhu Xi's commentaries, many Qing dynasty Ru very politely said they believed the great Song philosopher had sometimes been very wrong. Their recurrent complaint was that he had inadvertently contaminated Ru teachings with Buddhist and Daoist doctrines. Zhu Xi's bifurcation of existence into *qi* and *li* (Principle) was the main concern. When Principle subsequently

FIGURE 14   *Lady Tang breastfeeding her mother-in-law.*

Twenty-Four Paragons of Filial Piety (Ershisi xiao) was written in the early fourteenth century and remained popular thereafter. All the paragons were men serving their parents, except for Lady Tang, whose piety was shown to her husband's toothless mother who she breastfed until the old Dame finally died.

The sons did not get off any lighter. One dressed and behaved as an infant so his parents would not dwell on the fact they were getting old; another lay naked throughout the night so mosquitoes would not bother his parents. Impoverished Guo Jo was ready to bury his son so he would not compete for mother's food, although he found a chest of gold when digging the hole and they all lived happily ever after. And poor Yu Qianlou had to come to the aid of doctors who could not diagnose his father's complaint without a description of the taste of his excrement.

came to be identified with the heart-mind, Ruism virtually turned into Chan (Zen) and opened the way for the rampant excesses of the late Ming when anything and everything could be justified as being true to nature and heart-mind. Qing Ru rejected the existence of Principle as a fundamental metaphysical reality, sometimes reviving Zhang Zai as they returned to the solitary world of *qi* (Ng 1993). They made a strong case, for while *qi* is well established in the Classics, they do not mention *li*, at least not as a defining characteristic of existence.

To avoid the unfounded speculation of the Song and Ming, Qing Ru stressed the importance of establishing all truth claims in solid evidence. The main intellectual movement of the Qing is thus known as Evidential Studies (*kaozhengxue*). The name can be misleading if it conjures scientific notions of evidence, although subjects such as astronomy, mathematics, and geography were certainly included in the Qing research arsenal. Think rather of "evidence" in law, which is often drawn from documentary precedent and based on textual interpretation. As a verb, *kaozheng* means "to verify," but as a noun, it means "textual criticism," and the primary tools of Qing scholarship were methods of textual analysis including philology, paleography, phraseology, phonology, etymology, and epigraphy. The charismatic and quirky leaders of the late Ming were replaced by generations of very bookish Ru. Their biographies tend toward the bland, but their scholarship could be impressive, even by modern standards.

Qing Ru sought to undo the excesses of the Song and Ming dynasties by reviving the commentarial traditions of the Han, for which they had newfound respect. Evidential Studies is thus also known as Han Learning (*Hanxue*). They claimed that ritual was then paramount, just as it was the foremost concern of the Classics themselves. For instance, Huang Zongxi said in the early Qing that "the Six Classics are records of the Way, and rituals are the main structures" (Chow 1994: 52), while an encyclopedic study of rites from the eighteenth century asserted that "the intertwining coils of ritual are everywhere between Heaven and Earth" (Qin Huitian, cited in Zito 1997: 91). Kai-wing Chow has persuasively argued that one of the fundamental premises of Evidential Studies was that "the ancient sages had expounded moral doctrines not in elusive principles or theories but in concrete ritual-institutions (*li*)" (Chow 1994: 172). Again, a strong case can be made for reading the Classics in this light.

Much of the focus of Evidential Studies was on attempting to carefully uncover the original meaning of ritual texts from layers of commentary, counterfeiting, transmission error, and invention that had been silting over the books for millennia. The painstaking analysis of manuscripts, passages, and words revealed a great deal that is still valuable, such as the exposure of the Ancient Script *Documents* as a forgery. But this pedantic concentration on purifying the past meant the Qing was not noted for philosophical innovation; as Benjamin Elman's title suggests, it was a time when attention had shifted *From Philosophy to Philology*.

There were, nonetheless, unavoidable philosophical implications to the notion that ritual was the essence of Ru tradition. Their roots run back to the differences between Mengzi and Xunzi, discussed in Chapter 4. As we then saw, Mengzi maintained that everything was already "there in me," and virtuous life was for a person "to give full realization to his heart-mind" and to "understand his own nature." This was premised upon the essential goodness of human nature, which would become accepted Ru orthodoxy. Mengzi had greatly inspired the Ru revival of the Song and his authority would thus seem incontestable. In the Qing, however, as ritual came to take priority over the inherent nature of heart-mind, Xunzi's alternate position was revived. In this view, ritual was not intrinsic, but an external force imposed to regulate the wayward tendencies of human nature. Not everyone was willing to openly admit their debt to Xunzi, but his resurgent influence is unmistakable.

***

These general tendencies are exemplified in the work of Dai Zhen (1723–77), the most celebrated of all Qing Ru. Dai is as close to being a philosopher as any exponent of Evidential Studies, although in his own day he was better known for his skills in philology, trigonometry, astronomy, and hydrology. Dai was born into a small merchant family in Anhui province, and it was said he did not speak until he was eight, suggesting he had even more pent-up genius than Wang Yangming who had only remained silent six years. Stories like this add the only spice to the biography of this cordial but rather unexciting man. He was insatiably drawn to learning and his fame lies solely with his scholarship. Although he failed the metropolitan examinations six times, the emperor took pity and said he could skip them, a common concession made to aging tenacious failures. Dai was thus awarded his *jinshi* degree in 1775, just two years before he died peacefully at his friend's home.

Several of Dai Zhen's more philosophical works have survived, but his critical distance from Song-Ming Ru is only overt in his final book entitled A *Study of the Meaning of Terms in the Mengzi* (*Mengzi ziyi shuzheng*). In it, he adds his name to a list of Ru who had purged their tradition of heresy: "Mencius criticized Yangzi and Mozi. Han [Yu] criticized Laozi and the Buddhists. Now [Tai Zhen has] criticized what the Confucian texts have been saying since the Song dynasty" (Chin and Freeman 1990: 172).

Terms in Mengzi begins with a very mundane definition of Principle; it is no more than the distinctive qualities or properties that distinguish things. This quite deliberately opposes the speculations of Zhu Xi, where *li* had metaphysical independence from *qi*, and Wang Yangming, where it resided solely within the heart-mind. In both instances, says Dai, Principle is isolated from concrete reality, which allows its advocates to inject their own prejudices as they deliberate over a non-existent reality. "Of those who maintain that Principle is a thing received from Heaven and endowed in the heart-mind, there is no one who does not substitute personal opinion in place of it," he said (Chin and Freeman 1990: 75). In contrast; Dai denies that there is any Principle prior to, above, or outside of *qi* and he quite matter-of-factly says it is no more than those defining features that makes something what it is.

Dai Zhen then applied his no-nonsense dictum to morality. He was impatient with his predecessors who had employed the vagaries of Principle to argue there was a perfectly good human nature within us all just waiting to be liberated. For them, what hindered people was the intervention of desire, which was not a part of our true nature.

This, Dai said, was the nonsense of Buddhism that had subtly permeated the thinking of Ru since the Song: "The Principle they insist on preserving is nothing but an empty name and in the end amounts to nothing more than the eradication of impulses of feelings and desires. But how can such impulses be eradicated?" He maintained that desires and feelings were quite obviously integral to human nature and he prosaically noted it was simply impossible to "discard the way of nourishing life and still continue to live" (Chin and Freeman 1990: 173).

When Dai Zhen says that desires (*yu*) and feelings (*qing*) are intrinsic to human nature he is not for a moment reviving the moral relativism of the Taizhou school. Here, he cautiously crossed a precarious stretch of his philosophical terrain. Desire is natural but it is problematic and has the potential to put people at odds with one another; "selfishness arises from ... feelings and desires," and this can be socially devastating (Chin and Freeman 1990: 165). At this juncture, Dai was willing to admit his fondness for the long neglected and often rejected works of Xunzi, for he had "showed an appreciation for the profound influence of rites and righteousness" in delivering us from our great disposition for folly (Chin and Freeman 1990: 125). Yet while human nature can be problematic, Dai was not willing to say it was intrinsically bad, and in the end he rejected Xunzi in favor of Mengzi who was, of course, considered orthodox. He believed Xunzi had only considered base desire in defining human nature and had ignored human intelligence, which was equally natural. "Xunzi took rites and righteousness to be the means by which the sages taught the world to control men's natures in order to keep them from contention and rapacity, but he did not know how the ideas of rites and righteousness arose" (Chin and Freeman 1990: 92).

For Dai Zhen, sages were omniscient, the stupid were intractable, but most individuals had middling natures, had heart-minds that could appreciate the need to curb some desires to avoid conflict with other people, and could be readily persuaded to cultivate their capacity for accord. When it came to the role of ritual in curtailing human excess, Dai Zhen was in complete agreement with Xunzi: "Rites were ... devised to regulate men's feelings, either to diminish those feelings which were excessive or encourage those which were inadequate"; "the purpose of rites is to regulate man's crudities, to transform him so that he becomes cultured"; "those who become contemptuous [of rites] will do as they please without any restraints, which is the same as being animals; they are the ones who will lead the world into confusion" (Chin and Freeman 1990: 156–7).

Dai Zhen clearly believed people should modify their natural dispositions in order to conform to the Classical codes of ritual, but he awkwardly attempted to argue the rites were not foreign to human nature lest he be accused of siding with Xunzi against Mengzi. Ling Tingkan (1757–1809), a qualified admirer of Dai Zhen, took his predecessor's ideas to their logical conclusion. He boldly reversed the adjudication that had stood for nearly two millennia and frankly acknowledged that Xunzi had in fact been right all along. Like Xunzi, Ling had little faith in human nature and he believed that ritual was indispensable for shaping people's behavior in a manner contrary to the warp of their innate dispositions (Chow 1994: 191–7). Dai Zhen may not have gone this far, but the great political and social appeal of his teachings in a reactionary age was that they justified the rigorous imposition of ritual conduct and moved away from the introspective individualism of Principle Learning and Heart-Mind Learning.

***

Although Qing Ru were rediscovering Xunzi's views on humanity and the role of ritual in cultivating our imperfect selves, their vision was less comprehensive that that of Xunzi himself. As we saw in Chapter 4, Xunzi believed ritual had the potential to completely transform society, to bring Heaven to completion, and even to render everyone a sage. For most of the Qing, Ru had little interest in sagehood, and they were not pursuing utopian transformations of society. Rather, they were concerned with the more modest capacity for ritual to lift moral standards, improve social efficiency, and define Chinese cultural identity. Whereas Song-Ming Ru had very evidently pursued those ultimate transformations that (for our purposes) define religious traditions, Qing scholars were not overtly interested in such things. They may have purged Ru Learning of Buddhism and Daoism, but they did not provide any *religious* alternative. Consequently, as Judith Berling has observed, they created a vacuum that was partially filled by a resurgent interest in Buddhism, even among Ru themselves (Berling 1983: 214).

Was Qing dynasty Ru Learning at all religious? Modern exponents of New Ru Learning (Chapter 9) suggest it was not, and Mou Zongsan angrily claimed that by abandoning the quest for sagehood Evidential Studies had single-handedly killed Chinese philosophy (Mou 2015b: 468; Clower 2014: 180–7). More objectively, Tu Weiming has observed that Qing scholarship's "main concern is neither internal self-cultivation nor the transformation of society by ritual acts but scholarship as a way to be human" (Tu 1993: 118), and Liu Shuxian that "the key difference between the Qing scholars and Song-Ming Neo-Confucian philosophy is that the Qing scholars had totally lost the transcendent perspective and become exclusively humanist or naturalist" (Liu 2003: 3). Despite such views, which represent a consensus, Rodney Taylor has argued that "contrary to most interpretation," at least some exponents of Evidential Studies "can still be thought of as religious." Yet even he is obliged to add there were many exceptions and admit there was "much less attention given to discussions of sagehood in Qing thought" (Taylor 2004: 175, 173).

By the nineteenth century, some Qing scholars were themselves becoming frustrated with the seeming impotence of antiquarian textual studies. They indeed wanted to see the world transformed and from among their ranks the claim would be made, and made for the first time, that Ruism might actually be "a religion."

This was a time when the Qing was in decline and Western powers were a rapidly escalating threat. Among those initially trained in Dai Zhen's lineage of Evidential Studies, there emerged a renewed interest in the *Gongyang* commentary on the *Spring and Autumn Annals*. The *Gongyang*, you may recall (Chapter 5), was a Modern Script text that managed to extract esoteric and prophetic meaning from the dry and laconic lines of the *Spring and Autumn Annals*. Dong Zhongshu and many other Han Ru had been devoted to it, but it went into decline in the Later Han (along with the apocryphal literature to which it was related) due to its potential for fueling political unrest. Since the fall of the Han, the *Gongyang* had largely been ignored.

Evidential Studies had exposed the fact that certain Ancient Script versions of the Classics were in fact forgeries. There was no hidden agenda in this discovery. Subsequent thinkers, less scholarly but more visionary, began to make a major issue out of the Ancient Script – Modern Script distinction. They began crying conspiracy. China had been deceived for millennia by the Ancient Script Classics when the Modern Script texts in fact contained Kongzi's true teachings. And from the *Gongyang*, they knew that the Master had taught that the Way of the Ru was in fact the Way of the King (*wangdao*), a political vision that culminated in the realization of the utopian Great Peace and Great Unity. This is a theme we will pursue throughout the next chapter.

This chapter has arrived at the twilight of imperial China. Ru Learning today extends and refashions ideas already well established during the Ming and Qing. The more liberal representatives are the philosophers associated with New Ru Learning who emphasize self-transformation by cultivating the inner sage (*neisheng*). Most are heavily indebted to the thought of Wang Yangming. They tend to be politically moderate, defend liberal democracy, and would not be unduly disturbed by the social freedoms of the late Ming. They are discussed in Chapter 9.

The other modern manifestation of Ru Learning sees it as having a commitment to the Way of the King (*wangdao*), that is, to a political manifestation of Ru ideology. Two names stand out: Kang Youwei during the late nineteenth and early twentieth century, and Jiang Qing, who remains very active today. Significantly, both men wrote books on, and drew inspiration from, the *Gongyang* commentary. They provide the respective foci for Chapters 8 and 10.

PART FOUR

The Third Epoch: Modern China

As yet, a third epoch is just a possibility. It is something many modern exponents of Ruism are striving to realize, and something some impartial observers believe might well eventuate. This is an era when Ru tradition will require radical transformation insofar as a Classical education is no longer the pathway to government employment. It is also a time when the tradition must come to terms with Western political institutions and scientific claims to monopolize truth.

Chapter 8 looks at the turbulent decades between the fall of the empire and the Cultural Revolution and forges an essential link connecting the imperial past with recent revivals. Histories of Ruism tend to skim over this era, but it is essential to understand it in order to comprehend events that are unfolding today. This chapter weaves a multitude of movements around one concept: the Great Unity. This utopian ideal, attributed to Kongzi, was evoked again and again when constructing new sociopolitical models for post-imperial China. This chapter traces a pendulum swinging between extremes of Kongzi veneration and iconoclasm, culminating in the anti-Kongzi campaign of the 1970s. This campaign, I suggest, actually heralded the beginning of the current renaissance.

Chapter 9 is devoted to New Ru Learning, a philosophical tradition that centers around the teachings of individuals who left mainland China when the Communists came to power in 1949. The crucial "second generation" had moved to Hong Kong and Taiwan, while their "third generation" followers were mostly based in the United

States. I consider the motivation for bringing their ideas back to mainland China in the 1980s and examine how the actual "movement" of New Ru Learning was created in the process. The representative philosophies of Xiong Shili and Mou Zongsan are discussed in detail.

Chapter 10 is devoted to the twenty-first century. It looks at a wide range of contemporary revivals from advocates of various forms of Ru governance through to state celebrations of Kongzi's birthday, attempts to have Kongzi-religion officially recognized, the emergence of new places of worship and study, and popular movements for chanting the Classics. I conclude with two mass media representations of Kongzi and I use the public response to them as a segues to speculate on the fate of the Way of the Ru in the near future.

8

The Great Unity

Surely everyone in mainland China has heard of the Great Unity or *datong*. It is universally known in Taiwan as it is in the national anthem: "we advance into a state of *datong*." And in 2008, it very nearly went global when the World of Great Unity (*shijie datong*) was being considered as the theme of the Beijing Olympics (Leibold 2010: 21). At Kongzi's birthday celebrations in the preceding year, a government official proclaimed:

> The Olympic Games
> Joyfully arrive at our capital city.
> To the whole world,
> We are awe-inspiring
> The Great Unity (*datong*) is not a mere dream. (Billioud and Thoraval 2015: 210)

It is also well understood that the concept of the Great Unity comes from Kongzi. You need only watch Hu Mei's movie *Kongzi* (2010) to learn this. In a solemn scene early in the film, the Master reveals his vision for a perfect society. People would care for others as though they were their own parents and children. Everyone would diligently see to their allotted tasks. Orphans, widows, the old, sick, and weak would all be treated with kindness. This would be the Great Unity.

Neither the utopian image nor the term *datong* can be found in the *Analects*. Hu Mei is drawing her dialogue from the Kongzi of the *Liyun* ("Conveyance of Rites"), one of the books incorporated into the *Rites Records* (*Liji*). Although the chances of authenticity are perilously close to zero, some modern scholars nonetheless feel the Great Unity is almost definitive of the Way of the Ru. Indeed, one academic book published in 2012 actually does "define 'Confucianism' as a general system of social and political ethics that Confucius, Mencius, and their followers advocated to build a moral community of *datong shehui* (Great Unity society)" (Shin 2012: 74). The Great Unity is also seen as one of the most relevant legacies of Ru tradition for today. A recent book by two Korean authors advocates *The Great Equal Society* (their rendition of *datong*) as a "Confucian utopia" superior to liberal democracy (Kim and Kim 2014). Again, in a published conversation between Tu Weiming and Daisaku Ikeda, Ikeda refers to the *datong* as "a pillar of Chinese philosophy" that has "an invaluable gift to make to the world," to which Tu replied: "I agree that the concept … is certainly a globally significant Chinese legacy" (Tu and Ikeda 2011: 61).

Although the *Liyun*'s depiction of the Great Unity has been deemed to be "one of the most celebrated [passages] in Confucian literature" (de Bary, Chan, and Watson 1960: 175), it in fact only became prominent in modern times. Tu and Ikeda suggest as much and in context Ikeda spoke of "a pillar of Chinese philosophy set forth in the works of Kang Youwei, Tan Sitong, and Sun Yat-sen," some of the key figures of this chapter. As we will see, *datong* only came to the fore when Kongzi was making his entry into the modern world.

References to the *Liyun* were rare before the nineteenth century, and the *Rites Records* had been used with caution. Although the *Great Learning* and the *Doctrine of the Mean* had been extracted from it, an ever-increasing number of Ru came to suspect that, on the whole, the *Liji* was a forgery (Nylan 2001: 175; Liu and Habberstad 2014: 296–7). Zhu Xi, for instance, presumed the original Ru ritual corpus had been lost and so he concluded that "parts of [the *Liji*] can be believed, parts of it cannot" (Ching 2000: 74). As the *Liyun* smacked of Mohism and Daoism, it was regarded with suspicion.

The *Liji* was not the only Classic that had spent time on the sideline. The *Gongyang Commentary Spring and Autumn Annals* (*Chunqiu gongyang*) had also been largely ignored since the fall of the Han. Significantly, the *Gongyang* and the *Liyun* would be revived at much the same time. In the Han, the *Gongyang* had been interpreted to refer to an age of Great Peace (*taiping*), and this came to be equated with the *Liyun*'s Great Unity (*datong*) in the nineteenth century. With hindsight, it is easy to imagine why these texts had been eschewed. They have a utopian zeal unsettling to established political orders. It is no coincidence they became prominent at the very moment Kongzi was becoming a revolutionary.

These developments are primarily associated with Kang Youwei. This too is common knowledge that you can pick up from Evans Chan's recent film about Kang called *Datong* (2011) or his libretto for an opera of the same name (2014; see Chan 2015). Kang Youwei is focal to this chapter, but he was not the first to proclaim the Great Peace and the Great Unity. Although it is difficult to discern precisely how they resurfaced, it is very clear who was responsible for spreading these dangerous doctrines throughout China. It was Jesus's little brother.

Jesus's little brother condemns the Ru

In the late eighteenth century, China was at a peak. Massive in territory and population, it dominated world trade and kept foreigners confined to a few coastal trading ports where transactions were carefully regulated and heavily taxed.

By the mid-nineteenth century, China was a mess. Opium had been illegally imported by foreign powers to "balance trade," and when this was resisted, the British warships arrived. The scientific revolution had given the West a decided advantage in the art of killing. Qing authorities had no choice but to sue for peace, pay an indemnity, open their ports, and cede Hong Kong. This was in 1842. Over the next few decades, more treaty ports were forced open, foreign legations were established in Beijing, and the importation of opium was legalized.

Hong Xiuquan (1814–64) lived during this crisis. He came from a farming community in southern China where the foreign presence was centered. His family scraped together money for his education, and Hong did very well in the entrance examination. Then, in 1836, he set out for Guangzhou to sit the provincial exams, where three things happened. First, he became acquainted with the teachings of the Gongyang school briefly mentioned at the end of the previous chapter. The evidence for this is thin, but they were very active in this region (Boardman 1952: 116), and Hong was definitely introduced to the *Gongyang*'s doctrine of the Great Peace (*taiping*) and the *Liyun*'s Great Unity (*datong*) (Shih 1967: 210–14). Second, he picked up some Christian pamphlets and gave them a cursory glance. Third, he failed.

He failed again the following year. Despondent and exhausted, he had several terrifying dreams that included an old man lamenting that people were worshiping demons, Kongzi being whipped and reprimanded for leading the people astray, and an "elder brother" brandishing a sword and magic seal with which he was quelling demons. Some six years (and another two failures) later, Hong finally read those Christian tracts and realized the dreams revealed that he was himself the younger brother of Jesus, and God, their father, was telling Hong that his mission was to overthrow the demons who had overtaken the land: the Manchus, the idolatrous Buddhists and Daoists, and the philosophical and political imposters who were the Ru.

Hong began to preach and attract followers. His growing band thrived on persecution, and the Qing forces sent to suppress them invariably saw their numbers grow. After some major victories in 1851, they proclaimed they were ushering in a totally new religious and political order, the Heavenly Kingdom of Great Peace (*Taiping tianguo*). Two years later, they captured Nanjing, which they transformed into their new capital.

What is usually referred to as the Taiping uprising or rebellion was in fact a revolution. There had been countless Chinese rebellions that sought to overthrow the emperor and thus usurp the throne. The Taiping movement was unprecedented, however. It was, as Thomas Reilly has said, "the first movement to advocate not just the removal of the then-ruling emperor or the end of a particular dynasty but, along with this, the abolition of the entire imperial system and the institution of a whole new religious and political order" (Reilly 2004: 4–5). In challenging the legitimacy of imperial rule, the "Society of God Worshipers" (*Bai shangdi hui*), as they were also known, was equally the first to comprehensively condemn the Ru administrative edifice that had been instrumental in governing China for over two millennia.

Hong was uncompromising in his rejection of the Ru, but his attitude toward Kongzi was ambivalent. In his dream in which Kongzi was rebuked, he subsequently repented and was allowed into Heaven. Kongzi had his good points, God had to admit. He taught the truth, but he had to take some responsibility for his followers who had so thoroughly perverted his teachings (Spence 1996: 98).

Especially in their emergent phase, the Taipings were actually very dependant on the authority of the Classics and the sages. Following a precedent set by Jesuits in the late Ming, some missionaries continued to use "*Shangdi*" and "*tian*" to translate "God." As these words abound in the Classics, the Taipings believed the Classics attested to an ancient Chinese faith in the one true God. They were not rejecting the Classics, but rather forging a new *daotong* or "transmission of the way" that ran from Yao, Shun, Yu, Tang, Wen, Wu, the Duke of Zhou to Kongzi and even Mengzi before jumping two millennia to Hong Xiuquan. As they consolidated their power, the Taipings became less reliant on citing Classical sources, but they continued to employ their ideas and terminology (Shih 1967: chapter 6). Although the Taiping equivalent to the civil service examinations was based on the Bible and their own literature, the Four Books and Five Classics, suitably revised and purged of falsehood, were accepted as supplementary texts for students.

For Hong, acknowledging God as his father and Jesus as his brother was not converting to a foreign creed. Rather, it was a return to the foundation of Chinese religion that shared a common monotheistic source with the Christian faith. He wished to go back to an ideology that predated the monarchical adoption of Ru Learning and vanquish everything subsequent rulers and Ru had imposed on the land.

Taiping social values mirrored their theology. In the imperial order supported by Ru, the monarch, father of the people, occupied a pivotal sacred position and mediated with Heaven on behalf of humanity. The God Worshipers insisted God alone was "the universal Father of all in the mortal world" (de Bary, Chan, and Tan 1960: 26). The universal fatherhood of God rendered all people brothers and sisters and provided the justification for their claim that society should be egalitarian, without discrimination based on class or gender, and one in which people shared land equitably depending on their needs.

Hong regularly evoked "Kongzi's" doctrine of the Great Unity (*datong*) to encapsulate his new social order, and the *Liyun* passage was prominently cited in Taiping literature. For instance, "Proclamation on the Origin of the Way for the Enlightenment of the Age" (*Yuandao xingshi xun*) of 1852 quoted the most pertinent section, which reads:

When the Great Way (*datao*) prevailed, the world was common to all. They chose men of talent, virtue and ability, their words were sincere, and they cultivated harmony. Thus men did not love their own parents only, nor treat as children only their own sons. A competent provision was secured for the aged till their death, employment was given to the able-bodied, and a means for raising the young was provided. They showed kindness and compassion to widows, orphans, childless men, and those who were disabled by disease, so that they were all sufficiently maintained.

Men had their proper work, and women had their homes. They developed resources, disliking that they be wasted, but not for their own gratification. The labored with their strength, disliking that it should not be exerted, but not exerting it only for their own advantage. In this way selfish schemes were repressed and could not develop. Robbers, filchers, and rebellious traitors did not show themselves, and hence outer doors remained open, and were not shut. This was called the Great Unity (*datong*). (Legge 1885: vol. 27, 364–6, modified)

Turning this description of a past age into prophesy, Hong added: "But how can such a state of society be hoped for? Nevertheless, when disorder comes to the worst, order is elicited; when darkness is extreme, the light is found to spring up—this is the Way of Heaven" (Shih 1967: 119–20).

The Taipings became so powerful they feasibly could have taken China had they managed to enlist Western support. They briefly generated some foreign enthusiasm, but disillusion soon followed as the gulf between rhetoric and reality became apparent. The Taiping presence was disrupting trade, and the rebels' values were not conducive to Western economic interest. It was thus that Western troops rallied with the imperial forces, and by 1864, the year in which Hong died, the revolution was effectively over. It had cost some 20–30 million lives.

* * *

Once the Taipings were defeated, a more optimistic spirit settled, and there was growing enthusiasm for engaging with the wider world. But there were two urgent concerns. First, after the humiliation of being defeated by the West, China had to restore national dignity and pride. Second, this was impossible without modernization. There simply was no traditional reply to superior weapons, steamships, trains, telegraphic communication, and so on.

Modernization and China's extant education system were clearly incompatible. Simply acquiring Western commodities was no solution; China had to learn to manufacture them and use them professionally, which in turn demanded specialized scientific and technical training. A Classical education was quickly becoming an anachronism, yet renouncing the legacy of the sages ran the risk of sacrificing China's distinctive heritage so that the country was subsumed by Western cultural values. This would hardly restore dignity and pride.

One solution was, in effect, to replace Ruism with "Confucianism." That is, a distinction was now emerging between the way of Kongzi and the early sages and the subsequent Way of the Ru that had prevailed in imperial China—precisely the division that was central to Taiping theology. Kongzi was increasingly being identified with the essence of Chinese cultural values while institutionalized Ruism was being deemed to be incompatible with China's future.

This shift coincided with the Western invention of Confucianism, discussed in the first chapter. As I then mentioned, Wang Tao (1828–97) was important both to changing Chinese views and, as James Legge's collaborator, to emerging Western conceptions.

Wang is known as the "father of Chinese journalism," and his widely circulated writings had a massive impact. Although he passed the initial examinations, Wang abandoned his civil service aspirations and from 1849 worked for thirteen years as a translator for the London Missionary Society in Shanghai. He was accused of supporting the Taipings by sending tactical suggestions to their leaders, and it was even rumored he had attained the highest degree from the Taiping examination system (Tsui 2010: 125–6). True or not, he too saw Kongzi as championing the new world of the Great Unity.

Wang Tao maintained Kongzi was a reformer. In about 1870, he wrote: "The Way of the sages is valued only because it can make proper accommodations according to the times. If Confucius lived today, we can be certain he would not cling to antiquity and oppose making changes" (de Bary, Chan, and Tan 1960: 57). Two thousand years of Ru ritual practice, philosophical debate and service to the state were brushed aside in favor of a simple: "What would Kongzi do today?"

Wang Tao insisted that China must modernize and he said that "within a hundred years China will adopt all Western methods and excel in them." This was precisely what Kongzi would prescribe. At the same time, China would retain its cultural identity, which was the perennial heart of the "Way of Kongzi." Wang had a utopian vision of Kongzi paired with progress leading to the *datong*. "The Way of Confucius is the Way of Man. As long as humankind remains, the Way will remain unchanged ... I have said before that after a few hundred years the Way will achieve a Great Unity (*datong*) ... It will harmonize the various teachings of the world and bring them back to the same source" (de Bary, Chan, and Tan 1960: 56).

In the ensuing years, *datong* increasingly peppered Chinese discourse. While it evoked the sanction of the Sage, it invariably appeared in association with Christian or Western secular utopian ideals (Bernal 1976: chapter 1). These elements would fuse in Kang Youwei's monumental plan for the Great Unity for, as Zhang Junmai once observed, Kang's Kongzi was "the Jesus Christ of China, but in addition to this he had progressive ideas" (Chang 1962: 420). As we will see in this chapter, Kang Youwei's proposals pervaded the first half of the twentieth century. And in Chapter 10 we will witness his vision being resurrected by today's revivalists.

Kang Youwei's Great Unity

In 1898, Kang Youwei (1858–1927) convinced the young Qing Emperor to abandon millennia of absolute monarchy in favor of constitutional monarchy and to thoroughly reform the educational, economic, and military systems. As a part of this plan, Kang advised the emperor that every Buddhist and Daoist temple and academy be confiscated and converted into schools promoting the teachings of Kongzi—a kind of "Confucian fundamentalism" (Goossaert 2006: 313). He recommended setting up Kongzi churches throughout China, with clergy to lead the reading of Classics on Sundays. Kang felt it was necessary for China to be religiously united, to have something equivalent to, yet distinct from, Christianity in West. Kongzi was recast as the founder of religion and *Kongjiao* or Kongzi-religion was being proposed as the exclusive religion of the state (*guojiao*). As the symbol of national unity, Kongzi was to take the place previously occupied by the emperor, Son of Heaven. As such, Kang had turned Kongzi the sagacious teacher into Kongzi the emblem of Chinese national identity.

It took just over 100 days for conservatives to gain the support of the Empress Dowager in deposing the emperor and putting an end to these reforms. Although his brother and his follower Tan Sitong (see discussion later here) were executed, Kang managed to flee the country and continue to advocate his reforms from abroad.

But just how could Kang associate Kongzi with constitutional monarchy and a parliamentary system heading toward democracy? Wasn't Kongzi committed to the Heaven-sanctioned rule of sage-kings? Again, how do we reconcile Kongzi with modernization? Did he not look back to a past golden age rather that toward a utopian future made possible by rapid change and progress? To answer these questions, we need to retrace our steps to consider Kang's background and broader philosophical orientation.

***

Kang Youwei was born into a prominent scholarly family in Guangdong (the hub of Opium Wars and Taiping revolutionaries) and received a Classical education. He passed the entrance exams but failed at the provincial level and became dismissive of the whole examination process, although he would later obtain the highest *jinshi* degree. He now rejected Zhu Xi's commentaries on the Classics, saying they were "all empty and lacking in substance." At this stage he was drawn to Chan (Zen), and on one occasion he had an awakening reminiscent of that of Wang Yangming who he greatly admired and whose writings had introduced him to Buddhism. In meditation, he wrote, "I would suddenly come to the realization that the universe and the myriad things were all a part of me. A light dawned on me, and [I believed] I was a sage" (K'ang 1967: 33–4). He perhaps saw this as a step toward his youthful "desire to become the founder of a religion and of surpassing Confucius" (Hsiao 1975: 22). Kang believed he was destined by Heaven for greatness. Not surprisingly, his opponents could find him conceited, unrealistic, autocratic, and arrogant.

Although some have speculated Kang Youwei was inspired by Taiping ideology, he never acknowledged this in his writings (Hsiao 1975: 500). Kang rarely admitted to his sources. What he does say is that he next began to align himself with (others said plagiarize from) the thought of those scholars who were promoting the Modern Script Classics and rejuvenating the *Gongyang* commentary. They may well have been the source of Hong Xiuquan's own doctrines of the Great Peace and Great Unity, but here too the trail goes cold. We can but note a convergence of thought.

According to Kang Youwei, the Gongyang school had revealed the entire history of Ru Learning had been a massive conspiracy. Kang greatly admired Zisi and Mengzi, but even they only presented secondary interpretations of the Master's teachings. The Modern Script Classics, on the other hand, contained Kongzi's actual words as the commentaries on the *Spring and Autumn Annals* had been passed down by an inner circle of disciples. Because Dong Zhongshu had strictly based himself on these texts, the *Gongyang* in particular, he was seen by Kang Youwei as being superior even to Mengzi. Dong had persuaded emperor Wu to institute true Ru Learning as state religion, and "in Han times every family" followed Ru doctrine, he said. "The usurper" Wang Mang and arch-forger Liu Xin had undermined this, however, replacing the Modern Script Classics with counterfeit Ancient Script versions that omitted the Master's vision of a perfect world order. China was thus cast "in darkness for two thousand years" (Hsiao 1975: 80). Needless to say, Kang Youwei was a shoddy historian (Saussy 2008), but some of his fanciful ideas have proven surprisingly difficult to eradicate (e.g., see Nylan 1994; van Ess 1994).

Kang Youwei's philosophy was in fact very heavily indebted to Buddhism, Christianity, and recent Western theories of progress, but he sanctions all this through the exclusive authority of Kongzi. Kongzi, he said, "was the founder of a religion. He was a sagely king with spiritual intelligence. He was a counterpart of Heaven and Earth and nourished all things. All human beings, all events, and all moral principles are encompassed in his great Way. Thus he was the Great Perfection and Ultimate sage" (Chan 1963a: 728). No one before Kang had suggested Kongzi had founded a religion as such, and again China's great sage was quite deliberately being recast in the mold of the West's savior.

Kang Youwei presented Kongzi as a reformer who believed in social progress. What of *Analects* 7:1: "I transmit but do not innovate; I am ... devoted to antiquity?" "This is an interpolation, taken from a spurious" Ancient Script source, Kang conveniently retorted (Hsiao 1975: 83). The "real" Kongzi of the *Gongyang* tradition revealed that history progresses through three distinct phases in which the future will eclipse all things past.

The *Gongyang* itself makes no such claim, but Han commentaries on that commentary had teased out various patterns to history. Dong Zhongshu said the *Gongyang* revealed the rise and fall of kingdoms was determined by three-phase historic cycles (Arbuckle 1995). Toward the end of the Han, He Xiu (129–182) had proposed a linear three-phase progression, moving from periods of anarchy, through growing accord, to arrive at the *taiping* or Great Peace. For He, these were past ages reaching their zenith at the time of Kongzi, but there were also late-Han millennial movements proclaiming that the *taiping* would soon arrive (Hendrischke 2006: Introduction). The Taiping revolutionaries, it would seem, were modern inheritors of that expectation.

Kang Youwei also had a tripartite view of world transformation, but rather than Dong's eternal cycles or He's ancient history of linear development, he believed Kongzi had professed ongoing progress. Kang's descriptions actually sound suspiciously like Western theories of social evolution, although characteristically, he never acknowledged the debt (Pusey 1983: 15). Kongzi had thus apparently taught that human history advanced from the Age of Disorder through the Age of Rising Peace to ultimately arrive at the Age of Great Peace.

Confucius was born in the Age of Disorder. Now that communications have extended throughout the great earth and important changes have taken place in Europe and America, the world has entered the Age of Rising Peace. Later, when all groups throughout the great earth, far and near, big and small, are like one, when nations will cease to exist, when racial distinctions are no longer made, and when customs are unified, all will be one and the Age of Great Peace will have come. Confucius knew all this in advance. (Chan 1963a: 726)

Having prophetic foresight, Kongzi was aware that further social and political change would be necessary in the future. "History goes through an evolution, and humanity has its path of development ... Before the time is ripe, it cannot be forced," Kang said (Chan 1963a: 735). Kongzi lived in the Age of Disorder, and the reforms he sought to implement were perfectly appropriate for their day. The late nineteenth century had reached the Age of Rising Peace, however, and were he still alive, Kongzi would certainly "promote the principles of self-rule and independence and the system of parliamentarianism and constitutionalism" (Chan 1963a: 727).

Kang traced the origin of the Age of Disorder to the rise of absolute monarchy. Ru Learning in imperial China had been corrupted to reinforce this institution, despite the fact that Kongzi and Mengzi were preparing to replace it with a constitutional monarchy suited to the Age of Rising Peace. This was a necessary transitional step before arriving at the Age of Great Peace, which Kang Youwei said approximated the aspirations "of the socialist parties of various countries at present" (Hsiao 1975: 91).

***

Kang's theories explain his support for constitutional monarchy, which was a necessary transitional step to the Great Peace. His vision of that perfect world is contained in his remarkable work *Datong shu* or the *Book of the Great Unity*. Although it was completed in 1902, it was considered so radical, such "a mighty volcanic eruption and huge earthquake" (Liang 1959: 96), that only excerpts were published while Kang was still alive. The Age of Great Peace (*taiping*) was now equated with the arrival of the Great Unity or *datong*. While the *datong* is only briefly described in the *Liyun*, Kang's vision of the imminent Great Unity is a sweeping symphony of utopian imagination. And for Kang, it was no mere fantasy: "The arising of democracy, the flourishing of constitutions, the talk of unions and communism, all are the first signs of *datong*" (Thompson 1958: 86).

Datong shu begins with suffering and humaneness (*ren*). Kang sounds thoroughly Buddhist when insisting on the ubiquity of suffering; thoroughly Ru in declaring that a person who completely embraces humaneness (*ren*) cannot bear to see the distress of others. Our humaneness naturally extends to others because all beings are ultimately connected and united, something Kang had personally known since his mystical "awakening." This draws our compassion to those nearest us, needless to say, but it also reaches out to those in distant lands, to "savages," beasts, fish, insects, even grass and trees. "How about the living creatures on Mars, Saturn, Jupiter, Uranus,

Neptune? ... I wish to love (*ren*) them, [but] they are so far off I have no way to do it," he said (Thompson 1958: 66). *Ren* was a manifestation of a universal law of attraction so fundamental and pervasive that Kang quite literally equated it with ether and electricity. Today this sounds rather silly, but at the time some very reputable Western physicists were entertaining comparable kinds of electrical mysticism.

As *ren* is based on the ultimate unity of all beings, so inversely, suffering is caused by separation and distinction. Kang specifies division between states, classes, races, sexes, families, occupations, and species and advocates salvation simply by removing these spheres of distinction. For his day Kongzi might have promoted filial piety and loyalty to kings, but for the *datong* he apparently recommended abolishing familial and political boundaries in favor of small autonomous communities where men and women could change partners annually and leave the kids to be raised in public nurseries. In this highly industrialized world, where all property will be communal and where there will be no differentiation based on of class, gender or race, perfect harmony will at last prevail.

*** *

Although the complete *Datong shu* remained unpublished until 1935, many of its central ideas, including its idiosyncratic theory of the physics of *ren,* the dream of removing all social barriers to create a unified (and highly mechanized) utopia and a three-phase historic cycle culminating in the *datong*, were espoused as early as 1898 by Tan Sitong (1865–1898) in *Exposition on Ren* (*Renxue*). Tan had joined Kang during the Hundred Days' Reform but refused to flee during the coup d'etat. His martyrdom transformed him into a romantic icon of selfless devotion, and his book was widely read and had an inspirational effect.

In his Preface to *Renxue*, Liang Qichao (see discussion later here) said Tan was a disciple of Kang Youwei who wrote the book to "glorify the teaching" of his master (Chan 1984: 52). Allegedly, Tan was privy to an early draft of Kang's book. As both the discipleship and the mysterious draft have been questioned (Chan 1984: 15–16; Hsiao 1975: 49–54), it is not impossible that some similarities were rather due to Kang's *Datong shu* borrowing from Tan's *Renxue*; Kang was sometimes suspected of backdating work to cover his tracks. Tan was a creative synthesizer who presented a pioneering fusion of Ru Learning, Buddhism, and Christianity as well as making the first attempt to *philosophically* reconcile the Classics with Western science (Wright 1994).

According to Tan Sitong, Kongzi did not sanction monarchy, social hierarchy, or engendered authority. He denounced the Three Bonds and only endorsed friendship between equals. In some ways, Tan was more radical than Kang Youwei, and many of his criticisms anticipated the wholesale rejection of Kongzi that was about to erupt in China (see discussion to follow here), but he salvaged the Master by arguing that Ruism in imperial China was not true to his teachings. "The Ru have set their minds on obscuring the teaching of Confucius (*Kongjiao*) with Ruism," he said (Chan 1984: 185, modified). Ruism was thus a 2,000-year-old distortion that began with Xunzi and was perpetuated by state-sponsored Ru Learning: "Confucius thus betrayed, how very disheartened his soul must be in heaven!" (Chan 1984: 151).

Kongzi's religion

Although the Hundred Days' Reform saw the emperor locked away, Kang Youwei in exile, and Tan Sitong beheaded, the Empress Dowager knew change was inevitable, and the Qing court began to make plans to phase in constitutional monarchy.

The so-called New Policies (*xinzheng*) were a desperate attempt to salvage an empire. Insofar as the reforms relate to Ru Learning, they at first glance seem decidedly contradictory. On the one hand, in 1905 the civil service examinations were abolished, thus ending two millennia of recruiting officials based on their mastery of the Classics. On the other hand, Kongzi, the patron of that very education system and alleged author/editor of its texts, was promoted to an unprecedented status in the state sacrifices. Thus in 1906, the Manchu rulers decreed his ceremonies be elevated from the rank of Middle Sacrifice (*zhongsi*) to the highest echelon of Grand Sacrifice (*dasi*), which made rituals to him equal to those performed to Heaven and Earth. This was as close to god as Kongzi would ever get.

Beneath surface appearances, these seemingly discrepant reforms were united and reveal a new vision that endures to this day. In the past, the Ru were bureaucrats who had managed to excel in a torturously difficult series of examinations designed to weed out the vast majority of aspirants. They were the country's elite and, faced with the challenge of a new world, they were deemed to have failed. Insofar as Kongzi was primarily associated with this education system, his status had, if anything, been waning just as the Ru themselves were losing ground.

But, as we have seen with the Taiping revolutionaries and with Kang Youwei and Tan Sitong, Kongzi was increasingly being disassociated from the Ru apparatus of state. What the Manchus believed they now needed was not a small band of elite scholars, but a mass populace with specific skills, patriotism, and moral devotion to saving their country. This was Kongzi's new charter, and studying "his" Classics remained an integral part of the new school curriculum. Previously, Ru were responsible for performing sacrifices to Kongzi, but with the Sage's promotion this became the emperor's prerogative. When the emperor performed Grand Sacrifices to Heaven and Earth, the Grain, and the Imperial Ancestors, he was ritually centering those things vital to the realm. To them Kongzi's name was now added as an emblem of the nation itself. In a study of these reforms, Ya-pei Kuo perceptively highlights the legacy of this brief ritual innovation.

> For the rest of the twentieth century, Confucius would gradually fade from the centre stage of political ritual, but he remained one of the most prominent symbols of the Chinese nation ... Those who praised him upheld him as a national hero. Those who denounce him blamed him for the Chinese nation's cultural maladies. The assessment might fluctuate, but the linkage between Confucius and Chineseness would remain unbroken. (Kuo 2009: 146)

* * *

Two thousand years of imperial rule deserved a grand finale, but it ended with a fizzle. Sun Yat-sen has been mythologized as the revolution's hero, but the actual events leading to the formation of the Republic were quite nebulous. Sun was installed as provisional president in 1911, but Yuan Shikai (1859–1916), a Qing general who had made a pact with the revolutionaries, quickly forced his way into the presidency.

Kang Youwei's influence was now coming via his own presidency of the international Kongzi-Religion Society (*Kongjiao hui*), which was established in 1912 and which had over a hundred branches and a widely published journal. The society petitioned the parliament of the new Republic to establish *Kongjiao* as state religion. Their argument was that it would be cohesive insofar as Kongzi's legacy was synonymous with Chinese identity and that it would serve to match other countries' national religions.

Yuan Shikai was hardly the person Kang Youwei and his followers had in mind for the restoration, and cooperating with Yuan "greatly discredited the new Confucianist movement" (Hu 1934: 90). Yuan soon set his sights on becoming emperor and took to performing sacrifices to Heaven while dressed in imperial regalia (Figure 15). He also participated in sacrifices to Kongzi. When he died a few years later, the idea of a Kongzi state religion was tainted and seemed intrinsically opposed to the Republican cause. The Classics were dropped from school curricula, sacrifices to Heaven were terminated and those to Kongzi were confined to his hometown of Qufu and lacked any significant political association.

Kang Youwei's proposals had generated considerable debate as to whether *Rujiao* or *Kongjiao* in fact was, ever had been, or foreseeably could be a religion. The arguments were initially rather unsophisticated. Critics pointed out that since Kongzi was unwilling to discuss spirits, the afterlife and Heaven, it seemed evident "the doctrines of Confucius are not the words of a religionist" (Chan 1969: 14). The most comprehensive response to this was a book by Chen Huanzhang (1881–1933), entitled *Kongjiao lun* or *On Kongzi-Religion* (1912). Chen had inaugurated the Kongzi-Religion Society, of which he was chief executive, and his ideas amplify those the president Kang Youwei had been developing for some time. As early as 1886, Kang had made a yin-yang distinction between otherworldly religions (such as Christianity and Buddhism), which he termed *yinjiao*, and *yangjiao*, which were not world-negating. Later, in 1905, he wrote that "*jiao*, are of various sorts. Some instruct men by means of the divine way, others by means of the human way ... The essential significance of any *jiao* consists in making men avoid evil and do good" (Hsiao 1975: 113–14).

This very liberal definition of the essence of religion allowed Kang not only to define *Kongjiao* as religion but even to present it as a more evolved religious tradition. "As a founder of a religion Confucius presented an advanced stage in cultural progress," he wrote. "Now as men's intelligence gradually develops, divine authority gradually loses its hold on them. Confucianism therefore suits the present world best" (Hsiao 1975: 114). *Kongjiao*, as religion minus superstition, was eminently compatible with modernity.

FIGURE 15 *Sacrifice to Heaven in the early Republic.*

On December 23, 1914, Yuan Shikai officiated at the sacrifice to Heaven. This photograph was taken on the occasion, and the Altar of Heaven (Figure 4) is faintly discernable in the background. These boys carry peacock feathers and flutes that are distinctive features of row (*yi*) dances, also performed at Kongzi's ceremonies (compare Figure 19). Observers suspected Yuan was using Heaven and Kongzi as the central pillars for erecting a state religion. A few months later, he also participated in the sacrifices to Kongzi.

In the previous month, Yuan had announced: "Throughout our history for over two thousand years the moral teachings of Confucius have always been followed and he has been held in reverence as a most holy sage. During the creation of our new nation, he should be shown still higher honor and respect" (Johnston 1935: 153).

By 1912, Chen Huanzhang was refining these arguments to appeal to the leaders of China's new Republic:

There are all kinds of *jiao* (religions). Some instruct people by means of the divine way, some by means of the human way. Although they take different paths, they are the same in the sense that they are all *jiao* ... *Jiao*-founders of the savage world always appealed to ghosts and spirits ...; in the age of humanity, *jiao*-founders of the civilized world always emphasized moral values. This is the principle of evolution. (Chen 2013: 52)

Ru had their own scriptures, rituals, doctrines, and—in the form of schools—churches. Having established its religious credentials, Chen argued that *Kongjiao* had always been the de facto religion of China. "Since the time of Han Emperor Wu, Confucianism was the state religion; the whole country was Confucian," he said (Gan 2013: 28, 26), adding that it was as essential to the well-being of the nation as water was to the survival of fish. Chen believed that "the Chinese have the best religion—Confucianism," and that by rediscovering it "China shall be strong, the Great [Unity] of Confucius will come, and the world-state will appear" (Chen 1911: 726, 730).

Even if a liberal definition indicated that the teachings and practices of Kongzi and subsequent Ru were "religious"—and many critics were unwilling to grant even this much—this was not synonymous with conceding that *Rujiao* (or *Kongjiao*) was "*a* religion*," far less that it had ever served as the state religion of China. Ruism in the Han was very important for running the country, but it had not functioned as the religion of that dynasty. Kang's vision was thus deemed unprecedented; a reckless innovation rather than a revival of a national legacy. In 1913, a parliamentary proposal to install *Kongjiao* as state religion was crushed by an 8 to 40 vote. With this, Wing-tsit Chan concluded, "the failure of Confucianism to become a state religion was therefore complete" (Chan 1969: 13–14)—a conclusion that, remarkably, must now be reckoned premature, as we will see in the final chapter.

New culture, new Ru

When Yuan Shikai died, commanders in his army, along with sundry gangsters and local bullies, all began carving out separate power bases. This is known as the warlord period. Many of these warlords were keen on the idea of *Kongjiao* as state religion and they perpetuated their interests through the myriad "redemptive societies" I will be introducing in the next section. For the moment, we will follow the philosophers. In the midst of the chaos, intellectuals were also waging wars to determine China's future.

What was China going to do with Kongzi and Ru Learning? It is hardly surprising there was polarized opinion on this topic. Perhaps more unexpected, we can even see these extremes being expressed by one person. Liang Qichao's vacillating views were a prelude to things to come.

Liang Qichao (1873–1929), activist, scholar, and journalist, was an indefatigable writer and the most influential thinker of the early Republic. He was a friend and great admirer of Kang Youwei who he had assisted with his books upholding the Modern Script Classics and prophesying the Great Peace. He had also been Kang's confederate during the Hundred Days' Reform movement. After he fled to Japan, however, he witnessed firsthand a country's spectacular adaptation to modernity and he quickly turned his back on the past. He now cared not a whit whether a Classic be genuine or counterfeit; it was the very idea of bowing to the authority of ancient texts that he rejected. Liang had once hailed Kang's "great discovery" of social progression through three eras to arrive at the Great Peace as an independent invention of the principles of social Darwinism; he now kept Darwin and jettisoned his idiosyncratic Chinese counterpart. "And," as Joseph Levenson phrased it, "at last he comes out with it frankly: history is the story of struggle, race against race—there is no *datong* or *taiping*, he says, no Great [Unity], no Great Peace" (Levenson 1970: 91). Those who wished to promote *Kongjiao* as state religion were merely putting modern ideas into Kongzi's mouth, Liang said in 1902; they "love Confucius; they do not love truth" (Chan 1969: 9). He now denied that *Rujiao* had been a religion as "religion specifically refers to belief in super-stition," while Kongzi taught "none other than secular and social issues and moral principles" (Chen 2013: 53–4).

Liang's lucid writings disseminated by popular press inspired a new generation. He was not done yet, however. The devastation of World War I shattered his naïve faith in the inevitability of evolutionary progress. Liang suddenly saw the soullessness of mate-rial advance and proclaimed the West stood in need of spiritual salvation from China. He hastily dusted off Kongzi and Mengzi and brought them out of retirement. Darwin's ideas inappropriately applied to human society were bound to create the ruthless competi-tion that they predicted, he now realized. But, he insisted, human spiritual life was not bound by the same laws, and so "our problem is, under the conditions of this unprec-edented scientific progress, how can the Confucian ideal of equilibrium be applied so that every man may live a balanced life" (Levenson 1970: 207). And so it was that in 1913, "the almost inconceivable happens," and Liang was seen joining forces with the Kongzi-Religion Society and championing the view that *Rujiao* was the very essence of China and that it should be revived as the national religion (Levenson 1970: 196).

* * *

Liang Qichao's personal struggles with these issues were played out on a grand scale in the following decade. The disillusion with the events from the late empire until Yuan Shikai's death—many of which had been fueled by Kang Youwei's influence—led to enthusiasm for the New Culture Movement (*Xin wenhua yundong*), which had its focus in Peking University and which reached a political climax with student pro-tests on May 4, 1919 (hence it is by and large synonymous with the "May Fourth Movement"). Many of the key players had a Classical education but had turned against tradition; many others were schooled abroad and were well versed in Western philoso-phy and political thought. Their position was that modernization had become a matter of national life or death, and Ru tradition stood in the way. Previous discussion had been polite, but now the gloves were off.

Many of the critiques of the New Culture Movement had been rehearsed by Chinese anarchists studying in Japan and Paris (Zarrow 1990). An often overlooked pioneer was He-Yin Zhen (ca. 1884 – ca. 1920), an anarcho-feminist who wrote "On the Revenge of Women" (*Nüzi fuchou lun*) in 1907. Her well-informed analysis of the Classics and other prominent Ru texts led her to conclude that the "key concept" of Ruism was "none other than elevating men and depreciating women … When it comes to inflict-ing violence onto wives, the followers of Confucius are truly peerless." "All Confucian teachings," she concluded, "are teachings that kill people" (He-Yin 2013: 123–4).

Chen Duxiu (1879–1942), who would go on to become a cofounder of the Chinese Communist Party, continued this line of attack. Reacting to suggestions the constitution should acknowledge Ru ethical values, he observed that modern economic development demanded independence and freedom while Kongzi's views belonged to a feudal age dependant on hierarchy and dominance. He vocally opposed those advocating *Kongjiao* as a national religion and said: "Confucian religion and republicanism cannot coexist. To have one means to abandon the other" (Louie 1980: 6).

Chen focused on the Three Bonds in Ru tradition that placed rulers over subjects, fathers over families, and men over women, and listed the injustices that had accompanied them. As emperors were already a thing of the past, familism and patriarchy remained the primary targets of the New Culture Movement. Chen cataloged the countless restraints placed on women in the Classics and concluded: "These women have had no freedom and have endured a most miserable life. Year after year these many promising young women have lived a physically and spiritually abnormal life. All this is the result of Confucian teachings" (de Bary, Chan, and Tan 1960: 154).

Along with gender inequality, filial piety was constantly criticized. As a driving social force, *xiao* was seen to be detrimental to reform and modernization. Obediently following fathers was antithetical to progress that is dependant on the young surpassing the old. A filial son was prepared for nothing save unthinking acquiescence to the status quo. Wu Yu (1872–1949) targeted this issue and concluded that "the effect of the idea of filial piety has been to turn China into a big factory for the manufacturing of obedient subjects" (Chow 1960: 304).

The widespread desire for liberation from patriarchy and blind obedience to parents was made very apparent by the immense popularity of Ba Jin's autobiographical novel *Family* (*Jia,* 1931–2). In this book, the patriarchs upholding Ru ritual values are lascivious hypocrites whose self-serving demands lead to the death of several innocent young women. The struggle to rebel against their authority is depicted as a "struggle between parent and child for the right to freedom, love and knowledge" (Pa 2001: 237).

Another severe critic was Chen Duxiu's friend and colleague at Peking University, Hu Shi (1891–1962), a philosopher and essayist who championed liberal democracy and the supremacy of science.

> In the last two or three decades we have abolished three thousand years of eunuch system, one thousand years of foot-binding, six hundred years of the eight-legged essay, four or five hundred years of male prostitution, and five thousand years of judicial torture. None of the revolution was aided by Confucianism. (Chan 1969: 18)

The promise of liberation in these critiques had an electrifying effect on the educated youth of China. Straw effigies of Kongzi were burned and "down with Kongzi's shop," and "throw the old books into the toilet" were the slogans of the day. Hu Shi later reflected on this iconoclasm, saying:

> One of the great undertakings of the New Culture Movement was the liberation of thought. When we criticized Confucius or Mencius, impeached Cheng Yi and Zhu

Xi, opposed the Confucian religion and denied God, our purpose was simply to overthrow the canons of orthodoxy, to liberate Chinese thought, and to encourage a skeptical attitude and a critical spirit. (Grieder 1970: 230)

Hu Shi and Chen Duxiu both championed vernacular literature being used to replace the elitist, "stereotyped and monotonous literature of classicism" (Hu 1934: 54). Lu Xun (1881–1936), one of modern China's greatest authors, brilliantly captured the mood of the New Culture Movement with his first vernacular short story, "The Madman's Diary" (1918). His "madman," who has lapsed into an unsettling sanity in a deranged society, begins seeing a hidden message running through the Classics:

When I flick through the history books, I find no dates, only those fine Confucian principles "humaneness, righteousness, morality" snaking their way across each page. As I studied them again, through one of my more implacably sleepless nights, I finally glimpsed what lay between every line, of every book: "Eat people!" (Lu 2009: 24)

"*Ren* means 'eat people'" was a mantra still being chanted at the time of the Anti-Kongzi campaign of the 1970s (see discussion later here).

***

Just as Liang Qichao could easily slip between abandoning Kongzi and hailing him as China's savior, so too there were those who could sympathize with the New Culture Movement's critique of Ru tradition while promoting Kongzi revivalism. Old Ru conservatives might insist that all the talk denouncing the authority of emperors, fathers, and husbands was a load of "prattle" (Chang 1901: 44), but men like Kang Youwei, Tan Sitong, and Liang Qichao had in fact been in the vanguard of women's emancipation and social reform. Ru tradition, many believed, could shake off the shackles of the Three Bonds and, thus liberated, offer a morally rich alternative to rampant Westernization.

In 1917, the same year in which Chen Duxiu and Hu Shi were appointed, Liang Shuming (1893–1988) was also invited to take up a lectureship in Indian philosophy at Peking University. This was a significant moment, as many interpreters see Liang as a pioneer of *Xin Ruxue* (New Ru Learning), typically known as New Confucianism in English, to which the next chapter is devoted. Paradoxically, Guy Alitto's monograph on Liang was entitled *The Last Confucian*. Clearly there was a transition, a death and rebirth of Ru thought associated with Liang and his times. The last Confucian? The first New Confucian? It is a little embarrassing to learn that when asked late in his life, Liang replied that he had always considered himself to be primarily a Buddhist (Hanafin 2003).

Liang had a tremendous influence alternate to the New Culture Movement, but as he did not see himself as Ru first and foremost, he is often regarded as a forerunner rather than the founder of New Ru Learning. In 1922, Xiong Shili (1885–1968) joined Liang Shuming in the philosophy department of Peking University. Xiong is usually regarded as the true "spiritual leader" of the New Ru movement, and many considered him to be the most consummate philosopher of twentieth-century mainland China. Liang, however, thought his friend's ideas were "irresponsible tomfoolery" (Liang and Alitto 2013: 53).

There are many similarities in the thought of Liang and Xiong. Both develop their ideas out of an analysis of Buddhist "Consciousness Only" philosophy (*Weishi*, Sanskrit *Vijñaptimātra*), which was then undergoing a revival (Makeham 2014). Both too related to the "idealist" Ru tradition of Lu Xiangshan and Wang Yangming, which was itself deeply infused with Buddhist ideas. He Lin, also identified as a New Ru philosopher, insightfully reflected on this preference for Lu-Wang teachings:

> The thought of the Lu-Wang School stresses the self-consciousness of the individual person; it is more suitable to the new age, which stresses freedom of the individual and awakening the nation. The past fifty years were the time of opposition to the authority of tradition. To advocate self-consciousness and intuition inside one's inner heart-mind was helpful for opposing the authority of tradition, for getting rid of bonds and shackles. (Bresciani 2001: 219)

What is very evident and consistent in New Ru philosophy is that the millennia-old link joining Ruism with monarchy and familism is entirely broken. Indeed, by asserting that the inner realm of the heart-mind was their point of departure, they began their investigations free of any specific sociopolitical affiliation. When they returned to the world from introspective retreat, they espoused values that were thoroughly modern and entirely compatible with economic, scientific, and educational reform.

Both Liang and Xiong had been keen revolutionaries before they became academics. While they were eager to see China transform and embrace modernity, they also felt their country had something unique to offer the world and they resisted wholesale Westernization. This is clearly expressed in Liang's first and most important book, *Eastern and Western Cultures and Their Philosophies* (*Dongxi wenhua ji qi zhexue*) (1921), which became a best seller.

Liang blithely oversimplified the world by declaring that the West is oriented toward progress, India looks backwards and is world-negating, while China sits between these poles and seeks equilibrium and harmony. Liang definitely saw Chinese values as an antidote to rampant Western materialism, and he thus believed Chinese culture would supplant Western ways having once absorbed their benefits. He also believed Ru tradition could replace both Christianity—which he thought "a very stupid religion" with an untenable anthropomorphism (Meynard 2011: 47)—and Western secular philosophy by offering "a religion that has no tendency towards otherworldliness" (Alitto 1979: 116). Yet at a personal level, he felt India was in fact more spiritually advanced, although its path to salvation eschewed the sociopolitical world.

Liang saw the West, China, and India as representing three sequential stages of cultural evolution where China and India were like flowers that had bloomed prematurely without fully exploring the first phase of material adaptation that the West had so completely mastered. In his Buddhist reading, this reflects the advancement of the ego (the false sense of individual self), which at the lowest level is full of desire and is attached to worldly objects (the West), but as it progresses abandons selfish desire and communes harmoniously with other selves in the spirit or *ren* (China). Thus, he wrote, "Westerners have the 'self,' Chinese do not want the 'self' … [Chinese social relationships] enable a man to take no thought of himself, but to sublimate himself to others" (Grieder 1970: 141).

Ultimately, however, the individual renounces all desire and turns reflectively to realize complete non-attachment and the dissolution of the ego, which Liang saw as the great realization of Buddhism. This explains why Liang was so easily mistaken for an exponent of Ru Learning; he believed Ru ideals and values were destined to usher peace and unity into *this* world while the Buddhist way, which looks beyond the world, was necessarily unsuitable for solving sociopolitical problems. He thus said: "I converted to Confucianism because Buddhism is an other-worldly religion, and does not coincide with the human world. But I have still kept Buddhism in my heart. I have never changed on this" (cited in Billioud and Thoraval 2015: 119n. 10).

Liang's *Eastern and Western Cultures and Their Philosophies* began a vogue for defining an essential difference between Chinese and Western philosophies, which has not yet fully abated. Hu Shi reviewed the book and took great offense. "There is nothing more baseless and poisonous than the derision that Western civilization is materialistic and the praise that Eastern civilization is spiritualistic," he said (Kwok 1965: 97–8). Feng Youlan, who was a part of the Ru revival of this time, later reflected that he too had been caught up in searching for the defining differences between East and West but eventually came to suspect he was chasing phantoms created by comparing philosophies drawn from different historical and socioeconomic contexts (Feng 2000: 367–8). The East-West divide that Liang defined was nonetheless set to become a regular fixture of New Ru thought and, needless to say, it well suited the purpose of generating national pride.

The Ru underground

We have been following the intelligentsia of the new Republic. But what of the old intelligentsia, some 5 million literati who had suddenly lost their status along with their job prospects? Many of them found an alternate outlet in the Ru "redemptive societies" that flourished following the state's abandonment of Classical education.

"Redemptive society" was coined by Prasenjit Duara (2003) and has become commonplace among contemporary scholars who are only just beginning to excavate this very neglected episode in modern Chinese religious history. Collectively, these societies "constituted, by far, the largest group of organized religious congregations in Republican China" (Goossaert and Palmer 2011: 107), but as they were popular underground movements, they were until recently largely neglected by historians who had been preoccupied with events unfolding among political and intellectual elites. What follows is of necessity very general and incomplete.

A "redemptive society" is a religious association that seeks simultaneously to save individuals and the world as a whole; they are frequently movements that might otherwise be labeled "syncretistic" or "millenarian." The Taiping uprising began as one such movement. They were ubiquitous in the early Republic. Most of them had been banned by the Qing rulers, but many registered as religious associations after 1912. By mid-century, more then 300 had been identified, and both the Nationalists and Communist would feel compelled to curtail them. These societies had a history of being affiliated with warlords and attracting rebels.

The movements tended to expand the old Chinese adage that "the three teachings are one" (sanjiao heyi) to now recognize five great religious sages so that Jesus and Muhammad joined the ranks of Kongzi, Laozi, and Buddha. Each society had their own sacred texts, doctrines, and liturgies, but institutionally they resembled congregations of Christian churches more than they did anything in traditional Chinese religious history (Goossaert and Palmer 2011: 94).

For many displaced Ru, redemptive societies were a place where they could come together to express their collective identity and shared values. They often met on Sundays, they had sermons, prayers, and choirs, occasionally they even performed baptisms. They would meet in Kongzi temples or local halls where they would pay ritual respect to the Master with incense and prostrations, but they would also respectfully acknowledge other religious leaders as they anticipated the coming Great Unity (datong) that would soon draw the whole world together.

While they were virtually all ecumenical, each redemptive society had its own defining faith, Ru, Daoist, Buddhist, or Christian, although at times the declared religion seems no more dominant than the others to an outsider. Of particular interest to our story is the Worldwide Ethical Society (Wanguo daodehui) that was officially inaugurated in 1921. The movement was begun by a follower of Kang Youwei who had been prominent in the Kongzi-Religion Society, and Kang himself became president of the society in 1926, although he died within a year. Officials included prominent political figures, sympathetic Christian missionaries, and the head of the Kong family lineage. Their raison d'être was that the nation needed to rejuvenate its moral foundations to ensure it flourished, and branches of the society soon appeared in major cities. Its proclaimed charter was "promoting morality and [making] progress to the Great Unity (datong)." Although ecumenical, it maintained that Kongjiao was "the teaching of Great Unity, it penetrates everything, encompassing all other religions, and has the power to absorb all cultures in the world" (Tay 2012: 115, 120). This society still remains active in China as an illegal underground movement (Goossaert and Palmer 2011: 95–6).

Other forms of Ru revival were far less orthodox, however. There were movements that called themselves Rujiao or Kongjiao but that had elaborate pantheons and operated using the methods of the luantang or Phoenix Halls. "Wielding the phoenix" (fuluan) was a long-standing Daoist practice. It involved spirits communicating through a medium who used a peach-branch stylus and a planchette covered by a film of sand.

The automatic writer would inscribe a character that would be verified and recorded as the sand was wiped clean in preparation for the next character (Jordan and Overmyer 1986). Since the Tang dynasty, it had been common practice for aspiring Ru to stop by at a temple to ask such mediums about upcoming examination questions (Elman 2000: 319–22). Whole texts could also be transmitted in this fashion, the vast majority of which were morality books.

In the Republican era, the five religious founders, Kongzi, Jesus, and co., were regular communicators, while others like Tolstoy and George Washington made cameo appearances. Although traditional Ru would have recoiled in horror from the practice, many of these popular movements most definitely considered themselves "Ru" (Clart 2003). Indeed, societies practicing spirit writing were most likely to be so designated, which perhaps reflects a peculiar twist to Ru self-identity as scholars devoted to textual transmission (Jochim 2003: 72).

The defining characteristic of Ru Phoenix Halls was the liturgy that preceded the writing rather than the message itself. The officiants dressed in traditional Ru robes, used a "herald" as an announcer, and had distinctive ways of making pros-trations and offerings, all of which were appropriated from the rituals of Kongzi temples and Ru liturgical manuals. The spirits certainly did dwell on the importance of core Ru values—humaneness (ren), righteousness (yi), ritual propriety (li), filial piety (xiao), and so on—but so did those visiting Buddhist and Daoist Halls. At this juncture in history, Ru had no monopoly on virtue, or for that matter on the Classics and Kongzi.

In a sense, the Ru Phoenix Halls transposed the old meritocracy into a supernatural key. It was an education system where the spirits were teachers and the society mem-bers were students or disciples. The Jade Emperor presided over all. Depending on per-formance, the "student" received an appropriate grade of appointment. Examinations were based on moral achievement. The core feature of the redemptive societies of this period was the belief that the collapse of Chinese society was due to a lapse in righteousness, and the spirits were incessantly lecturing on the importance of virtuous living. Many Halls kept a record of member's good and bad deeds in a "ledger of merit and demerit" and this was used to determine the appointment an individual would be posthumously given. Ultimately, salvation was achieved by becoming a god, but still there were grades; an earth god, a city god, a temple god or, for outstanding achieve-ment, an appointment as a celestial god.

To give some sense of the self-identity of these Ru Phoenix Halls, I will quote from one of their liturgical manuals. Although this is from a Taiwanese work from 1979, it nicely shows how gods and mediums can be incorporated into Ru practice.

This hall takes Confucianism as its tradition, and the gods as [the source of its] teachings. It relies on the flying phoenix to awaken the human mind. It uses filial piety, brotherly love, loyalty, and trustworthiness as the basis of establishing the self, and propriety, righteousness, frugality, and a sense of shame as the root of purifying it . . .

This Hall takes as its mission to proclaim and promote the morality of Confucius and Mencius, to revive Chinese culture, to guide the lives of the people, and to lead people towards goodness so that they may be good citizens. (Clart 2003: 22)

The most widespread of the spirit-writing movements was Yiguandao or the Way of Pervading Unity, which today remains the third most popular faith in Taiwan after Buddhism and Daoism. It began on the mainland in 1917 and had attracted some 13 million followers by the 1940s. It was the first thing the Communists targeted when they came to power. Although sometimes also outlawed in Taiwan, it continued to thrive. Yiguandao was not originally Ru but increasingly became so. Again, with time the practice of spirit writing was supplemented by classes to study and recite the Classics and other scriptures (Jochim 2009). Today, they promote themselves as behaving "in accordance with the Great *Dao* as taught by Confucius" and upholding principles whereby "the world will be transformed; everyone will live as one family. Thereafter, the *datong*—the ideal world of Confucius—will be achieved" (Hwang n.d; cf. Lu 2008: 175–6).

Yiguandao was but one of a multitude of Ru organizations whose seeds would return to the mainland when the winds changed. In Chapter 10, I will be considering some current forms of Ru revival that are very possibly taking up the mantle of the Republican-era redemptive societies (Billioud 2010: 209–14, 217). If this is so, then the line of transmission is one that moved from the mainland to Taiwan when the Communists came to power, from whence it returned in the more benign atmosphere of the 1990s. This is a highly significant history waiting to be written.

Redemptive Societies were considered to be a significant threat to the major political parties. To contain them, party leaders believed they needed to develop ideologies that alternatively fulfilled China's spiritual needs. The remainder of this chapter focuses on the two supreme sages respectively upheld by the Nationalists and the Communists: Kongzi and Mao Zedong.

Kongzi for fascists

In 1919, a few years after Yuan Shikai's death, when the New Culture Movement was at its peak, Sun Yat-sen revived the Chinese Nationalist Party (Guomindang, hereafter GMD). Two years later, the Chinese Communist Party (CCP) was formed, with its members filling a left wing of the GMD.

Everyone was still talking about the *datong*. Li Dazhao (1888–1927), who cofounded the CCP with Chen Duxiu, prophesized that "all tracks of human evolution are consistently following one line [which] … leads to Great Unity (*datong*)" (Lu 2011: 176). In 1925, Guo Moruo (1892–1978), an acclaimed author who would become very influential in the CCP, wrote a short story in which Karl Marx meets Kongzi in a temple, which leads the sagely spirit to declare: "This ideal world of yours and my Great Unity unexpectedly coincide" (Guo 1999: 81). Even the young Mao Zedong was saying, "*datong* is our goal" (Hua 2009: 76).

The Great Unity was also being espoused by Sun Yat-sen (Sun Zhongshan, 1866–1925). Sun Yat-sen's childhood hero was the revolutionary Taiping leader Hong Xiuquan. During his schooling in Hawaii he became a Christian, and he said it was "mostly from the church that I learned the truth of revolution" (Goossaert 2011: 182). He also declared the inspiration for his life's work as a revolutionary was "a development and a continuation of the ancient Chinese doctrines of Confucius" (Gregor 1981: 55). Hong, Jesus, and Kongzi fuse in Sun's philosophy.

In an effort to keep the GMD united and to retain Soviet support, Sun took a position between the communist left and the right who opposed communism. He endorsed "communism," although not Marxism that insisted on class struggle as the driving force of history. Sun envisioned a communism based on harmonious cooperation, and the Great Unity of the *Liyun* was his model. He said that although communism was a new Western theory, China had espoused it thousands of years ago. "Marxism … is not communism," he insisted, adding: "While no country in the West has practiced communism, China during the days of Hong Xiuquan gave the theory a trial" (Sun n.d.: 36). Presumably, the millennia-old communist philosopher was Kongzi and his ideals were trialed in the Taiping quest to establish the *datong*. Alluding to the *Liyun*, Sun also said: "When the Great [Unity] doctrine is practiced, the world is the public property of all. In other words, Confucius perceived the value of a socialized world" (Sun n.d.: 57).

Like Liang Qichao, Sun believed that humans could transcend the Darwinian struggle for existence by evolving toward harmonious cooperation: "What is the end of human evolution? It is the aim indicated by Confucius when he said: 'When your goal has been reached, you can live on earth as in the heavens'" (Sun 1918: 99)—which, needless to say, Kongzi never said. To achieve a perfectly harmonious society, Sun believed it was vital to reform individuals so that they abandon self-interest in favor of the greater good. To this end, he constantly stressed the importance of traditional Ru moral values. Thus: "The most important virtues are: first, filial piety (*xiao*) and loyalty (*zhong*); next humaneness (*ren*) and love (*ai*); thirdly, trustworthiness (*xin*) and righteousness (*yi*); and lastly, love of peace (*heping*)" (Sun n.d.: 46).

Sun compressed his revolutionary vision into his renowned "Three Principles of the People" (*sanmin zhuyi*): national consciousness or Nationalism (*minzu*), people's rights or Democracy (*minquan*), and people's livelihood or Socialism (*minsheng*). While he avowed democracy, he had witnessed the dangers of rampant Western capitalism and saw socialism as a necessary countermeasure. He thus upheld the "communism" of Kongzi's Great Unity. He said:

The *sanmin* Doctrine means a government "of the people, by the people, and for the people"—that is, the state is the common property of all the people, its politics are participated in by all, and its profits are shared by all. Then there will be not only communism in property, but communism in everything else. Such will be the ultimate end of the Doctrine of Livelihood, a state which Confucius calls *datong* or the age of "Great [Unity]." (Sun n.d.: 139)

It is thus the national anthem of the Republic of China (Taiwan) begins: "The Three Principles of the People, the foundation of our party. Using this, we establish the Republic, using this, we advance into a state of *datong*."

* * *

When Sun Yat-sen died in 1925, a deep fissure opened in the GMD dividing the communist left and anticommunist right. Chiang Kai-shek (Jiang Jieshi, 1887–1975) secured control over the party by instigating the massacre of hundreds of thousands of communist supporters, thus beginning a civil war between the GMD and the CCP. "*Datong*" and "communism" were about to become doctrinal poles.

Chiang used ideology in his war. For Sun, the Three Principles of the People was more a goal than an ideology, and Chiang saw the need for theoretical infrastructure. In 1925, Dai Jitao (1891–1949) had published a pamphlet entitled *The Philosophical Foundations of Sun Yat-senism* (*Sun Wen zhuyi zhi zhexue jichu*), arguing Ru Learning was the basis of Sun's thinking and that Sun was essentially a sage continuing the "transmission of the Way" (*daotong*) (Mast and Saywell 1974). Chiang echoed these sentiments when he said the Three Principles had "inherited the ethical thought of Yao, Shun, Yu, Tang, King Wen, King Wu, Duke of Zhou, Confucius, and other ancient sages and raises this thought to a new phase of development" (Zheng 2001: 208).

Chiang Kai-shek's thinking was especially indebted to Chen Lifu (1900–2001), the "official representative of the Guomindang in matters of philosophy" (Feng 2000: 251). Communists claimed that Chen Lifu and his brother actually controlled the GMD and had a slogan: "The Party belongs to the Chens" (Ch'en 1994: 214). Although Chen is often overlooked in histories of Ruism in the twentieth century, he most definitely deserves our attention.

Chen had no formal background in philosophy or politics and he attributed his fondness for Ru Learning to his mother who died when he was ten. Chen later went to the United States to train as a mining engineer, but when he returned, in 1926, he was persuaded by Chiang Kai-shek to work for the GMD. It was only after this date that Chiang began showing interest in Ruism. The two men sometimes lived together, discussing China's future over meals; "we were very close," Chen recalled late in life (Ch'en 1994: 24). Chen threw himself into to making propaganda speeches on Sun Yat-sen's "Three Principles," but he was struck by a lack of national zeal. The key to promoting nationalism, he decided, was to revive those Ru moral values that had once made China great and unique. By preaching these ideals to large audiences, Chen Lifu claimed to have won back thousands of young people from the Communists (Chen 1986: ii).

Chen contested the Marxist view of history. He wrote several books espousing a hybrid philosophy fusing the cosmology of the *Changes* (*Yijing*) with "vitalism," a Western scientific view that replaced the dead matter of materialism with a life force struggling to fulfill its destiny. "Benevolence and love are the expression for the life-begetting motive of the universe," Chen said (Chen 1948: 65). He made it quite clear he wrote these books primarily to challenge communist philosophical premises (Ch'en 1994: 247). In his alternate view of cosmic and social evolution, the universe was unfolding toward the Great Unity of the *Liyun*, which was being made manifest by the "mild and benevolent measures of the Guomindang Government" (Chen 1948: 120, 134).

Chen took the *Great Learning*'s dictum that rectifying the state and the world began with self-cultivation to mean nationalism must begin with fundamental lessons in morality. He began promoting the Classics as the basis of education, and in 1929 Ru Learning was formally reinstated in school curricula. He traveled to schools explaining the essence of the Four Books and started to rearrange their content to form a systematic textbook. He also advocated children being taught to rote-learn the Four Books while their memories were at a peak (Chen 1986: v–vi). Troops in the army were likewise urged to study them, and a widespread "read the Classics" movement emerged in the 1930s. For all these educational reforms, there were vocal liberal critics (Billioud and Thoraval 2015: 33–4).

In 1934, Chiang Kai-shek upped the ante by launching the New Life Movement (*xin shenghuo yundong*), which he hoped would satisfy the spiritual needs then driving people into Redemptive Societies (Ownby 2008: 38). As such, it has been described as "primarily a religious movement" that "attempted to provide a comprehensive system of transformative and ultimately salvific power" (Oldstone-Moore 2000: 4); Chiang himself described it as a "spiritual revolution" (Chiang 1943: 30). Chen Lifu has been suspected of ghostwriting Chiang's inaugural speech on "The Essentials of the New Life Movement," delivered in 1934. The speech certainly echoed Chen Lifu's view that the listlessness of the nation was due to moral failure. "In order to develop the life of our nation, protect the existence of our society, and improve the livelihood of our people, it is absolutely necessary to wipe out" immorality, he said. This was the goal of the New Life Movement that proceeded by promoting a new quartet of Ru virtues, namely *li* (ritual), *yi* (righteousness), *lian* (integrity), and *chi* (sense of shame).

These four virtues were basically taken to mean all people should obey their leader and the law, appreciate the difference between right and wrong, and correct themselves when they transgressed (de Bary and Lufrano 2000: 341–4). This was not Ru Learning being employed to refine noble persons (*junzi*); it was rather an ideological fumigant being sprayed over the morally infected masses who Chiang described as being unbearably filthy, lazy, decrepit, hedonistic, barbaric, and deprived of reason (Dirlik 1975: 954). At a very basic level, Chiang wanted to stop people smoking, littering, slurping, slouching, and leaving buttons undone, but more generally he wanted them obedient, orderly, healthy, and fighting fit. Although the etymology of Ru might suggest "soft" (Chapter 1), Chiang required a hard "muscular Confucianism" to wage his war (Oldstone-Moore 2015: 48). By overcoming "social disorder and individual weakness" the New Life Movement manifesto declared that people would "become more military-minded" (de Bary and Lufrano 2000: 344).

Chiang's government has been described as a form of "Confucian fascism" (Wakeman 1997). Fascism is a totalitarian regime in which individuals are expected to completely surrender themselves to the higher cause of the nation as defined by the leader. They are typically military dictatorships. Chiang was a military man, the Generalissimo, who said "the most important point of fascism is absolute trust in a sagely, able leader. Aside from complete trust in one person, there is no other leader or ism" (Eastman 1972: 6). He likewise advocated "the abandonment of the small self in favor of the large self," which meant "individuals must lose themselves in the state." This was his understanding of Sun Yat-sen's "Three Principles of the People," and for his authority he too turned to the *Liyun*'s description of the *datong* (Chiang 1943: 178, 181).

Chiang's utopian vision culminated in *China's Destiny*, meant for mass education (some sources say a million copies were printed), and *Chinese Economic Theory* written for officials. The latter is more informative. It argues that Western economic theory (be it capitalist or Marxist) is driven by human desires, whereas Chinese economic theory has its foundation in human nature (*xing*). Ruism is said to define Chinese economics, and the book is saturated with references to the Classics and Ru Learning. It asserts that "human nature is naturally benevolent and loving," which in turn is "based on the idea that men are not individual separate entities." This is quickly interpreted to mean all people must totally surrender themselves to the greater good of the nation and assume military responsibilities. Chiang could make the promise of the *datong* sound like a threat: "In the world of the 'Great Unity' when human nature is developed to the highest point, no one will be able to earn a living by sitting idle" (Chiang 1947: 265, 245, 289).

***

In 1937, the battle between the GMD and the CCP was interrupted by the need to join forces against Japanese invasion. In a bizarre twist, Japan too was promoting "Confucian fascism." Rather than equating Ru tradition with the Chinese nation, Japanese propaganda insisted it was coterminous with East Asia. By claiming that Japan alone remained faithful to the Way, *Jukyo* (Japanese for *Rujiao*) could be used to justify imperialism (Smith 1959: chapter 4; Paramore 2016: chapter 6). As one of Japan's Chinese "running dogs" said, "The Japanese are shedding their blood in order to help Chinese civilization which is dying because the revolution destroyed Confucianism" (Taylor 1940: 73–4). And from this collision of Ru fascisms splintered the grotesque utopia of Manchukuo (1932–45). This short-lived Japanese puppet state in northern China was said to actualize the "Kingly Way" of Ru governance. The last Qing emperor was installed as nominal regent and his reign was named, you guessed it, *datong*, the "Great Unity." The Manchukuo government proudly paraded the *Liyun*'s description of the *datong* as a credo for their nation (Manchoukuo Government 1933: 17–18).

By the time Japan surrendered in 1945, the GMD was depleted. In 1949, the Communists claimed victory and the Nationalists retreated to Taiwan. Before pursuing the events that unfolded on the mainland, let me finish the story of the partnership between Chiang Kai-shek and Chen Lifu.

Chen blamed himself for the defeat and left for New Jersey to become a chicken farmer. Twenty years later, he returned to Taiwan to work with Chiang on the Chinese Cultural Renaissance Movement (*Zhonghua wenhua fuxing yundong*), which began in 1967. The fact that this movement was launched immediately following the outbreak of the Cultural Revolution on the mainland indicates this was really a continuation of the New Life Movement and the ongoing ideological battle between the GMD and CCP. In 1968, Chiang delivered a speech in which he said: "Today the Chinese Communist bandits are in the process of insanely destroying Chinese culture, and they view Confucianism as the enemy ... We should instead esteem Confucius as great and sincerely believe in the eternally valid nature of Confucianism" (Fetzer and Soper 2013: 47–8).

In Taiwan, Chen Lifu was exceptionally influential. Tu Weiming observed: "His voice was heard not only in the schools but also in the army. Through television, radio, and the printed media, his ideas penetrated virtually every corner of the island country. Despite the resentment of liberal intellectuals, he was perhaps the best-known missionary for the Confucian faith." As deputy, Chen served under Chiang who headed the Kongzi and Mengzi Learning Society (*Kong meng xuehui*) and he was a regular contributor to its journal. Chen wrote books for schools on the interpretation of the Four Books, promoted rote-learning the Classics, and pushed to have *Rujiao* made state religion. He had a reputation for being honest, incorruptible, and sincere, but he was very much the fundamentalist. In Tu's words: "The kind of message Chen Lifu delivered is a combination of cultural chauvinism, nationalism, ethnocentrism, anthropocentrism, and political conservatism" (Tu 2010: 72).

Some of Chen's views can be gleaned from his *Interconnecting Thread of the Way in the Four Books* (*Sishu daoguan*, 1966), which he had been working on since 1929. This book heavily influenced compulsory components of Taiwanese school curricula promoting Ru values, and it was criticized for distorting the Classics to fit the "GMD's political agenda" (Makeham 2005: 197–8). Schoolchildren were basically obliged to rote-learn a "bag of virtues" wherein patriotism loomed large (Jochim 2003: 62–3). In *Interconnecting Thread,* the Four Books are rearranged to form a single coherent doctrine that is woven around Chen's own commentary. It builds to a blueprint for "humane government," which is essentially a form of virtuous autocracy. Occasionally, quotations from Sun Yat-sen and Chiang Kai-shek are added to those of the sages, none too subtly suggesting the Nationalist leaders were rightfully continuing the "transmission of the Way" (*daotong*). Chen once said: "The late president [Chiang Kai-shek] mentioned several times, the doctrines of Confucius and Mencius are the theoretical foundation of the Three Principles of the People. It behooves us to work harder for the practice of the Three Principles of the People to realize the essence of the doctrines of Confucius and Mencius" (Lee 2004: 44–5). Unsurprisingly, critics claimed the movement aimed to turn Chiang Kai-shek "into a sacred figure and make him into the transmitter of the *daotong*" (Makeham 2008: 203).

There are well over a thousand quotations in *Interconnecting Thread*, all of them from the Four Books, except the final climactic one that, once again, is the *Liyun* passage describing the Great Unity. Given the indelible association between the *datong* and Sun Yat-sen's "Three Principles," we are left with the impression that the fulfillment of the teachings of the Four Books was being implemented by the GMD. Ignoring the recent violence that had left China split in two, Chen concluded by suggesting that the teachings of Kongzi explained why China had lived for millennia as one harmonious family. Chinese culture could thus benefit all humanity—unless the Communists prevailed, and then, he added, beware the "Yellow Peril" (Chen 1986: 594).

Although there have been many vocal critics of Chen Lifu in Taiwan, especially since the lifting of martial law and the introduction of multi-party elections, many of his methods are currently being revived in mainland China. This will become apparent in Chapter 10. For the moment, however, our story must return to 1949 and the events that followed the Communist victory.

The Helmsman and the Sage

China had suffered under the GMD since the 1930s. Government corruption was rife, inflation was out of control, poverty was rampant, and warlords threatened the land. A master strategist like the "Great Helmsman" Mao Zedong (1893–1976) flourished in such terrain, and the events that ensued are the stuff myths are made of: the 10,000 km Long March to relocate the Red Army after defeat by the Nationalists in 1934; the subsequent life of devoted compatriots and egalitarian social reformers living in caves cut in cliffs in Yan'an; comrades gathering together to study Mao's words on how the peasant masses were the true leaders of the nation. From such things, Mao "created stories that were mythic in character, and that were repeated again and again like incantation" (Apter and Saich 1998: 35–6). By 1949, the Communists were victorious and Mao announced the formation of the People's Republic of China (PRC).

Insofar as the CCP was doctrinally driven by Mao's interpretation of Marxism-Leninism, there was no place for ideological dissent. Mao's words became the new Classics; they were studied, memorized, internalized, recited, embodied, ritualized. His sayings collected in the "Little Red Book" possibly surpass the Bible as the most widely distributed book in human history—by some estimates, twice as many copies were printed as there then were people on Earth. Many observers have commented on the religious nature of Maoism, and Ru thought was accordingly treated as heresy (e.g., Landsberger 1996; Young and Ford 1977; Leese 2013). Mao was especially keen to distance himself from any ideology patronized by the GMD, and he condemned "those who worship Confucius, the study of the Confucian canon, the old ethical code and the old ideas in opposition to the new culture and new ideas" (Mao 1965: 369). Initially, everything associated with Ruism was abandoned to rot. All public ceremony to Kongzi ceased and any remaining temples or shrines were converted into schools, culture centers, or storage depots.

When the Communists took over, many of those who would become the leading exponents of the next generation of New Ru Learning departed for Taiwan and Hong Kong. The real creativity in Ru thought left the mainland with the Diaspora, as we will see in the next chapter. For those that remained, there was the choice of silence or the dangerous option of seeking reconciliation between Maoism and Ru thought. Liang Shuming and Xiong Shili both had genuine sympathies for Mao's reforms and wished only to question his materialist metaphysics. Feng Youlan (1895–1990) and He Lin (1902–92) are also counted as exponents of New Ru Learning. While they may have had private reservations, for all appearance they became unreserved converts to Maoism (see Zhang 2015a: chapter 5).

Liang Shuming was frequently targeted. His delusions of sagehood did not help matters (Alitto 1979: 59). Liang highly valued his own opinion and was forthright in expressing it. Liang and Mao had once been close, but they had a falling-out in 1953. In that year at a government meeting, Mao publically abused Liang for supporting the fascist ideals of Chiang Kai-shek and Chen Lifu. "You stink!" he said before adding that Liang was a murderous, hypocritical, greedy schemer who had never done a single thing for the Chinese people (Alitto 1979: 1–2). Mao then went to the trouble of publishing a "Criticism of Liang Shuming's Reactionary Ideas" in which he said: "Confucius ... had the faults of not being democratic and of lacking a self-critical spirit, in a way rather like Mr. Liang. Confucius ... came close to being a despot and reeked of fascism. I hope ... you Mr. Liang ... won't follow Confucius' example" (Mao 1977: 127). For a while, writing anti-Liang articles was all the rage. By 1958, a repentant Liang was saying: "The rule of Chairman Mao makes me full of admiration to the point of prostrating before him. He is so capable and intelligent, he is extraordinary, and there are no words to describe him" (Bresciani 2001: 243n. 22). Just as this otherworldly Buddhist had previously advocated Ruism for *this* world, he now supported Maoism in the sociopolitical domain while continuing to reserve Buddhism for "transcending the world." He thus cheekily said, "I acknowledge Marxism-Leninism, unfortunately, Marxism-Leninism does not acknowledge me" (Hanafin 2003: 191). These sentiments were apparently quite sincere and long after Mao's death Liang still maintained Mao had been the greatest person in all of Chinese history (Liang and Alitto 2013: 90).

When anti-Kongzi sentiment ran high, there was a tendency to call upon Feng Youlan as whipping boy. This was because he was regarded as the foremost authority on Chinese philosophy and his *History of Chinese Philosophy* (1934) with its high appraisal of Kongzi was very well known both in China and abroad. When the Communists came to power, Feng applauded the demise of the Ru, but he always tried to put in a good word for Kongzi. He had little room to maneuver and was constantly attacked. After prolonged self-examination he pleaded guilty to having "defended the 'Confucian shop'," thereby serving the interests of the "Guomindang reactionaries ... and other political swindlers" (Feng 1974: 88). From his autobiography written late in life, it seems his confessions were genuine (Feng 2000: 191).

Xiong Shili miraculously managed to avoid being censored prior to the Cultural Revolution. He had friends in high places, including Premier Zhou Enlai who gently nurtured his reeducation. I will be examining Xiong's early and most important works in the next chapter. Here I am concerned with his writings after 1949. Although he retained his earlier metaphysical premises, Xiong was now in agreement with Mao's dismissal of Ruism as feudalistic and intrinsically opposed to democracy. Xiong abandoned everything and everyone save Kongzi. Indeed, in his amazing work of revisionist history, *An Inquiry on the Ru* (*Yuanru*, 1956), he even disavowed half of Kongzi. Apparently, at the age of fifty, Kongzi for all intents and purposes became a communist when he decided to abolish private property and class distinction and usher in the Great Unity (*datong*). Kongzi's erroneous earlier ideas were recorded by others in the *Analects*, but he himself recorded his mature thought when writing and revising the Six Classics. Unfortunately, his "followers," slave-Ru who wished to exploit the masses, tried to disguise the Master's message by tampering with the Classics and fabricating Ancient Script editions. They concealed Kongzi's *datong* to perpetuate absolute monarchy. Even Mengzi and Dong Zhongshu had been in on it. Sun Yat-sen was brilliant, but he was still fettered by feudalist ideas. Readers are left to surmise that the CCP was finally realizing Kongzi's Great Unity.

***

Mao withdrew his frontal attacks on heresy in 1956 and instead encouraged free expression of divergent opinion; "let the hundred flowers bloom and a hundred schools of thought contend," he famously said. Whatever his intent, in practice this served to flush out closet dissenters. In the late 1950s there was a flurry of conferences on China's philosophers, especially Kongzi, but scholarship was now reduced to evaluating past thinkers to see if they passed or failed the test of agreeing with Marxism-Leninism-Maoism. Was Kongzi a materialist (✓) or idealist (✗); did he teach humaneness (*ren*) toward all (✓) or just the slave-owning class (✗)? (Louie 1980: chapter 2). It was a tedious exercise and Mao was becoming impatient.

He was tired of debate. Experts advised him on gradual steps for modernizing China, but Mao was ready to risk a dash for utopia. By harnessing the power of hundreds of millions of workers, the Great Leap Forward would exponentially increase China's agricultural and industrial productivity, he believed. More than half a billion people were resettled in People's Communes (*renmin gongshe*) where everything was collectively owned.

Marx and Engels had left no practical guidelines for organizing communist societies, and only two abortive attempts had ever been made to establish Marxist communes. From where, then, did Mao derive his model? This is necessarily speculative, but the evidence points toward Kang Youwei. The young Mao had "worshipped" Kang and knew some of his work by heart (Snow 1968: 137). In a famous article written in 1949, Mao referred to the ideal communist society as the "Great Unity," adding that "Kang

Youwei wrote *Datong shu* ... but he did not and could not find the way to achieve [the *datong*]" (Mao 1961: 414). According to Yang Jisheng, "Mao believed he had found that [way] in the communes" (2012: 172).

There are many obvious correspondences between Kang's *datong* and the principles governing People's Communes—"the structural similarities between Kang's plan and the rural commune of Communist China are too obvious to require comment," said Kang's biographer Hsiao Kung-chuan (1975: 470). We know Kang's *Datong shu* was at least consulted "as the guideline for the People's Commune" (Hua 2009: 76). It is perhaps also significant that the two defining terms Mao used to characterize communes were that they were "great" (*da*) and held in "common" (*gong*). These are key words from the opening line of the *Liyun* passage on the *datong*: "When the great (*da*) *Dao* was in practice, the world was common (*gong*) to all" (see Chi 1967).

The thesis that the People's Commune was the bastard offspring of Kang Youwei's Great Unity is necessarily conjectural. Mao was hardly about to publicly associate with a social ideal attributed to Kongzi. Were this proven, then realizing the Great Unity is apparently a very risky business. Adding to the Taiping body count, as many as 45 million lives were lost in the Great Leap Forward.

In the wake of this disaster, there was a brief window in which Kongzi's contributions to China's progress were being reconsidered. Between 1961 and 1962, his teachings were again being discussed and his life publicly celebrated, although participants later became the target of attack. The Kong family mansions in Qufu were open to the public, attracting tens of thousands of daily visitors (Louie 1980: 51). Once he had caught his breath, Mao stepped in to remind China that class struggle must remain the key to progress. The Cultural Revolution was about to erupt.

In the sweeping destruction of the past that was the Cultural Revolution (1966–76), philosophical debate was replaced by the army. As one paper reported it, "Confucianism should be eradicated and put to death immediately ... Red Guards have buried Confucianism, once and for all." Portraits of Kongzi were carried through the streets reading: "I am an ox, a demon, a snake, and a devil" (Bush 1970: 377–8). In his hometown of Qufu, China's first anti-Kongzi ceremony was staged. His statue was taken from the temple and plastered with the words "Number One Bastard" (*touhao dahuaidan*). It was then paraded by truck through the streets to the sound of chanting, with known sympathizers forced to flank the vehicle. The statue was subsequently thrown onto a bonfire, the temple was raided, and the adjoining family cemetery was desecrated (Wang 2002). The discussion was over.

If Kongzi was mentioned during the Cultural Revolution, it was in venomous tones. He was the archetypal reactionary, a fraud, a feudal mummy, a defender of slavery, murderer, purveyor of poison, wielder of an "invisible knife that killed without leaving a trace of blood" (Gregor and Chang 1979: 1077–8). It at first seems rather peculiar, therefore, that in 1973, when Mao was fatally ill, the infamous Gang of Four (Mao's wife and her three associates) felt it necessary to launch an anti-Kongzi campaign. As Wm. Theodore de Bary aptly observed, for this campaign to proceed, "Confucius had first to be resurrected before he could be pilloried and crucified" (de Bary 1991b: ix).

Who was there left praising Kongzi? Consider, for example, the cases of those pioneers of New Ru Learning we have already met. Liang Shuming had been harassed and his wife beaten by Red Guards who had occupied his home and burned his books. Although renowned for being stubborn, proud, and self-righteous, even he could do little more than mutter he did not think everything Kongzi said was total rubbish. Xiong Shili, equally arrogant and sometimes considered a little mad, suffered from physical abuse and the mental affliction of seeing his friends imprisoned, tortured, and lynched. He wrote of his hatred of the Cultural Revolution on his socks and handkerchiefs and neglected his health to hasten his death, in 1968. He Lin had been converted to Maoism and joined the campaigns to criticize Liang Shuming, although he was still subsequently sentenced to reeducation through two years of farm labor. And if Feng Youlan was not in his heart fully converted to extremist Maoism, he faked it well, for he joined the anti-Kongzi campaign, contributed articles, and was advisor to the Gang of Four (Feng 1974).

There was something very telling in this campaign. No one was espousing Kongzi, yet the Gang of Four saw him everywhere. To understand the events of this time we need to pause and identify a shift that had occurred in Mao's thinking. The early Mao had optimistically anticipated the imminent realization of a utopian communist society. His view of history seems to have been based on Kang Youwei's three ages (the ages of disorder, rising peace, and great peace) but reworked so there was peace at both the beginning and end, in accord with Marxist theory that said communism resided at both poles of human history (primitive communism, slave society, feudalism, capitalism, communism). Mao said:

> The life of humankind is made up of three great eras—an era in which humankind lived in peace, and era in which humankind lived at war, and another era in which humankind lived in peace. We are at present at the dividing line between the second and third eras. Humankind's era of wars will be brought to an end by our own efforts, and beyond doubt the war we wage is part of the final battle. (Knight 1996: 180–1)

As the era of peace never seemed to get any closer, Mao's optimism wavered and eventually turned. His rhetoric by the time of the Cultural Revolution had radically changed and he spoke of struggle and revolution as perpetual principles that would endure till the sun had cooled and the earth died. Even communism was no longer a terminus; it was but a station along an endless road of social revolution.

During the anti-Kongzi campaign, "Kongzi" was synonymous with "reactionary" and the campaign's real purpose was to tar opponents with the brush of association (Figure 16). Kongzi's name was no longer being connected with long since discredited aspects of his teachings (feudalism, elitism, patriarchy, familism), but with the core of essential concepts retained by the most progressive Ru: humaneness (*ren*) and harmony (*he*). In Mao's new vision of history, these things hindered social progress as genuine advance was only achieved by overcoming opposition through struggle.

FIGURE 16 *Criticize Kongzi.*

In 1974, Beijing residents were greeted by this huge poster attacking Kongzi thought.

Ru had been an all-male intellectual elite who kept well clear of manual labor and combat (recall, Ru may have originally meant "weakling"). In the 1970s, images of Kongzi portrayed him as scrawny, doddery, cowardly, and crafty, typically executed in sickly grey tones (Sommer 2007).

In stark contrast, the vibrant hues of this poster depict labor-toned young men and women ready to openly confront their enemy. They smash a placard representing the old regime while embracing a copy of Mao's sayings.

The caption reads: "Workers, Peasants and Soldiers are the Main Force for Criticizing Lin Biao and Kongzi." (Lin Biao was the initial target of the campaign against Kongzi thought. Although he had died, his name continued to be paired with Kongzi's).

Far from eulogizing the Great Peace and Great Unity as he had done earlier in his career, Mao later became rhapsodic when using the language of opposition, war, conflict, and perpetual revolution. At a time when prominent fellow party members (Deng Xiaoping among them) where recognizing the urgent need for stability, the Gang of Four retaliated by branding them followers of Kongzi. As James Gregor and Maria Chang insightfully observed, the legacy of the latter Mao and his allies "was on-going class struggle, and their principal opponent was Confucianism in whatever guise, for Confucianism advocated collective harmony, propriety, and benevolence" (Gregor and Chang 1979: 1091).

***

By highlighting the affiliation between Kongzi and social values that many longed for and considered desirable, the anti-Kongzi campaign was its own undoing. With Mao's death and the arrest of the Gang of Four in 1976, policy steadily turned from struggle and revolution toward economic and industrial development dependant on a stable and harmonious workforce.

In an ironic twist, as Kam Louie has noted, the campaign had instigated "the greatest revival of Confucius's teaching in Chinese history. Every university, school, factory, commune, even kindergarten had to study *The Analects* as 'negative material'." For instance, 2.5 million pocket-sized comic-books, as well as 700,000 posters, were printed of just one new illustrated life of Kongzi. The Sage was back on the best-seller list, albeit in a biography entitled *The Evil Life of Dickhead Kong* (the slang connotation of *Kong lao'er zui'e de yisheng*, 1974). As Louie further observed, "this flogging of his corpse only had the effect of making Confucius spring back to life as soon as the beating was over" (Louie 2011: 82).

The fundamental association of Kongzi with unity, harmony, and benevolence has stuck. While it is has taken time to adjust the policy and rhetoric of the CCP, ever increasingly Kongzi is being rehabilitated as someone who can help guide China toward the future.

We will pick up the story of the Ru revival in twenty-first-century China in Chapter 10. But first we need to follow those exponents of Ru Learning who left the mainland in 1949. These exiles were not merely helping keep the tradition alive but were in fact developing some of the most sophisticated philosophies in all of Chinese history.

9

New Ru Learning

Are we on the threshold of a new great epoch in the Way of the Ru? Mou Zongsan, the pivotal figure of this chapter, certainly thought so. He did not base his claim on dispassionate observation. Rather, he proclaimed it as a rallying cry to save China.

Mou called this modern revival the third epoch (*disanqi*) of Ru Learning. As we have seen, the first epoch was the formative era spanning the Zhou and Han dynasties when Ruism was asserting itself against other indigenous philosophies. The second was the Song-Ming revival when the tradition was refashioned to meet the challenge of the foreign Buddhist faith. The current third epoch was precipitated by the arrival of the Western world, science, democracy, and communism. Whenever Mou spoke of this third epoch, it was in the present; it was "what needs to happen now" (Chan 2011: 80). He would say to his students: "Where does this third epoch fall? On your shoulders? On my shoulders? This is the mission of our age" (Clower 2014: 187).

In the 1980s, the notion of a third epoch was taken up by Tu Weiming who himself had been inspired to pursue philosophy by Mou. Tu, however, was observing developments that now had some history. With more detachment, he noted that Mou and his contemporaries had generated a groundswell that feasibly could generate a third epoch. "The real challenge" remained the same: "How a revived Confucian humanism might answer questions that science and democracy have raised" (Tu 1993: 158).

More recently, there has been a tendency to associate the rather nebulous "third epoch" with a more clearly defined movement stretching back to the 1920s. It is known as the New Ru School (*xin rujia*) or New Ru Learning (*Xin ruxue*) both usually translated as New Confucianism. Here we must proceed very cautiously.

The invention of New Ru Learning

New Ru Learning was basically invented by a committee. It was the by-product of a packaging process occurring in the 1980s. China was ready to import back to the mainland philosophies that had been flourishing among exiles in Hong Kong and Taiwan.

Their ideas were now seen to have value for helping China recover in the post-Mao era; they could restore cultural continuity after recent attempts to obliterate the past, they could promote nationalism, remedy social problems, and perhaps even boost the economy.

Certainly, some of the thinkers identified as pioneers of New Ru Learning had been voicing their views since the 1920s. We have already met several of them as original and creative philosophers, but we are about to encounter them again as founders and forefathers. In reality, they lacked any real shared identity and were at times quite at odds with one another. The New Ru movement was an ingenious concoction that turned fragmentary developments into a well-defined commodity. It was a fabrication, but one that has helped shape modern Chinese history.

The actual term *Xin rujia* was coined by Feng Youlan, but that was just his way of describing Ru of the Song and Ming dynasties. In 1941, He Lin started to use it to refer to contemporary thinkers, but he did not mention names, let alone lineages. In 1958, Mou Zongsan and three others soon to be classified as exponents of *Xin ruxue* together published a manifesto that showed clear signs of growing collective identity, but they did not link themselves to any specific predecessors and others of their generation (now also classified as exponents of *Xin ruxue*) had declined to support them. It was only in the 1980s that we see the first faltering attempts to delineate an actual movement.

The definitions of New Ru Learning that began to emerge ran something like this. First, and rather obviously, it was a movement in which exponents primarily identified with Ru tradition. Furthermore, they claimed Ruism was the quintessence of Chinese culture and thus integral to China's future. More specifically, they acknowledged the Song-Ming tradition of Ru scholarship that was based on the unity of heart-mind (*xin*) and nature (*xing*). To ensure this tradition was correctly understood and perpetuated, New Ru emphasized the importance of the *daotong* or legitimate "transmission of the Way."

Second, again obviously, there was something decidedly "new" about this type of Ru thought. Their philosophies responded to China's current challenges and engaged with the Western traditions that had generated them. *Xin ruxue* thus incorporated Western philosophy in much the same way as the Song revival had absorbed Daoist and Buddhist metaphysics, all the while tending to polarize the East-West intellectual divide. The Western philosophers who were engaged tended to be idealists and vitalists; Kant, Hegel, Bergson, and Whitehead were favorites. The new synthesis was offered as something that could overcome the political, social, cultural, and moral predicaments of the modern age, and it was presented as a religious, or at least spiritual, path to China's salvation (Makeham 2003: 29–31).

The trouble is, very few of the philosophers conscripted into the ranks of New Ru Learning actually conform to the definition, which was primarily modeled on Mou Zongsan. A movement was born, nonetheless. In 1987, a committee was formed to make a thorough investigation of *Xin ruxue*. The impetus for that committee was the reconstruction of China's political and cultural image in the wake of the Cultural

Revolution. The CCP saw aspects of Ru thought being extremely useful for building Marxism with "Chinese characteristics" and it welcomed the Ru emphasis on virtue, harmony, and accord. The Party was keen to bring home philosophies being developed in Taiwan and Hong Kong so as to adopt their strengths. It was also keen to gain some control over the disconcerting tendency of thinkers outside the mainland to conflate Ru tradition with liberal democracy.

Fang Keli (b. 1938) was primarily responsible for directing the decade-long study of Contemporary New Ru Learning (*Dangdai xin ruxue*). It was the largest and most expensive humanities project ever funded by China's Ministry of Education. Fang's own position was that ancient and historically influential traditions such as Ruism provided the uniquely Chinese foundations on which the country's Marxism should be built. He was entirely willing to acknowledge the positive contributions of the past, but there was a qualification. "We should highly value these precious legacies and subject them to critical inheritance so they can serve as important traditional resources for molding a new ideology and psycho-spiritual civilization," he said (Makeham 2008: 248). Fang spoke of this as "using the past to serve the present," which he endorsed in much the same manner as he sanctioned "using the foreign to serve China." In both cases the resource must be "critically inherited" and made to serve China's current needs. Fang no more wished for a revival of Ruism as such than he wanted to see China thoroughly Westernized.

Fang was the head of a team of forty-seven academics from eighteen institutes responsible for studying and evaluating the New Ru. The volumes that were published are on the whole fair and balanced yet have a decidedly Marxist tone and tend to approach their subjects as worthy reactionaries. What Fang and others had not anticipated was that their research would spark an enthusiasm for Ru Learning that would flare into advocacy and revival. By the 1990s, *Ruxue* was being discussed side by side with Marxism and liberalism as a significant discourse for shaping the future of China. Kang felt the need to write that "Confucianism was the ideology of feudal society in the past, and cannot possibly have a leading role in the society building and modernization of the country ... Even though in the past Confucianism played a role of a quasi-religion, we today absolutely cannot approve that Confucianism will again become a religion" (Bresciani 2001: 433). By the time Fang had written these words, the flames of "*Ruxue* fever" were out of control.

For the moment, our concern with Fang Keli and the research committee must begin with a basic and preliminary question that they had to confront: Just who were these exponents of New *Ruxue*? Initially they identified ten individuals: Liang Shuming, Zhang Junmai, Xiong Shili, Feng Youlan, He Lin, Qian Mu, and Fang Dongmei, who formed the so-called first generation, and Tang Junyi, Mou Zongsan, and Xu Fuguan, who constituted the second generation. At a later date, Ma Yifu was added to the first generation and four younger scholars were identified as forming a third generation: Tu Weiming, Yu Yingshi, Cheng Zhongying, and Liu Shuxian.

This corps of fifteen individuals created a coterie that has shaped subsequent discussion, East and West. Its visibility has undoubtedly contributed to the revival of

Ruism in China, but it is historically suspect. I will not examine all of these individuals. Rather, I will focus on just one individual from each of the "three generations"—Xiong Shili, Mou Zongsan, and Tu Weiming—as well as examining the manifesto Mou wrote with the other two second-generation representatives. The reasons for my selection will become apparent as this chapter unfolds.

The mind of Xiong Shili

Of the designated members of the first generation of New Ru Learning, Xiong Shili is the only one who actually conforms to the movement's description. The others were primarily Buddhists, Hegelians, Marxists, pluralists, or philosophically uncommitted historians. Ma Yifu was certainly dedicated to Ru Learning, but he was not really "new"—he was something of a relic of the world of Song-Ming scholarship.

Xiong Shili is considered the "founder" of New Ru Learning, but in truth he is the only candidate left standing. The second generation was in fact the real hub that defined the movement, and Xiong Shili became prominent because he had inspired all three second-generation exponents.

Xiong was from a poor rural family and largely self-educated. His introduction to Ru thought came primarily from his father, a village tutor who died when Xiong was only ten. Xiong was considered a troublesome youth, sometimes living in abandoned temples where he would wander naked smashing Bodhisattvas, a strangely apt prelude to his mature philosophical iconoclasm. In his late teens he joined the revolutionary movement but eventually became uneasy among his comrades and felt they lacked a deep moral commitment to the goals for which they fought. In his late works, he would finally show how Ru Learning was the foundation for authentic revolution.

At the age of thirty-five, disillusioned, anguished, and deploring the human condition, he turned to Buddhism and in particular *Weishi* or "Consciousness only" Buddhist philosophy (Sanskrit *Vijñaptimātratā*, better known as *Yogācāra* or "yoga practice"). This had not been a major force in Chinese history but it was then undergoing a revival after the recovery of lost texts from Japan. Xiong was preparing an outline of *Weishi* doctrine, and on the basis of his draft and the recommendation of his teacher he was offered a lectureship at Peking University in 1922. He thus became Liang Shuming's colleague, as mentioned in the previous chapter. Xiong retained this position until he retired in 1954, but he was frequently absent due to long convalescences from mental exhaustion and teaching stints at Ma Yifu's and Liang Shuming's academies.

Xiong never finished that introduction to *Weishi* Buddhism. Instead, in 1932 he published *New Treatise on Weishi* (*Xin weishi lun*) in which he uses *Weishi* as a foil for his own ideas. The reader can feel the creative shoots of Xiong's thinking sprouting between the architectural cracks in *Weishi*, but once his ideas have fully emerged, *Weishi* had been reduced to a crumbling philosophical ruin. As *Weishi* teachings are very complex yet unnecessary to the gist of Xiong's thesis, I will spare you those details.

Everyone assumed Xiong had turned to Ru Learning to critique Buddhist doctrine. Xiong said this was not what had happened. Rather, he said, his frustration with Buddhism drove him "to seek within myself." Only later did he realize what he had personally discovered perfectly aligned with what Kongzi had espoused in his commentaries on the *Yijing*. Thus, he said, "what I have obtained from Confucius has not been through books, but through personal experience" (Makeham 2015: xviii).

Xiong's primary concern was the relationship between absolute Reality and the world as we know it. He certainly disagreed with the idea of a creator-God separate from creation, but even Buddhism had driven a wedge between absolute and mundane realms. This may not be true of all forms of Buddhism, especially those schools that emerged in China (such as Tiantai, Huayan, and Chan), but Xiong was arguing against Buddhisms of Indian origin where absolute Reality was said to be totally distinct from the inconstant, illusionary world we inhabit.

Xiong had no tolerance for this kind of dualism. He said only one thing exists. Absolute Reality is all there is. The world we know is that very Reality, although we misconstrue what we perceive and imagine it to be made of discreet, individual things. His favorite analogy for the relationship between Reality and the universe composed of seemingly separate phenomena was the association between an ocean and waves. The ocean is manifest to us as a multitude of individual waves, yet waves are no more than momentary transformations of a single, indivisible ocean.

Xiong used the established Chinese philosophical polarity of *ti* (essence, substance) and *yong* (manifestation, function) to discuss the relationship between the One and the many. In his analogy, the ocean is substance while waves are particular manifestations or functions of that substance. Or, to offer another example, if we take clay to be substance, then a cup or a bowl or a sculpture made from clay would be various functions. Xiong said absolute or Original Reality (*benti*) is the one unique substance and all of phenomenal reality should be understood as functions of that substance. We can no more separate the "ten thousand things" from Original Reality than we can isolate waves from an ocean or cups and bowls from clay.

As his ocean analogy suggests, Xiong's Reality is constantly transforming and yet essentially unchanging: "Change is unchanging because change is always constant" (Xiong 2015: 157). This is where Xiong turned to the fluid cosmology of the *Classic of Changes* (*Yijing*) rather than static Buddhist notions of ultimate Reality. As change is intrinsic to Reality, all the separate individual things we discern are in fact "nothing but instant upon instant of ceasing and arising, arising and ceasing" (Xiong 2015: 106). They are only "illusionary" to the extent that we see them as being autonomous rather than as fleeting moments of Reality.

We usually see the world as consisting of various physical and mental things. Xiong, of course, said this was not strictly so, but it nonetheless relates to a *yin-yang* pulse in the transformations of Reality. The *Yijing* says that "contraction (*qu*) and expansion (*shen*) impel each other on" (Lynn 1994: 81), and Xiong maintained that contraction tends toward physicality while expansion moves in the direction of mental phenomena. In his words, "Material *dharmas* [elements of existence] are when the movement of constant transformation is contracting; mental *dharmas* are when the movement of the constant transformation is expanding" (Xiong 2015: 110). But Xiong was not at all introducing a mind-matter dualism. He was saying, rather, that the constant transformation of a single Reality has innumerable moments of contracting and expanding, which we mistakenly conceptualize as discreet "mental" and "material" phenomena. Thus, in the case of contraction, "countless points of movement are *illusorily* constituted, the tendency of which *seems to be* toward solidifying" (Xiong 2015: 97). Reality itself is an infinitude of instantaneous transformations that people apprehend as objective things.

While Xiong considers mental and material phenomena equally to be fluctuations in undifferentiated Reality, he nonetheless does privilege mind over matter. This is because Original Reality in fact is *xin* or heart-mind:

> If one were only to say that the Reality of the heart-mind is constant transformation, one could not be reproached for implying that the heart-mind is Reality. And so, if one were to regard this heart-mind as not descending into the material but to be the expression of the power of constant transformation's self-nature ... then there would be nothing to stop one saying that the heart-mind is not different from Reality. In other words, the heart-mind is not different from the constant transformation that is Fundamental Reality. (Xiong 2015: 178)

Xiong is thus saying that all the myriad things of the universe are inseparable from Original Reality which is heart-mind or consciousness. This he boldly asserted in his opening sentence of the *New Treatise*: "My aim in writing this treatise is to awaken those who study the learning that is concerned with fundamental wisdom to understand that Reality is not ... detached from one's own heart-mind" (Xiong 2015: 21).

From what I have said, it is obvious that Xiong sometimes spoke of heart-mind in different ways. There is Original heart-mind (*benxin*) that is identical with Original Reality (*benti*), and there is the everyday customary mind (*xixin*) that misconstrues that same Reality as the phenomenal world. Xiong does not totally dismiss the latter orientation. Appropriately applied, it generates knowledge essential for life, and the obvious benefits of science are among the great achievements of the customary mind. Xiong had no gripe with science except insofar as it claimed to be the supreme arbitrator of truth. Science is by nature confined to interpreting a world composed of discrete things, which bars it from apprehending Reality as a totality. Science excels at generating "knowledge": "As for what is termed 'knowledge,' it has always been developed on the basis of looking outward at things. In the universe that constitutes our everyday lives, because we regard that which our sense detect to be real cognitive objects external to our mind, so we distinguish and deal with them accordingly" (Xiong 2015: 25). But knowledge (*zhishi*) is not "wisdom" (*zhi*, one of the Five Constant Virtues). Wisdom is "the self's recognizing the self, with absolutely nothing concealed.

Correspondence with true realization is called wisdom because it differs from the mundane world, which is established on the basis of discernment" (Xiong 2015: 21).

New Treatise was published when Xiong was at Peking University, the hub of the New Culture Movement with all its enthusiasm for science and Western education (Chapter 8). Xiong threw down a challenge by arguing that this kind of knowledge was secondary to learning to apprehend wisdom, which alone could provide a secure foundation for authentic morality. China's woes could not be solved by science, and therefore Ru Learning remained paramount. He said that "if one wants to realize inherent mind, then one must value learning," but clarified that "self-recognition or self-creativity is collectively referred to as 'awakening'—and it is this alone that constitutes true learning'" (Xiong 2015: 308–9).

True learning is not the accumulation of factual information or rational argumentation, but rather the heart-mind's direct "intuition" of its own Reality. How would this promote morality? Xiong draws on stock Ru assumptions that will by now be very familiar to readers. First, heart-mind is identical to nature (*xing*): "heart-mind is not different from the nature" (Xiong 2015: 308). Next, virtue is inherent in our nature: "the five virtues [presumably humaneness, righteousness, ritual, wisdom and trustworthiness] are endowed in the inherent nature" (Xiong 2015: 316). In a later rewrite of *New Treatise*, Xiong particularly emphasizes the supreme virtue of *ren*: "Humaneness (*ren*) is the original heart-mind. It is the original [Reality] common to man, Heaven, Earth, and all things ... From Confucius to Mencius to the teachers of the Song and Ming periods, all directly pointed to humaneness which is the original heart-mind. The substance of humaneness is the source of all transformations and the foundation of all things" (Chan 1963a: 768–9).

Thus, Original Reality is heart-mind, which is nature, which is also humaneness. In his later works, Xiong brings politics into his converging cosmos; there is no separation between knowing and acting, between inner awakening and enlightened ruling. Since the Song dynasty, Ru had discussed the relationship between "inner sageliness" (*neisheng*) and "outer kingliness" (*waiwang*), but this pair had been neglected since the fall of the empire. Xiong returned them to the philosophical discussion and they have remained pivotal ever since. Xiong's own definition will suffice: "The study of internal sageliness solves the important problems of the universe and life ... The study of external kingliness solves important problems in society and politics" (Ng 2003: 223).

Just as Reality itself is unchanging in its eternal transformation, so too we must achieve stillness through social and political activity. People should "not renounce activity and seek quietude; likewise they should not let themselves be taken up by activity and lose their quietude" (Bresciani 2001: 132). Kongzi, the author of the *Changes*, was, after all, also Kongzi the socialist revolutionary, as we saw Xiong arguing in Chapter 8.

The full reach of Xiong's ever-conflating universe is seen in the following passage:

The great rule for becoming Sage Within and King Without is all here: substance and phenomena are not two divided realities ... Heaven and humans are not two divided realities ... Human life is not divided from its ultimate source, as waves are not divided from the great mass of seawater ... Heart-mind and things are not two divided realities ... Knowing and acting are not two divided realities. (Bresciani 2001: 131–2)

Some applaud Xiong for having "solved the difficult metaphysical problem of the separation between ontological substance and phenomena" (Ng 2003: 239). Others point out that while Xiong was quick to proclaim his solution to this problem was "subtle and profound," he regularly presents "the metaphor of the ocean and its waves to substitute for the expected arguments" (Yu 2002: 134). And, it has to be said, his metaphor is most unfortunate. The fact that *every* wave in an ocean is generated by something *other* than ocean (e.g., wind, seismic activity) is not at all suggestive of a self-transforming Original Reality. Waves are *not* ocean; they are waves of energy passing through the ocean's surface. It makes no more sense to say that waves are inseparable from ocean than it does to say electricity is inseparable from copper wire.

Be this as it may, Xiong's followers believed he had established the foundations on which Ru Learning could be reestablished in an age of science and democracy. To meet that challenge, however, there were two shortcomings to Xiong's philosophy that needed to be addressed.

The first requisite was a more thorough investigation into the limits of science, which in turn required a greater understanding of Western philosophy. Xiong was well aware there were Western thinkers who had critiqued the naïve Enlightenment view that science was based on evidence directly deriving from reality, but he knew his grasp of the relevant sources was limited. Xiong could see that Immanuel Kant was seminal in this regard and he particularly encouraged the young Mou Zongsan to engage with Kant. The importance of this will become apparent a little later.

The other perceived shortcoming was Xiong's politics. Did he really make a pact between Kongzi and Mao Zedong in his later works (Chapter 8)? Probably not. He never used Maoist or Marxist jargon, and his image of Kongzi as a socialist revolutionary seems closer to Sun Yat-sen's socialism. Even this much made his followers uneasy. Mou Zongsan could not accept his beloved teacher was so inclined. It was, he said, an "expedient strategy," as under Mao "the only way [for Xiong] to save Confucius was to admit that Confucius supported socialism and the idea of revolution" (Ng 2003: 250n. 61). The scant available evidence on Xiong's private views, however, suggest his publications do in fact approximate his convictions (Liu 2003: 59–60, 70–1n. 10). Here, his disciples would not follow. The next generation of New Ru philosophers were all advocates of liberal democracy. Tu Weiming has observed that "those who are attuned to the Confucian message inevitably discover that Confucian personality ideals (the authentic person, the worthy, or the sage) can be realized more fully in a liberal democratic society than in either traditional imperial dictatorship or a modern authoritarian regime" (Tu 2010: 105). Many contemporary revivalists in mainland China would contest Tu's verdict, but his observation certainly holds for the philosophers discussed in the remainder of this chapter.

Xiong's three most renowned followers believed they understood how Ru Learning could embrace and yet enrich democracy and science. And they were ready to declare this to the world.

A declaration to the world

In 1958, Tang Junyi, Xu Fuguan, and Mou Zongsan, the so-called second generation, together with Zhang Junmai, produced a manifesto that is often seen as a defining moment in the history of New Ru Learning. Liu Shuxian hails it "a landmark for the emergence of the Contemporary Neo-Confucianism Movement" (Liu 2003: 26), while Nicholas Bunnin sees it as actually "giving rise to the Movement of Contemporary New Confucianism" (Bunnin 2002: 11). Something like this may well have been the authors' intention, but they were first to admit their manifesto was initially a flop.

The work in question is "A Manifesto [or Declaration] on Chinese Culture Respectfully Announced to the People of the World" (*Wei zhongguo wenhua jinggao shijie renshi xuanyan*). Several immediate questions arise regarding its intent and authorship.

Although it is professedly written "as an aid to Western intellectuals in appreciating Chinese culture" (Chang 1962: 455), it was initially published in Chinese in two Taiwanese journals, Xu Fuguan's *Democratic Review* (*Minzhu Pinglun*) and *National Renaissance* (*Zaisheng*). The English translations that appeared a few years later— one an awkward abridgement appended to Zhang's *Development of Neo-Confucian Thought*, the other in a Taiwanese journal so obscure few have ever sighted it—are not suggestive of an urgent desire to communicate with the West. Rather, the critique seems to have been primarily directed toward Chinese people who embraced Western values and themselves wished to turn their back on China's past. Addressing the declaration to "the people of the world" accentuated the otherness of those who had chauvinistically imposed their culture on China while failing to understand the tradition they were usurping. In short, the Manifesto is crafted to generate national pride and revive select aspects of traditional Chinese cultural. As Serina Chan observed, "Chinese cultural nationalism penetrates the 1958 Declaration" (2011: 236).

If the Manifesto's intended readership is uncertain, so too is its authorship. It seems clear the initial idea for writing it came from Zhang Junmai and that Tang Junyi produced the first draft. According to Zhang's preface to his translation, Tang then sent his draft to Mou Zongsan and Xu Fuguan, and the final version thereafter emerged from their collaborative revisions. In the other English translation, however, a preface says this draft was first sent to Xie Youwei (1903–76), who was identified as a fifth author. John Makeham sees the omission of Xie's name as part of "the retrospective creation of the New Confucian identity" (Makeham 2003: 45n. 11), while Umberto Bresciani more explicitly says Xie was dropped because he "was otherwise little involved with their propaganda movement for New Confucianism" (Bresciani 2001: 535n. 3). Clearly, the major authors had an agenda for consolidating a specific form of revival. Zhang mentions that "in order not to delay the publication too much we have not been able to approach for endorsement many of those who hold similar views" (Chang 1962: 456); he fails to mention that Qian Mu, now counted among the exponents of New Ru Learning, had refused to sign and neglects to explain why Xie's name had been dropped.

The authors of the Manifesto were undeniably seeking to consolidate a revival, even perhaps to initiate a movement. Makeham does not hesitate to assert that it "can be seen to represent a group of Confucian scholars speaking collectively, thereby lending the group a cohesion and shared identity" (Makeham 2003: 28). It surely indicates concord and collegiality, but it is erroneous to suggest the Manifesto played a major role in the actual creation of what came to be known as *Xin ruxue*. The Manifesto does not make any explicit link with so-called first-generation exponents such as Liang Shuming and Xiong Shili; it sits awkwardly with the full gamut of names later recruited to the movement and, quite frankly, except for a noncommittal response from a few Chinese Catholics and a dismissive review by Hu Shi, when it first appeared, the Manifesto was totally ignored. Xu Fuguan was himself forced to admit that it "did not bring about any concrete results" (Bresciani 2001: 538n. 28).

Liu Shuxian has said that although they recognized the need for East-West synthesis, "the scholars who signed the document are deeply convinced that the Confucian tradition is the most open, inclusive, and creative one among various traditions which may serve as the best vehicle for us to look towards the future of mankind" (Liu 1991: 383). It should be added that even though the Ru tradition they endorse is a very specific interpretative lineage, they take pains to argue that it is the essence, the perennial heart, and "the root of Chinese thought" (Chang 1962: 461). Given that they were also promoting democracy, it is rather ironic that their views were set in opposition to then common Chinese opinion, were not well supported by peers, and would have be totally unintelligible to the vast majority of the Chinese population. Their arguments may or may not be good political and moral philosophy, but they were decidedly uneven as an account of Chinese history and the country's cultural diversity. The Manifesto must therefore be seen as a piece of cultural essentialism designed to advance the authors' own vision for reconstructing China.

Although "most Chinese and Western scholars now cannot appreciate this point of view"—indeed, even though it was absent from the *Analects* and most of the Classics and had been downplayed since the Qing dynasty—the "root of Chinese thought," we are told, was the doctrine of *xinxing* ("heart-mind" and "nature"). Their understanding of this followed the tradition of Wang Yangming and reflected the more recent interpretative innovations of Xiong Shili. As Heaven (*tian*), heart-mind (*xin*), and nature (*xing*) are one, cultivating the heart-mind discloses the moral essence of human nature, which is identical with Reality. Thus, "human nature reflects the nature of Heaven; the morality of man is also that of Heaven. What man does to perfect his own nature is also what gives praise to the manifold manifestations of the universe" (Chang 1962: 464).

The Manifesto makes it clear that in saying *xinxing* was the heart of China the authors believed that Chinese culture was fundamentally religious. *Xinxing* arises from "a primordial religious passion to ethico-moral principles" and while it lacks God, it is "yet pervaded by [religious] sentiments, and hence is quite different from occidental atheism" (Chang 1962: 461). In the year following the publication of the Manifesto, Mou added:

> On our view, a culture cannot be without its most fundamental inner spirit. This is the driving force for cultural creation; within it is that which renders the culture unique. On our view, this driving force is religion, regardless of mode. Accordingly, we can say this: the fundamental driving force of the life of a culture should lie in religion. (Chan 2011: 265–6)

The heart-mind of Heaven immanent as human heart-mind and human nature was the religious essence of Chinese culture and the source of Chinese moral values. As such, it served as a measure for evaluating foreign cultures. China was by disposition tolerant and open-minded—it only rejected "barbarians" because "objectively China's culture was more advanced than theirs" (Chang 1962: 468)—and so China would welcome science and democracy introduced from the West. These must first pass through the filter of *xinxing*, however, and develop organically from within: "It is erroneous to think that [China's] culture contains neither the seeds of democracy nor such tendencies, or that it is hostile to science and technology" (Chang 1962: 469).

The Manifesto says democracy was latent in Ru tradition. "Confucianists ... championed the conception that the nation belonged not to one man but to the people," and so "it then follows that a constitution must be drawn up, in accordance with the popular will" (Chang 1962: 472). Given there was "no doubt the Chinese people do aspire for a democratic government" (Chang 1962: 473), the authors felt obliged to clarify why recent political events had not seen this realized, and they were at pains to show precisely why communism should not and could not endure. The Manifesto's views on liberal democracy were expanded in the following years by Mou and Tang, as we will see in the next section.

As for science, China was not without its own achievements, but, for good reason, these had fallen short of the triumphs of the West. In an argument reminiscent of Xiong Shili (and anticipating Mou Zongsan's more extensive analysis), the Manifesto maintains that the pursuit of science "demands the suspension, at least temporarily, of all ... moral activities, transcending evaluations and moral judgment." In order for science to flourish, the heart-mind must turn away from the self-reflection that discloses our moral self, and instead focus on the external world so as to "illuminate the laws of the universe." In China, therefore, "the privation of ... a scientific spirit was the result chiefly of the obsession with the fulfillment of moral principles, which prevented any objective assessment of the world" (Chang 1962: 469–70).

Despite the West's spectacular material achievements, the Manifesto says that in a most fundamental way the West needs to learn from China and from the doctrine of *xinxing*. In the tradition of Liang Shuming, the authors proceed from a simplistic distinction between China and the West and employ a line of argument to which

Gloria Davies has referred as "the well-established Sinophone tradition of defending China's spiritual superiority against the technological or scientific superiority of the West" (Davies 2007: 25). Rather than pursuing progress and devoting the heart-mind to empirical and conceptual analysis, they say the West needs to learn that authentic wisdom is only achieved by direct "intuition" of the heart-mind. This intuition will reveal our underlying unity with all things and so generate genuine compassion for others guided by the gentle restraints of *li* or ritual decorum. Finally,

> The human existence as formed by "establishing Man as the Ultimate" is that of a moral being which, at the same time, attains a higher spiritual enlightenment … thereby attaining "harmony in virtue with Heaven." Hence, this human existence is simultaneously moral and religious existence. Such a man is, in politics, the genuine citizen of democracy, in epistemology, one who stands above the physical world. Not being bound by his concepts, his intellectual knowledge does not contradict his spiritual appreciation. (Chang 1962: 483)

Like Christianity, Ruism teaches universal love and offers religious insights relevant to all humanity, but in the modern "global family" it would actually be "better to rely more on *Ru* thought." This moment of spiritual one-upmanship is derived from the fact that Christianity's doctrine of salvation is reserved for converts, while Ruism is free from such exclusivist dogma. Ru tradition teaches that "all human beings can attain sagehood and be equal to Kongzi. What that means is that the teaching of the *Ru* and the religions of all people are not in opposition" (Chan 2011: 276).

The Manifesto is a significant document for accessing ideas shared by a small circle of like-minded friends. It would have faded into obscurity, however, were in not for ensuing events. In particular, it was the subsequent status of one of the signatories, Mou Zongsan, and following this the retrospective creation of the New Ru School in the 1980s, that saw the proclamation being revered as the Manifesto definitive of all that was to follow. Mou's "ideological control" over the Manifesto is quite evident (Chan 2011: 264), and the brief reference to the resonance between *xinxing* and "Kant's 'ethical' metaphysics" (Chang 1962: 463) can be seen as a prelude to Mou's primary philosophical achievement.

Mou Zongsan encounters Immanuel Kant

Mou Zongsan (1909–95) stands out in the second generation. Indeed, he is foremost among all the supposed exponents of New Ru Learning and is considered by many to be the greatest Chinese philosopher of the modern era.

Mou Zongsan was born into a farming family of modest means in Shandong province. He would later recall how content he was in this natural environment as well as reflecting on his intractable character as a young student. He disliked authority and "loathed" and was "disgusted" by the affected ways of his schoolteachers. This impatience with those he deemed unworthy remained with him; in later life he saw it as having "no tolerance for smug academics" (Mou 1915: 26).

Mou had no real inclination towards Ru philosophy when he entered Peking University and he initially focused on mathematical logic and the New Realism of Bertrand Russell. On the side, however, he was drawn to the works of Alfred North Whitehead which, surprisingly, roused him to delve deeper into one of the Classics: "As for my interest in the cosmology ... [of] the *Yijing,* the credit for inspiring that must go to Whitehead" (Mou 2015a: 71). A comparativist was born.

Mou would outgrow Whitehead who he felt lacked the capacity to understand "inner being" (Mou 2015a: 78). Then, in 1932, he met Xiong Shili. His first impression was of a man who was "unabashedly impolite and utterly aggressive." He quickly reframed this as complete authenticity and being "principled without any duplicity," and he knew he had found his master and his role model (Mou 2015a: 119). Over their sixteen-plus years of close association, on occasion living together—at which time Xiong "admonished me and guided me day and night and enlightened me a great deal" (Chan 2011: 11)—Mou came to develop a profound admiration for Ru Learning. In 1939 he met his life-long friend Tang Junyi who introduced him to Hegel and the possibilities of in-depth comparative philosophy. Late in life, he would reflect that Xiong had been his only teacher and Tang his one friend (Mou 2015a: 118n. 2).

Mou briefly worked with two others counted as exponents of New Ru Learning, but he soon fell out with them. Although Zhang Junmai was a cosignatory of the Manifesto, Mou thought him "a mediocre person" and at times a "muddleheaded boring fool" (Mou 2015a: 139, 137). He also disliked Liang Shuming and stormed out on him over a minor matter, never to reconnect. He was repelled by the way Liang's followers placed him "on a pedestal of sagehood" (Mou 2015a: 142), yet seemed comfortable enough when his own followers later did so to him. There is perhaps a reason sages traditionally appear centuries apart.

Mou and Xiong were again living together as the Communists were securing China, and they parted in the summer of 1949. Mou felt the "loss" of the mainland like his own death. His commiseration for others blurred with self-pity and his own healing fused with China's recovery. Mou detested communism: "From its very roots, Communism is demonic heresy and should be thoroughly eradicated" (Clower 2014: 112). This fiend was destroying China, and Mou's self-regeneration was synonymous with saving *his* China. He wrote:

My country, the Chinese people, cultural life, and the distinctions between Chinese and foreign ... were my religion at the time. I indeed had religious zeal then. I absolutely opposed anyone who charted a different path by violating or negating my "religion," and anyone who failed to follow my "religion" to fulfill his or her duty to establish a nation that would most perfectly realize the Chinese people's *xing*-nature. (Mou 2015a: 166)

While he was more moderate in later life, Mou remained very confident in his ability to guide China's recovery by promoting what *he* deemed to be the essence of Chinese culture.

For the decade following 1949, when Mou was teaching philosophy in Taiwan, his thought was preoccupied with anticommunist plans for China's reconstruction. By the time he moved to Hong Kong, in 1960, when he was fifty-one, his raging nationalism had abated and he thereafter proceeded to produce his greatest philosophical works.

Mou Zongsan would say later in his life that nothing he wrote before he was fifty should be read (Su 2004: 335). I will take him at his word. The Manifesto thus nicely serves to mark the beginning of his mature thought. For the half-decade following its appearance, Mou and Tang Junyi both continued to write on political philosophy. It is quite misleading when Jiang Qing (Chapter 10) accuses the second generation of New Ru Learning of neglecting politics, and a few years before his death Mou declared that his unwavering concern had always been "how to bring forth outer kingliness from inner sageliness" (Clower 2014: 77).

Mou was a fierce critic of traditional Ru notions of outer kingliness, however. The Manifesto had acknowledged the shortcomings of Ru political theory—"It was a weakness of their ideologies that they did not formulate theories of effective transfer of the throne to those of high moral integrity" (Chang 1962: 472)—but Mou and Tang were subsequently to develop what has been deemed to be "the most systematic, if not searing, critiques of [Ru political philosophy] put forward in the 20th century" (Fröhlich 2010: 168).

Mou and Tang believed Ru *political* tradition had been a failure and had been detrimental to China. They were both staunch advocates of liberal democracy and continued to argue, as the Manifesto had briefly done, that the germ of democracy had been present in early Ru philosophy. What was needed was a new exposition to show how this could be effectively delivered into the political arena. This was not a straightforward transfer, however.

Mou's analysis of politics is very similar to his views on science. He readily acknowledged Western superiority in science and politics and he attributed this to China's preoccupation with morality. He, of course, esteemed this moral awareness, but it could become an obstacle if it was mishandled. Zhu Xi orthodoxy took much of the blame. Zhu had based his understanding of the moral self on the empirical "investigation of things." In this approach, the external world was used to access our interior nature which Mou called "studying the ordinary in order to understand the ultimate" (Mou 2015b: 417). This conflation of inner and outer realms hindered both the true development of science and politics on the one hand and of morality on the other.

Mou followed the Lu-Wang tradition that instead maintains our nature (*xing*) is manifest in the heart-mind (*xin*). Our moral nature is apprehended by intuitive introspection, not by the analysis of external evidence. But reason applied to empirical evidence is precisely what is required of science, as it is of sound politics. To get around this, Mou, like his teacher Xiong Shili, clearly separated two orientations of the heart-mind. Sometimes Mou uses Xiong's metaphor of the ocean and waves, but his favorite refrain was "one mind opening two gates." That is, the heart-mind can dwell on its own original nature or alternatively it can be directed toward making vital discriminations in the external world.

For Mou, even perfect inner awareness is insufficient for developing science and politics. Science: "God does not make atomic bombs; though he be omniscient, he does not have scientific knowledge" (Clower 2014: 218). Politics: "A sage who wants to be president must leave behind the status of sage and obey the laws and rules required of a president" (Mou 2015b: 290). Just as a preoccupation with morality and the introspective heart-mind had hindered China developing the atomistic analysis of the external world required of science, so too Chinese politics had foundered due to the absence of clear conceptual differentiation between morality and politics.

To establish either science or politics, the mind must restrain itself (ziwo kanxian, "self negation") from direct self-intuition lest the potential for genuine science and politics be "swallowed" by morality. The error of past Ru had been to naively assume that outer kingliness (waiwang) would automatically and spontaneously emerge from cultivating inner sageliness (neisheng), precisely the false premise that lay behind China's education system and meritocracy. It failed to the extent that politics is not a simple outgrowth of morality. Indeed, to ensure people have an environment in which to genuinely engage their moral selves, politics must be detached from individuals (even the most sagacious rulers) and use constitutions and laws to create space to protect individual freedom.

***

Having espoused his defense of liberal democracy in *The Way of Politics and the Way of Government* (*Zhengdao yu zhidao*, 1961), Mou thereafter turned to primarily focus on the world of the inner sage. Mou was a prolific writer, and his philosophy is not easy. His critics find him obscure, which Mou acknowledged and attributed to his intuitive way of thinking. His magnum opus is the three-volume *Metaphysical Reality of Heart-Mind and Nature* (*Xinti yu xingti*, 1968–9), but the most popular introduction to his thought is *Nineteen Lectures on Chinese Philosophy* (*Zhongguo zhexue shijiu jiang*, 1983). It is still hard going.

Mou believed that Ru religious insight was urgently needed to counter the growing tendency to treat science as the only and ultimate way of ascertaining truth – "modern people wear science like a protective amulet and . . . want to get rid of Heaven" (Clower 2014: 133). The discriminating mind provides essential information about the external world and has produced the undeniable benefits of science, but it cannot lead to moral awareness. This can only occur when our heart-mind functions as original heart-mind introspectively apprehending its own true nature.

Thus far, Mou echoed Xiong Shili. Where he surpassed his mentor was in developing these ideas so that they took their place on a global philosophical stage. Xiong had a very limited understanding of Western philosophy, whereas Mou took to it effortlessly and was drawn to those considered notoriously difficult. Xiong must, nonetheless, be credited with encouraging the young Mou's comparative inclinations, and a letter he wrote to him in the early 1940s can be seen as defining Mou's philosophical crusade:

> You wish to elucidate Kant and make a return to this path. This is a worthwhile effort. Yet the three concepts that Kant called God, the soul and the free will are too fragmented. Wouldn't it be fantastic if you did away with God and the soul and became good at elucidating the free will! (Chan 2011: 36)

Mou did not just make casual comparisons between Ru thought and Immanuel Kant (1724–1804), whose major works he translated into Chinese; he spun a rich and original system based on deep philosophical dialogue. This was, so to speak, Mou's considered response to a topic raised in the Manifesto: "What the West can learn from Oriental thought." As Stephen Schmidt has noted, Mou is esteemed in China for having show that "Confucianism is one of the great intellectual and spiritual traditions of the world and has a substantial contribution to make to modern humankind. As such, it is neither outdated nor backward, although it does need to be reformulated in a new and more precise—more 'philosophical' in the Western sense of the discipline—kind of way" (Schmidt 2011: 274–5).

Mou was drawn to Kant because he saw him as "the best bridge" for "reconciling Chinese and Western philosophy" (Clower 2014: 116). At a time when Western science was in its ascent, Kant had challenged science's monopoly on truth by arguing that empirical knowledge is never simply presented to us, but is always filtered by the workings of the mind. Kant himself described this as a Copernican revolution in philosophy, while Arthur Schopenhauer said Kant had awakened the Enlightenment from an intellectual dream so that philosophers came to the startling realization that "the beginning and end of the world are to be sought not without us, but rather within" (Schopenhauer 1958: vol. 1, 420–1). Kant also argued the source of authentic morality was not the outer world but the inner reaches of the mind. This much obviously resonated with Mou's understanding of Ru Learning. But Kant maintained other views that, were they true, spelled disaster for many Chinese schools of thought. Kant's simultaneous resonance and discord with Ru Learning generated Mou's most creative thinking.

Song-Ming Ru had argued that the sagacious heart-mind could directly apprehend the absolute nature of existence. For Kant, this was impossible. Kant's most famous contribution was to show that we can never actually know things external to ourselves. We receive information through our senses, but it is our mind that orders this raw data so as to make it meaningful. What we know are *phenomena*. We thus never directly apprehend things "out there," which Kant calls *noumena* or things-in-themselves. Perhaps God knows noumena through divine intuition, Kant admitted, but he carefully argued it was impossible to prove whether in fact God actually exists. But God, along with freedom and the immortal soul, were nonetheless *practical* necessities, as we shall soon see.

Kant's ultimately real world was theoretically accessible only to the intellectual intuition of a transcendent deity while we humans are limited to knowing things mediated through our senses (as well as things we can know a priori through reason). This presented a real challenge for Ru Learning, and Mou observed that the fundamental "difference between Kant and Confucianism is that Kant thinks only God has intellectual intuition while humans do not" (Mou 2015b: 462). Mou's response was an attempt to show there was no absolute separation between noumenal and phenomenal realities, and thus that the human heart-mind could partake of those intuitive capacities that Kant had reserved for God alone.

Kant had rejected the possibility of knowing God through the world of our senses or through reason, but he snuck God in through the back door of morality. For Kant, morality was not dependant on the phenomenal world—it was not, for example, something people invent to help regulate their interaction with others. Rather, morality arises directly from our inner self as our conscience simply commands us, in much the same manner as when Mengzi said our nature (xing) elicits our goodness. With this much, Mou said, "Confucianism takes the same approach as Kant" (2015b: 402). But Kant went further. We know *freedom* through our experience of moral choice. We understand the *immortality of the soul* when we constantly fall short of the moral perfection toward which we are driven—an immortal soul is a necessity for reaching the highest good. And insofar as virtue does not always bring immediate happiness, as we understand it should, we know *God* as the arbitrator who ultimately balances all virtue with happiness. These are not proofs that freedom, the soul or God actually exist, but Kant said there was a compelling *practical* reason why we should accept them: they were necessities integral to our moral being.

Mou was unimpressed. He disliked all these divisions—virtue separated from happiness, the human soul from God, a future kingdom of God from this world. "Kant invokes three postulates—free will, God's existence, and the immortality of the soul— without allowing them to be one" (Mou 2015b: 460). Although Mou conceded ultimate Reality (ti) could legitimately be spoken of as having various aspects—such as Heavenly ti (tianti), nature ti (xingti), heart-mind ti (xinti)—these were actually just different ways of looking at one single Reality. "Moral order is cosmic order, and conversely, cosmic order is moral order" (Mou 2015b: 459).

In short, Mou was saying humans can take the place of Kant's God. Kant missed this because he saw humans being limited to what they are rather than seeing them for what they might be "from the perspective of self-realization through practice." If the heart-mind, human nature, and "the Way of Heaven and earth" are ultimately inseparable, then humans have the capacity for intellectual intuition of things-in-themselves and "endowing humans with intellectual intuition means Kant's three postulates must be one" (Mou 2015b: 462).

Many have found Mou's claim that the heart-mind can apprehend ultimate Reality to be most inspiring. But is it true? Mou bristled whenever the question was raised. Kant had rejected such claims as "mysticism," to which Mou curtly replied: "This view of Kant is very inappropriate" (2015b: 464). At the end of *Nineteen Lectures*, having subjected his audience to his torturously intellectual analysis, Mou readily dismissed those who say "show me the proof" for having "an intellectualist attitude" (2015b: 467).

Again, when Mou once overheard Feng Youlan referring to innate moral knowledge (*liangzhi*) as a "hypothesis," he was so enraged he instantly dismissed everything Feng had ever written on the history of Chinese philosophy (Mou 2015a 122–3). These are not the responses of a philosopher but of someone guard-dogging dogma.

The only real proof Mou does offer can be summarized in just one word: China. He is prone to statements like: "When Kant spoke about things-in-themselves he was speaking in relation to God, but in China it is different" (Clower 2014: 142); "Kant may not acknowledge human intellectual intuition, but that does not mean the Chinese must deny it" (Mou 2015b: 461); "If it is true that human beings cannot have intellectual intuition, then the whole of Chinese philosophy must collapse completely, and the thousands [of] years of effort must be in vain" (Tang 2002: 333). To borrow a distinction from Kant, this is not pure reason but practical reason; Chinese traditions need to be correct in order to restore China's philosophical pride.

In Mou's vision, China can accept the benefits of Western science and democracy yet remain proudly Chinese because China reciprocates by advancing the West's philosophical and religious understanding. Kant had shown that morality was autonomous from science, but Mou felt Western philosophical traditions had fettered Kant and his successors. "Only through comparison with Chinese philosophy can the imperfection and incompletion of Kantian philosophy be revealed," he said; and again, "if we wish to move Kantian philosophy a step forward, we must allow it and Chinese philosophy to mutually agitate" (Mou 2015b: 316, 323)

Mou's dialogue with Kant was meant to be synonymous with China's dialogue with the West. Mou said Kant was "the best medium" for "absorbing Western culture" (Clower 2014: 55), and Mou's own encyclopedic surveys of the history of Chinese philosophy might suggest he himself was well positioned to speak on behalf of China. In reality, however, Mou carefully cherry-picked China's past so that it conformed to "Mou Zongsan." "China" is almost Mou's alter ego. Mou presented his philosophy as Ru Learning, but he was not at all reserved in expelling great Ru of the past for their alleged failings. Without hesitation, he dismissed Cheng Yi and Zhu Xi. Along with most modern exponents of Ru Learning, Mou preferred the interpretations of Lu Xiangshan and Wang Yangming, but he felt even they fell short. Only Cheng Hao and Hu Hong (1105–61) had completely grasped "perfect teaching," he said, and so he promptly promoted them to first rank among the authentic transmitters of the Way (*daotong*). As Jason Clower has observed, Mou evaluates past Ru against a single criterion, their "fidelity to truth as Mou conceives it" (Clower 2014: 25). In this way, China was Ru Learning was Mou Zongsan.

To some extent, Mou was well served by his cockiness. Like Kang Youwei, Liang Shuming, and Xiong Shili, he was very capable of assuming the posture of a sage. Serina Chan has observed both Xiong and Mou "shared a kind of intellectual arrogance and spiritual elitism, expressed as overt contempt ... for thinkers and scholars deemed uninitiated in the moral metaphysical truth they saw imbedded in *Ruxue*" (Chan 2011: 293). Mou's critics took exception to his air of authority befitting a cult leader, his aggressiveness toward those who dared challenged him, and his claim to moral superiority based on his monopoly on truth. For better or worse, these very qualities can nonetheless help consolidate an ideologue's status, as a glance to the mainland at the time Mou was writing his main works will readily confirm.

Mou's disciples are frequently very passionate and loyal followers. His impact is undeniable, and his sweeping encyclopedic synthesis of the gamut of Chinese thought along with key Western thinkers is surely the most ambitious and embracive of all Ru philosophies. Were it not for Mou Zongsan's celebrity, Xiong Shili would not have become a "founder," the Manifesto would be yet another dusty, forgotten document, and the philosophers of the New Ru Learning "movement" would have virtually no cohesion. It was Mou's gravitational pull that drew all this into shared orbit, thus creating a conspicuous commodity to be exported back to the mainland. As John Makeham has said, "One might well argue that without Mou there would be no New Confucian movement" (Makeham 2003: 8).

The return of the repressed

Following the death of Mao Zedong in 1976, anti-Ru sentiment in the PRC began to subside. The first sign of this was a symposium on Ru studies held at Shandong University, close to Kongzi's hometown. The inventory of Ru institutions, seminars, journals, and publications that have sprung up in the interim is enormous. Between 1979 and 1990, for example, 14 Ru-related organizations had been established in China, but by the turn of the century the figure had grown exponentially to around 100 (Makeham 2008: 48–9). All have government approval and many receive government support. As we have seen, the invention of the New Ru Learning movement was a part of this regeneration.

It is widely recognized that Tu Weiming, designated one of the third-generation exponents of New Ru Learning, was instrumental in launching the mainland revival of the late twentieth century. Umberto Bresciani maintained that "if, after thirty years of interruption, China has seen a rebirth of interest in Confucian studies, it would be due to a large extent to [Tu Weiming's lecture tours]" (2001: 410), John Makeham said Tu "contributed more than any other individual to promoting a renewed interest in *ruxue* through his lectures and networking in China" (2008: 43), while Suzanne Ogden claimed that "Tu Weiming is almost single-handedly responsible for the revival of Confucianism in China" (Ogden 2002: 43n. 4).

Tu Weiming (pinyin Du Weiming) was born in Kunming in 1940 to parents inclined toward literature and art rather than philosophy. They moved to Taiwan in 1949 when Tu was nine years old, and in his mid-teens one of his teachers stimulated his interest in the Four Books. When he was seventeen, that teacher in turn introduced him to his own teacher, who was none other than Mou Zongsan. Tu found Mou to be brilliant and inspiring and he would regularly visit him at home to join small discussion groups. He says: "If I were to identify a single person as my mentor, Mou Zongsan is certainly the one. Without my fateful encounter with him, I might have … pursued a career in science, engineering, or medicine" (Tu and Ikeda 2011: 16). This is high praise indeed given the very prestigious list of Tu's later mentors and teachers while he was completing a doctorate at Harvard University. Tu went on to teach at Princeton University (1968–71), the University of California (1971–81), and, since 1981, Harvard University.

In 1980, Tu spent a year as a visiting scholar at Beijing Normal University during which time he also traveled to lecture in eighteen cities. He returned in 1983 and again in 1985 when he offered a course on Ru philosophy at Peking University – the last time a course like this had been offered was in 1923 when Liang Shuming was lecturing to students who he could not dissuade from their belief that *Ruxue* was dead (Tu 2010: xi). After the revival built momentum, it is impossible to discern any one individual directing events, but Tu remains a tireless ambassador for Ruism in China and he is currently Director of the Institute for Advanced Studies at Peking University.

Tu's preference for the Lu-Wang lineage is subtly evident in his work, but for the most part he is a careful and insightful scholar not prone to partisanship. Tu is a great advocate of interreligious and intercultural dialogue and believes Ruism has a genuine contribution to make to resolving world political, social, moral, and environmental problems. He is a diplomat for Ru culture on the whole rather than someone promoting a particular lineage in the transmission of the Way (*daotong*). His finesse has greatly contributed to his success.

This is not the place to examine Tu's exemplary scholarship. Nor will I dwell on his deeper concerns, which are not directed toward reviving Ruism per se, but rather to ensuring that Ru moral and religious insight contributes to a global dialogue for achieving an authentic and sustainable humanism. The following passage serves as a concise statement of his more expansive orientation:

> The so-called Third Epoch of Confucian Humanism may have been wishful thinking of a small coterie of academicians, but the emergence of a new inclusive humanism with profound ethical-religious implications for the spiritual self-definition of humanity, the sanctity of the earth, and a form of righteousness based on immanent transcendence has already been placed on the agenda in cultural China. (Tu 2010: 27)

He believes this in an urgently needed corrective to the "Faustian drive" of the West, which has the capacity to push humanity to self-destruction.

Bearing in mind Tu's broader vision, I am here concerned with his specific influence in late twentieth-century China. Effective advocates are sensitive to the expectations of their audience, and Tu's impact was driven by two things China was craving: a strong national identity and wealth.

As China began to stabilize politically and grow economically in the 1980s, the ongoing relevance of Ru tradition was once again being debated. There were many who still shared the sentiments of the New Culture Movement (Chapter 8) and felt that Ruism was obsolete. For example, Bo Yang (Guo Yidong, 1920–2008) was a poet, essayist, historian, and social critic who Chiang Kai-shek had imprisoned for a decade for translating a Popeye cartoon allegedly meant to lampoon him. After his release in 1977, Bo Yang vocally campaigned for human rights and democracy. In 1985, he published *The Ugly Chinaman* (*Choulou de Zhongguoren*), which blamed the decline of China on Ru Learning, which was, he said, nothing more than 2,500 years of footnotes to Kongzi. It was a stagnant pool, a fetid soy-fermenting vat that quickly reduced any fresh intellectual peach that fell into it into a shriveled turd (Yang 1992: 21–2). This book became very popular on the mainland and sold around half a million copies before it was banned.

Following on its heels in 1988, a six-part television series entitled *River Elegy* (*Heshang*) was seen by hundreds of millions of people on China Central Television (CCTV). It too was soon banned. It was blamed for fueling the pro-democracy protests in Tiananmen Square, and members of the production crew subsequently were arrested or fled the country. The Yellow River was more than a symbol as it had been the capricious artery along which many of China's land-locked capital cities had been built. This had made China insular an inward-looking land that built a Great Wall of separation. Thriving Western nations, on the other hand, had been coastal and opened onto an ocean spanning the world. Yet even the Yellow River, choked with sediment (the imperial legacy) and swelling turbid and uncontrollable (recent political upheavals), finally must let go and join the sea. The film emphasized Ru culture as a major source of silt in Chinese history and, alluding to Tu Weiming's recent lectures, it was critical of those anticipating a "third flowering" of Ruism. It was time for the Yellow River to release itself into the blue waters of a modern global democratic community.

While Tu Weiming was quite appreciative of many of the concerns of *River Elegy*, he could not accept the wholesale condemnation of Ru Learning or the naïve eulogizing of Western civilization that, after all, had "brought humanity to the brink of self-destruction" (Tu 1991: 305). Tu's lectures appealed to those who alternatively believed that Ru tradition remained essential to China's future. Tu himself has said that reviving China will entail regenerating Chinese culture, and that "the core element in the revitalization of the national culture is the revitalization of *ruxue* thought" (Makeham 2008: 15). This is perhaps not representative of Tu's generally more moderate stance, but the rivers of Tu's lectures were themselves feeding the swelling waters of nationalism.

By the 1990s, Ruism was widely being held up as the enduring essence of Chinese culture. John Makeham has compiled an evocative medley of slogans. He notes

the frequent, almost ritualistic, invocation of the following mantras: the spirit of *ruxue* became the Chinese people's national spirit; *ruxue* is the spirit of China's overall culture; the *ruxue* tradition is the foundation of the Chinese nation's identity; *rujia* thought is the main guiding force in China's cultural tradition; *ruxue* was the mainstream of thought in traditional culture; *ruxue* is the spirit of China's overall culture; *rujia* culture is the mainstream of Chinese culture; *ruxue* is the main artery of Chinese culture; and so on. (2008: 112–13)

At the same time as age-old Ru tradition was being identified with the essence of Chinese culture, it was also being presented as the ideal companion for a modern market economy. After two and half millennia, the penny dropped: Ruism generates wealth. Tu recalls he initially reacted to this claim with "astonishment" and was reluctantly drawn into the discussion (Tu 2010: xiv), but he nonetheless devoted considerable energy to exploring the nexus between Ruism and capitalism. It is important to stress he does not justify Ru moral values by calculating cash returns, but he has tried to show they are not a hindrance to, and very likely facilitate, modern economic growth. He has thus argued core Ru ideals—such as disciplined self-cultivation, seeing the wider community as an extension of the self, and augmenting family responsibility to loyalty to superiors—are exceptionally well suited to a capitalist work ethic.

"Ru capitalism" has become a major focus of research. In China, there is considerable critical interest in the ideas of the German sociologist Max Weber (1864–1920) who in *The Protestant Ethic and the Spirit of Capitalism* (1905) argued for a direct link between Puritan Christian doctrines and the emergence of capitalism and who later, in his *Religion of China* (1915), explained why Ruism was particularly ill-suited to nurturing the capitalist ethos. Weber's arguments seemed suspect when Japan and the Four Mini-Dragons (Singapore, Hong Kong, Taiwan, and South Korea) rapidly developed capitalist economies, as each had been shaped by Ru tradition. When mainland China began to join their ranks, it seemed increasingly possible that Weber had missed the mark entirely and that Ru culture might not only be compatible with, but a vital stimulus to, capitalist growth. In Tu's words,

> In the 1980s ... the Confucian ethic was promoted as a motivating force to generate a spirit of capitalism. This forcefully refuted the assertion that Confucianism was feudalistic. Rather, Confucianism was believed to be compatible with a modern form of life and instrumental in facilitating East Asian modernization ... The idea of an "elective affinity" between Confucian ethics and the rise of Japan, South Korea, Taiwan, Hong Kong, Singapore, Mainland China, and Vietnam is widely accepted. (Tu 2011: 79)

The compatibility between capitalism and Ruism is not confined to economic theory. Since the 1980s, people in China have developed a gusto for the way of the *rushang* or the "Ru entrepreneur." Countless conferences and business training seminars have been devoted to this, although there is considerable ambiguity as to just what they are advocating. Certainly key Ru values such as self-cultivation and self-reliance, humaneness, justice, righteousness, duty, and loyalty are assumed and agreed on, but there is variance as to whether priority should be given to ensuring businesspeople conduct themselves in accord with Ru values or, alternatively, whether these values are desirable primarily because they generate wealth. An exponent of the former position said he saw business not just as a way of "making money but as a sacred undertaking" in which entrepreneurs "pay the profit back to society, bringing peace, stability, and happiness" (Cheung and King 2004: 252). The latter stance was more evident in views of another businessperson: "Morality is an inner spirit, yet it is capable of being transformed into external material wealth . . . Morality is not 'worthless,' since it can be transformed into money" (Makeham 2008: 326).

* * *

The Ru revival of the late twentieth century was cautiously welcomed by the CCP. As we saw at the beginning of this chapter, the New Ru Learning movement was itself invented by a government-sponsored committee, and this greatly enhanced the visibility of contemporary Ru tradition. But as momentum built, the question had to be asked: Just how compatible was Ruism with Chinese Communism? This became the focus of numerous colloquia during the mid-1990s.

There was a vast array of opinion, but I will briefly observe three broad categories. The first was the easy option that simply avoided conflict and said they were on the whole compatible. Although Tu Weiming did not himself endorse this view, he was willing to acknowledge there was some substance to the arguments of those who did. He lists some of the frequently noted commonalities.

Apparently Confucian rationalism is compatible with Marxist materialism. By focusing on the world here and now, Confucians, like Marxists, are committed to the transformation of the world from within. They both emphasize social praxis and education as important to their political mission. They both stress the importance of economic well-being for all, especially for the underprivileged and marginalized, and they also share ideas of equality and distributive justice. In a sense, Confucianism may be regarded as Marxist in its life-orientation. Indeed, some scholars have noted that Confucianism provided fertile soil for Chinese acceptance of Marxism. Arguably, the indigenization of Marxism in China turned it into an ideology with Chinese characteristics. (Tu 2011: 77)

Another obvious point of convergence that has been regularly noted is that "Kongzi's" ideal of the Great Unity (datong) could be seen as the utopian goal toward which Chinese Communism was striving. Coercion aside, there was, after all, good reason why many exponents of Ru Learning who remained in mainland China after 1949 converted to Marxism-Maoism, just as there was some substance to the anti-Kongzi campaign's claims that high-level Party members were furtive followers of the Sage.

These commonalities were comfortably noted in the conciliatory mood of the early 1990s, but by mid-decade, strain was showing. The compatibility model put both traditions on equal footing and undermined Marxism's capacity to critically assess Ru ideology. Fang Keli, who we met earlier heading the major research team investigating Xin ruxue, was the most high-profile spokesperson for a second position. Kang was a committed Marxist who welcomed the legacy of China's past in much the same way as he welcomed Western culture; both had value but both must pass through the filter of Chinese Marxism and be "critically inherited." He maintained Tu Weiming was attempting to revive Ru Learning as the "grammar" of Chinese culture, when in fact Marxism provided that grammar and Ruism was a resource that should merely enrich its "vocabulary." Fang certainly welcomed minor accommodation but he was very resistant to challenges to the deep structure of Chinese political thought (Makeham 2008: 247–52).

The third position was the one Fang Keli feared. It maintained that as *the* authentic expression of Chinese national character, Ru Learning should become the ultimate arbitrator of the country's social and political decisions. This raises two further questions: Could Marxism be dethroned and could Ruism take its place?

If Tu's recent observations are correct, Marxism-Maoism is already dead in the water. He suggests Ruism, socialism, and liberalism are the only contenders left standing; "Maoism, the former guiding principle for loyal members of the Chinese Communist party, has faded from the scene" (Tu 2011: 78). Daniel Bell, one of the most astute observers of "China's New Confucianism," likewise notes a conspicuous silence currently surrounding Marxism and a concern to deal with socioeconomic challenges without recourse to overt ideology:

> The main reason Chinese officials and scholars do not want to talk about Communism is that hardly anybody really believes that Marxism should provide guidelines for thinking about China's political future … Even the "Communist" government won't be confined by Marxist theory if it conflicts with the imperative to remain in power and to provide stability and order in society. For practical purposes, it is the end of [Marxist] ideology in China. (Bell 2008: 8)

If this is so, how far might Ruism rise? In 1993, Tu wrote: "Surely, the CCP is not about to abdicate power to restore a "Confucian system," but many of its leaders now recognize that Confucianism has made many valuable contributions to Chinese life … and that China today still has much to gain and much to learn from its own cultural heritage" (reprinted in Tu 2010: 294). Fifteen years later, Bell was less reserved in his prediction: "It is not entirely fanciful to surmise that the Chinese Communist Party will be relabeled the Chinese Confucian Party in the next couple of decades" (Bell 2008: 12).

Is it possible that Ru notions of governance will actually be officially endorsed by the Chinese government? And, failing that, in what other forms might Ru revival be embodied? In the following chapter I will address these questions as the final episode of our story brings us into the twenty-first century.

10

A spirit without a body

In 1966, the Red Guards were busy desecrating the Three Kongs: Kongzi's temple, the adjoining mansions, and the Kong family cemetery. Twenty years later, this trio became a brand name. It was a modest start. "Three Kong" was a new line of local beer being produced by a state-owned brewery in Qufu.

Now, after another thirty years, Kongzi has become the export label of the nation.

China is increasingly utilizing "soft power" to generate enthusiasm for Chinese culture abroad. The main arm of global outreach is a network of "Confucius Institutes" (*Kongzi xueyuan*). These institutes, which predominantly focus on teaching the Chinese language, are closely affiliated with the CCP's Ministry of Education and since their inception in 2004 have been established in over ninety countries. "Confucius" has become China's trademark.

At the 2008 Olympic Games, Kongzi was again presented to the world. He infused the opening ceremony in Beijing. The curtain raiser commenced with 2,008 drummers dressed in ancient costume chanting the opening lines of the *Analects*: "Is it not a joy to have friends come from afar?" (1:1) as well as "all within the four seas are brothers" (12:5). Other Ru references included human bodies forming the giant character for "harmony" (*he*), bamboo strips (i.e., Classical texts) being paraded by "disciples," and projected images of the Four Treasures of the Scholar's study: brush, ink-stick, paper, and ink-stone. One journalist watching the ceremony aptly described it as "a coming-out for Confucius" (Leibold 2010: 16).

Two years later, Kongzi was again spotted promoting world harmony and peace, although this time with less eloquence. The so-called "Confucius Peace prize" (*Kongzi hepingjiang*) was inaugurated to protest the 2010 Nobel Peace Prize given to Liu Xiaobo, who remains an imprisoned activist for human rights and democratic reform. The first Confucius Peace Prize was instead offered to Lien Chan, who many believed was working to reunite the PRC and Taiwan. It was a fiasco, and Lien had no interest in receiving his prize. The Ministry of Culture disbanded the organizers within the year and claimed the government had never endorsed the project, but many remain suspicious. While China's alternative peace prize was a debacle, it remains significant that Kongzi was the reflex substitute for Alfred Nobel.

Kongzi is literally becoming a part of modern China's landscape as statues of the sage proliferate. Initially, these were being donated by Hong Kong proselytizers. The first one was erected in Qufu in 1984 and seemed to be just a monument marking the place where Kongzi had once lived. Next, they started to appear at various Ru temples throughout China. Their numbers continued to increase, as did their size, and they began materializing in public arenas such as universities. Then, one night in 2011, a 9.5 meter, 17 ton bronze Kongzi mysteriously arrived in Tiananmen Square. This was almost beyond belief, as the only other individual represented in the Square is Mao Zedong. Three months later, the sculpture just as mysteriously disappeared, and no one in authority has yet explained why. It was perhaps too much, but a message had nonetheless been delivered: Kongzi could feasibly stand at the symbolic center of twenty-first-century China (Figure 17).

FIGURE 17 *Kongzi in Tiananmen Square.*

On the night of January 13, 2011, this massive bronze statue of Kongzi appeared in Tiananmen Square. On the night of April 20, it vanished. There has been no official explanation and thus a great deal of speculation. An obvious theory is the Party decided it was excessive. Another is that an opinion poll revealed that 70 percent of respondents disliked it. The most prosaic possibility is that it was always intended for a courtyard inside the National Museum and it was temporarily parked outside while refurbishments were being completed.

Whatever the truth, the fact remains that for three months there stood in Tiananmen Square a sculpture of Kongzi significantly larger than the iconic portrait of Mao Zedong.

But is he just a logo? What depths of change lie beneath surface display? How Ru is China? How Ru might it become? These are the questions I want to address in this final chapter. The data I will be looking at are diverse and include top-down plans to form a Ru government and grassroots movements for reciting the Classics, revivals of rituals to venerate Kongzi, and movies and best-selling books promoting his life and teachings. The sites of activity range from universities, private academies, and historic temples to small halls, parks, restaurants, the mass media, and cyberspace. The evidence is ubiquitous yet uncoordinated, fragmentary, at times factional.

Despite this diversity, and despite the fact that the revival of the last few decades seems to sprout from earth scorched bare by the Cultural Revolution, none of what we are now witnessing is particularly new. In the first sections I will be examining recent attempts to establish Ruism as state religion, but as one of the main advocates has said, "Frankly speaking, everything that we want to do today is nothing more than a continuation of Kang Youwei's work and a completion of his still-unaccomplished ideals" (Kang 2013: 71). The push to see Ruism recognized as religion, discussed in the subsequent section, is being partially driven by a Hong Kong society that maintains an unbroken link to Kang Youwei's campaigns. The seeds of revival blowing across the Taiwan Straight derive from the old stock of redemptive societies and the GMD's deployment of Ru tradition. Although rarely acknowledged, the legacy of Chen Lifu's pedagogy is becoming very evident in mainland China. The methods and goals have changed little; the real question is how well they will thrive in a new season.

I commence this chapter with the most ambitious and comprehensive of all revival projects: Jiang Qing's proposal to totally reform China's government and replace it with one constructed on Ru values and principles. Jiang is without doubt the most influential contemporary mainland exponent of Ru Learning, and his thinking often permeates seemingly disparate movements in much the same manner as Kang Youwei's thought had swayed an earlier generation. As Yong Chen has observed, "Behind all of these revival movements, there is a central figure who … has stood out among the other revivalists because of his strong commitment to a holistic revitalization of Confucianism. This figure is none other than Jiang Qing, the widely disputed utopian thinker and 'Confucian fundamentalist' " (Chen 2012: 175).

The kingly way of Jiang Qing

Jiang Qing's (b. 1953) critics claim he is "advancing a utopian vision that is tantamount to a return to the middle ages (or even earlier!)" (Makeham 2008: 275), and to some extent Jiang would agree with their assessment. He sees himself as a latter-day Dong Zhongshu working to reinstate Ruism following its persecution by Mao, a latter-day First Emperor. He has a snowball's chance in hell of seeing his plan fully implemented, but perhaps his comprehensive model is better seen as an archetype, a beacon of idealism to guide reformers rather than a political destination to actually be reached. Jiang is tolerated by the government and freely allowed to promote his views. He has developed an enthusiastic following and generated a substantial body of literature reviewing his ideas. It is not unthinkable that some of his ideas, in less radical guise, will become manifest in future Chinese political practice.

Jiang Qing was born into a financially comfortable and intellectually inclined family in Guizhou province in southwest China. His father was a high-ranking Party official, and the young Jiang was a committed Maoist who joined the People's Liberation Army in 1974. He diligently read Marx, Engels, and Mao, but on the sly he also read the Classics that his grandmother had taught him to appreciate. Following Mao's death, Jiang enrolled in university where he was exposed to other Western philosophies, and in 1980 he controversially published an article that argued that Marx's true views upheld liberty, democracy, and human rights rather than perpetual class struggle. Jiang's thesis expressing similar views promptly failed. He then submitted a successful second thesis on the humanism of Kongzi, a theme marking a major shift in his thought.

Disenchanted with politics, he turned to the study of religion, to meditation, and to nature. He was fond of Daoist texts and studied Buddhism deeply, yet he felt these faiths lacked the capacity to resolve worldly problems. He came very close to converting to Christianity before he encountered the writings of Tang Junyi and thence Xiong Shili, Liang Shuming, Xu Fuguan, and Mou Zongsan. He now saw his mission as returning New Ru Learning (*Xin ruxue*) to the mainland while advocating its compatibility with liberal democracy.

The shock of the massacre of unarmed civilian protesters in Tiananmen Square in 1989 shattered Jiang's trust in liberal democracy's capacity to solve China's problems. It also broke his association with New Ru Learning. He felt their focus on cultivating the inner self had neglected the political charter of Ru tradition; they devoted themselves to nurturing the inner sage (*neisheng*), but they had not attended to the duties of the outer king (*waiwang*). The exponents of New Ru Learning had been so preoccupied with what he calls Heart-Mind and Nature Ru Learning (*xinxing ruxue*) that they had cast aside Political Ru Learning (*zhengzhi ruxue*), which Jiang was about to take up as his cause. After the Tiananmen events, he wrote to Mou Zongsan:

> The last year's political upheaval has driven me to the political teachings of Confucianism. Now I recognize that the most challenging issues faced by China today are the issues of outward kingliness (*waiwang*), and there is no hope to revive Confucianism if we do not turn to such issues. It would be difficult for the general public to accept Confucianism if its political teachings cannot provide a solid theoretical foundation for the subsequent political development in China. Hence, the crucial point of development of contemporary Confucianism is to reconstruct a new outward kingliness to which I will dedicate myself from now on. (Yu and Fan 2011: 249)

Jiang challenges the premise of liberal democracy that maintains that the sovereignty of the people is the highest good. He argues that this evolved out of an earlier Western worldview based on the sovereignty of God. With secularization, "the people" came to assume God's place and become a quasi-sacred locus of authority. But, says Jiang, this is tantamount to elevating human desire to a transcendent principle: "Democratic politics amounts to the politics of desire" (Jiang 2013a: 33).

Here, Jiang Qing takes a stand against Mengzi whose views had been considered orthodox throughout imperial China. *If* Mengzi was correct when he said human nature was good, then liberal democracy just might work. But Jiang insists Mengzi was wrong. "When Xunzi says men are bad by nature or Dong Zhongshu says human nature is neutral, they are both in accord with Confucius's position" (Jiang 2011: 26). Unless they are exemplary individuals who have cultivated the raw stuff of their nature, we can depend on people to vote for what will best serve short-term self-interest. Jiang offers environmental problems as an illustration of the failure of liberal democracy. Real solutions demand a commitment to values that are contrary to the immediate interests of individuals; they require the recognition of moral values that transcend "the people."

Rather than pandering to what people immediately want and desire, Jiang's Kingly Way (*wangdao*) is based on the priority of moral values that reflect ultimate human potential and the ideal of a harmonious relationship between Heaven, earth, and humanity. He does not hesitate to call this a sacred legitimacy or to admit he is seeking to implement a state religion:

> The [Kingly Way] includes sacred legitimacy, which can correct the flaws inherent in the recognition of the will of the people as the sole form of legitimacy. Sacred legitimacy can restrain popular legitimacy so that it does not get inflated. The will of the people is subject to the universal restraint of religious morality, which embodies the Way and the principle of Heaven. Thus, it may overcome the extreme secularization of democracy and the flaws in human desires and to realize sacred values in political life. (Jiang 2013a: 37)

Why should modern China again take up an ancient faith? Jiang's response to this wavers. Sometimes he argues in absolute terms that Kongzi espoused perfect sagacious wisdom and therefore that his kingly way "is the best possible form of government that human beings have ever invented" (Jiang 2013a: 42–3). This would suggest it should ideally replace liberal democracy at a global level, yet this sits uncomfortably with Jiang's main justification for implementing his scheme in China: it is quintessentially Chinese and demarcates China from the West.

> To talk of broad Confucianism (Confucian religion [*rujiao*]) is to refer to Chinese culture and civilization. This is the only term by which China can be compared to other cultures and civilizations … Thus, when we talk about Confucian constitutionalism today we are talking about Chinese constitutionalism. There is no other Chinese constitutionalism outside Confucian constitutionalism, bar Western constitutionalism. For Chinese constitutionalism to be Chinese, it must be Confucian. (Jiang 2013a: 48)

Jiang says China should be governed in accord with the decree of Heaven (*tianming*). An immediate problem is that both the *Documents* and *Mengzi* say that "Heaven sees with the eyes of its people; Heaven hears with the ears of its people" (*Mengzi* 5A5; *Shujing*, "Great Declaration"). The modern Ru tendency to read this as a justification for liberal democracy is, he says, a serious misunderstanding: "In a Confucianist perspective, Heaven is Heaven and human is human." In emphasizing this point, Jiang defines *tian* in a manner that is not at all in keeping with Ru tradition, but that shows definite affinity with Christian thought. His *tian* is essentially God (*shangdi*), "a metaphysical, sacred and personal Heaven" (Jiang 2013a: 47–8). *Tian*, the ultimate origin of all that exists, continues to sustain existence as it differentiates into the trinity of Heaven, earth, and humanity. In his view, there is thus both a transcendent Heaven and a manifest Heaven: "There must be a Heaven, which is the one principle above the subprinciples of the triad of Heaven-earth-humanity," he said (Jiang 2013a: 189).

Ideally, the three realms would be harmonized by the rule of a sage-king. "Only the sage king can embody the will of Heaven" (Jiang 2013a: 51), and sovereignty should reside with him rather than the will of the people. Today, in the absence of such a king, the best possible solution is to govern according to the words past sages left for posterity. "The ancient sage kings and Confucius, Mencius and Xunzi were created by Heaven" (Hong 2011: 200), and their words, suitably interpreted and applied by scholar-officials, are the key to establishing an ideal government in modern China.

Jiang Qing's model of government mirrors his cosmology. Just as there is *tian* presiding over the trinity of Heaven-humanity-earth, so too there is to be an Academy of scholars overseeing three parliamentary houses, the House of the Ru (*tongruyuan*) representing Heaven and sacred legitimacy, the House of the Nation (*guotiyaun*) representing earth and cultural legitimacy, and the House of the People (*shuminyuan*) that represents popular legitimacy or the will of the people.

The members and leadership for the House of the People would be chosen using methods similar to those employed in electoral democracies. The people are to have their say, but their views must vie with sacred authority and China's accumulated cultural history. The House of the Ru would be composed of scholars who had trained in the Academy and who were assigned positions in the House based on examination results or personal recommendation. They would be presided over by an outstanding Ru. The House of the Nation represents China's cultural heritage. Jiang has faith in blood and lineages, and so descendants of past rulers, patriots, and worthies are to be included along with retired high-ranking officials and chosen representatives of Daoism, Buddhism, Islam, Tibetan Buddhism, and Christianity. Where feasible, the leader of this House would be a lineal descendant of Kongzi. This heir to Kongzi would also serve as the symbolic monarch and head of state, figuratively recognizing the place of the sage-king in China.

The three houses are not equal, and the House of the Ru is given more power befitting its representation of sacred authority. Any House can put a bill forward and it will pass if two houses support it. The House of the Ru has the additional power of veto, however. Thus, to use Jiang's own example, if the House of the Nation and the House of the People both voted to pass a bill allowing same-sex marriage, the House of the Ru would block it using its power of veto (Jiang 2013a: 41).

Standing above the three houses, like Jiang's transcendent *tian* above the triad of Heaven, humanity, and earth, is the Academy. The Academy fulfills the educational and ceremonial duties traditionally associated with the Ru, but it also has a supervisory responsibility and can remove individuals from office and even dismiss a government. The Academy is the highest form of legitimacy, but it does not interfere in the daily running of the state and would only step in during a crisis. It is nonetheless the religious heart of the whole system. "The Academy regulates politics by embodying the Way of Heaven and uses a sacred, religious-ethical principle to limit state power . . . The aim [of the Academy] is to ensure that the state authorities do not infringe Confucian values and to guarantee that they act according to sacred, moral values" (Jiang 2013a: 57).

Jiang Qing's plan will not be fully implemented, of course, but the true worth of his ideas lies in their capacity to inspire others. In the following sections it will become apparent that his influence is almost ubiquitous in the multiple manifestations of contemporary Ru revival in China. Daniel Bell's prediction is, I suspect, a safe bet: "We will be still debating Jiang Qing's ideas one hundred years from now, just as we are still debating Kang Youwei's ideas today" (Bell 2013: 24).

The varieties of state-Ru relationship

Two further advocates of state Ru religion who are often bracketed together with Jiang Qing are Kang Xiaoguang and Chen Ming. Their more moderate proposals have a greater chance of success, and some of their ideas are showing signs of influencing contemporary Chinese political practice.

Kang Xiaoguang (b. 1963), a professor with the Institute for Advanced Historical and Social Research, Renmin University (Beijing), is a thinker who is regularly consulted and whose opinion holds sway. Following the Tiananmen incident of 1989, he became deeply aware of the need to establish "civil society" in China. His initial research had focused on specific issues such as the Falun Gong movement and ineffective rural poverty relief, but he came to see such problems as symptoms of China's underlying spiritual fragmentation (Gaenssbauer 2011). From 2002 on, he thus began to argue that China needed to embrace Ruism as a unifying national religion. "Only if Confucianism becomes a religion that deeply penetrates into the daily lives of the Chinese people can it be considered a genuine revival. For this reason, the revival of national culture is the revival of Confucianism" (Ownby 2009: 107).

In 2005, Kang gathered together his various articles on Ru religion and published *Humane Government: A Third Road for the Development of Chinese Politics* (*Renzheng: Zhongguo zhengzhi fazhan de disantiao daolu*). It argues that the quintessential Ru virtue of humaneness or benevolence (*ren*) should be the foundation of Chinese politics: "China needs benevolent government, and benevolent government is good politics for China." Seeming to assume Ru tradition has a monopoly on *ren*, he insists that "if benevolent government is the best politics, then no party that does not believe in Confucianism is entitled to come into power" (Kang 2006: 95–6).

The strategy he proposes is for smooth and gradual change, although the transformation would be nonetheless radical: "to Confucianize the CCP at the top and society at the lower level" (Kang 2006: 115). Kang is critical of liberal democracy, and many of his arguments in favor of authoritarian Ru politics are very similar to those of Jiang Qing. His methods of implementation differ, however. He is more realistic in that he is not proposing a totally new system of government; rather, he wishes to saturate the CCP with Ru doctrine. The existing Party schools would be retained, but the curriculum would be changed so that the Five Classics and Four Books would replace Marxist literature. Promotions would be based on examinations testing candidates' knowledge of Ru texts and "benevolent government will be realized the day the CCP is turned into a community of Confucian scholars and Confucianism replaces Marxism" (Kang 2006: 115).

Kang's other prong for reform works from below by introducing Ru curricula into the national education system from primary school to university. "In the long term," he says, "the key is to establish Confucianism as the state religion" (Kang 2006: 116). In this regard, Kang Xiaoguang, like Jiang Qing, sees himself as an heir to Kang Youwei's mission from over a century earlier (Kang 2013). More surprisingly, he also sees himself inheriting the legacy of Chiang Kai-shek, and he commends the Nationalist leader for his deployment of Ru tradition.

While Kang has been very influential, he comes across as being far less devout than Jiang Qing, and he is actually not particularly knowledgeable of Ru tradition. As Stephen Angle has observed, he is rather utilitarian in his rationale, and "all of the talk of religion is motivated by its usefulness towards achieving the ends of a stable Confucian authoritarianism" (Angle 2012: 44). He speaks of the centrality of *tian* but gives no hint as to what he takes this to mean, and his philosophy has grown without any deep engagement with Ru philosophy.

Many of his arguments are concerning. He operates using a remarkable degree of essentialism and argues Ruism is the absolute core of Chinese culture even if "9,999 out of 10,000" Chinese people today "have not even any superficial knowledge about Confucianism" (Kang 2006: 114). Apparently Chinese culture is entirely independent of the Chinese people. Kang seems willing to ignore the complexity of Chinese history and the diversity of current opinion for the sake of a simple solution. Angle is surely correct when he says: "We cannot conclude that the Chinese people today have any strong reason to endorse the authority of Kang's version of Confucian government," although given Kang's indifference to what the majority believe, he is unlikely to be unduly perturbed by this (Angle 2012: 45).

***

Chen Ming, a professor of philosophy at the Capital Normal University (Beijing), offers a proposal more moderate than those of Jiang Qing and Kang Xiaoguang. He feels their models for reform are not only highly unlikely to gain government support but also run the risk of being religiously and socially divisive.

Chen launched the journal *Yuandao* ("Original Dao") in 1994, and while it is described as a forum promoting traditional culture, in practice it primarily runs articles encouraging various kinds of Ru revival. Generating such discussion is itself part of Chen's strategy. "In contrast to Jiang Qing's top-down approach," Chen says that he "stresses the importance of the bottom-up approach, that is to rely on the societal influence on the state, to reconstruct and promote Confucianism" (Chen 2009: 103).

Chen has borrowed a concept from the sociologist Robert Bellah who famously analyzed political discourse in America as a form of "civil religion." Although the U.S. Constitution separates church and state and strictly relegates religion to the private sphere, it is nonetheless very apparent that American politics assumes a shared religious orientation that becomes very evident in speeches and national celebrations. Bellah calls these shared beliefs, symbols, and rituals "civil religion," and Chen's proposal is to develop Ruism as China's civil religion. As he puts it, "Looking at Confucianism as a civil religion … brings Confucianism back to the politics of society where it originated and allows people to examine the social function of Confucianism as a religion, transforming the Confucian religion into something like … Protestantism that [exists] in the society independent of the state." Chen believes Ru tradition is particularly well suited to this task because it has always been a peculiarly secular kind of religion. "While it can be said that the religiousness of Confucianism is weak," he wrote, "it can be said to be strong if one takes into consideration its import on the secular lives of ordinary Chinese" (Chen 2009: 104).

Chen Ming distances himself from "fundamentalist Confucianism" and insists that a thriving nation and human well-being take priority over any doctrinal orthodoxy. In contrast to Jiang Qing and Kang Xiaoguang, he supports constitutional democracy and maintains that Ru civil religion would not compromise political and religious freedom.

Chen has been criticized for reducing Ru religion "to nothing more than a body of truncated symbols" (Chen 2009: 105) on the one hand, and on the other for being rather naïve as to how civil religion might be manifest in political practice. For example, he wrote a paper praising Chiang Kai-shek's Chinese Cultural Renaissance movement, suggesting it offered a model to be emulated and claiming it could take some of the credit for Taiwan's subsequent economic growth. Taiwanese Ru Learning scholars had to remind him of the realities of the movement that, as we have seen, was primarily a ultraconservative anticommunist response to the Cultural Revolution.

Nonetheless, and for better or worse, Chen's proposal is a real possibility. As Anna Sun recently observed, "It may fairly be asked whether Confucianism might not develop in a comparatively weak political direction, as a de facto civil religion, as a cultural resource for nationalism, and as a form of life for people … who endorse Confucian moral values and social practices. These developments make it not implausible to suppose that, for China, the twenty-first century may prove to be the Confucian century" (Sun 2013: 172).

Sun is aware that her prediction requires qualification, however. A civil religion, at least as Bellah described it, is not made to measure. Rather, it emerges organically and unselfconsciously. Nor would it be "Ruism as a civil religion," but instead Chinese civil religion that indirectly reinforced Ru values. But even this remains problematic. Chinese moral values have multiple sources that have been competing and blending for millennia. A Chinese civil religion might express and reinforce moral values compatible with Ruism, but this need not mean those values are therefore exclusively Ru. Bellah himself recently spoke alternatively of "Confucianism as a central but non-exclusive part of an open Chinese civil religion" that would also draw on Buddhism, Daoism, and Christianity (Yang and Sun 2014: 10). An embryonic form of Chinese civil religion indeed already exists, but the extent to which it will come to be explicitly associated with Ru tradition remains unclear at this stage (see Ivanhoe and Kim 2016).

* * *

The ideas being promoted by Jiang Qing, Kang Xiaoguang, and Chen Ming are now showing signs of making inroads into political reality. Xi Jinping (b. 1953), China's current leader, warmly acknowledges Kongzi and Ru Learning. In the last few years, stunned Western observers have responded with headlines such as these: "The Chinese Communist Party's Confucian Revival"; "Xi Launches Cultural Counter-Revolution To Restore Confucianism as China's Ideology"; and "Confucius Says, Xi Does." A *Time* headline from October 30, 2014, goes so far as refer to "The Chinese President's Love Affair with Confucius" (Figure 18).

Like all good headlines, they sensationalize some truth. Xi's speech that generated the most comment was one he gave in 2014 at an international conference coinciding with Kongzi's 2,565th birthday. Xi certainly acknowledged that "studying Confucius and Confucianism is an important approach to understanding the national characteristics of the Chinese as well as the historical roots of the spiritual world of the present-day Chinese," but he invariably places Kongzi and Ru Learning within a spectrum of Chinese intellectual traditions working in "harmonious co-existence." Xi spoke of the CCP having "consciously absorbed nutrition from the teachings of Confucius to those of Sun Yat-sen," but he quietly reminded his audience that Marxism remained the prevailing ideology and that "people have to make the past serve present needs" (Xi 2014a).

In his speeches, Xi regularly quotes the Four Books, Five Classics, and later Ru texts, but he also cites other philosophies as well as drawing many passages from Chinese historical and literary works (see Zhang 2015). To date, he is acknowledging traditional Chinese culture on the whole rather than overtly privileging Ru tradition. There is, however, reason to suspect Ru values might increasingly loom large.

Xi Jinping is perhaps the most powerful Chinese leader since Mao, and his personality cult is thriving. His folksy image is that of a devoted family man and an affable man of the people who is also cultured, idealistic, and irreproachably moral. He enjoys his nickname Xi dada, "uncle Xi" or even "daddy Xi," which is officially encouraged. But Xi has carefully consolidated his position and he is now probably the world's most powerful leader. "Xi dada" might be affectionate, but it also resonates with the Ru notion of the emperor as father of the people as well as Chiang Kai-shek's claims that he led China like a father guiding his children (Fenby 2003: 225). Xi dada is a great advocate of soft power that utilizes "the unique charm of Chinese culture," and his style of rule is itself a kind of charming, soft autocracy (Xi 2014: 179).

Ru doctrine is particularly evident in Xi's tough stance on official corruption. He advocates using learning to instill moral values and he acknowledges Kongzi as the champion of this approach (Xi 2014: 454–5). He insists Party members study not only Communist material but also delve into China's historical resources, and an eleven-volume textbook on traditional culture is currently being used for training officials. Xi maintains "traditional Chinese culture is both extensive and profound, and to acquire the essence of various thoughts is beneficial to the formation of a correct worldview, outlook on life and sense of values" (Xi 2014: 453).

FIGURE 18 *Statue of Kongzi with arms open to the "Chinese Dream."*

Xi Jinping's vision for China's future is encapsulated by the catch-phrase "Chinese Dream." This 19-meter statue of Kongzi stands with arms open to a huge obelisk (behind the camera) with the words "Chinese Dream" written on the front and "core socialist values" on the back. The obelisk's base inscribes a lengthy quotation from Xi Jinping.

The obvious message is that Kongzi and the CCP now embrace one another. Although the two colossal edifices were not officially sponsored, the fact that they stand in the beach-side city of Beidaihe, where the Beijing government holds its summer retreat, is highly significant. They are part of a complex built by a member of the CCP who was formerly a general.

In a speech given at Peking University, he likewise exhorted students to study not only to acquire knowledge but also to cultivate morality and virtue, learn right from wrong, and become honest and sincere. He maintains these are socialist values, but it is surely significant that most of his quotations are drawn from Ru sources (Xi 2014: 190–4).

While they are far more sophisticated and belong to a very different age, Xi Jinping's efforts bear some resemblance to Chiang Kai-shek's attempts to use Ru Learning to promote traditional values and uplift moral standards. But Xi is unlikely to specifically align the CCP with Ruxue as this would compromise the authority of Marxist ideology, which in turn would open the possibility that an alternate form of governance might better suit modern China. For now, this is off the table.

Ru religion revisited

Even if the Chinese government does not formally align itself with Ru tradition, many revivalists feel it is nonetheless important that *Rujiao* be officially recognized as a religion; if not state religion then at least a religion acknowledged by the state. There are still only five approved religions in China—Buddhism, Daoism, Islam, (Protestant) Christianity, and Catholicism—but *Rujiao* increasingly receives de facto acknowledgment in government-sanctioned surveys and reports on Chinese religion.

Hong Kong is different. As a Special Administrative Region, it is not governed by the mainland's policy on religion, and *Rujiao* is classified as a sixth religion. It was in fact in Hong Kong that Kang Youwei's push to establish Kongzi-religion (*Kongjiao*) was in a small way successful. I mentioned in Chapter 8 that Chen Huanzhang had, in 1912, inaugurated the Kongzi-religion Society (*Kongjiao hui*) of which Kang was president. In 1930, Chen moved to Hong Kong and founded a similar organization, the Kongzi-religion Academy (*Kongjiao xueyuan,* known in English as the Confucian Academy). This Academy was primarily responsible for the subsequent recognition of *Rujiao* as religion in Hong Kong. It is still active, and the current president is Tang Enjia, a very wealthy Ru entrepreneur (*rushang*). The Academy's influence is increasingly felt on the mainland where it has contributed to various academic and charitable projects as well as the renovation of temples and the raising of over 1,000 statues of Kongzi.

While the Kongjiao Academy devotes much of its attention to education through its primary and secondary schools, it is evident that its broader goals are still in keeping with those of Kang Youwei. Their main objective remains promoting *Rujiao* as the nation's primary religion, and their recent (unsuccessful) push to convince the government to annually celebrate Kongzi's birthday with a public holiday was a symbolic gesture in this direction. The Kongjiao Academy stresses the nexus between *Rujiao* and national unity and identity. As Sébastien Billioud and Joël Thoraval have observed, "The Academy reveals a patriotism that, for all its different agenda, can easily be integrated with the official ideological discourse coming from the mainland" (Billioud and Thoraval 2008: 102).

The Kongjiao Academy's quest to have *Rujiao* recognized as a religion has recently been revived on the mainland by Zhou Beichen (b. 1965). Zhou's interest in philosophy led him to New Ru Thought and thence to Jiang Qing, who he came to accept as his teacher. He helped Jiang establish his Yangming Abode (described later) and lived there from 1996 to 2003. When he left, he decided to take up the mantle of Kang Youwei and Chen Huanzhang and once again seek to establish Ru religion in China. In 2009, with financial support from the Hong Kong Kongjiao Academy, he opened a place of worship in Shenzhen called the Hall of the Sage Kongzi (*Kongsheng tang*). The main area has an altar to Kongzi and is used for rituals, text reading, and the performance of ceremonial music. This is a prototype, and the hope is it will be replicated throughout China. Early response has been enthusiastic, with several thousand people becoming involved in the first few months. It seems to be warmly accepted by the government, and the long-term hope is that this kind of Ru ceremonial practice will encourage the state to recognize the religious attributes of Ru tradition (Billioud 2010: 209–14).

***

Zhou Beichen is well aware that for Ruism to be acknowledged as "a religion" it must look like one. This means it must satisfy the CCP's understanding of religion (*zongjiao*), which is an inherently Western concept essentially modeled on Christianity, as we saw in Chapter 1. Temples, rituals, and a community of worshipers are thus vital to the *Rujiao* cause, but they are not well established, as we shall now see.

The occasion when the state comes closest to recognizing the religious dimensions of Ru tradition is when Party members partake in the annual rituals to Kongzi in Qufu (Figure 19). The vicissitudes of these ceremonies have swung wildly for over a century. As we saw in Chapter 8, they peaked at the very end of the empire, were briefly revived by Yuan Shikai, and were on occasion patronized by the Republican government, in each case providing "the prevailing regime with some sort of symbolic and moral authority" (Billioud and Thoraval: 2009. 85). They came to an abrupt end with the Communist takeover, and it was only fortune that saved the Qufu temple complex from complete destruction. After Mao's death, the CCP edged ever closer to associating with the annual rituals to Kongzi. In 1984, the Party established the Kongzi Foundation (*Kongzi jijinhui*) in Qufu and encouraged tourists to travel there. By 1989, a formal Kongzi Festival (*Kongzi wenhua jie*) was in place and received UNESCO support. In 2004, the ceremonies were made into a major national occasion. They were broadcast live on CCTV, and local government officials played an active part in the celebrations. This has been the practice every year since. Public enthusiasm for the event seems to have peaked in the patriotic build-up to the Beijing Olympics, however, and it has attracted less attention in more recent years.

The annual ceremony to commemorate Kongzi's birth has, since 2004, largely been an occasion for mass partying and Party sloganing about unity and harmony. The main ceremony is essentially an act of collective flower arrangement, with each delegate in turn placing a bouquet at the altar and thrice bowing to the Master's statue. This is a

FIGURE 19 *Kongzi's birthday ceremony, Qufu.*

This photograph was taken in 2007 during the annual International Confucius Cultural Festival that incorporates the ceremonies celebrating Kongzi's birthday. The dancers are outside the Hall of Great Perfection (*Dacheng dian*). The statue of Kongzi lies directly inside the main entrance (center). His Four Associates (depicted in Figure 6) are set against the side walls.

The ornate "dragon pillars" seen here signified Kongzi's status—the *Rites Records* stipulated that "ornament formed a mark" of distinction (Legge 1885: vol. 27, 400). Likewise, the numbers of rows of dancers signified rank. Today, Kongzi receives eight rows, a number he had himself implied was the preserve of kings (*Analects* 3:1).

Although row (*yi*) dance was used in various contexts, the peacock feathers and flute carried by dancers evoke Kongzi's teaching. The flute obviously represents music. The feathers epitomize beautiful pattern, and the early word for "pattern" (*wen*) also referred to the refined ritualized patterns of human behavior. *Wen* thus also meant "culture," and significantly, Kongzi Temple (*Kongmiao*) is largely synonymous with Culture Temple (*wenmiao*).

far cry from the solemn rituals of imperial times that were performed by Ru who had devoted their life to study, and which involved animal sacrifice. Observers of the 2007 ceremony noted the crowds were largely apathetic when viewing the choreographed traditional culture displays but were soon whipped into frenzy by a suggestively clad Korean rock singer. The event, they said, ended in "complete pandemonium" (Billioud and Thoraval 2009: 89–91).

The media circus of the annual Qufu celebration is not conducive to displays of sincere reverence and heartfelt remembrance. Honest acts of commemoration are currently modest affairs. A few days after the 2007 ceremony in Qufu, about forty people partook in a ritual to honor Mengzi. Mengzi's hometown, Zoucheng, is only about 30 km from Qufu, and as his temple attracts far fewer tourists, it retains an air of tranquility (Figure 7). The alternative ceremony performed by committed activists was simple and brief, but it was nonetheless a solemn expression of genuine sentiment (Billioud and Thoraval 2009: 91–3).

The ritual veneration of Kongzi is currently finding some expression outside of major state-sponsored events. Thus far this has been minor and scattered. There were some 1,500 active temples to Kongzi (*Kongmiao*) at the end of the empire. Today, a few hundred remain in various states of disrepair, but as of 2011, only thirty-nine were registered as "national cultural heritage sites" in China. Those that are not tourist destinations or museums are more ritually active, partially out of economic necessity. As they receive less government support, they require paying "customers." The most common ritual practices are burning incense, bowing to the tablet or image of Kongzi, and writing prayers on prayer cards (*xuyuan qian*), the latter being a recent innovation adapted from Japanese Shinto temples. Rather than being a focal point of Ru devotion, most people participate in a casual way and purchase a prayer card in the hope of getting some good luck, especially on exams (a function performed by the god Wenchang in imperial times). The respect is genuine even if most people are uncertain whether the offerings actually work, but a passing participation in temple ritual is not an indication of serious commitment to Ru tradition (Sun 2013: chapter 8).

There are a few other small rituals that might be mentioned here. Although in 2010 a marriage was performed in strict accordance with the *Rites Records* at Zhou Beichen's Hall of the Sage Kongzi (Chen 2012: 77), it is more common for the occasional couple to wed before a portrait of Kongzi. This has no precedent in the Classics or tradition, but it is very similar to the once widespread convention of taking marriage vows before a portrait of Mao Zedong.

The examples I have thus far considered—unrealized proposals for grand reform and rituals that tend to lack conviction save for tiny pockets of genuine piety—seem only to reinforce Billioud's observation that Ru revival has "remained a largely scattered, ill-defined and non-integrated phenomenon encompassing completely different realities" (Billioud 2010: 214). And they collectively highlight something that is increasingly being noted: the resurrection of the Ru spirit has revived a tradition that no longer occupies a body.

A spirit without a body

If Ru beliefs and values do not find their representation as the religion of the state, then in what other forms might their revival be embodied? Because of centuries of intimate association with the administration of the Chinese empire, Ruism developed very little in the way of alternative institutional superstructure. With the exception of private academies, elite havens for Ru in waiting, the social structure that had held the community of Ru together was the state. There were no Ru equivalents to monasteries, temple communities, or churches; Ru had no clergy, priesthood, or rite of initiation for converts. True, the microcosmic Ru community was the family, the archetype for the macrocosm of the state, but there was precious little to be found in between.

Joseph Levenson identified the dilemma over half a century ago. He said: "It is no use waving a cheerful good-bye to Imperial China, as though the bureaucratic monarchy were inessential ... and pretending that Confucianism is essentially undisturbed" (Levenson 1972: xi). More recently Yu Yingshi has employed an extremely apt metaphor for the situation in which Ru culture finds itself today: it is like a wandering spirit that no longer has a body to occupy. John Makeham's excellent study of contemporary Ru discourse takes its title from Yu's metaphor: *Lost Soul*. Summarizing Yu's position, he says "that although *ruxue* was now freed from the institutional shackles to which traditional *ruxue* had been tied (and which had also enabled it to be given expression), it was now without a body, a home, a specific identity" (Makeham 2008: 2). Kang Xiaoguang also alludes to this wandering spirit: "Once the traditional political system fell apart, Confucianism also lost its vehicle and was left in a situation of separation of the soul from the body" (Kang 2006: 116).

Failing a miraculous resurrection in the body of the state, Ru revival will, nonetheless, have to work through other types of religious community. In this regard, it is poorly prepared.

*　*　*

As many of the revivalists we have discussed have been academics, universities are an obvious "body" to consider. Despite a period when Maoist ideology redefined universities, they are today, as they by and large have been since the 1920s, modeled on Western universities. This clearly places limits on would-be proselytizers. As a spokesperson for the People's University in Beijing said: "The official line is ... Confucius is neither praised nor criticized, he is studied" (Billioud and Thoraval 2007: 9).

Universities can, of course, draw together people who feel the subject they study has a spiritual or religious contribution to make to society, but this must be framed in the language of secular theory. As Mou Zongsan once said about his life as a university academic, "I had no choice but to draw my spirit inward and immerse myself in scholarly research" (Clower 2014: 125). Sébastien Billioud and Joël Thoraval have observed that although sagehood has remained a New Ru Learning ideal, the "ideal could less and less be practically implemented [when] transformed into a pure philosophical enterprise conducted in a Western-style institution" (Billioud and Thoraval 2015: 137).

Many revivalists therefore long for an independent forum for like-minded people with a broader understanding of what is meant by "learning" (*xue*). For this they have an excellent precedent in the quintessential Ru establishment of the academy (*shuyuan*). Several first-generation exponents of New Ru Learning had established academies;

Zhang Junmai opened his *Minzu Wenhua* ("National Culture") Academy in Dali in 1938, Ma Yifu began his *Fuxing* ("Return to Nature") Academy in Leshan in 1939, and Liang Shuming established his *Mianren* ("Exhort Humaneness") Academy in Chongqing in 1942. All of these were short-lived, however. The formation of the New Asia College (New Asia "Academy" is more accurate, *Xinya shuyuan*) by Qian Mu and Tang Junyi in Hong Kong in the early 1950s might also be counted here, although it was incorporated into the Chinese University of Hong Kong in 1963 and so was obliged to comply with British colonial university guidelines.

There is currently a lot of renewed enthusiasm for establishing academies in China. Most of these are not Ru *shuyuan*, however, but are rather writers associations. While some of the famous Ru academies of dynastic China have been restored, they are preserved as historical sites and tourist attractions, and the few that involve any teaching are attached to universities and the constraints of secular education.

There are, however, a handful of independent Ru Learning academies. Jiang Qing was again in the vanguard. In 1996, he purchased 100 acres in remote Guizhou, the region where Wang Yangming had once sat in contemplation. The buildings for his Yangming Abode (*Yangming jingshe*) were completed in 2000, and invited visitors come to ceremonially honor Kongzi, read and study the Classics, sing together, and hear Jiang Qing teach. It is, says Jiang, a place of self-cultivation "intended to safeguard the spiritual values of Confucianism" (Chen 2012: 73). Unlike modern universities, his academy is devoted to learning that leads to self-transformation rather than the acquisition of information and skills to be utilized in the workplace.

Peace and Harmony Academy (*Pinghe shuyuan*) in Zhuhai consists of two vast apartments in a modern city block. It was founded in 2005 by a man who had once been a follower of the Baha'i faith and a successful businessman. Unlike Jiang, with whom he maintains a friendly relationship, he has no scholarly background and is less focused on religious and political aspects of Ru Learning. The policy statement on the academy's website proclaims: "In order to build a harmonious society, it is imperative to revitalize Chinese culture; in order to revitalize Chinese culture, *shuyuan* should be the pathway. Pinghe Academy is created for this exact purpose." Similar sentiments about the importance of academies are expressed on the website for the Yunshen Academy in Wuhan, which adds: "We need thousands, tens of thousands of *shuyuan* to transmit Chinese culture" (Chen 2012: 73, 74).

Although academies are an ideal Ru institution, they are currently not making a major impact simply because, as the last quotation suggests, so many would be required for this to occur. In the late Qing dynasty, for instance, there were over 7,000 academies. Today, they are not easy to establish insofar as they require considerable sponsorship, and obtaining approval is difficult (the obstacles are more bureaucratic than political). In contrast to imperial times, modern academies are not a pathway to employment, and so they will never attract large numbers. As one advocate said, "Confucian academies, which carry on the Confucian Dao ... aim to attract the elite ... [who] have no need to worry about jobs" (Hong 2011: 191). At this stage, it seems unlikely that academies will be a major force for revival.

A vastly less expensive option is the "virtual academy." These websites often have very impressive lists of academics acting as editorial consultants, yet an online forum also has the liberty to move from objective study to advocacy. Among others, there is Confucius2000 founded by a group of young intellectuals in 2001; China Kongzi, which is maintained by the China Kongzi Foundation; Yuandao, which was founded by Chen Ming; Rujiao China; and the Rujiao Revival Forum. There are also countless other smaller sites that range from the conservative to the peculiar, such as the virtual Academy of Eminent Virtue (*Junde shuyuan*), which promotes the not uncommon view that the Classics anticipated modern mathematical and scientific discoveries (Billioud and Thoraval 2008: 98–9; Smith 2008: 209–11). It is difficult to accurately measure the impact of these websites, but a one-week sample taken for Confucius2000 in 2010 indicated it was averaging over 20,000 visits per day (Sun 2013: 211n. 19).

Websites and online discussion groups are without doubt very significant domains for contemporary Ru revival. They are, however, disembodied forums that can only offer to resurrect Ru spirit in a virtually corporeal form. In the following section, I will turn to consider Ru movements that, in contrast, seek to engage participants in a thoroughly somatic manner. It is at this level that Ru culture is becoming very popular indeed.

Taking it to the people

Rather than gambling on academies and hoping their influence will permeate society, an alternative would be to begin at a mass level, trusting that an increased enthusiasm for Ru values would eventually make academies truly viable. This is precisely the approach of Yidan School (*Yidan xuetang*), a nonprofit organization founded by Pang Fei (b. 1973) in 2001. Pang had pursued Chinese, Western, and Indian philosophies in his personal quest for "truth." After completing his Master's degree in philosophy, however, he came "back to earth" and realized intellectual pursuit was akin to materialist pursuit, and both were contrary to the fundamental priorities of self-cultivation and care for others. Yidan School has an almost anti-intellectual tenor and espouses principles such as "privilege action, silence is golden" and "less empty talk" (Billioud 2011: 290). The relatively uneducated rural population is targeted for future expansion, and the countryside is seen as the key to a successful spiritual revolution just had it had once been vital to the Communist political revolution.

While Pang's ultimate goal is to set up institutions modeled on traditional academies (*shuyuan*), his organization meanwhile operates as a less formal *xuetang* or "learning hall," a term that evokes the traditional "schools" of imperial China (Figure 2). It is a successful strategy that has attracted about 5,000 volunteer staff who have allegedly enticed over half a million people to participate in their activities. Volunteers are ranked and are promoted according to their contribution, the highest becoming teaching masters or managers. The organization is thus expanding and its stated objective is to eventually reach every person in China.

Yidan School is text-based, with the Four Books heading the curriculum, but it has a decidedly unacademic attitude toward these works. Rather, the texts are approached ritually by practitioners seeking embodied engagement. This orientation is contrasted with ordinary reading that only allows people "to see the ancient sages, but not really to encounter them" (Billioud 2011: 302). Groups meet, often in parks or other natural settings, and begin with traditional exercises and breathing techniques to center the body and mind and to purify participants' *qi*. Following this, reading begins (collectively, alternating, or solitary), with emphasis placed on a slow tempo and variation of rhythm. Cognitive engagement with the text is not important. What is vital is the "*incorporation* of the text, an experience of savoring and impregnation, facilitated by physical exercises, breathing, and slowness" (Billioud and Thoraval 2007: 14).

* * *

The most widespread of all forms of Ru revival is the movement for teaching children to recite the Classics (Figure 20). Accurate figures are not available, but estimates always exceed one million, often hover around 10–20 million, and can swing as high as 100 million (Billioud 2010: 217n. 65). The movement has now extended well beyond the initial focus on children. In a survey of the "Renaissance of Traditional Cultures in Contemporary China" directed by Kang Xiaoguang, "chanting traditional classics" was by far the activity respondents had most engaged in. Kang's data was obtained from more than 2,000 people in 10 cities, and although half his sample were actively involved in cultural revival, it is still very impressive that almost 85 percent reported having participated in recitation (Kang 2012: 59–60).

Rote-learning the Classics was the standard method of instruction in imperial China. As we have seen, Chen Lifu had revived the practice both on the mainland and, after 1970, in Taiwan. The modern children's recitation movement was launched in Taiwan in the 1980s by Wang Caigui (b. 1949) who had been a disciple of Mou Zongsan. Wang said his teaching method ultimately sought to nourish "the moral intelligence of sages" and "cultivate the rectitude of the heart-mind, of nature and of action" (Billioud and Thoraval 2007: 15). He believes that between the ages of 4 and 13 children are not yet capable of comprehending the Classics, but they have a great capacity for rote-learning. His aim is therefore to inscribe the texts within children through constant recitation so they will be ever-present at a later date when they can reflect upon their meaning.

Wang's methods were introduced to the mainland in 1993. A proposal to establish schools for the recitation of Classical literature was presented to the Chinese People's Political Consultative Conference in 1995, and the government subsequently implemented the recommendation. A twelve-volume textbook of readings was published, the works selected being prose and poetry reflecting Chinese cultural heritage generally. In 2004, an alternative text was produced by a subsidiary of the Ministry of Education, and in this case Ru sources were exclusively used. Despite an impressive

FIGURE 20 *Chanting the Classics.*

(Above) Students wearing traditional costume while chanting to celebrate Teachers Day in Lanzhou, Gansu, September 10, 2014. No one quite knows why September 10 was designated Teachers Day in the PRC, and there are now proposals to align it with Kongzi's birthday (September 28), as it is in Taiwan.

(Below) Adults dressed in traditional costume reading the Classics outside the Kongzi temple in Hangzhou, Zhejiang. This was during the mid-Autumn festival for 2012, which fell the day before Kongzi's birthday.

list of organizations said to have provided editorial assistance, the real editor was none other than Jiang Qing. In his preface, Jiang makes no apology for interpreting "Chinese cultural classics" to be the Six Classics, Four Books, and other Ru works. "If a person does not know the content of these classics, that person cannot be seen as a Chinese in the cultural sense," he wrote. Recalling that for him "Chinese culture" means "Ru culture," the following passage reveals just how significant he believes recitation might be:

> The renaissance of Chinese culture must start with children. Through reciting Chinese cultural classics, children are implanted with the seeds of the principles and teachings of sages and worthies. When they grow up, they can naturally understand the ideas about self-cultivation and self-fulfillment articulated by sages and worthies throughout history, i.e., teachings about "inner sagehood and outer kingliness," about the fulfillment of the self and others, about human nature and Heaven … Furthermore, they can integrate the sagely teachings into their personal biographies and actively participate in the creation of great history and culture, and in the end strive to appreciate and merge with the transformation of Heaven and earth. (Chen 2012: 65–6)

The publication of this textbook quickly precipitated heated exchange in journals, newspapers, forums, and blogs. Critics claimed it was archaic pedagogy, indoctrination, and an attempt to impose ultraconservative ideology; defenders retreated to arguments about "Chineseness" and the need for moral rectification. Jiang Qing surveyed the battlefield and, apparently believing there is no such thing as bad press, was delighted: "Now Confucianism is a public discourse. This proves that Confucian tradition has regained its vitality" (Chen 2012: 68).

Classics recitation has gone well beyond the bounds of set curricula and designated institutions, however. It is a ubiquitous phenomenon found in schools, study groups, informal gatherings, or at home with private tutors. The Four Books are certainly the most frequently used texts, but Ru works are not the only sources. Indeed, the curricula is not even limited to Chinese classical literature, and it is sometimes possible to hear Shakespeare's sonnets being recited by children who know not a word of English. Despite what those sympathetic to Jiang Qing's view might wish, this cannot always be considered a practice exclusively devoted to Ru Learning.

The recitations are generally quite different to the slow and varied method of Yidan School; they are rather fast, regular, robotic, and monotonous. The children are not forcefully drilled to memorize, and the ability to recall the texts is allowed to naturally develop. Some teachers also complement recitation with education in "ritual" by encouraging small gestures such as bowing to adults and proper deportment. Training children in traditional *li* (ritual, protocol) is currently big business, and a seventeenth-century text entitled *Rules for Students and Children* (*dizi gui*) is a twenty-first-century best seller (Sun 2013: 170).

Not surprisingly, the reasons parents give for sending their children to Classics recitation vary. Some go mainly for fun, and parents who attend with their children often say they enjoy the occasions. At the other extreme are parents who place children in private schools and believe recitation gives their child an educational advantage so that they learn faster and become better socially adjusted.

As with Yidan School, Billioud and Thoraval here too see a comparison to be made with *qigong* movements. They note that participants say "there is an objective power resulting from 'incorporation' of the text, a power that can be experienced by each person as in the case of *qi*" (Billioud and Thoraval 2007: 17). Indeed, Vincent Goossaert and David Palmer have observed that "the Confucian revival became a truly mass movement in Mainland China" at precisely the time of "the collapse of the *qigong* movement," and so suggest it is in fact filling a void created by *qigong*'s demise (Goossaert and Palmer 2011: 295).

In this regard, these authors also suggest mass Classics recitation movements are possibly taking on the characteristics of the "redemptive societies" that mushroomed in the early Republican era, discussed in Chapter 8. As I then noted, these have been poorly studied, but we are perhaps now seeing the resurgence of the esoteric kinds of Ru movement that flourished almost a century ago. It is significant that Yidan School promotes the teachings of Wang Fengyi (1864–1937) a prominent figure in the Worldwide Ethical Society (*Wanguo daodehui*), of which Kang Youwei had been inaugural president (Chapter 8), while Wang Caigui's methods have had a profound impact on Taiwanese redemptive societies where Classics recitation has substituted for spirit writing (Goossaert and Palmer 2011: 294). Further research is needed to untangle and trace the lines of transmission, but David Palmer may well be correct when he argues that "redemptive societies are the *main* social expression of Confucian revivalism" in the modern era (Billioud 2010: 214).

* * *

A recurrent theme of Classics recitation is that is not necessary to be well educated or to be able to understand the texts; there is no need to be familiar with centuries of commentary and exegesis or versed in philosophy. As we have seen, the movements tend to focus on children and uneducated people living in the countryside.

At first, this seems antithetical to the academic world of New Ru Learning. How could any save the intellectual elite hope to cope with Mou Zongsan's philosophy? But beneath all the complexity of his arguments, Mou was seeking direct intuition of "original heart-mind," and he believed people living simple lives were very proximate to this realization: "Real living is living for living's sake, engaged in the activities that sustain us—life immersed in itself. Only a farmer leads such existence, what I call 'life in itself' " (Mou 2015a: 29–30).

Billioud and Thoraval relate an intriguing story of a visit to a vegetarian restaurant in Shenzhen owned by a woman with a deep commitment to Ru values. In her teens she had been in a dance troupe of the People's Liberation Army and had subsequently discovered, in succession, wealth, wildness, and Buddhism. Her life was again transformed when she came upon Wang Caigui's recitation CDs, and her vegetarian restaurant (a favorite haunt for small religious groups in China) thereafter became a hub promoting the practice. The authors observed she also had works by Mou Zongsan in her library. How did this restaurateur untangle Mou's labyrinthine philosophy? Apparently, she didn't. She did not see him as a philosopher: "Master Mou is a sage (*shengxian*), not a scholar (*xuezhe*). He indicates the way for all humanity." Just as Mou had been transformed from philosopher to sage, so too his texts took on a scriptural quality that required a unique kind of reading. As another follower of Wang Caigui who was active in encouraging young people to read Mou said, "When one reads Mou Zongsan, one must come to a unity of reading and effort (*gongfu*). One must not read like so many professors, who read in a unilateral (*pianmian*) way. You can't read Mou like you read Kant" (Billioud and Thoraval 2008: 97).

The reading and recitation of esteemed texts in a manner that transcends ordinary semantic content is hardly unique to contemporary Ru practice. It is, for example, evident in ancient Vedic chants that had no "meaning" (Staal 1990), in carefully intoned Daoist scriptures written in a "hidden language" only gods could understand (Bokenkamp 1997: 385–92), and in modern yoga studios where students chant Patañjali's *Yoga Sūtra* without understanding a word. It is tempting to see here nothing but aesthetics mixed with an affective response to vocal rhythm, but in their respective contexts the practices acquire specific significance and reinforce unique movements. The magic of incanting the Classics might have a simple physiological explanation, but if participants experience this as the power of the sages' words, recitation can be a strong force legitimizing and energizing revival at a broader social, cultural, and political level.

Kongzi for mass consumption

Is a major Ru renaissance representative of the overall aspirations of the Chinese people? Does all the talk about Kongzi and *Rujia* being synonymous with Chineseness resonate, or is it just revivalist mythmaking? One way of assessing this is to look at just how well Kongzi sells.

What I will be considering in this final section are not the creations of philosophers or activists. Rather, Yu Dan (b. 1965) hosts popular television shows, and Hu Mei (b. 1958) is a prominent film director. Both recently turned their attention to Kongzi. What their depictions lack in accuracy they make up for with popular appeal. These two women have manufactured the most instantly available and widespread images of Kongzi in Chinese history.

Hu Mei's film *Kongzi* (English release *Confucius*) was created with one eye on the box office and the other on the CCP. It was made with government backing, it is very patriotic, and it was intended for release in 2009 to correspond with the celebrations of the sixtieth anniversary of the founding of the PRC. Yet it very obviously tried to appeal to popular taste by casting celebrity Chow Yun-fat as Kongzi, reinventing him as a brilliant military tactician so he could feature in epic battle scenes and even throwing in some romance.

The message of the movie, clearly announced in a set of captions overlaying the concluding frames, is that Kongzi, renowned for being one of history's greatest advocates of moral philosophy and egalitarian education, stands as the symbol of Chinese civilization. He is a national icon whose teachings on personal virtue, social harmony, and civil order have much to contribute to the country today.

Yet Kongzi is not presented as a sage, and his words are not put forward as being infallible or having the scriptural authority they enjoyed in the past. The very human nature of his humanity is seen in the most notable scene in the film in which he meets Nanzi, the wife of the Duke of Wei. The *Analects* no more than mentions that a disciple was displeased the encounter had occurred, to which Kongzi replied by swearing he had done nothing wrong (6:28)—an enigmatic response more than capable of fueling gossip for millennia. Subsequent commentary was standard fare slandering any woman venturing into the political domain, and Nanzi was portrayed as a powerful, manipulative, and dangerous woman harboring murderous intent toward the Duke's son and, for good measure, involved in an incestuous affair (Englert and Ptak 1986).

Nanzi's reputation shifted with changes to women's status. Li Zhi had praised her during the liberal decades of the late Ming (Li 2016: 66–7) and at the time of the New Culture Movement Nanzi was seen to suggest that the sage was moved by and approved of romantic love (Chen 2007: 29). Lin Yutang (1895–1976) was enticed by this idea and wrote a play entitled "Kongzi Met Nanzi" that was first performed in Qufu in 1929. The Kong family's outrage added to its appeal, and it was thereafter performed in many large cities. In the play Nanzi is both powerful and beautiful, as the early sources suggest, but she is also refined, intelligent, witty, creative, free-spirited, and spontaneous in a manner that is contrasted with the rigid ritualism of Kongzi. She is proudly sexual and insists sexuality is the source of all art and life. Kongzi comes away humbled by Nanzi saying, "I have lived fifty-six years and today for the first time, I begin to understand the real meaning of art and life ... This is real ceremony, real music" (Lin 1936: 43–4).

Hu Mei's Nanzi is akin to the Nanzi of Lin's play (and some of the Kong family were again outraged) (Figure 21). She arranges to meet Kongzi because she genuinely recognizes the value of his teachings, and he agrees to the audience because he appreciates that she is the intelligence behind the throne. Their encounter is a sensual philosophical dance where she advocates beauty and love and he responds upholding virtue and righteousness. She seductively asks whether his claim that true humaneness (*ren*) is to love people (12:22) would extend to a woman of her reputation; she quotes the *Odes* on gentlemen seeking beauty and reminds him that this Classic celebrated romance and love. When she asks to meet again, the reason he gives for declining acknowledges that he has been touched by her wisdom and her charm: "I have yet to meet the man who is as fond of virtue as he is of the beauty of women," a clever deployment of a passage occurring twice in the *Analects* (9:18 and 15:13). When she is assassinated (we must assume at the hands of the Duke's son), she dies with a smile of contentment fondly recalling her meeting with Kongzi.

The case of Nanzi illustrates the stance of the film as a whole and a position that is held by many in China today: Kongzi is a figure who is revered for his contribution to shaping the character of the nation, he is undoubtedly a great moral philosopher and educator, but his teachings must be reworked to conform to modern values and be extended to better embrace the complexities of human reality.

While the Nanzi sequence seems to try to make Kongzi more relevant to modern mores, the final scenes pander to political expectation. After years in exile the elderly Kongzi is invited back to Lu and returns in an emotional scene where he formally bows saying: "my beloved motherland, I am back in your arms." This certainly

FIGURE 21 Kongzi *movie poster.*

Shanghai commuters nonchalantly wait for buses beside a movie poster suggestively pairing Kongzi and Nanzi. In the past this would have been considered blasphemous.

Kongzi has always been defined by his iconographic associates. The *men* whose image or tablet accompanied Kongzi into temples illuminated the Master and embodied the "transmission of the Way" (*daotong*). Needless to say, they had exemplary moral reputations.

Traditionally, Nanzi was seen to be the antithesis of these men. In Hu Mei's movie, her unique and intimate connection with Kongzi inverted millennia-old stereotypes. Few people seemed to care one way or the other.

evokes a patriotic spirit and surely made many viewers think of the government's recent recall of Kongzi following his "exile" under Mao. The film, however, inserts a qualification to his return that is totally out of keeping with the Kongzi we know from the early sources. He says he will return on the proviso he can "just teach and not be troubled with politics." The message many have detected is that philosophers, historians, and other upholders of Kongzi are performing a valuable service in build-ing national spirit and encouraging virtuous living, but they need to respect limits and refrain from meddling in politics (useful sources include Lee et al. 2011, Ou 2010, and Ash n.d.).

Although a *Shanghai Daily* headline simply read "Confucius says: Flop," Hu Mei's film was not a total failure. A record-breaking 2,500 release prints were distributed nationwide, and it was seen by millions. The government response was warm, but moviegoers were not particularly enthralled. There is a message here. If you intend selling Kongzi to the masses, you need a genius for marketing and a product for which consumers hanker.

* * *

Where Hu Mei fell short, Yu Dan excelled. Her TV series and the companion volume entitled *Professor Yu Dan Explains the Analects of Kongzi* (2006), since translated into twenty-eight languages, were a cultural phenomenon. More than 1.5 million copies of the book sold in the first forty days, and sales eventually exceeded 10 million. Daniel Bell has grasped the essential comparison: "The last book out of China to attract so much attention has been, well, let me think ... Mao's *Little Red Book*" (Bell 2008: 163). Quite simply, it is the most successful book interpreting a philosopher or religious thinker in human history.

The secret to Yu Dan's success was repackaging Kongzi's words to appeal to a very large and lucrative market. Her book captured an audience attracted to "motivational" and "self-help" genres, and she presents the *Analects* as a guide to personal success and happiness, a kind of "Chicken Soup for the Chinese Soul."

Yu Dan has no real training as a philosopher or cultural historian, but is a professor of media studies. She was nonetheless invited in 2006 to offer a series of seven lectures on the *Analects* for a popular show called *Lecture Hall*, which seeks to make academic expertise accessible to the public and which screens on state-owned CCTV. Yu Dan excels in this role and she has a certain charisma that has led several commentators to describe her as the Chinese Oprah.

Most people would find it daunting to try to present ideas that had challenged some of the greatest minds in Chinese history in a way that was accessible to millions of viewers and readers. Yu Dan does it with ease. First, she dismisses the entire tradition of the Ru:

What we can learn from Confucius today is not the "Confucian Learning" set out by Emperor Wu; it is not the solemn, dignified, ritualized "Confucian religion" that stands alongside Daoism and Buddhism in China; nor is it the Confucianism of the scholars, full of deep argumentation and fettered by textual research.

What we can take away from the Analects of Confucius are simple truths that every person knows in his or her heart, though they may not let them out through their mouths. (Yu 2010 5–6)

Yu Dan repeatedly emphasizes that the truths that Kongzi taught do not require extensive training, a Classical education, or a "lifetime's laborious study to understand." Rather, he "offers us simple truths that will help us develop our inner hearts and souls and allow us to make the right choices as we go through life's journey" (Yu 2010: 31, 32). To stress this point, later editions of her book where retitled *The Analects from the Heart* (*Lunyu xinde*).

A defining feature of her book is this focus on the "inner" person. The passage of our entire life is defined in this way. Thus she says: "What we call growing and maturing is a process by which the inner heart gradually becomes stronger through experience, and we acquire the ability to take external things and transform them into inner strength" (Yu 2010: 178). The chapters deal with themes such as being happy even when poor or disadvantaged (chapter 1), being courageous through misfortune and maintaining a positive attitude (chapter 2), selecting the right way to relate to friends and colleagues (chapter 3), choosing and finding good friends (chapter 4), having realistic ambitions and not getting bogged down or stressed (chapter 5), and journeying successfully through the various stages of life (chapter 6). Passages from the *Analects* are selected to illuminate her argument, and then, almost invariably, a story or anecdote or fable is found to, in turn, illuminate the chosen passage. These illustrative tales, which are taken from around the globe and often have no more authenticity than hearsay, occupy more space than the *Analects* do.

It is no surprise academics with expertise in philosophy have been critical of her interpretations, but even if her reading of the *Analects* is often superficial and sometimes plain wrong, does this really matter? After all, if millions of people feel their lives have been enriched, what harm is done? Yu Dan wants people to be happy. She says, "The happiness that Confucius and his disciples enjoyed can be a wellspring of happiness for us today. This is probably the greatest lesson that Confucius can give us, and his greatest gift" (Yu 2010: 96). Although Kongzi himself in fact never prioritized happiness, can we begrudge Yu Dan her vision?

The problem is Yu Dan's view on happiness. She praises the disciple Yan Hui who was so poor he had insufficient food for his family and yet could still find happiness. She advocates "the kind of happiness that cannot be taken away by poverty" (Yu 2010: 22), and in one of the very few sections where she skirts anywhere near political issues, she says that rather than obsessing over the gross national product, more attention should be given to measuring gross national happiness, which comes from our inner selves. The problem here is that careful cross-cultural research has clearly shown that the "money can't buy happiness" hypothesis is true *only* for people living above the poverty line. Poverty most certainly can and invariably does buy misery, as does the violation of human rights.

The most recurrent and alarming criticism of Yu Dan is that in reinterpreting the *Analects* in terms of our inner selves and the quest for happiness she has totally abandoned the sociopolitical dimension of Kongzi's teachings. Michael Nylan and Thomas Wilson rightly observe that "Yu Dan's work offers nary a hint that roughly a third of the *Analects* that deals with social justice and economic redistribution" (Nylan and Wilson 2010: 222), while Daniel Bell hammers home the dangers of this oversight:

> Her account isn't as apolitical as it seems. By telling people that they shouldn't complain too much, that they should worry first and foremost about their inner happiness, by downplaying the importance of social and political commitment, and by ignoring the critical tradition of Confucianism, Yu Dan deflects attention from the economic and political conditions that actually cause people's misery, as well as the sorts of collective solutions needed to bring about substantial improvement to people's lives. In actual fact, her account is complacent, conservative, and supportive of the status quo. (Bell 2008: 174)

Conclusion

Hu Mei and Yu Dan work through mass media; their portraits of Kongzi are out there to be viewed by those who are interested and ignored by those who are not. Public response to their work is therefore a useful measure of the mood of the people. More specifically for our purposes, they offer a very imprecise census of the common disposition toward proposals to reinstate Ru Learning in education and government.

Yu Dan was successful in large part because her Kongzi was so thoroughly apolitical. His refashioned teachings are directed toward individuals and the day-to-day challenges they face in life. Her book remains popular and may do so for some time yet, but the appeal is driven by the personal interests and needs of her readers, not by larger social, political, or religious concerns. Her Kongzi seems to lack any authority save that as a life coach who might be quickly replaced were he found to be no longer effective. And, significantly, Yu Dan's subsequent series for *Lecture Room* was on the Daoist philosopher Zhuangzi (2007). The companion volume sold 15,000 copies the day it was released.

Hu Mei's Kongzi could not totally avoid politics, although as we have seen, she presents him as renouncing this aspect of his life in his final years. The government intent and expectation was that her film would engender nationalism, but many found his incessant moralizing and commitment to ancient protocol uninspiring. Would Chinese viewers have perhaps preferred outlandish fantasy as an alternative way to reflect on the problems of corruption and immoral greed? We know the answer. James Cameron's environmental sci-fi epic *Avatar* was screening at the same time as *Kongzi* was released in China, and even with the government buying up and giving away free tickets and pulling *Avatar* from some cinemas, it still managed to outsell *Kongzi* 10:1.

My reading of Yu Dan's success and the less than glowing response to Hu Mei's film suggest that, despite a general respect and admiration for Kongzi, there is little widespread zeal for any kind of formal revival of his teaching. My own observations corroborate this. In 2006, I discussed the question "Is Kongzi relevant to 21st century China?" with about 120 students at a university in Yunnan province, some 40 of them electing to submit a written response. While all save one gave an affirmative reply, there was almost unanimous agreement that Kongzi's ideas must be critically assessed. They particularly admired him as a great patron of education and for his emphasis on personal morality and virtue in governing, but they were very quick to reject what they saw as elitist, archaic, and patriarchal aspects to his thought.

In brief, the predominant view in China is that Kongzi is a great national hero, the quintessential teacher, and someone who was uncommonly virtuous and wise. He was not, however, an infallible sage, and his words are not an ultimate authority deserving of religious reverence. The push to install *Rujiao* or *Kongjiao* as state ideology cannot, therefore, be said to reflect a current consensus of opinion.

Further evidence supporting this comes from a most unlikely source. Kang Xiaoguang wrote an article based on a survey designed to measure "the renaissance of traditional cultures in contemporary China." His article title, however, specified a "renaissance of traditional *Confucian* culture" as he simply assumed that "Chinese traditional culture [is] centered on Confucianism" (Kang 2012: 33). The editors of the book in which the article appeared felt obliged to draw attention to the fact that Kang had overlooked the very statistics he presented (Tamney and Yang 2012). Of those surveyed, there was in fact significantly more admiration for Mao Zedong's philosophy (82.4 percent) than Kongzi's (57.9 percent) and far more respondents identified with Buddhism (32.1 percent) than Ru tradition (14.5 percent). This, by the way, is a surprisingly generous figure, as an independent survey found 16.7 percent belief in Buddhism but only .2 percent belief in Confucianism (Sun 2013: 116). But then again, you may recall that Kang himself had said "9,999 out of 10,000" Chinese people today "have not even any superficial knowledge about Confucianism," which would yield only .01 percent! Whatever the exact minority, we are left wondering just how the few manage to determine the Chinese psyche as a whole. Perhaps it is not consciously realized by the majority, but this then leaves us wondering what Kang could possibly have hoped to achieve by surveying popular opinion.

* * *

Are there solid *historical* grounds for claiming that Ru tradition or Confucianism (*Kongjiao*) defines Chineseness? I think not. As we have seen, the supremacy of Ru Learning in early dynastic China has been greatly exaggerated (Chapter 5). Ruism certainly did dominate education and official recruitment from the Song dynasty onward (Chapters 6 and 7), but we need always remember that, in John Dardess' words, there "was a surprisingly small statistical base for Chinese Confucianism, something which is too often lightly equated or confused with Chinese civilization in general" (Dardess 1983: 15). It is one thing to acknowledge that Ru Learning has been a mighty force in shaping Chinese history, quite another to say that it defines what it is to be Chinese.

As we have seen, the assumption that "Confucianism" was definitive of China's national character emerged alongside the terminological transition from Ruism (*Ruxue, Rujiao*, etc.) to Confucianism (*Kongjiao*). Before Western intrusion, Ruism primarily operated as an intellectual tradition bound up with the administration of state. It did not define the Chinese people, but rather a small elite distinct from the rest of the populace. It was only with the collapse of the imperial system and the need to demarcate China from the West that Kang Youwei and his sympathizers sought to elevate *Kongjiao* (Confucius-ism) as the country's faith and cast it in a form of a religion comparable to Christianity. Since that time, the conflation of China and Confucianism has in some circles become almost reflexive.

The problem with equating Ru tradition with Chineseness is that it erases China's rich cultural and intellectual heritage. Suzanne Ogden has suggested that anyone advocating any -ism defining China probably needs to attend an introductory class in Chinese Studies: "China is a big country, and there are lots of people" (Ogden 2002: 54). It is a land where cherries make easy picking. In the early twentieth century, China's artistic tradition was said to define the "national essence" (*guocui*) (Hon 2013). At much the same time, anarchists were arguing Daoism demarcated China's authentic core. "Legalism" was singled out during Mao's reign (Wu 1983: 7). Not surprisingly, the chosen nucleus invariably matched the revivalists' agenda. Later in the twentieth century, even *qigong* enthusiasts were saying that *qigong* "was what made China China" (Ownby 2008: 13). The candidates go on and on.

***

Whenever a Chinese government aligns itself with Ruism, it invariably does so to strengthen nationalism and uplift moral standards. This can be effective if it takes the form of an unofficial "civil religion," but when it is perceived to be coercive, it succeeds primarily in generating resistance.

In a peculiar reversal of their mid- to late-twentieth-century stances, the CCP is currently edging ever closer to Ru tradition as Taiwanese politicians are stepping back. The association between Ruism and Chiang Kai-shek's autocratic rule tainted the tradition so that it has now largely disappeared from Taiwanese political discourse (Fetzer and Soper 2013), just as it vanished from Japan after "the Confucian brand was damaged ... [by] its association with fascism" (Paramore 2016: 188). Although Taiwan's recent president Ma Yingjiu belonged to the GMD party, he showed no more that a polite appreciation for Ru tradition. Taiwan's new president could not depart further from the conservative Ru stereotype of a Chinese ruler governing the nation like a father does his family: Tsai Ing-wen of the Democratic Progressive party is a woman of Hakka and aboriginal descent, unmarried, childless, and a very strong supporter of gay and lesbian rights.

There would be a very strong backlash were mainland Chinese leaders to utilize Ru Learning in a heavy-handed and overbearing manner. This would come from conservative Marxists, it would come from democratic liberals, and, most importantly, it would come from prominent advocates of Ru Learning.

As we saw in Chapter 9, many distinguished exponents of New Ru Learning recommend liberal democracy as the form of government most compatible with their aspirations. They are quite opposed to autocratic regimes posing as the "Kingly Way." Tu Weiming once observed: "The most serious damage to the public image of Confucianism did not come from frontal attack organized by the liberals, anarchists, socialists and other Westernizers. It came from the extreme right ... who used Confucian ethics to stabilize their control" (Tu 1993: 154). The peril of patrons remains a very real risk in mainland China. Yu Yingshi, one of the designated third-generation exponents of New Ru Learning, has recently warned that were the CCP "to support Confucianism [it would amount] to the kiss of death for Confucianism" (Yu 2015).

***

If it does not establish itself as state ideology or state religion, in what other body might the Ru spirit survive? Universities will of course continue to provide an important home for the philosophers, but unlike education in imperial times, they will constitute only a small fraction of faculties and they will be expected to present their views as objective discourse. Something more is needed to reach wide audiences.

Phenomena such as Yu Dan's lectures and book on the *Analects* or the mass movement for reciting the Classics have extended to tens of millions of people. Both have had a sweeping impact, but both are "fevers," and their heat will soon dissipate. Every blockbuster must make way for its successor, and the enthusiasm for Classics chanting will surely decline as did the "*qigong* fever" that preceded it. Enduring movements require institutional stability; they demand a robust body.

I suspect we may be witnessing Ru tradition metamorphosing in preparation for a new incarnation. The transformation was inaugurated by Kang Youwei in the late nineteenth century, it was perpetuated by Chen Huanzhang in the first half of the twentieth century, and it is now something to which Zhou Beichen and others are devoting themselves. This is to see Ruism officially recognized, or at least achieve de facto acceptance, as "a religion."

I have taken care to stress that in imperial and pre-imperial times, Ruism was *not* "a religion," even though it was a tradition with profoundly religious concerns (Chapter 1). Although it was never China's state religion, the machinery of state was nonetheless a host body in which it thrived. What was intuited as the empire fell was that if Ruism had a soul or spirit, it must prepare to depart the body in which it had traditionally resided.

In this regard, some of Kang Youwei's suggestions were rather astute. True, he hoped to install Kongjiao as state religion, but by recasting the faith in the mold of Christianity, by seeking to institute a "Kongzi church" (*Kongjiaohui*), and recommending the widespread establishment of Kongzi temples and shrines, missionaries, and services with teaching and singing, he was equally seeking to equip the Way of the Ru with an organizational form that could function independently of the state.

The academies that began emerging in the late 1930s and which have been recently revived by Jiang Qing and a few others represent one possible base for developing autonomous Ru religious communities, although their rather elite status does not currently encourage proliferation. Redemptive societies such as the Worldwide Ethical Society, the influence of which continues to resurface in movements like Yidan School, offer another model for Ru "churches." The proselytizing influence of the Kongzi-religion society in Hong Kong, as well as various sectarian movements in Taiwan, will almost certainly continue to feed developments on the mainland.

In November 2015, the Chinese Church of Kongzi (*Zhonghua Kongshenghui*) was formed with the aim of consolidating and spreading the Way of the Sage in China through education and the proliferation of temples along the Shenzhen model. Jiang Qing is chairman, while Kang Xiaoguang and Chen Ming are among an impressive array of consultants. Although it is not yet claiming to be "a religion," the term *shenghui,* "holy association" or "church," along with the emphasis on spiritual values and the need to multiply places of worship is surely a significant step in this direction (Figure 22).

The final challenge to Ruism adopting the body of religion will be the government's willingness to allow that the tradition in fact constitutes one of China's religions.

FIGURE 22   *Logo of the Chinese Church of Kongzi.*

The bell is an allusion to *Analects* 3:24: "The Empire has long been without the Way. Heaven is about to use the Master as the wooden tongue for a bell." Within a cosmology reverberating the trigrams of the *Changes*, this bell resonates Kongzi's message of humaneness (仁, *ren*).

Official policy is becoming increasingly relaxed, and this now seems a real possibility (Goossaert and Palmer 2011: 344–50).

In the opening pages of this book, I cited Wilfred Cantwell Smith's pithy observation: "The question 'is Confucianism a religion?' is one the West has never been able to answer, and China never able to ask." When he wrote these words in 1963, he was already half-wrong. As we have seen, Chinese thinkers began debating the question in earnest in the early twentieth century, and the discussion continues. And the West may have its answer in due course. But for now, my answer to the question "Is Confucianism a religion?" must be: soon, perhaps.

Glossary

Academy 書院 *Shuyuan. Shuyuan*, literally "book schools," were private or semi-independent educational institutions. They emerged to encourage learning purely for self-cultivation but eventually became fettered to the examination system.

Authenticity 誠 *Cheng. Cheng* can mean "sincerity," but in Ru philosophy it suggests remaining faithful to our intrinsic human nature, which comes closer to the English "authenticity" or "integrity."

Chen Lifu 陳立夫 (1900–2001). The most influential promoter of Ru values and education in the Guomindang.

Cheng Hao 程顥 (1032–1085) and **Cheng Yi** 程頤 (1033–1107). The "two Chengs" were brothers who began the great Ru revival known as Way Learning *(Daoxue)*.

Classic of Filial Piety 孝經 *Xiaojing*. A little text in which Kongzi lectures Zengzi on the importance of filial piety. It had quasi-canonical status and was formally added to the canon in the Song.

Classic 經 *Jing*. "Classic" does not fully capture *jing*, which connotes a sacred text or scripture. *Jing* literally signifies vertical weaving threads and the Classics exposed the "warp" of existence. See Five Classics.

Dong Zongshu 董仲舒 (c. 179 – c. 104). The most celebrated exponent of Ruism in the Han. He was traditionally said to have masterminded Ru Learning being patronized by the state.

Evidential Studies 考證學 *Kaozhengxue*. Largely overlapping with Han Learning, its exponents focused on applying new methods of textual analysis to the "evidence" of the Classics.

Filial Piety 孝 *Xiao*. The virtue of humaneness was based on concrete relationships, and the quintessential human relationship was between a parent and a child. Learning to be a reverential child was considered the root of all moral cultivation.

Five Classics 五經 *Wujing*. The "Five" Classics eventually came to incorporate nine books.

Odes
    Shijing 詩經 *Odes Classic*
Documents
    Shujing 書經 *Documents Classic*
Changes
    Yijing 易經 *Classic of Changes*
Rites
    Liji 禮記 *Rites Records*
    Zhouli 周禮 *Rites of Zhou*
    Yili 儀禮 *Ceremonies and Rites*
Spring and Autumn *Chunqiu* 春秋
    with *Gongyang Commentary* 公羊傳
    with *Guliang Commentary* 穀梁傳
    with *Zuo Commentary* 左傳

Five Constant Virtues 五常 *Wuchang*. The virtues are *ren* 仁 humaneness, *li* 禮 ritual, *yi* 義 righteousness, *Zhi* 智 wisdom, and *xin* 信 trustworthiness. Mengzi grouped the first four while Dong Zhongshu added the fifth.

Four Books 四書 *Sishu*. The crux of the curriculum for the final six centuries of imperial China, the Four Books are:
Lunyu 論語 *Analects*
Daxue 大學 *Great Learning*
Zhongyong 中庸 *Doctrine of the Mean*
Mengzi 孟子

Four Correlates 四配 *Sipei*. From the thirteenth century, Four Correlates were installed in Kongzi temples and received secondary sacrifices. Three of them, Zengzi, Zisi, and Mengzi, were associated with the Four Books. The fourth, Yan Hui, had been Kongzi's favorite disciple.

Great Unity 大同 *Datong*. An ideal briefly described in the *Rites Records*. It has been focal to Chinese utopian thought since the late nineteenth century.

Han Learning 漢學 *Hanxue*. The predominant Ru orientation of the final Qing dynasty. It rejected Song-Ming metaphysical speculation and sought to reconnect with the commentarial traditions of the Han.

Han Yu 韓愈 (768–824). The most revered Tang dynasty exponent of Ruism. He was regarded as a herald of the Song dynasty renaissance.

Heart-mind 心 *Xin*. Xin is "heart," but as it was associated with both feeling and thought, it is translated "heart-mind." Xin became paramount with Mengzi and Xunzi, and its significance was the crux of the divergence between Lixue and Xinxue schools.

Heart-mind Learning 心學 *Xinxue*. The tradition deriving from Lu Xiangshan and Wang Yangming, who maintained that Principle and heart-mind were identical.

Heaven 天 *Tian*. Tian mean "sky" or "Heaven," but for most Ru it was not a separate domain, but rather an inherent force or order informing events unfolding in the world.

Humaneness 仁 *Ren*. The quintessential Ru virtue. It is a profound care for others within the context of specific embodied relationships. See also *shu* and *zhong*.

Inner Sage, Outer King 內聖外王 *Neisheng waiwang*. This pair of terms, which actually derive from the Daoist *Zhuangzi*, came to define two Ru orientations: inner self-cultivation and worldly political transformation.

Jiang Qing 蔣慶 (b. 1953). The most conspicuous and influential advocate of Ru revival in contemporary China.

Kang Youwei 康有為 (1858–1927). A tireless advocate of Kongzi Religion *(Kongjiao)* in the late Qing and early republic. Many current reformers claim to continue his quest.

Kongjiao 孔教 "Kongzi religion." An alternative to *Rujiao* that emerged in the late nineteenth century when institutionalized Ruism came under fire.

Kongzi 孔子 (551–479) or Master Kong. Recognized as the ultimate sage, the first teacher and the author-editor of all the Classics. "Confucius" derives from Kongfuzi 孔夫子, which was actually very uncommon in written Chinese.

Learning 學 *Xue*. The one thing Kongzi admitted he excelled at, *xue* was definitive of the Way of the Ru. It involved reading and study, but as Classics were scriptural traces of sages, this was understood to be a path to moral self-transformation.

Lu Xiangshan 陸象山. The assumed name of Lu Jiuyuan (1139–1193). He argued against Zhu Xi, his contemporary, and anticipated the teachings of Wang Yangming. Together they were thus said to establish a Lu-Wang School.

Luxuriant Gems on the Spring and Autumn Annals 春秋繁露 *Chunqiu fanlu*. A book attributed to Dong Zongshu. While only sections reflect Dong's own views, it is our best source for Ru thought in the Han.

Mandate of Heaven 天命 *Tianming*. Rulers came to power by Heaven's mandate and the rise and fall of dynasties evinced *Tian*'s response to the virtue of rulers. Historical records revealed this process (or perhaps just revealed that victors wrote the histories).

Mengzi 孟子 (Mencius, 372?–289?). Regarded as the "second sage" after Kongzi. The *Mengzi*, a book recoding his teachings, was one of the Four Books paramount to Ru Learning from the Song dynasty onward.

Mou Zongsan 牟宗三 (1909–1995). Often regarded as the greatest exponent of Ru Learning in the twentieth century.

Nature 性 *Xing*. Human nature has been central to Ru thought since the time of Mengzi and the *Zhongyong*. It was a pivotal yet controversial concept. Whether it was good, bad, or mixed was an ongoing issue.

New Ru School 新儒家 *Xin Rujia*. Although individuals counted as exponents of *Xin Ruexue* 新儒學 (New Ru Learning) had been active since the 1920s, a movement as such was a retrospective creation of the 1980s.

Noble Person 君子 *Junzi*. Becoming a *junzi* was the goal toward which Ru realistically strived. Sagehood was an absolute but remote possibility.

Principle 理 *Li*. An inherent "pattern" that directs the formation of all things; "order," "reason," and "coherence" are other translations. It became central to Ru philosophy in the Song dynasty.

Principle Learning 理學 *Lixue*. Largely synonymous with Way Learning.

Qi 氣 . The basic stuff of all existence, physical and mental. It is more than dead matter and has generative potential and is thus sometimes translated "material force" or "vital force."

Quiet Sitting 靜坐 *Jingzuo*. A type of meditation developed by Song dynasty exponents of *Ruxue*. It was complimentary and preparatory to studying the Classics.

Reflections on Things at Hand 近思錄 *Jinsilu*. Compiled by Zhu Xi (with Lü Zuqian) in 1175, it is an anthology of quotations from Zhou Dunyi, Zhang Zai, Cheng Hao, and Cheng Yi with Zhu Xi's commentary. It became the orthodox primer for studying the Four Books.

Reverence / Concentration 敬 *Jing*. *Jing* initially referred to awe experienced in the presence of the sacred. It can mean "reverence," but during the Song this was primarily seen as the apprehension of our own nature and so connoted inner "concentration."

Ritual 禮 *Li*. *Li* is ritual in a broad sense extending to propriety, decorum, and manners. In pre-imperial times, Ru were essentially regarded as ritual masters. While they were later primarily recognized as "scholars," ritual was pivotal to the texts they studied.

Ru 儒 "scholar" or "Classicist". The word that is usually translated as "Confucian." "Confucianism" variously translates *Rujia* 儒家 (Ru school), *Rujiao* 儒教 (Ru teaching) and *Ruxue* 儒學 (Ru learning).

Sage 聖人 *Shengren*. More literally "holy person" or saint. Sages were morally perfect with an uncanny clarity of mind. Their faultless wisdom now remains inscribed in Classics.

Shu 恕 consideration or empathy. A essential aspect of *ren*. It is the awareness of the needs of others based on our experience of our own needs.

Sima Qian 司馬遷 (145–86). China's most revered historian who wrote *Records of the Historian (Shiji)*. The *Shiji* achieved near canonical status and every Ru was expected to be familiar with it.

Supreme Ultimate 太極 *Taiji*. *Ji* refers to the ridge of a roof, hence it is the ultimate point, the apex, the extremity. As a ridge is inseparable from the two sides of a roof (i.e., as *yin* and *yang* converge it *ji*), some believe "supreme polarity" is a preferable translation.

Taizhou School 泰州學派 *Taizhou xuepa*. A radical offshoot of Wang Yangming's teachings, named after founder Wang Gen's hometown.

Three Bonds 三綱 *Sangang*. *Sangang* more literally means "three guidelines": the ruler "guides" the ruled, fathers guide sons, and husbands guide wives.

Transmission of the Way 道統 *Daotong*. A legitimate line of succession in the Way of the Ru. Invariably, adjudicators were seeking to historically legitimize their own stance.

Tu Weiming 杜維明 (Pinyin Du Weiming, b. 1940). A leading scholar of Ru tradition who holds professorships at both Peking and Harvard Universities. He has been very instrumental in reviving interest in Ruism in mainland China since the 1980s.

Wang Gen 王艮 (1483–1541). Founder of the Taizhou school, a popular "leftist" movement that flourished in the late Ming.

Wang Yangming 王陽明. The assumed name of Wang Shouren (1472–1529). Despite Zhu Xi's orthodoxy, Wang alternative theories were immensely influential in late dynastic China, and his thinking heavily informs Ru Learning today.

Way Learning 道學 *Daoxue*. A movement begun by Cheng Hao and Cheng Yi and brought to a "great completion" by Zhu Xi. It is usually referred to as Neo-Confucianism in English.

Xiong Shili 熊十力 (1885–1968). Often regarded as the greatest exponent of Ru philosophy in mainland China in the twentieth century. While not really a founder, he inspired many key thinkers of the so-called New Ru school.

Xunzi 荀子 (313?–238? BCE). The third great pre-imperial Ru philosopher following Kongzi and Mengzi. His ideas profoundly influenced the state implementation of Ru Learning.

Yang Xiong 揚雄 (53 BCE–18 CE). A mid-Han thinker who sought to return Ru tradition to the thought of Kongzi and Mengzi and whose concerns anticipated the revival of the Song.

Yinyang wuxing 陰陽五行 or *yinyang* and the "five processes" (wood, fire, earth, metal, water). A model of existence that radically transformed every aspect of Chinese thought, including Ru Learning. It emerged around the time of unification (221 BCE).

Zengzi 曾子 (Zeng Shen, 505–435). A disciple of Kongzi traditionally believed to have compiled the *Great Learning* and the *Classic of Filial Piety*. His is one of the Four Correlates.

Zhang Zai 張載 (1020–1077). Identified by Zhu Xi as a patriarch of Daoxue. He was particularly revered for his *Western Inscription*.

Zhong 忠. Zhong is (with *shu*) an aspect of humaneness *(ren)*. Although it narrowly suggests "loyalty" to superiors, it more generally signifies "devoted care" to the needs of others.

Zhou Dunyi 周敦頤 (1017–1073). Identified by Zhu Xi as a patriarch of Daoxue. He was esteemed for his *Diagram of the Supreme Ultimate Explained*, which provided Zhu with a cosmology.

Zhu Xi 朱熹 (1130–1200). Zhu defined Ru orthodoxy for the final six centuries of imperial China. He was seen to have brought the revival of the Song to a "great completion," and his commentaries on the Four Books and Classics were officially adopted.

Zisi 子思 (Kong Ji, 483?–402?) . Traditionally believed to be Kongzi's grandson, a disciple of Zengzi and the author of the *Doctrine of the Mean*. He is one of the Four Correlates.

References

Adler, Joseph A. 2004. "Varieties of Spiritual Experience: *Shen* in Neo-Confucian Discourse." In *Confucian Spirituality: Volume Two*, edited by Tu Weiming and Mary Evelyn Tucker, 120–48. New York: Crossroad.

Adler, Joseph A. 2008. "Divination and Sacrifice in Song Neo-Confucianism." In *Teaching Confucianism,* edited by Jeffrey L. Richey, 55–82. Oxford: Oxford University Press.

Adler, Joseph A. 2014a. *Reconstructing the Confucian Dao: Zhu Xi's Appropriation of Zhou Dunyi*. Albany: State University of New York Press.

Adler, Joseph A. 2014b. "Confucianism as Religion / Religious Tradition / Neither: Still Hazy After All These Years." http://www2.kenyon.edu/Depts/Religion/Fac/Adler/Writings/ Still%20Hazy%20-%20Minzu.pdf.

Adler, Joseph A. 2016. "On Translating *Taiji*." In *Returning to Zhu Xi: Emerging Patterns within the Supreme Polarity*, edited by David Jones and Jinli He, 51–81. Albany: State University of New York Press.

Alitto, Guy S. 1979. *The Last Confucian: Liang Shu-ming and the Chinese Dilemma of Modernity*. Berkeley: University of California Press.

Ames, Roger T. and David L. Hall. 2001. *Focusing the Familiar: A Translation and Philosophical Interpretation of the Zhongyong*. Honolulu: University of Hawai'i Press.

Ames, Roger T. and Henry Rosemont (trans.) 1998. *The Analects of Confucius: A Philosophical Translation*. New York: Ballantine Books.

Angle, Stephen C. 2012. *Contemporary Confucian Political Philosophy*. Cambridge: Polity Press.

Apter, David E. and Tony Saich. 1998. *Revolutionary Discourse in Mao's Republic*. Cambridge, MA: Harvard University Press.

Arbuckle, Gary. 1987. "A Note on the Authenticity of the *Chunqiu fanlu*." *T'oung Pao*. 75: 226–34.

Arbuckle, Gary. 1991. *Restoring Dong Zhongshu (BCE 195–115): An Experiment in Historical and Philosophical Reconstruction*. PhD dissertation. University of British Columbia.

Arbuckle, Gary. 1994. "The *Gongyang* School and Wang Mang." *Monumeta Serica*. 42: 127–50.

Arbuckle, Gary. 1995. "Inevitable Treason: Dong Zhongshu's Theory of Historical Cycles and Early Attempts to Invalidate the Han Mandate." *Journal of the American Oriental Society*. 115: 585–97.

Asad, Talal. 2002. "Reading a Modern Classic: W.C. Smith's 'The Meaning and End of Religion.'" In *Religion and Media*, edited by Hendrik de Vries and Samule Veber, 131–48. Stanford, CA: Stanford University Press.

Ash, Alec. no date. "A Conversation on 'Confucius' with Daniel Bell." *The China Beat*. http://www.thechinabeat.org/?p=1455.

Barrett, T. H. 1996. *Taoism Under the T'ang: Religion and Empire during the Golden Age of Chinese History*. London: Wellsweep.

Bell, Daniel A. 2008. *China's New Confucianism: Politics and Everyday Life in a Changing Society*. Princeton, NJ: Princeton University Press.

Bell, Daniel A. 2013. "Introduction." In Jiang Qing, *A Confucian Constitutional Order: How China's Ancient Past Can Shape Its Political Future*, edited by Daniel A. Bell and Ruiping Fan, 1–24. Princeton, NJ: Princeton University Press.

Berkowitz, Alan J. 2000. *Patterns of Disengagement: The Practice and Portrayal of Reclusion in Early Medieval China*. Stanford: Stanford University Press.

Berkowitz, Alan J. 2014. "Biographies of Recluses: Huangfu Mi's *Accounts of High-Minded Men*." In *Early Medieval China: A Sourcebook*, edited by Wendy Swartz, Robert Ford Campany, Yang Lu, and Jessy J. C. Choo, 333–49. New York: Columbia University Press.

Berling, Judith A. 1980. *The Syncretic Religion of Lin Chao-en*. New York: Columbia University Press.

Berling, Judith A. 1983. "When They Go Their Separate Ways: The Collapse of the Unitary Vision of Chinese Religion in the Early Ch'ing." In *The Meeting of Minds: Intellectual and Religious Interaction in East Asian Traditions of Thought*, edited by Irene Bloom and Joshua A. Fogel, 209–36. New York: Columbia University Press.

Bernal, Martin. 1976. *Chinese Socialism to 1907*. Ithaca, NY: Cornell University Press.

Bielenstein, Hans. 1986. "Wang Mang, the Restoration of the Han Dynasty, and Later Han." In *The Cambridge History of China, Volume 1: The Ch'in and Han Empires. 221 B.C. – A.D. 220*, edited by Denis Twitchett and Michael Loewe, 223–90. Cambridge: Cambridge University Press.

Billioud, Sébastien. 2010. "Carrying the Confucian Torch to the Masses: The Challenge of Structuring the Confucian Revival in the People's Republic of China." *Oriens Extremus*. 49: 210–24.

Billioud, Sébastien. 2011. "Confucian Revival and the Emergence of 'Jiaohua Organizations': A Case Study of Yidan Xuetang." *Modern China*. 37: 286–314.

Billioud, Sébastien and Joël Thoraval. 2007. "*Jiaohua*: The Confucian Revival in China as an Educative Project." *China Perspectives*. 4: 4–20.

Billioud, Sébastien and Joël Thoraval. 2008. "*Anshen liming* or the Religious Dimension of Confucianism." *China Perspectives*. 3: 88–106.

Billioud, Sébastien and Joël Thoraval. 2009. "*Lijiao*: The Return of Ceremonies Honoring Confucius in Mainland China." *China Perspectives*. 4: 82–100.

Billioud, Sébastien and Joël Thoraval. 2015. *The Sage and the People: The Confucian Revival in China*. Oxford: Oxford University Press.

Biot, Édouard. 1851. *Le Tcheou-li ou Rites des Tcheou*. 3 volumes. Paris: Imprimerie Nationale.

Birch, Cyril (ed.) 1965. *Anthology of Chinese Literature from Early Times to the Fourteenth Century*. New York: Grove Weidenfeld.

Birch, Cyril (trans.) 1980. *The Peony Pavilion*. Bloomington: Indiana University Press.

Bloom, Irene (trans.) 1987. *Knowledge Painfully Acquired: The K'un-chih chi by Lo Ch'in-shun*. New York: Columbia University Press.

Boardman, Eugene Powers. 1952. *Christian Influence upon the Ideology of the Taiping Rebellion, 1851–1864*. Madison: University of Wisconsin Press.

Bodde, Derk. 1961. "Myths of Ancient China." In *Mythologies of the Ancient World*, edited by Samuel Noah Kramer, 369–408. New York: Anchor Books.

Bokenkamp, Stephen R. 1997. *Early Daoist Scriptures*. Berkeley: University of California Press.

Bol, Peter. 1992. *"This Culture of Ours": The Intellectual Transitions in T'ang and Sung China*. Stanford, CA: Stanford University Press.

Bol, Peter. 2008. *Neo-Confucianism in History*. Cambridge, MA: Harvard University Press.

Bresciani , Umberto. 2001. *Reinventing Confucianism: The New Confucian Movement*. Taipei: Taipei Ricci Institute for Chinese Studies.

Brook, Timothy. 1998. *The Confusions of Pleasure: Commerce and Culture in Ming China*. Berkeley: University of California Press.

Bujard, Marianne. 2011. "State and Local Cults in Han Religion." In *Early Chinese Religion: Part One: Shang Through Han (1250 BC – 220 AD)*, edited by John Lagerwey and Marc Kalinowski, 777–811. Leiden: Brill.

Bunnin, Nicholas. 2002. "Introduction." In *Contemporary Chinese Philosophy*, edited by Chung-ying Cheng and Nicholas Bunnin, 1–13. Malden, MA: Blackwell.

Bush, Richard C. 1970. *Religion in Communist China*. Nashville: Abingdon.

Cai, Liang. 2010. "Who Said, 'Confucius Composed the *Chunqiu*'? – The Genealogy of the '*Chunqiu*' Canon in the Pre-Han and Han Periods." *Frontiers in the History of China*. 5: 363–85.

Cai, Liang. 2014. *Witchcraft and the Rise of the First Confucian Empire*. Albany: Sate University of New York Press.

Cai, Liang. 2015. "When the Founder Is Not a Creator: Confucius and Confucianism Reconsidered." In *Varieties of Religious Invention: Founders and their Functions in History*, edited by Patrick Gray, 62–82. Oxford: Oxford University Press.

Campany, Robert Ford. 2003. "On the Very Idea of Religions (in the Modern West and in Early Medieval China)." *History of Religions*. 42: 287–319.

Cao, Xueqin and Gao E. 1982. *The Story of the Stone: Volume 4: The Debt of Tears*, translated by John Minford. Harmondsworth: Penguin.

Chaffee, John W. 1995. *The Thorny Gates of Learning in Sung China: A Social History of Examinations*. Albany: State University of New York Press.

Chan, Evans. 2015. *Datong: The Chinese Utopia*. Hong Kong: East Slope.

Chan, Joseph. 2013. "On the Legitimacy of Confucian Constitutionalism." In Jiang Qing, *A Confucian Constitutional Order: How China's Ancient Past Can Shape Its Political Future*, edited by Daniel A. Bell and Ruiping Fan, 99–112. Princeton, NJ: Princeton University Press.

Chan, N. Serina. 2011. *The Thought of Mou Zongsan*. Leiden: Brill.

Chan, Sin-wai (trans.) 1984. *An Exposition of Benevolence: The Jen-hsüeh of T'an Ssu-t'ung*. Hong Kong: Chinese University Press.

Chan, Wing-tsit (trans.) 1963a. *A Source Book in Chinese Philosophy*. Princeton, NJ: Princeton University Press.

Chan, Wing-tsit (trans.) 1963b. *Instructions for Practical Living and Other Neo-Confucian Writings by Wang Yang-ming*. New York: Columbia University Press.

Chan, Wing-tsit (trans.) 1967. *Reflections on Things at Hand: The Neo-Confucian Anthology Compiled by Chu Hsi and Lü Tsu-ch'ien*. New York: Columbia University Press.

Chan, Wing-tsit. 1969. *Religious Trends in Modern China*. New York: Octagon.

Chan, Wing-tsit. 1986a. "Biography of Chu Hsi." In *Chu Hsi and Neo-Confucianism*, edited by Wing-tsit Chan, 595–601. Honolulu: University of Hawai'i Press.

Chan, Wing-tsit (trans.) 1986b. *Neo-Confucian Terms Explained*. New York: Columbia University Press.

Chan, Wing-tsit. 1987. *Chu Hsi: Life and Thought*. Hong Kong: The Chinese University Press.

Chan, Wing-tsit. 1989a. *Chu Hsi: New Studies*. Honolulu: University of Hawai'i Press.

Chan, Wing-tsit. 1989b. "Chu Hsi and the Academies." In *Neo-Confucianism and Education: The Formative Stage*, edited by Wm. Theodore de Bary and John W. Chaffee, 389–413. Berkeley: University of California Press.

Chang, Carson. 1962. *The Development of Neo-Confucian Thought*, vol 2. New York: Bookman.

Chang, Chih-tung. 1901. *China's Only Hope: An Appeal*, translated by Samuel I. Woodbridge. Edinburgh: Oliphant, Anderson & Ferrier.

Ch'en, Ch'i-yün. 1986. "Confucian, Legalist, and Taoist Thought in Later Han." In *The Cambridge History of China, Volume 1: The Ch'in and Han Empires. 221 B.C. – A.D. 220*, edited by Denis Twitchett and Michael Loewe, 766–807. Cambridge: Cambridge University Press.

Chen, Huan-chang. 1911. *The Economic Principle of Confucius and His School*. New York: Faculty of Political Science of Columbia University.

Chen, Jo-shui. 1992. *Liu Tsung-yüan and Intellectual Change in T'ang China, 773–819*. Cambridge: Cambridge University Press.

Chen, Lai. 2015. "Mysticism in the Confucian Tradition." *Studies in Chinese Religions*. 1: 20–45.

Chen, Li Fu. 1986. *The Confucian Way: A New and Systematic Study of "The Four Books"*. London: Routledge & Kegan Paul.

Chen, Li-fu. 1948. *Philosophy of Life*. New York: Philosophical Library.

Ch'en, Li-fu. 1994. *The Storm Clouds Clear over China: The Memoir of Ch'en Li-fu*. Stanford, CA: Hoover Institution Press.

Chen, Ming. 2009. "Modernity and Confucian Political Philosophy in a Globalizing World." *Diogenes*. 56: 94–108.

Chen, Ming. 2013. "On Confucianism as a Civil Religion and Its Significance for Contemporary China." *Contemporary Chinese Thought*. 44, 2: 76–83.

Chen, Xiaoming. 2007. *From the May Fourth Movement to Communist Revolution: Guo Moruo and the Chinese Path to Communism*. Albany: State University of New York Press.

Chen, Yong. 2012. "Renewing Confucianism as a Living Tradition in 21st Century China: Reciting Classics, Reviving Academies and Restoring Rituals." In *Mapping Religion and Spirituality in a Postsecular World*, edited by Giuseppe Giordan and Enzo Pace, 63–84. Leiden: Brill.

Chen, Yong. 2013. *Confucianism as Religion: Controversies and Consequences*. Leiden: Brill.

Cheng, Anne. 2001. "What Did It Mean to Be a *Ru* in Han Times?" *Asia Major*. 14: 101–18.

Cheng, Zhongying. 1991. *New Dimensions of Confucian and Neo-Confucian Philosophy*. Albany: Sate University of New York Press.

Cheung, Tak Sing and Yeo-chi King. 2004. "Righteousness and Profitableness: The Moral Choices of Contemporary Confucian Entrepreneurs." *Journal of Business Ethics*. 54: 245–60.

Chi, Wen-shun. 1967. "The Ideological Source of the People's Communes in Communist China." *Pacific Coast Philology*. 2: 62–78.

Chiang, Kai-shek. 1943. *The Collected Wartime Messages of Generalissimo Chiang Kai-shek, 1937–1945. Volume One: 1937–1940*. New York: John Day.

Chiang, Kai-shek. 1947. *China's Destiny and Chinese Economic Theory*. New York: Roy Publishers.

Chin, Ann-ping and Mansfield Friedman (trans.) 1990. *Tai Chen on Mencius: Explorations in Words and Meaning*. New Haven, CT: Yale University Press.

Ching, Julia (trans.) 1972. *The Philosophical Letters of Wang Yang-ming*. Canberra: Australian National University Press.

Ching, Julia. 1986. "Chu Hsi on Personal Cultivation." In *Chu Hsi and Neo-Confucianism*, edited by Wing-tsit Chan, 273–91. Honolulu: University of Hawai'i Press.

Ching, Julia. 2000. *The Religious Thought of Chu Hsi*. Oxford: Oxford University Press.

Chow, Kai-wing. 1993. "Purist Hermeneutics and Ritual Ethics in Mid-Ch'ing Thought." In *Cosmology, Ontology, and Human Efficacy: Essays in Chinese Thought*, edited by R. J. Smith and D. W. Y. Kwok, 179–204. Honolulu: University of Hawai'i Press.

Chow, Kai-wing. 1994. *The Rise of Confucian Ritualism in Late Imperial China: Ethics, Classics, and Lineage Discourse*. Stanford, CA: Stanford University Press.

Chow, Tse-tsung. 1960. *The May Fourth Movement: Intellectual Revolution in Modern China*. Cambridge, MA: Harvard University Press.

Chu, Roy Guey. 1998. "Rites and Rights in Ming China." In *Confucianism and Human Rights*, edited by Wm. Theodore de Bary and Tu Weiming, 169–78. New York: Columbia University Press.

Clark, Anthony E. 2008. *Ban Gu's History of Early China*. New York: Cambria Press.

Clart, Philip. 2003. "Confucius and the Mediums: Is There a 'Popular Confucianism'?" *T'oung Pao*. 89: 1–38.

Clower, Jason (trans.) 2014. *The Late Works of Mou Zongsan: Selected Essays on Chinese Philosophy*. Leiden: Brill.

Connelly, Edward F. 1978. *Xiong Shili and His Critique of Yogācāra Buddhism*. PhD dissertation. Australian National University.

Cook, F. H. 1977. *Hua-yen Buddhism: The Jewel Net of Indra*. Philadelphia: Pennsylvania State University Press.

Cook, F. H. 1979. "Causation in the Chinese Hua-yen Tradition." *Journal of Chinese Philosophy*. 6: 367–85.

Cook, Scott. 2012. *The Bamboo Texts of Guodian: A Study and Complete Translation*, 2 vols. Ithaca, NY: Cornell University Press.

Csikszentmihalyi, Mark. 2004. *Material Virtue: Ethics and the Body in Early China*. Leiden: Brill.

Csikszentmihalyi, Mark and Tae Hyun Kim. 2014. "The Formation of the *Analects*." In *The Analects*, edited by Michael Nylan, 152–65. New York: Norton.

Cua, Antonio S. 1982. *The Unity of Knowledge and Action: A Study in Wang Yang-ming's Moral Psychology*. Honolulu: University of Hawai'i Press.

Dardess, John W. 1983. *Confucianism and Autocracy: Professional Elites in the Founding of the Ming Dynasty*. Berkeley: University of California Press.

Davies, Gloria. 2007. *Worrying about China: The Language of Chinese Critical Inquiry*. Cambridge, MA: Harvard University Press.

Dawkins, Richard. 2007. *The God Delusion*. London: Transworld.

de Bary, Wm. Theodore. 1981. *Neo-Confucian Orthodoxy and the Learning of Mind-and-Heart*. New York: Columbia University Press.

de Bary, Wm. Theodore. 1991a. *Learning for One's Self: Essays on the Individual in Neo-Confucian Thought*. New York: Columbia University Press.

de Bary, Wm. Theodore. 1991b. *The Trouble with Confucianism*. Cambridge, MA: Harvard University Press.

de Bary, Wm. Theodore (trans.) 1993. *Waiting for the Dawn: A Plan for the Prince. Huang Tsung-hsi's Ming-i tai-fang lu*. New York: Columbia University Press.

de Bary, Wm. Theodore, Wing-tsit Chan, and Chester Tan (trans. and eds.) 1960. *Sources in Chinese Tradition: Volume 2*. New York: Columbia University Press.

de Bary, Wm. Theodore, Wing-tsit Chan and Burton Watson (trans. and eds.) 1960. *Sources in Chinese Tradition: Volume 1*. New York: Columbia University Press.

de Bary, Wm. Theodore and Richard Lufrano (eds.) 2000. *Sources in Chinese Tradition: From 1600 through to the Twentieth Century*. 2nd ed. New York: Columbia University Press.

Dimberg, Ronald G. 1974. *The Sage and Society: The Life and Thought of Ho Hsin-yin*. Honolulu: University of Hawai'i Press.

Dirlik, Arif. 1975. "The Ideological Foundations of the New Life Movement: A Study in Counterrevolution." *Journal of Asian Studies*. 34: 945–80.

Dirlik, Arif. 1995. "Confucius in the Borderlands: Global Capital and the Reinvention of Confucianism." *Boundary 2*. 22: 229–73.

Duara, Prasenjit. 2003. *Sovereignty and Authenticity: Manchukuo and the East Asian Modern*. Lanham, MD: Rowman and Littlefield.

Dubs, Homer H (trans.) 1955. *The History of the Former Han Dynasty*, volume 3. Baltimore: Waverly Press.

Durkheim, Émile. 1961. *The Elementary Forms of the Religious Life*. New York: Collier Books.

Durrant, Stephen W. 1995. *The Cloudy Mirror: Tension and Conflict in the Writings of Sima Qian*. Albany: State University of New York Press.

Durrant, Stephen, Li Wai-yee and David Schaberg (trans.) 2016. *Zuo Tradition / Zuozhuan: Commentary on the "Spring and Autumn Annals."* Seattle: University of Washington Press.

Eastman, Lloyd E. 1972. "Fascism in Kuomintang China: The Blue Shirts." *The China Quarterly*. 49: 1–31.

Ebrey, Patricia Buckley. 1986. "The Economic and Social History of Later Han." In *The Cambridge History of China, Volume 1: The Ch'in and Han Empires. 221 B.C. – A.D. 220*, edited by Denis Twitchett and Michael Loewe, 608–48. Cambridge: Cambridge University Press.

Ebrey, Patricia Buckley (trans.) 1991a. *Chu Hsi's Family Rituals: A Twelfth-Century Chinese Manual for the Performance of Cappings, Weddings, Funerals, and Ancestral Rites*. Princeton, NJ: Princeton University Press.

Ebrey, Patricia Buckley. 1991b. *Confucianism and Family Rituals in Imperial China: A Social History of Writing about Rites*. Princeton, NJ: Princeton University Press.

Einstein, Albert. 1956. *Ideas and Opinions*. New York: Crown.

Eliade, Mircea. 1954. *The Myth of the Eternal Return or, Cosmos and History*. Princeton, NJ: Princeton University Press.

Elman, Benjamin A. 1984. *From Philosophy to Philology: Intellectual and Social Aspects of Change in Late Imperial China*. Cambridge, MA: Harvard University Press.

Elman, Benjamin A. 1990. *Classicism, Politics, and Kinship: The Ch'ang-chou School of New Text Confucianism in Late Imperial China*. Berkeley: University of California Press.

Elman, Benjamin A. 2000. *A Cultural History of Civil Examinations in Late Imperial China*. Berkeley: University of California Press.

Elman, Benjamin A. 2002. "Rethinking 'Confucianism' and 'Neo-Confucianism' in Modern Chinese History." In *Rethinking Confucianism: Past and Present in China, Japan, Korea, and Vietnam*, edited by Benjamin A. Elman, John Duncan and Herman Ooms, 518–54. Los Angeles: Asia Pacific Monograph Series.

Elman, Benjamin A. 2013. *China's Examinations and Meritocracy in Late Imperial China*. Cambridge, MA: Harvard University Press.

Englert, Siegfried and Roderich Ptak. 1986. "Nan-Tzu, or Why Heaven Did Not Crush Confucius." *Journal of the American Oriental Society*. 106: 679–86.

Eno, Robert. 1990. *The Confucian Creation of Heaven: Philosophy and the Defense of Ritual Mastery*. Albany: State University of New York Press.

Fan, Ruiping. 2011. "Jiang Qing on Equality." In *The Renaissance of Confucianism in Contemporary China*, edited by Ruiping Fan, 55–74. Dordrecht: Springer.

Fenby, Jonathan. 2003. *Generalissimo: Chiang Kai-shek and the China He Lost*. London: Free Press

Feng, Youlan. 2000. *The Hall of Three Pines: An Account of My Life*. Honolulu: University of Hawai'i Press.

Feng, Yu-lan. 1974. "A Criticism of Confucius and Self-Criticism of My Own Past Veneration of Confucius." In *Selected Articles Criticizing Lin Piao and Confucius*, 88–106. Beijing: Foreign Languages Press.

Fetzer, Joel S. and J. Christopher Soper. 2013. *Confucianism, Democratization, and Human Rights in Taiwan*. Lanham, MD: Lexington.

Fingarette, Herbert. 1972. *Confucius: The Secular as Sacred*. New York: Harper Torchbooks.

Forke, Alfred (trans.) 1962. *Wang Ch'ung: Lun-heng*, 2 vols. New York: Paragon Book Gallery.

Fröhlich, Thomas. 2010. "'Confucian Democracy' and Its Confucian Critics: Mou Zongsan and Tang Junyi on the Limits of Confucianism." *Oriens Extremus*. 49: 167–200.

Fung, Yu-lan. 1948. *A Short History of Chinese Philosophy*. New York: Macmillan.

Fung, Yu-lan. 1953. *A History of Chinese Philosophy: Volume II: The Period of Classical Learning*. Princeton, NJ: Princeton University Press.

Gaenssbauer, Monica. 2011. *Confucianism and Social Issues in China—the Academician Kang Xiaoguang*. Bochum/Freiburg: Projekt Verlag.

Gan, Chunsong. 2013. "Kang Youwei, Chen Huanzhang, and the Confucian Society." *Contemporary Chinese Thought*. 44, 2: 16–38.

Gardner, Daniel K (trans.) 1990. *Learning to Be a Sage: Selections from the* Conversations of Master Chu, Arranged Topically. Berkeley: University of California Press.

Gardner, Daniel K. 1995. "Ghosts and Spirits in the Sung Neo-Confucian World: Chu Hsi on *Kuei-shen*." *Journal of the American Oriental Society*. 115: 598–611.

Gardner, Daniel K (trans.) 1996. "Zhu Xi on Spirit Beings." In *Chinese Religions in Practice*, edited by Donald S. Lopez, 106–22. Princeton, NJ: Princeton University Press.

Gardner, Daniel K. 2003. *Zhu Xi's Reading of the Analects: Canon, Commentary, and the Classical Tradition*. New York: Columbia University Press.

Gardner, Daniel K. 2004. "Attentiveness and Meditative Reading in Cheng-Zhu Neo-Confucianism." In *Confucian Spirituality: Volume Two*, edited by Tu Weiming and Mary Evelyn Tucker, 99–119. New York: Crossroad.

Gardner, Daniel K. 2007. *The Four Books: The Basic Teachings of the Later Confucian Tradition*. Indianapolis: Hackett.

Gingell, William Raymond (trans.) 1852. *The Ceremonial Usages of the Chinese B.C. 1121 as Prescribed in the "Institutes of the Chow Dynasty Strung as Pearls …"* London: Smith, Elder, & Co.

Girardot, Norman J. 1976. "The Problem of Creation Mythology in the Study of Chinese Religion." *History of Religions*. 15: 289–318.

Girardot, Norman J. 2005. *The Victorian Translation of China: James Legge's Oriental Pilgrimage*. Berkeley: University of California Press.

Goldin, Paul R. 2005. *After Confucius: Studies in Early Chinese Philosophy*. Honolulu: University of Hawai'I Press.

Goldin, Paul R. 2007. "Xunzi and Early Han Philosophy." *Harvard Journal of Asiatic Studies*. 67: 135–66.

Goldin, Paul R. 2008. "When *Zhong* 忠 Does Not Mean 'Loyalty'." *Dao*. 7: 165–74.

Goossaert, Vincent. 2006. "1898: The Beginning and End for Chinese Religion?" *The Journal of Asian Studies*. 65: 307–36

Goossaert, Vincent. 2011. "The Social Organization of Religious Communities in the Twentieth Century." *In Chinese Religious Life*, edited by David A. Palmer, Glen Shive, and Philip L. Wickeri, 172–90. Oxford: Oxford University Press.

Goossaert, Vincent and David A. Palmer. 2011. *The Religious Question in Modern China*. Chicago: University of Chicago Press.

Graham, A. C. 1958. *Two Chinese Philosophers: Ch'eng Ming-tao and Ch'eng Yi-ch'uan*. London: Lund Humphries.

Graham, A. C. (trans.) 1981. *Chuang-tzu: The Inner Chapters*. London: Unwin.

Graham, A. C. 1989. *Disputers of the Tao: Philosophical Argument in Ancient China*. Chicago: Open Court.

Gray, John Henry. 1878. *China: A History of the Laws, Manners and Customs of the People*. London: Macmillan.

Gregor, A. James. 1981. "Confucianism and the Political Thought of Sun Yat-Sen." *Philosophy East and West*. 31: 55–70.

Gregor, A. James and Maria Hsia Chang. 1979. "Anti-Confucianism: Mao's Last Campaign." *Asia Survey*. 19: 1073–92.

Gregory, Peter N. 2002. *Tsung Mi and the Sinification of Buddhism*. Honolulu: University of Hawai'i Press.

Grieder, Jerome B. 1970. *Hu Shih and the Chinese Renaissance: Liberalism in the Chinese Revolution, 1917–1937*. Cambridge, MA: Harvard University Press.

Grimm, Tileman. 1982. "Academies and Urban Systems in Kwangtung." In *The City in Late Imperial China*, edited by G. William Skinner, 475–98. Stanford, CA: Stanford University Press.

Guo, Moruo. 1999. "Marx Enters the Confucian Temple," translated by Matthew Finkbeiner and John Timothy Wixted. *Renditions*. 51 : 77–86.

Guo, Qitao. 2005. *Ritual Opera and Mercantile Lineage: The Confucian Transformation of Popular Culture in Late Imperial Huizhou*. Stanford, CA: Stanford University Press.

Hall, David L. and Roger T. Ames. 1987. *Thinking Through Confucius*. Albany: State University of New York Press.

Halperin, Mark. 2006. *Out of the Cloister: Literati Perspectives on Buddhism in Sung China, 960–1279*. Cambridge, MA: Harvard University Asian Centre.

Hanafin, John J. 2003. "The 'Last Buddhist': The Philosophy of Liang Shuming." In *New Confucianism: A Critical Examination*, edited by John Makeham, 187–218. New York: Palgrave.

Handlin, Joanna F. 1983. *Action in Late Ming Thought: The Reorientation of Lü K'un and Other Scholar-Officials*. Berkeley: University of California Press.

Henderson, John B. 1991. *Scripture, Canon, and Commentary: A Comparison of Confucian and Western Exegesis*. Princeton, NJ: Princeton University Press.

Hendrischke, Barbara, 2006. *The Scripture on Great Peace: The Taiping Jing and the Beginnings of Daoism*. Berkeley: University of California Press.

He-Yin, Zhen. 2013. "On the Revenge of Women." In *The Birth of Chinese Feminism: Essential Texts in Transnational Theory*, edited by Lydia H. Liu, Rebecca E. Karl and Dorothy Ko, 105–46. New York: Columbia University Press.

Ho, Peng Yoke. 1985. *Li, Qi and Shu: An Introduction to Science and Civilization in China*. Hong Kong: Hong Kong University Press.

Holloway, Kenneth W. 2009. *Guodian: The Newly Discovered Seeds of Chinese Religious and Political Philosophy*. Oxford: Oxford University Press.

Hon, Tze-ki. 2013. *Revolution as Restoration: Guocui Xuebao and China's Path to Modernity, 1905–1911*. Leiden: Brill.

Hong, Xiuping. 2011. "The Characteristics and Prospects of the Confucian Academy: A Commentary on Jiang Qing's Ideas about the Confucian Academy." In *The Renaissance of Confucianism in Contemporary China*, edited by Ruiping Fan, 185–204. Dordrecht: Springer.

Hsiao, Kung-Chuan. 1975. *A Modern China and a New World: K'ang Yu-Wei, Reformer and Utopian, 1958–1927*. Seattle: University of Washington Press.

Hu, Shi. 1928. "Wang Mang, the Socialist Emperor of Nineteen Centuries Ago." *Journal of the North-China Branch of the Royal Asiatic Society*. 59: 218–30.

Hu, Shih. 1929. "The Establishment of Confucianism as a State Religion During the Han Dynasty." *Journal of the North-China Branch of the Royal Asiatic Society*. 60: 20–41.

Hu, Shih. 1934. *The Chinese Renaissance*. Chicago: University of Chicago Press.

Hu, Shih. 1968. *The Development of the Logical Method in Ancient China*. New York: Paragon.

Hu, Zhihong. 2008. "The Obscuration and Rediscovery of the Original Confucian Thought of Moral Politics: Deciphering Work on the Guodian, Shangbo and the Transmitted Versions of *Ziyi*." *Frontiers of Philosophy in China*. 3: 535–57.

Hua, Shiping. 2009. *Chinese Utopianism: A Comparative Study of Reformist Thought with Japan and Russia, 1898–1997*. Stanford, CA: Stanford University Press.

Huang, Ray. 1981. *1587, a Year of No Significance: The Ming Dynasty in Decline*. New Haven, CT: Yale University Press.

Huang, Siu-chi. 1944. *Lu Hsiang-shan: A Twelfth Century Idealist Philosopher*. New Haven, CT: American Oriental Society.

Huang, Siu-chi. 1999. *Essentials of Neo-Confucianism: Eight Major Philosophers of the Song and Ming Periods*. Westport, CT: Greenwood Press.

Huang, Tsung-hsi. 1987. *The Records of Ming Scholars*, edited by Julia Ching. Honolulu: University of Hawai'i Press.

Hutton, Eric L. (trans.) 2014. *Xunzi: The Complete Text*. Princeton, NJ: Princeton University Press.

Hwang, Shih-ming (trans.) n.d. "A Brief Introduction to Yi-guan Dao." http://www.taousa.org/classic-texts/7A-Brief-Introduction-to-Yi-Guan-Dao-I-Kuan-Tao.pdf.

Idema, Wilt L. 2009. *Filial Piety and Its Divine Rewards: The Legend of Dong Yong and Weaving Maiden with Related Texts*. Indianapolis, IN: Hackett.

Inglehart, Ronald, et al. (eds.) 2004. *Human Beliefs and Values: A Cross Cultural Sourcebook Based on the 1999–2002 Values Surveys*. Mexico: Siglio Veintiuno Editores.

Isaacson, Walter. 2007. *Einstein: His Life and Universe*. New York: Simon & Schuster.

Israel, Jonathan I. 2007. "Admiration of China and Classical Chinese Thought in the Radical Enlightenment (1685–1740)." *Taiwan Journal of East Asian Studies*. 4: 1–25.

Ivanhoe, Philip J. (trans.) 2009. *Readings from the Lu-Wang School of Neo-Confucianism*. Indianapolis, IN: Hackett.

Ivanhoe, Philip J. and Sungmoon Kim (eds.) 2016. *Confucianism, a Habit of the Heart: Bellah, Civil Religions, and East Asia*. Albany: State University of New York Press.

James, William. 1902. *The Varieties of Religious Experience: A Study in Human Nature*. New York: Longmans, Green.

Jensen, Lionel. 1997. *Manufacturing Confucianism: Chinese Tradition and Universal Civilization*. Durham, NC, and London: Duke University Press.

Jiang, Qing. 2011. "From Mind Confucianism to Political Confucianism." In *The Renaissance of Confucianism in Contemporary China*, edited by Ruiping Fan, 17–32. Dordrecht: Springer.

Jiang, Qing. 2013a. *A Confucian Constitutional Order: How China's Ancient Past Can Shape Its Political Future*, edited by Daniel A. Bell and Ruiping Fan. Princeton, NJ: Princeton University Press.

Jiang, Qing. 2013b. "Blessed Are the Meek and the Peacemakers." *Contemporary Chinese Thought*. 44: 39–60.

Jochim, Christian. 2003. "Carrying Confucianism into the Modern World: The Taiwan Case." In *Religion in Modern Taiwan: Tradition and Innovation in a Changing Society*, edited by Philip Clart and Charles B. Jones, 48–83. Honolulu: University of Hawai'i Press.

Jochim, Christian. 2009. "Popular Lay Sects and Confucianism: A Study Based on the Way of Unity in Postwar Taiwan." In *The People and the Dao: New Studies in Chinese Religion in Honor of Daniel L. Overmyer*, edited by Philip Clart and Paul Crowe, 83–107. Monograph Series, 60. Sankt Augustin: Monumenta Serica.

Johnston, Ian (trans.) 2013. *The Book of Master Mo*. London: Penguin.

Johnston, Reginald Fleming. 1935. *Confucianism in Modern China*. New York: D. Appleton-Century.

Jones, David (ed.) 2008. *Confucius Now: Contemporary Encounters with the Analects*. Peru, IL: Open Court.

Jordan, David K. and Daniel Overmyer. 1986. *The Flying Phoenix: Aspects of Chinese Sectarianism in Taiwan*. Princeton, NJ: Princeton University Press.

Josephson, Jason Ānanda. 2012. *The Invention of Religion in Japan*. Chicago: University of Chicago Press.

Kang, Xiaoguang. 2006. "Confucianization: A Future in the Tradition." *Social Research*. 73: 77–120.

Kang, Xiaoguang. 2012. "A Study of the Renaissance of Traditional Confucian Culture in Contemporary China." In *Confucianism and Spiritual Traditions in Modern China and Beyond*, edited by Yang Fenggang and Joseph Tamney, 33–96. Leiden: Brill.

Kang, Xiaoguang. 2013. "Confucianism and Conceiving a Cultural Renaissance in the New Century." *Contemporary Chinese Thought*. 44, 2: 61–75.

K'ang, Yu-wei. 1967. "Chronological Autobiography of K'ang Yu-wei." In *K'ang Yu-wei: A Biography and a Symposium*, edited by Jung-pang Lo, 17–174. Tuscon: University of Arizona Press, 1967.

Karlgren, Bernhard. 1950. "The Book of Documents." *Bulletin of the Museum of Far Eastern Antiquity*. 22: 1–81.

Karlgren, Bernhard. 1974. *The Book of Odes: Chinese Text, Transcription and Translation*. Stockholm: Bulletin of the Museum of Far Eastern Antiquities.

Kasoff, Ira E. 1984. *The Thought of Chang Tsai (1020–1077)*. Cambridge: Cambridge University Press.

Keenan, Barry C. 2011. *Neo-Confucian Self-Cultivation*. Honolulu: University of Hawai'i Press.

Keenan, John P. 1994. *How Master Mou Removes Our Doubts: A Reader-Response Study and Translation of the Mou-tzu Li-hou lun*. Albany: State University of New York Press.

Kern, Martin. 2000. *The Stele Inscriptions of Ch'in Shih-huang: Text and Ritual in Early Chinese Imperial Representation*. New Haven, CT: American Oriental Society.

Kim, Young-oak and Kim, Jung-kyu. 2014. *The Great Equal Society: Confucianism, China and the 21st Century*. Hackensack, NJ: World Scientific Publishing.

Kim, Yung Sik. 2000. *The Natural Philosophy of Chu Hsi (1130–1200)*. Philadelphia: American Philosophical Society.

Kleeman, Terry F. 1994. *A God's Own Tale: The Book of Transformations of Wenchang, the Divine Lord of Zitong*. Albany: State University of New York Press.

Knapp, Keith Nathaniel. 2005. *Selfless Offspring: Filial Children and Social Order in Medieval China*. Honolulu: University of Hawai'i Press.

Knechtges, David R. 1978. "Uncovering the Sauce Jar: A Literary Interpretation of Yang Hsiung's 'Chü Ch'in Mei Hsin'." In *Ancient China: Studies in Early Civilization*, edited by David T. Roy and Tsuen-hsuin Tsien, 229–52. Hong Kong: Chinese University Press.

Knight, Nick. 1996. "From Harmony to Struggle, from Perpetual Peace to Cultural Revolution: Changing Futures in Mao Zedong's Thought." *China Information*. 11: 176–95.

Knoblock, John and Jeffrey Riegel (trans.) 2000. *The Annals of Lü Buwei*. Stanford, CA: Stanford University Press.

Ko, Dorothy. 1994. *Teachers of the Inner Chambers: Women and Culture in Seventeenth-Century China*. Stanford, CA: Stanford University Press.

Kohn, Livia. 1990. "Introduction to the Life of Chen Tuan." *Taoist Resources*. 2: 1–31.

Kohn, Livia. 1995. *Laughing at the Tao: Debates amongst Buddhists and Taoists in Medieval China*. Princeton, NJ: Princeton University Press.

Kramers, Robert P. 1986. "The Development of the Confucian Schools." In *The Cambridge History of China, Volume 1: The Ch'in and Han Empires. 221 B.C. – A.D. 220*, edited by Denis Twitchett and Michael Loewe, 747–65. Cambridge: Cambridge University Press.

Ku, Mei-kao. 1988. *A Chinese Mirror for Magistrates: The Hsin-yu of Lu Chia*. Canberra: Australian National University.

Kuhn, Dieter. 2009. *The Age of Confucian Rule: The Song Transformation of China*. Cambridge, MA: Harvard University Press.

Kuhn, Thomas. 1962. *The Structure of Scientific Revolutions*. Chicago: University of Chicago Press.

Kuo, Ya-pei. 2009. "'The Emperor and the People in One Body': The Worship of Confucius and Ritual Planning in the Xinzheng Reforms, 1902–1911." *Modern China*. 35: 124–54.

Kutcher, Norman. 1999. *Mourning in Late Imperial China: Filial Piety and the State*. Cambridge: Cambridge University Press.

Kwok, D.W.Y. 1965. *Scientism in Chinese Thought, 1900–1950*. New Haven, CT: Yale University Press.

Lagerwey, John. 2010. *China: A Religious State*. Hong Kong: Hong Kong University Press.

Lam, Joseph S. C. 1998. *State Sacrifices and Music in Ming China: Orthodoxy, Creativity, and Expressiveness*. Albany: State University of New York Press.

Landsberger, Stefan R. 1996. "Mao as the Kitchen God: Religious Aspects of the Mao Cult during the Cultural Revolution." *China Information*. 11: 196–214.

Lau, D. C. (trans.) 1963. *Lao Tzu: Tao Te Ching*. Harmondsworth: Penguin.

Lau, D. C. (trans.) 1970. *Mencius*. Harmondsworth: Penguin.

Lau, D. C. (trans.) 1979. *Confucius: The Analects*. Harmondsworth: Penguin.

Lee, Joseph Tse-Hei, Ronald K. Frank, Yu Renqiu and Xu Bing. 2011. *From Philosopher to Cultural Icon: Reflections on Hu Mei's "Confucius" (2010)*. Social and Cultural Research, Occasional Paper No. 11. Hong Kong: Centre for Qualitative Social Research.

Lee, Pauline C. 2000. "Li Zhi and John Stuart Mill: A Confucian Feminist Critique of Liberal Feminism." In *The Sage and the Second Sex: Confucianism, Ethics, and Gender*, edited by Chengyang Li, 113–32. Chicago: Open Court.

Lee, Pauline C. 2012. *Li Zhi: Confucianism and the Virtue of Desire*. Albany: Sate University of New York Press.

Lee Seung-hwan. 2004. *A Topography of Confucian Discourse: Politico-Philosophical Reflections on Confucian Discourse Since Modernity*. Paramus, NJ: Homa & Sekey.

Lee, Thomas H. C. 2000. *Education in Traditional China: A Handbook*. Leiden: Brill.

Leese, Daniel. 2013. *Mao Cult: Rhetoric and Ritual in China's Cultural Revolution*. Cambridge: Cambridge University Press.

Legge, Helen Edith. 1904. *James Legge: Missionary and Scholar*. London: Religious Tract Society.

Legge, James (trans.) 1865. *The Shoo King or the Book of Historical Documents*. The Chinese Classics, volume 3. Oxford: Clarendon Press.

Legge, James (trans.) 1871. *The She King or the Book of Poetry*. The Chinese Classics, volume 4. Oxford: Clarendon Press.

Legge, James (trans.) 1872. *The Ch'un Ts'ew with the Tso Chuen*. The Chinese Classics, volume 5. Oxford: Clarendon Press.

Legge, James. 1880. *The Religions of China: Confucianism and Taoism Described and Compared with Christianity*. London: Hodder and Stoughton.

Legge, James (trans.) 1885. *The Li Ki*. The Sacred Books of the East, edited by F. Max Müller, vols. 27 & 28. Oxford: Oxford University Press.

Leibold, James. 2010. "The Beijing Olympics and China's Conflicted National Form." *The China Journal*. 63: 1–24.

Levenson, Joseph R. 1970. *Liang Ch'i-ch'ao and the Mind of Modern China*. Berkeley: University of California Press.

Levenson, Joseph R. 1972. *Confucian China and Its Modern Fate: A Trilogy*. 3 volumes bound as one. Berkeley: University of California Press.

Lewis, Mark Edward. 1999a. *Writing and Authority in Early China*. Albany: State University of New York Press.

Lewis, Mark Edward. 1999b. "The *Feng* and *Shan* Sacrifices of Emperor Wu of the Han." In *State and Court Ritual in China*, edited by Joseph P. McDermott, 50–80. Cambridge: Cambridge University Press.

Lewis, Mark Edward. 2009a. *China between Empires: The Northern and Southern Dynasties*. Cambridge, MA: Harvard University Press.

Lewis, Mark Edward. 2009b. *China's Cosmopolitan Empire: The Tang Dynasty*. Cambridge, MA: Harvard University Press.

Li, Chenyang. 2002. "Fang Dongmei: Philosophy of Life, Creativity, and Inclusiveness." In *Contemporary Chinese Philosophy*, edited by Chung-ying Cheng and Nicholas Bunnin, 263–80. Malden, MA: Blackwell.

Li, San-pao. 1993. "Ch'ing Cosmology and Popular Precepts." In *Cosmology, Ontology, and Human Efficacy: Essays in Chinese Thought*, edited by Richard J. Smith and D. W. Y. Kwok, 113–39. Honolulu: University of Hawai'i Press.

Liang, Ch'i-ch'ao. 1959. *Intellectual Trends in the Ch'ing Period*. Cambridge, MA: Harvard University Press.

Liang, Shu Ming and Guy S. Alitto. 2013. *Has Man a Future? Dialogues with the Last Confucian*. Heidelberg: Springer.

Lin, Yutang. 1936. *Confucius Saw Nancy and Essays about Nothing*. Shanghai: Commercial Press.

Li, Zhi. 2016. *A Book to Burn and a Book to Keep (Hidden): Selected Writings*, edited and translated by Rivi Handler-Spritz, Pauline C. Lee and Haun Saussy. New York: Columbia University Press.

Liu, J. J. Y. 1975. *Chinese Theories of Literature*. Chicago: University of Chicago Press.

Liu, James T. C. 1973. "How Did a Neo-Confucian School Become the State Orthodoxy?" *Philosophy East and West*. 23: 483–505.

Liu, Shu-hsien. 1978. "The Function of the Mind in Chu Hsi's Philosophy." *Journal of Chinese Philosophy*. 5: 195–208.

Liu, Shu-hsien. 1991. "A Critical Review of Contemporary Neo-Confucian Thought with a View to Modernization." In *The Triadic Cord: Confucian Ethics, Industrial East Asia and Max Weber*, edited by Tu Weiming, 377–94. Kent Ridge, Singapore: Institute of East Asian Philosophies.

Liu, Shu-hsien. 2003. *Essentials of Contemporary Neo-Confucian Philosophy*. Westport, CT: Praeger.

Liu, Yonghua. 2013. *Confucian Rituals and Chinese Villagers: Ritual Change and Social Transformation in a Southeastern Chinese Community, 1368–1949*. Leiden: Brill.

Liu, Yucai and Luke Habberstad. 2014. "The Life of a Text: A Brief History of the *Liji* (Rites Records) and Its Transmission." *Journal of Chinese Literature and Culture*. 1: 289–308.

Loewe, Michael (ed.) 1993. *Early Chinese Texts: A Bibliographic Guide*. Berkeley: Society for the Study of Early China.

Loewe, Michael. 2011. *Dong Zhongshu, a "Confucian" Heritage and the Chunqiu fanlu*. Leiden: Brill.

Louie, Kam. 1980. *Critiques of Confucius in Contemporary China*. New York: St. Martin's Press.

Louie, Kam. 2011. "Confucius the Chameleon: Dubious Envoy for 'Brand China.'" *Boundary 2*. 38: 77–100.

Lu, Xiufen. 2011. "The Confucian Ideal of Great Harmony (*Datong*), the Daoist Account of Change, and the Theory of Socialism in the work of Li Dazhou." *Asian Philosophy*. 21: 171–92.

Lu, Xun. 1976. "The Picture-Book of the Twenty-Four Acts of Filial Piety." In *Dawn Blossoms Plucked at Dusk*, edited and translated by Gladys Yang and Hsien-yi Yang. Peking: Foreign Languages Press.

Lu, Xun. 2009. *The Real Story of Ah-Q and other Tales of China: The Complete Fiction of Lu Xun*. London: Penguin.

Lu, Yunfeng. 2008. *The Transformation of Yiguan Dao in Taiwan: Adapting to a Changing Religious Economy*. Plymouth: Lexington Books.

Lufrano, Richard John. 1997. *Honorable Merchants: Commerce and Self-Cultivation in Late Imperial China*. Honolulu: University of Hawai'i Press.

Lynn, Richard John (trans.) 1994. *The Classic of Changes: A New Translation of the I Ching as Interpreted by Wang Bi*. New York: Columbia University Press.

McDermott, Joseph P. 1999. "Introduction." In *State and Court Ritual in China*, edited by Joseph P. McDermott, 1–19. Cambridge: Cambridge University Press.

McDermott, Joseph P. 2006. *A Social History of the Chinese Book: Books and Literati Culture in Late Imperial China*. Hong Kong: Hong Kong University Press.

McMullen, David. 1987. "Bureaucrats and Cosmology: The Ritual Code of T'ang China." In *Rituals of Royalty: Power and Ceremonial in Traditional Societies*, edited by David Cannadine and Simon Price, 181–236. Cambridge: Cambridge University Press.

McMullen, David. 1988. *State and Scholars in T'ang China*. Cambridge: Cambridge University Press.

Machle, Edward J. 1993. *Nature and Heaven in the Xunzi: A Study of the Tian Lun*. Albany: State University of New York Press.

Mair, Victor (ed.) 1994. *The Columbia Anthology of Traditional Chinese Literature*. New York: Columbia University Press.

Major, John S., Sarah A. Queen, Andrew Seth Meyer and Harold D. Roth (trans.) 2010. *The Huainanzi: A Guide to the Theory and Practice of Government in Early Han China*. New York: Columbia University Press.

Makeham, John. 2003. "Introduction," "The Retrospective Creation of New Confucianism," and "The New *Daotong*." In *New Confucianism: A Critical Examination*, edited by John Makeham, 1–21, 25–53, and 55–78. New York: Palgrave.

Makeham, John. 2005. "Indigenization Discourse in Taiwanese Confucian Revivalism." In *Cultural, Ethnic, and Political Nationalism in Contemporary Taiwan: Bentuhua*, edited by John Makeham and A-chin Hsiau, 187–220. New York: Palgrave.

Makeham, John. 2008. *Lost Soul: "Confucianism" in Contemporary Chinese Academic Discourse*. Cambridge, MA: Harvard University Asia Centre.

Makeham, John (ed.) 2014. *Transforming Consciousness: Yogācāra Thought in Modern China*. Oxford: Oxford University Press.

Makeham, John. 2015. "Translators Introduction." In *New Treatise on the Uniqueness of Consciousness*, by Xiong Shili, xi–lxviii. New Haven, CT: Yale University Press.

Malmqvist, Göran. 1971–7. "Studies in Gongyang and Guuliang Commentaries." *Bulletin of the Museum of Far Eastern Antiquities*. 43: 67–222; 47: 19–69; 49: 33–215.

Manchoukuo Government. 1933. *Manchoukuo Handbook of Information*. Bureau of Information and Publicity.

Mao, Tse-tung. 1961. "On the People's Democratic Dictatorship." In *Selected Works of Mao Tse-tung*, vol. 4, 411–24. Beijing: Foreign Language Press.

Mao, Tse-tung. 1965. "On New Democracy." In *Selected Works of Mao Tse-tung*, vol. 2, 339–84. Beijing: Foreign Language Press.

Mao, Tse-tung. 1977. "Criticism of Liang Shu-ming's Reactionary Ideas." In *Selected Works of Mao Tse-tung*, vol. 5, 121–30. Beijing: Foreign Languages Press.

Mast, Herman and William G. Saywell. 1974. "Revolution out of Tradition: The Political Ideology of Tai Chi-t'ao." *The Journal of Asian Studies*. 34: 73–98.

Meskill, John. 1982. *Academies in Ming China: A Historical Essay*. Tuscon: University of Arizona Press.

Meynard, Thierry. 2011. *The Religious Philosophy of Liang Shuming: The Hidden Buddhist*. Leiden: Brill.

Meynard, Thierry. 2015. *The Jesuit Reading of Confucius: The First Complete Translation of the Lunyu (1687) Published in the West*. Leiden: Brill.

Miller, Harry (trans.) 2015. *The Gongyang Commentary on the Spring and Autumn Annals: A Full Translation*. New York: Macmillan.

Miyazaki, Ichisada. 1981. *China's Examination Hell: The Civil Service Examinations of Imperial China*. New Haven, CT: Yale University Press.

Mou, Zongsan. 1981. "Confucianism as Religion." In *Chinese Essays on Religion and Faith*, edited by Douglas Lancashire, 21–43. San Francisco: Chinese Material Centre.

Mou, Zongsan. 2015a. *Autobiography at Fifty: A Philosophical Life in Twentieth Century China*. San Jose, CA: Foundation for the Study of Chinese Philosophy and Culture.

Mou, Zongsan. 2015b. *Nineteen Lectures on Chinese Philosophy: A Brief Outline of Chinese Philosophy and the Issues It Entails*. San Jose, CA: Foundation for the Study of Chinese Philosophy and Culture.

Murray, Julia K. 1997. "Illustrations of the Life of Confucius: Their Evolution, Function and Significance in Late Ming China." *Artibus Asiae*. 57: 73–134.

Murray, Julia K. 2009. "'Idols' in the Temple: Icons and the Cult of Confucius." *Journal of Asian Studies*. 68: 371–411.

Murray, Julia K. 2015. "The Sage's New Clothes: Popular Images of Confucius in Contemporary China." In *The Sage Returns: Confucian Revival in Contemporary China*, edited by Kenneth J. Hammond and Jeffrey L. Richey, 157–93. Albany: State University of New York Press.

Ng, On-cho. 1993. "Toward an Interpretation of Ch'ing Ontology." In *Cosmology, Ontology, and Human Efficacy: Essays in Chinese Thought*, edited by Richard J. Smith and D. W. Y. Kwok, 35–58. Honolulu: University of Hawai'i Press.

Ng, Yu-kwan. 2003. "Xiong Shili's Metaphysical Theory about the Non-Separability of Substance and Function." In *New Confucianism: A Critical Examination*, edited by John Makeham, 219–51. New York: Palgrave.

Nivison, David S. 1975. "Protest against Conventions and Conventions of Protest." In *Confucianism and Chinese Civilization*, edited by Arthur F. Wright, 227–51. Stanford, CA: Stanford University Press.

Nongbri, Brent. 2013. *Before Religion: A History of a Modern Concept*. New Haven, CT: Yale University Press.

Nylan, Michael. 1994. "The *Chin Wen / Ku Wen* Controversy in Han Times." *T'oung Pao*. 80: 83–145.

Nylan, Michael. 1999. "A Problematic Model: The Han 'Orthodox Synthesis' Then and Now." In *Imagining Boundaries: Changing Confucian Doctrines, Texts, and Hermeneutics*, edited by Kai-wing Chow, On-cho Ng, and John B. Henderson, 17–56. Albany: State University of New York Press.

Nylan, Michael. 2001. *The Five "Confucian" Classics*. New Haven, CT: Yale University Press.

Nylan, Michael. 2007. "Classics without Canonization: Learning and Authority in Qin and Han." In *Early Chinese Religion: Part One: Shang Through Han (1250 BC–220 AD)*, edited by John Lagerwey and Marc Kalinowski, 721–76. Leiden: Brill.

Nylan, Michael and Thomas Wilson. 2010. *Lives of Confucius*. New York: Doubleday.

Ogden, Suzanne. 2002. *Inklings of Democracy in China*. Cambridge, MA: Harvard University Press.

Oldstone-Moore, Jennifer. 2000. *The New Life Movement of Nationalist China: Confucianism, State Authority and Moral Formation*. PhD Dissertation. University of Chicago.

Oldstone-Moore, Jennifer. 2015. "Scientism and Modern Confucianism." In *The Sage Returns: Confucian Revival in Contemporary China*, edited by Kenneth J. Hammond and Jeffrey L. Richey, 39–63. Albany: State University of New York Press.

Ou, Anthony. 2010. "Confucius vs. Avatar: Rethinking Confucian Advocacy in the 21st Century." *Political Reflections*. 1, 3: 61–6.

Ownby, David. 2008. *Falun Gong and the Future of China*. Oxford: Oxford University Press.

Ownby, David. 2009. "Kang Xiaoguang: Social Science, Civil Society, and Confucian Religion." *China Perspectives*. 4: 101–11.

Pa, Chin. 2001. *The Family*, translated by Sidney Shapiro. Honolulu: University Press of the Pacific.

Palmer, David A. 2007. *Qigong Fever: Body, Science, and Utopia in China*. New York: Columbia University Press.

Paramore, Kiri. 2016. *Japanese Confucianism: A Cultural History*. Cambridge: Cambridge University Press.

Peng, Guoxiang. 2016. "Spiritual and Bodily Exercise: The Religious Significance of Zhu Xi's Reading Methods." In *Returning to Zhu Xi: Emerging Patterns within the Supreme Polarity*, edited by David Jones and Jinli He, 325–42. Albany: State University of New York Press.

Petersen, Willard. 1998. "Confucian Learning in Late Ming Thought." In *The Cambridge History of China: Volume 8: The Ming Dynasty, 1368-1368, Part 2*, edited by D. Twitchett and F. W. Mote, 708–1001. Cambridge: Cambridge University Press.

Pinker, Steven. 2011. *The Better Angels of Our Nature: Why Violence Has Declined*. London: Penguin.

Puett, Michael. 2001. *The Ambivalence of Creation: Debates Concerning Innovation and Artifice in Early China*. Stanford, CA: Stanford University Press.

Puett, Michael. 2003. "Determining the Position of Heaven and Earth: Debates over State Sacrifices in the Western Han Dynasty." In *Confucian Spirituality: Volume*

One, edited by Tu Weiming and Mary Evelyn Tucker, 318–34. New York: Herder and Herder.

Puett, Michael. 2010. "Centering the Realm: Wang Mang, the *Zhouli*, and Early Chinese Statecraft." In *Statecraft and Classical Learning: The Rituals of Zhou in East Asian Tradition*, edited by Benjamin A. Elman and Martin Kern, 129–54. Leiden: Brill.

Pung, Kwang Yu. 1893. "Confucianism." In *The Worlds Parliament of Religions*, edited by John Henry Barrows, vol. 1, 374–439. Chicago: Lakeside Press.

Pusey, James Reeve. 1983. *China and Charles Darwin*. Cambridge, MA: Harvard University Press

Queen, Sarah A. 1996. *From Chronicle to Canon: The Hermeneutics of the Spring and Autumn, According to Tung Chung-shu*. Cambridge: Cambridge University Press.

Queen, Sarah A. 2003. "The Way of the Unadorned King: The Classical Confucian Spirituality of Dong Zhongshu." In *Confucian Spirituality: Volume One*, edited by Tu Weiming and Mary Evelyn Tucker, 304–17. New York: Herder and Herder.

Queen, Sarah A. and John Major (trans.) 2016. *The Luxuriant Gems of the Spring and Autumn Annals: Attributed to Dong Zhongshu*. New York: Columbia University Press.

Rawski, Evelyn Sakakida. 1979. *Education and Popular Literacy in Ch'ing China*. Ann Arbor: University of Michigan Press.

Reilly, Thomas H. 2004. *The Taiping Heavenly Kingdom: Rebellion and the Blasphemy of Empire*. Seattle: University of Washington Press.

Rosemont, Henry and Roger T. Ames (trans.) 2009. *The Classics of Family Reverence: A Philosophical Translation of the Xiaojing*. Honolulu: University of Hawai'i Press.

Roth, Harold D. 1999. *Original Tao: Inward Training and the Foundations of Taoist Mysticism*. New York: Columbia University Press.

Russell, Bertrand. 1922. *The Problem of China*. London: George Allen & Unwin.

Saussy, Haun. 2008. "Reading for Conspiracy: Kang Youwei's Restoration." *Chinese Literature: Essays, Articles, Reviews*. 30: 125–32.

Schmidt, Stephen. 2011 "Mou Zongsan, Hegel, and Kant: The Quest for Confucian Modernity." *Philosophy East and West*. 61: 260–302.

Schneider, Laurence A. 1971. *Ku Chieh-kang and China's New History*. Berkeley: University of California Press.

Schopenhauer, Arthur. 1958. *The World as Will and Representation*. Indian Hills, Colorado: Falcon's Wings Press.

Schwartz, Benjamin I. 1985. *The World of Thought in Ancient China*. Cambridge, MA: Harvard University Press.

Shaughnessy, Edward L (trans.) 1996. *I Ching: The Classic of Changes*. New York: Ballantine Books.

Sheridan, James E. 1975. *China in Disintegration: The Republican Era in Chinese History, 1912–1949*. New York: Free Press.

Shih, Vincent Y.C. 1967. *The Taiping Ideology: Its Sources, Interpretations and Influences*. Seattle: University of Washington Press.

Shin, Doh Chull. 2012. *Confucianism and Democratization in East Asia*. Cambridge: Cambridge University Press.

Shryock, John K. 1966. *The Origin and Development of the State Cult of Confucius: An Introductory Study*. New York: Paragon.

Skiena, Steven and Charles Ward. 2013. *Who's Bigger: Where Historical Figures Really Rank*. Cambridge: Cambridge University Press.

Smith, Joanna Handlin. 2009. *The Art of Doing Good: Charity in the Late Ming*. Berkeley: University of California Press.

Smith, Jonathan Z. 1982. *Imagining Religion: From Babylon to Jonestown.* Chicago: University of Chicago Press.

Smith, Jonathan Z. 2010. "Tillich['s] Remains." *Journal of the American Academy of Religion.* 78: 1139–70.

Smith, Richard J. 1992. *Chinese Almanacs.* Hong Kong: Oxford University Press.

Smith, Richard J. 2008. *Fathoming the Cosmos and Ordering the World: The Yijing (I Ching, or Classic of Changes) and Its Evolution in China.* Charlottesville: University of Virginia Press.

Smith, Warren W. 1959. *Confucianism in Modern Japan: A Study of Conservatism in Japanese Intellectual History.* Tokyo: The Hukuseido Press.

Smith, Wilfred Cantwell. 1963. *The Meaning and End of Religion: A New Approach to the Religious Traditions of Mankind.* New York: Macmillan.

Snow, Edgar. 1968. *Red Star over China.* New York: Grove Press.

Sommer, Deborah. 2002. "Destroying Confucius: Iconoclasm in the Confucian Temple." In *On Sacred Grounds: Culture, Society, Politics, and the Formation of the Cult of Confucius,* edited by Thomas A. Wilson, 95–133. Cambridge, MA: Harvard University Press.

Sommer, Deborah. 2003. "Ritual and Sacrifice in Early Confucianism: Contacts with the Spirit World." In *Confucian Spirituality: Volume One,* edited by Tu Weiming and Mary Evelyn Tucker, 197–219. New York: Crossroad.

Sommer, Deborah. 2007. "Images for Iconoclasts: Images of Confucius in the Cultural Revolution." *East-West Connections: Review of Asian Studies.* 7: 1–23.

Spence, Jonathan D. 1996. *God's Chinese Son: The Taiping Heavenly Kingdom of Hong Xiuquan.* New York: Norton.

Staal, Frits. 1990. *Ritual and Mantras: Rules without Meaning.* New York: Peter Lang.

Standaert, Nicolas. 1999. "The Jesuits Did NOT Manufacture Confucianism." *East Asian Science, Technology and Medicine.* 16: 115–32.

Steele, John (trans.) 1917. *The I-li or Book of Etiquette and Ceremonial,* 2 vols. London: Probsthain.

Streng, Frederick J. 1982. "Three Approaches to Authentic Existence: Christian, Confucian, and Buddhist." *Philosophy East and West.* 32: 371–92.

Streng, Frederick J. 1985. *Understanding Religious Life.* Belmont, CA: Wadsworth.

Su, Esther C. 2004. "A Review of *The Complete Works of Mou Zongsan.*" *Dao: A Journal of Comparative Philosophy.* 3: 335–41.

Sun, Anna. 2013. *Confucianism as a World Religion: Contested Histories and Contemporary Issues.* Princeton, NJ: Princeton University Press.

Sun, Yat-sen. 1918. *Memoirs of a Revolutionary: A Program of National Reconstruction for China.* Philadelphia: David McKay Company.

Sun, Yat-sen. no date. *San Min Chu I: The Three Principles of the People.* http://larouchejapan.com/japanese/drupal-6.14/sites/default/files/text/San-Min-Chu-I_FINAL.pdf

Tam, Wai Lun. 2011. "Communal Worship and Festivals in Chinese Villages." In *Chinese Religious Life,* edited by David A. Palmer, Glenn Shive, and Philip L. Wickeri, 30–49. Oxford: Oxford University Press.

Tamney, Joseph B. and Fenggang Yang. 2012. "Introduction: Nationalism, Globalization, and Chinese Traditions in the Twenty-First Century." In *Confucianism and Spiritual Traditions in Modern China and Beyond,* edited by Yang Fenggang and Joseph Tamney, 1–29. Leiden: Brill.

Tang, Renfeng. 2002. "Mou Zongsan on Intellectual Intuition." In *Contemporary Chinese Philosophy,* edited by Chung-ying Cheng and Nicholas Bunnin, 327–46. Malden, MA: Blackwell.

Tay, Wei Leong. 2012. *Saving the Chinese Nation and the World: Religion and Confucian Reformation, 1880s–1937*. MA dissertation. National University of Singapore.

Taylor, George. 1940. *The Struggle for North China*. New York: Institute of Pacific Nations

Taylor, Rodney L. 1979. "Meditation in Ming Neo-Confucianism: Kao P'an-lung's Writings on Quiet Sitting." *Journal of Chinese Philosophy*. 6: 149–82.

Taylor, Rodney L. 1990. *The Religious Dimensions of Confucianism*. New York: State University of New York Press.

Taylor, Rodney L. 1997. "Chu Hsi and Meditation." In *The Meeting of Minds: Intellectual and Religious Interaction in East Asian Traditions and Thought*, edited by Irene Bloom and Joshua A. Fogel, 43–74. New York: Columbia University Press.

Taylor, Rodney L. 2004. "Confucian Spirituality and Qing Thought." In *Confucian Spirituality: Volume Two*, edited by Tu Weiming and Mary Evelyn Tucker, 163–79. New York: Crossroad.

Taylor, Romeyn. 1998. "Official Religion in the Ming." In *The Cambridge History of China, Volume 8: The Ming Dynasty, Part 2: 1368–1644*, edited by Denis C. Twitchett and Frederick W. Mote, 841–92. Cambridge: Cambridge University Press.

Teng, Aimin. 1986. "On Chu Hsi's Theory of the Great Ultimate." In *Chu Hsi and Neo-Confucianism*, edited by Wing-tsit Chan, 93–115. Honolulu: University of Hawai'i Press.

Thompson, Lawrence G. (trans.) 1958. *Ta T'ung Shu: The One-World Philosophy of K'ang Yu-wei*. London: George Allen & Unwin.

Thomsen, Rudi. 1988. *Ambition and Confucianism: A Biography of Wang Mang*. Aarhus: Aarhus University Press.

Tien, David W. 2010. "Metaphysics and the Basis of Morality in the Philosophy of Wang Yangming." In *Dao Companion to Neo-Confucian Philosophy*, edited by John Makeham, 295–314. Dordrecht: Springer.

Tillich, Paul. 1959. *Theology of Culture*. Oxford: Oxford University Press.

Tillman, Hoyt Cleveland. 1992. *Confucian Discourse and Chu Hsi's Ascendancy*. Honolulu: University of Hawai'i Press.

Tillman, Hoyt Cleveland. 2004. "Zhu Xi's Prayers to the Spirit of Confucius and Claim to the Transmission of the Way." *Philosophy East and West*. 54: 489–513.

Tiwald, Justin and Bryan W. Van Norden (eds.) 2014. *Readings in Later Chinese Philosophy: Han Dynasty to the 20th Century*. Indianapolis, IN: Hackett.

Tjan, Tjoe Som (trans.) 1949-52. *Po Hu T'ung: The Comprehensive Discussions in the White Tiger Hall*. 2 vols. Leiden: E. J. Brill.

Tsui, Wai. 2010. *A Study of Wang Tao's (1828–1897)* Manyou suilu *and* Fusang youji *with Reference to Late Qing Chinese Foreign Travels*. PhD dissertation: University of Edinburgh.

Tu, Weiming. 1976. *Neo-Confucian Thought in Action: Wang Yang-ming's Youth (1472–1509)*. Berkeley: University of California Press.

Tu, Weiming. 1985. *Confucian Thought: Selfhood as Creative Transformation*. Albany: State University of New York Press.

Tu, Weiming. 1989. *Centrality and Commonality: An Essay on Confucian Religiousness*. Albany: State University of New York Press.

Tu, Weiming. 1991. "Deathsong of the River: Whither Chinese Culture." In *Deathsong of the River: A Reader's Guide to the Chinese TV Series Heshang*, edited by Su Xiaokang and Wang Luxiang, 301–9. Ithaca, NY: Cornell University East Asia Series.

Tu, Weiming. 1993. *Way, Learning and Politics: Essays on the Confucian Intellectual*. Albany: State University of New York Press.

Tu, Weiming. 2010. *The Global Significance of Concrete Humanity: Essays in Confucian Discourse in Cultural China*. New Delhi: Centre for Studies in Civilizations.

Tu, Weiming. 2011. "Confucian Spirituality in Contemporary China." In *Confucianism and Spiritual Traditions in Modern China and Beyond*, edited by Fenggang Yang and Joseph Tamney, 75–96. Leiden: Brill.

Tu, Weiming and Daisaku Ikeda. 2011. *New Horizons in Eastern Humanism: Buddhism, Confucianism and the Quest for Global Peace*. London: I. B. Tauris.

Tylor, Edward Burnett. 1958. *Religion in Primitive Culture*. New York: Harper Torchbooks.

van Ess, Hans. 1994. "The Old Text / New Text Controversy: Has the 20th Century Got It Wrong?" *T'oung Pao*. 80: 146–70.

Van Norden, Bryan W. (ed.) 2002. *Confucius and the Analects: New Essays*. Oxford: Oxford University Press.

Wakeman, Frederic. 1997. "A Revisionist View of the Nanjing Decade: Confucian Fascism." *The China Quarterly*. 150: 395–432.

Waley, Arthur (trans.) 1996. *The Book of Songs / Shijing: The Ancient Chinese Classic of Poetry*, edited with additional translations by Joseph R. Allen. New York: Grove Press.

Walton, Linda. 1993. "Southern Sun Academies as Sacred Places." In *Religion and Society in T'ang and Sung China*, edited by Patricia Buckley Ebrey and Peter N. Gregory, 335–63. Honolulu: University of Hawai'i Press.

Wang, Liang. 2002. "The Confucius Temple Tragedy of the Cultural Revolution." In *On Sacred Grounds: Culture, Society, Politics, and the Formation of the Cult of Confucius*, edited by Thomas A. Wilson, 376–98. Cambridge, MA: Harvard University Press.

Wang, Shaoguang. 2013. "Is the Way of Humane Authority a Good Thing? An Assessment of Confucian Constitutionalism." In Jiang Qing, *A Confucian Constitutional Order: How China's Ancient Past Can Shape Its Political Future*, edited by Daniel A. Bell and Ruiping Fan, 139–58. Princeton, NJ: Princeton University Press.

Watson, Burton. 1958. *Ssu-ma Ch'ien: Grand Historian of China*. New York: Columbia University Press.

Watson, Burton (trans.) 1961. *Records of the Grand Historian of China*. 2 vols. New York: Columbia University Press.

Watson, Burton (trans.) 1964. *Han Fei Tzu: Basic Writings*. New York: Columbia University Press.

Watson, Burton (trans.) 1989. *The Tso Chuan: Selections from China's Oldest Narrative History*. New York: Columbia University Press.

Watson, Burton (trans.) 1993. *Records of the Grand Historian: Qin Dynasty*. New York: Columbia University Press.

Weber, Max. 1951. *The Religion of China: Confucianism and Taoism*. New York: Free Press.

Wechsler, Howard J. 1985. *Offerings of Jade and Silk: Ritual and Symbol in the Legitimization of the T'ang Dynasty*. New Haven, CT: Yale University Press.

Weinstein, Stanley. 1987. *Buddhism under the T'ang*. Cambridge: Cambridge University Press.

Wilhelm, Richard (trans.) 1967. *The I Ching or Book of Changes*. New York: Bollingen.

Wilson, Thomas A. 1995. *Genealogy of the Way: The Construction and Uses of the Confucian Tradition in Late Imperial China*. Stanford, CA: Stanford University Press.

Wilson, Thomas A. 2002a. "Sacrifice and the Imperial Cult of Confucius." *History of Religions*. 43: 251–87.

Wilson, Thomas A. 2002b. "Ritualizing Confucius/Kongzi: The Family and State Cults of the Sage of Culture in Imperial China." In *On Sacred Grounds: Culture, Society, Politics, and the Formation of the Cult of Confucius*, edited by Thomas A. Wilson, 43–94. Cambridge, MA: Harvard University Press.

Wilson, Thomas A. 2014. "Spirits and the Soul in Confucian Ritual Discourse." *Journal of Chinese Religions.* 42: 185–212.

Wittenborn, Allen (trans.) 1991. *Further Reflections on Things at Hand: A Reader.* New York: University Press of America.

Wright, David. 1994. "Tan Sitong and the Ether Reconsidered." *Bulletin of the School of Oriental and African Studies.* 57: 551–75.

Wu, Tien-wei. 1983. *Lin Biao and the Gang of Four: Contra-Confucianism in Historical and Intellectual Perspective.* Carbondale: Southern Illinois University Press.

Xi, Jinping. 2014. *The Governance of China.* Beijing: Foreign Languages Press.

Xi, Jinping. 2014a. "Xi Jinping's Speech in Commemoration of the 2,565th Anniversary of Confucius' Birth." http://library.chinausfocus.com/article-1534.html

Xiong, Shili. 2015. *New Treatise on the Uniqueness of Consciousness*, translated by John Makeham. New Haven, CT: Yale University Press.

Yang, Bo. 1992. *The Ugly Chinaman and the Crisis of Chinese Culture*, translated and edited by Don J. Cohn and Jing Qing. Sydney: Allen & Unwin.

Yang, C. K. 1961. *Religion in Chinese Society: A Study of Contemporary Social Functions of Religion and Some of Their Historical Factors.* Berkeley: University of California Press.

Yang, Fenggang and Anna Sun. 2014. "An Interview with Robert N. Bella, July 8, 2013." *Review of Religion and Chinese Society.* 1: 5–12.

Yang, Hsien-yi and Yang, Gladys (trans.) 1979. *Selections from the Records of the Historian Written by Szuma Chien.* Beijing: Foreign Languages Press.

Yang, Jisheng. 2012. *Tombstone: The Great Chinese Famine, 1958–1962.* New York: Farrar, Straus and Giroux.

Yang, Xiong. 2013. *Exemplary Figures: Fayan*, translated by Michael Nylan. Seattle: University of Washington Press.

Yao, Xinzhong (ed.) 2003. *RoutledgeCurzon Encyclopedia of Confucianism.* London: Routledge, 2003.

Yao, Xinzhong and Paul Badham. 2007. *Religious Experience in Contemporary China.* Cardiff: University of Wales Press.

Ye, Yang (trans.) 1999. *Vignettes from the Late Ming: A Hsiao-p'in Anthology.* Seattle: University of Washington Press.

Young, L. C. and Ford, S. R. 1977. "God Is Society: The Religious Dimensions of Maoism." *Sociological Inquiry.* 47: 89–97.

Yu, Anthony. 2005. *State and Religion in China: Historical and Textual Perspectives.* Peru, IL: Open Court.

Yu, Dan. 2010. *Confucius from the Heart: Ancient Wisdom for Today's World.* London: Pan Books.

Yu, Erika and Fan Meng. 2011. "A Confucian Coming of Age." In *The Renaissance of Confucianism in Contemporary China*, edited by Ruiping Fan, 241–57. Dordrecht: Springer.

Yu, Jiyuan. 2002. "Xiong Shili's Metaphysics of Virtue." In *Contemporary Chinese Philosophy*, edited by Chung-ying Cheng and Nicholas Bunnin, 127–46. Malden, MA: Blackwell.

Yü, Ying-shih. 1986. "Morality and Knowledge in Chu Hsi's Philosophical System." In *Chu Hsi and Neo-Confucianism*, edited by Wing-tsit Chan, 228–54. Honolulu: University of Hawai'i Press.

Yu, Ying-shi. 2015. "The Chinese Communists Are Not Confucianists." https://chinachange.org/2015/07/01/the-chinese-communists-are-not-confucianists/

Zarrow, Peter. 1990. *Anarchism and Chinese Political Culture*. New York: Columbia University Press.

Zeitlin, Judith T. 1994. "Shared Dreams: The Story of The Three Wives' Commentary on The Peony Pavilion." *Harvard Journal of Asiatic Studies*. 54: 127–79.

Zhang, Fenzhi. 2015. *Xi Jinping: How to Read Confucius and Other Classical Thinkers*. New York: Beijing Mediatime Books.

Zhang, Xingxing. 2015a. *Selected Essays on the History of Contemporary China*. Leiden: Brill.

Zheng, Yuan. 2001. "The Status of Confucianism in Modern Chinese Education, 1901– 48: A Curricular Study." In *Education, Culture and Identity in Twentieth-Century China*, edited by Glen Peterson, Ruth Hayhoe and Yonglin Lu, 193–216. Ann Arbor: University of Michigan Press.

Ziporyn, Brook. 2013. *Beyond Oneness and Difference: Li and Coherence in Chinese Buddhist Thought and Its Antecedents*. Albany: Sate University of New York Press.

Zito, Angela. 1997. *Of Body and Brush: Grand Sacrifice as Text/Performance in Eighteenth-Century China*. Chicago: University of Chicago Press.

Zufferey, Nicolas. 2003. *To the Origins of Confucianism: The Ru in Pre-Qin Times and During the Early Han Dynasty*. Bern: Peter Lang.

Index

Note: Page numbers in bold refer to illustrations